Oil and Gas

A Practical Handbook

Consulting Editor **Geoffrey Picton-Turbervill**

Consulting editor
Geoffrey Picton-Turbervill

Publisher
Sian O'Neill

Marketing manager
Alan Mowat

Production
John Meikle, Russell Anderson

Publishing directors
Guy Davis, Tony Harriss, Mark Lamb

Oil and Gas: A Practical Handbook
is published by
Globe Law and Business
Globe Business Publishing Ltd
New Hibernia House
Winchester Walk
London Bridge
London SE1 9AG
United Kingdom
Tel +44 20 7234 0606
Fax +44 20 7234 0808
Web www.gbplawbooks.com

Printed by Antony Rowe

ISBN 978-1-905783-23-6

Table of contents

Preface

Geoffrey Picton-Turbervill
Ashurst LLP

Oil and gas are likely to continue to be key drivers of the world economy for the foreseeable future. Notwithstanding the sort of economic downturn and price volatility that we have been experiencing in 2008 and 2009, the long-term growth in economies such as India and China, and the demand for oil and gas for transportation, power generation, petrochemical products and other industrial uses is likely to continue to drive demand. As existing reservoirs are depleted, the search for oil and gas is taking the industry to new regions using technological advances to explore for and produce hydrocarbons in increasingly hostile environments. New discoveries are often remote from demand centres, posing new challenges in terms of transportation, whether by ship or pipeline.

This book is an introduction to the legal and commercial elements of the oil and gas chain, from resource to market, and is aimed at providing a practical overview of the suite of legal agreements likely to be encountered by a practitioner involved in the oil and gas business. It does not seek to provide an in-depth analysis of each area covered (many are themselves the subject of separate books), but is intended to help those who are newer to the area to get a broad understanding of each element of the chain.

Written by experienced industry practitioners, the book starts at the exploration stage with several chapters covering the relationship between governments and international energy companies and the nature of upstream joint venture arrangements; it covers transportation of oil and gas by pipeline and ship, and gas and crude oil sales agreements; there are chapters covering the issues involved in commingling, allocation and attribution, and gas balancing, as well as terminalling and processing; and the book includes chapters on international boundary delimitation, financing of upstream developments, and buying and selling upstream assets.

I hope it will be of interest and benefit to anyone wanting to get a better understanding of the oil and gas chain, from resource to market, and the legal and commercial issues which it involves.

Geoffrey Picton-Turbervill is a partner in the energy, transport and infrastructure department in London and heads Ashurst's global energy team. Ashurst is an international commercial law firm with its head office in London and other offices in Europe, the Middle East, Asia and the United States. Ashurst has a dedicated energy practice and specialises in advising international energy companies, governments and government agencies, and financial institutions on international energy projects.

After qualifying as a lawyer, Geoffrey was seconded to an international oil and gas company where he gained wide experience of work in that sector, and in 1994 to 1995 he was based with his family in New Delhi, India, where he opened Ashurst's liaison office. He is a member of the Energy Institute, the International Bar Association, the UK Energy Lawyers Group and the Association of International Petroleum Negotiators, and is a regular speaker at international energy conferences.

Geoffrey has 22 years' experience of working in the international oil and gas industry, advising on mergers and acquisitions, greenfield projects and commercial agreements. Over the last couple of years Geoffrey has advised on transactions in many different jurisdictions, including the United Kingdom, Ireland, the Netherlands, Kuwait, Libya, Iran, Iraq, India, Brunei, Egypt and the former Soviet Union. He regularly acts for international energy companies and governments, and is recognised in independent guides as a leading energy lawyer.

Territorial delimitation and hydrocarbon resources

Mhairi Main Garcia
Ashurst LLP

This chapter examines whether the combination of territorial delimitation and hydrocarbon resources is a toxic mix. It considers what constitutes sovereignty and territory and the mechanisms available for settlement of disputes. The issues relating to maritime delimitation and disputes and the risks confronted by oil and gas companies operating in contested boundary areas are then examined in greater depth.

1. Introduction

"The frontiers that divide States are among the most fundamental elements regulating their relationships. For they limit and define the authority each wields."[1]

Territorial sovereignty and territorial limitations are of fundamental importance in international law, as sovereignty represents "the basic constitutional doctrine of the law of nations, which governs a community consisting primarily of states having a uniform legal personality".[2]

The discovery of oil and gas increases the economic and political pressures to settle territorial disputes and define boundaries. The United Nations Convention on the Law of the Sea 1982 (the Convention) confers on coastal states sovereign rights "for the purpose of exploring and exploiting, conserving and managing the natural resources".[3] As a result, where there is a dispute concerning which state has sovereignty over a territory, or a boundary is uncertain or disputed, resolving that territorial dispute or defining that boundary will be key to resolving who has rights over the resources. This is particularly important where there is a risk that oil and gas deposits are located in a disputed area.

2. Dispute resolution and the international legal order

The principle of the sovereign equality of states is enshrined in Article 2 of the Charter of the United Nations (the UN Charter). Article 2 goes on to provide that all states must fulfil their obligations in good faith in accordance with the UN Charter and must settle their disputes by peaceful means in such a manner that international peace, security and justice are not endangered. However, there is no obligation under

---

1 Evan Luard, *Conflict and Peace in the Modern International System*, State University, 2nd Edition, 1988, at p 68.
2 Ian Brownlie, *Principles of Public International Law*, Oxford University Press, 5th Edition, 1999, at p 289.
3 Articles 56 and 77, the Convention.

general international law to settle disputes. Formal or judicial settlement of disputes is subject to the consent of the parties involved.

Article 33(1) of the UN Charter sets out the means by which states may resolve disputes, namely negotiation, enquiry, mediation, conciliation, arbitration, judicial settlement, resort to regional agencies or arrangements, or other peaceful means of their own choice. In addition, for states party to the Convention, Article 279 of the Convention requires that they settle any dispute between them concerning the interpretation or application of the Convention by peaceful means in accordance with Article 2 of the UN Charter and must seek a solution by the means indicated in Article 33(1) of the UN Charter.

States are reluctant to refer their disputes for resolution by third parties, since this may be seen as giving up sovereign rights that may lead to unpredictable decisions and a lengthy and costly decision-making process, which may further aggravate relations between the relevant states. In practice, therefore, most territorial disputes are settled by negotiation and the majority of maritime boundaries have been settled by negotiation between states.

Where negotiation fails, it is relatively unusual for the resolution of territorial disputes to be sought through armed aggression. The majority of such disputes, where mutually conflicting claims have been put forward, rather lead to a war of words and political tensions between the states concerned. As a result, notwithstanding the reluctance to resort to a third-party process, disputes can and are resolved, subject to the consent of the states concerned, by referring the matter to a process involving a third party, as prescribed under Article 33(1) of the UN Charter.

2.1 Mediation and conciliation

Mediation involves a third party, usually an independent third state or an individual or international organisation, which can assist the parties in a dispute by bringing about an amicable solution. One successful example of a dispute resolved through meditation is the dispute between Argentina and Chile relating to their maritime boundary and island sovereignty. In this case, Pope John Paul II acted as mediator. On January 9 1979 Chile and Argentina signed the Act of Montevideo formally requesting mediation by the Vatican and renouncing the use of force. The mediation, although tested during tumultuous political times in Argentina and Chile, was ultimately successful and led to the 1984 Treaty of Peace and Friendship.

Conciliation is listed both under Article 33(1) of the UN Charter and Article 284 of the Convention as a means of dispute resolution open to states. It involves the intervention of a third party to examine the claims of the parties. The parties are not bound by any proposed settlement, but if they do accept the settlement as binding, it may be transposed into a formal agreement. The dispute between Iceland and Norway regarding the continental shelf area between Iceland and Jan Mayen is an example of a successful conciliation. The conciliation commission that was established recommended a joint development zone.[4] The recommendation was

4 Conciliation Commission on the continental shelf area between Iceland and Jan Mayen: Report and Recommendations to the Governments of Iceland and Norway (23 ILM 797 (1981)).

subsequently adopted in the 1981 Agreement on the Continental Shelf between Iceland and Jan Mayen.[5] However, in practice, conciliation is rarely used.

2.2 Arbitration

Arbitration and judicial settlement lead to binding dispute resolution between the parties. Arbitration can be ad hoc where an arbitral tribunal is established to hear a particular dispute or class of disputes, or it can be in accordance with the procedures set out under Annex XII of the Convention. Two of the perceived advantages of arbitration over judicial settlement are the speed of decisions and the option of keeping the arbitral award confidential. Arbitration was the forum of choice in the *Guinea v Guinea-Bissau* and *Eritrea v Yemen* disputes,[6] and recently the dispute between Guyana and Suriname.[7]

The Permanent Court of Arbitration (PCA) is an intergovernmental organisation established in 1899. It provides services for the resolution of disputes involving various combinations of states, state entities, intergovernmental organisations, and private parties. Whilst the PCA heard a number of cases during its first 30 years of existence, it has only recently witnessed a renaissance in its use as an arbitral forum.

2.3 Judicial settlement

Judicial settlement can either be through the International Court of Justice, established under the UN Charter, or the International Tribunal for the Law of the Sea (ITLOS), established under the Convention. In practice, states have resorted to the International Court of Justice rather than ITLOS. The International Court of Justice has established a growing body of law in relation to territorial disputes and maritime delimitation, interpreting the Convention and general principles of law, and developing a general body of customary international law relating to territorial delimitation.

3. Territorial sovereignty

> *"The legal competence of states and the rules for their protection depend on and assume the existence of a stable, physically delimited, homeland."*[8]

Disputes concerning territory relate to which state has sovereignty over a particular territory and disputes concerning boundaries relate to the limits of that sovereignty. Territorial questions therefore involve traditional rules regarding modes of acquisition of title, whilst boundary questions involve those rules which are relevant to the delimitation and maintenance of boundaries.

The primary criterion for determining territorial sovereignty is the continuous and peaceful display of state activity in relation to other states, demonstrated by "an

5 Agreement on the Continental Shelf between Iceland and Jan Mayen, *Iceland v Norway*, October 22, 1981, 21 ILM 1222 (1982).

6 *Guinea v Guinea Bissau Maritime Delimitation Case* (1985), 77 ILR 636 and *Eritrea v Yemen*, First Award (Territorial Sovereignty and Scope of the Dispute), October 9 1998, 114 ILR 1, Second Award (Maritime Delimitation), December 17 1999, 119 ILR 417.

7 *In the Matter of an Arbitration Award between Guyana and Suriname*, Award of the Arbitral Tribunal (September 17 2007) (available at http://www.pca-cpa.org/upload/files/GuyanaSuriname%20Award.pdf).

8 Ian Brownlie, above at note 2, at p 106.

intentional display of power and authority over the territory, by the exercise of jurisdiction and State functions, on a continuous and peaceful basis. The latter two criteria are tempered to suit the nature of the territory and the size of its population, if any."[9]

There is, however, no one single mode of acquisition of territory. The following methods define general modes of acquisition, on which an assessment can be based, whilst bearing in mind that the methods can overlap:

- cession and transfer in accordance with a treaty;
- the title of successor states in accordance with the principle of *uti possidetis*, whereby colonial frontiers inherited by new states on independence must be respected "according to which existing boundaries are the pre-emptive basis for determining territorial jurisdictions in the absence of mutual agreement to do otherwise".[10] The principle originates from practice in Latin America, but has also been used in Asia[11] and Africa,[12] and the former Yugoslavia;[13]
- where there is continuity of boundaries;
- renunciation or relinquishment of title where, in the absence of cession, title is renounced in favour of another state or a power or disposition is conferred on another state or group of states;
- adjudication where a judicial decision or arbitral award constitutes a valid basis of title;
- acquisition by effective occupation, where a state intentionally occupies or acquires sovereignty over a territory that is *terra nullius* and not at that time under the sovereignty of any state;
- prescription, where the territory is not *terra nullius*, where a territory previously belonged to a state and has been taken over by another state with the former's acquiescence: it must be undisturbed, uninterrupted and unchallenged;[14]
- accretion, through a change in the shape of the land by natural processes;
- annexation by an official act signifying the extension of territory; and
- subjugation.

Claims to sovereignty may also be justified on considerations of national justice, which include strategic claims, based on the claimant's security; geographical claims, where the territory is geographically part of the claimant's land area; claims based on ethnic, religious or linguistic groupings; and historical claims.

4. Law of the sea and maritime boundaries

Maritime boundaries and their delimitation have historically been regulated by

---

9 *Eritrea v Yemen*, First Award, above at note 6, at para 239.

10 Robert Jackson (ed), *Sovereignty at the Millennium*, Blackwell Publishers, 1999, at p 25.

11 See *Case concerning the Temple of Preah Vihear (Cambodia v Thailand), Merits*, Judgment of June 15 1962: ICJ Reports 1962, p 6.

12 See for example the *Guinea v Guinea-Bissau* case, above at note 6.

13 Opinions No 2 and No 3, Conference on Yugoslavia, Arbitration Commission, 92 ILR 62.

14 See Chamizal Arbitration between the United States and Mexico, Minutes of Meeting of the Joint Commission, June 10 1911, 5 AJIL 782 (1911).

customary international law. The 1958 Geneva Conventions codified a number of key principles. However, it was not until 1982 that a comprehensive regime was recognised under the Convention. The Convention entered into force on November 16 1994.

Today, therefore, maritime boundaries are primarily governed in accordance with the Convention and/or customary international law. Where a state is not a party to the Convention, customary international law will apply, which in turn includes a number of key principles under the Convention, since it is generally accepted that a number of provisions of the Convention now form part of customary international law. As of December 19 2008, 157 states have ratified or acceded to the Convention.[15]

4.1 Territorial sea and contiguous zone

The sovereignty of a coastal state extends to an "adjacent belt of sea known as the territorial sea" including the air space over the territorial sea as well its bed and subsoil (Article 2 of the Convention). All states have the right to establish the breadth of their territorial sea up to a limit not exceeding 12 nautical miles, measured from baselines determined in accordance with the Convention, which are normally the low-water line along the coast as marked on large-scale charts officially recognised by the coastal state.[16] With the exception of permitting safe passage to ships of all states, a state is entitled to exercise full sovereignty over its territorial sea. This includes rights to natural resources and rights to exploit hydrocarbon resources.

The 'contiguous zone' is a zone adjacent to the territorial sea which may not extend beyond 24 nautical miles from the territorial sea baselines.[17] Within the contiguous zone, a state may prevent infringement of its customs, fiscal, immigration or sanitary laws and regulations within its territory or territorial sea; and may punish infringement of these laws and regulations committed within its territory or territorial sea.

4.2 Continental shelf and exclusive economic zone

The continental shelf of a coastal state comprises the seabed and subsoil of the submarine areas that extend beyond its territorial sea throughout the natural prolongation of its land territory to the outer edge of the continental margin, or to a distance of 200 nautical miles from the territorial sea baselines, where the outer edge of the continental margin does not extend up to that distance.[18] The International Court of Justice has confirmed that this principle of prolongation of land territory as reflected in the Convention is a matter of customary international law.[19]

The coastal state may exercise sovereign rights over the continental shelf (which includes the seabed and subsoil) for the purpose of exploring it and exploiting its natural resources; such rights are exclusive and do not require exploration or exploitation by the coastal state. Moreover, pursuant to Article 77 of the Convention, these rights do not depend on occupation or on any express proclamation. The

15 http://www.un.org/Depts/los/reference_files/status2008.pdf.
16 Article 5, the Convention. A full assessment of baselines is beyond the scope of the chapter.
17 Article 33, the Convention.
18 Article 76(1), the Convention.
19 *Continental Shelf (Libyan Arab Jamahiriya/Malta)*, Judgment, ICJ Reports 1985, p 13, at p 55, para 77.

Convention reflects the jurisprudence of the International Court of Justice and in particular its judgment in the *North Sea Continental Shelf* cases, where the International Court of Justice held that "the rights of the coastal State in respect of the area of continental shelf that constitutes a natural prolongation of its land territory into and under the sea exist *ipso facto* and *ab initio*, by virtue of its sovereignty over the land, and as an extension of it in an exercise of sovereign rights for the purpose of exploring the seabed and exploiting its natural resources. In short there is an inherent right".[20] The International Court of Justice further confirmed that there is no requirement for any special legal process or acts in order to exercise such rights.

This 'exclusive economic zone' was introduced under the Convention and normally corresponds to the continental shelf, extending to a maximum distance of 200 nautical miles from the territorial sea baselines. Within the exclusive economic zone, in accordance with Article 56 of the Convention, coastal states have "sovereign rights for the purpose of exploring and exploiting, conserving and managing the natural resources ... of the waters superjacent to the seabed and of the seabed and its subsoil, and with regard to other activities for the economic exploitation and exploration of the zone ...". These rights must be exercised in accordance with the provisions under the Convention which govern the continental shelf.

Under the Convention, the rights of the coastal state in relation to exploitation of resources in its exclusive economic zone and continental shelf extend specifically to oil- and gas-related activities:

- *Artificial islands, installations and structures:* under Articles 60 and 80, the coastal state has the exclusive right to construct and to authorise and regulate the construction, operation and use of artificial islands, installations and structures in its exclusive economic zone and continental shelf.
- *Drilling:* under Article 81, the coastal state has the exclusive right to authorise and regulate drilling on the continental shelf for all purposes.
- *Pipelines:* in accordance with Article 79, all states have the freedom to lay submarine cables and pipelines on the continental shelf of another state, subject to the coastal state's right to take reasonable measures for the exploration of the continental shelf, the exploitation of its natural resources and the prevention, reduction and control of pollution. The coastal state must give its consent to the delineation of the course for laying pipelines and may establish conditions in respect of such pipelines.
- *Resource deposits transcending a boundary:* under Article 142, activities relating to resource deposits which lie across limits of national jurisdiction must be conducted with due regard to the rights and legitimate interests of any coastal state across whose jurisdiction such deposits lie.

4.3 Islands and rocks

Irrespective of size, islands enjoy the same status and maritime rights as other land territory:

"In accordance with article 121(2) of the Convention, which reflects customary

---

20 *North Sea Continental Shelf*, Judgment, ICJ Reports 1969, p 3, at p 22, para 19.

international law, islands, regardless of their size, in this respect enjoy the same status, and therefore generate the same maritime rights, as other land territory."[21]

Pursuant to Article 121(1) of the Convention, an island is "a naturally formed area of land, surrounded by water, which is above water at high tide". On the other hand, low-tide elevations (which are submerged at high tide) and rocks, do not attach maritime zones under the Convention. Rocks are distinguished from islands under Article 121(3) of the Convention, which provides that rocks cannot sustain human habitation or an economic life of their own.

Evidence of *effectivités* (the effectiveness of acts of occupation) is necessary in order to consolidate a claim to title over islands. Sovereignty over minor maritime features such as islands may be established on the basis of a relatively modest display of state powers in terms of quality and quantity.[22] In the *Indonesia v Malaysia* case, the International Court of Justice indicated that "in the case of very small islands which are uninhabited or not permanently inhabited ... *effectivités* will indeed generally be scarce".[23] However, "if the contestation is based on the fact that the other Party has actually displayed sovereignty, it cannot be sufficient to establish the title by which territorial sovereignty was validly acquired at a certain moment; it must also be shown that the territorial sovereignty has continued to exist and did exist at the moment which for the resolution of the dispute must be considered as critical. This demonstration consists in the actual display of State activities, such as belongs only to the territorial sovereign."[24] The mere presence of individuals on an island is by itself insufficient to confer title on the claimant state to which they adhere.

In assessing *effectivités*, it should be borne in mind that "[i]t is quite natural that the establishment of sovereignty may be the outcome of a slow evolution, of a progressive intensification of State control".[25] Even limited activity in the *Anglo-Norwegian Fisheries* case represented a "consideration not to be overlooked, the scope of which extends beyond purely geographical factors: that of certain economic interests peculiar to a region, the reality and importance of which are clearly evidenced by long usage".[26]

More recently, the International Court of Justice held in the *Nicaragua–Honduras* case, that evidence relating directly to the offshore oil exploration activities of the parties had no bearing on the islands in dispute. It was nonetheless willing to take into account land-based acts on the islands related to oil concessions under the category of public works in considering the question of *effectivités* supporting title over the islands. In this case, the erection of an antenna in the context of authorised oil exploration activities and payment of taxes in respect of such activities were

---

21 *Maritime Delimitation and Territorial Questions between Qatar and Bahrain, Merits*, Judgment, ICJ Reports 2001, p 40, at p 97, para 185.

22 *Case concerning Territorial and Maritime Dispute between Nicaragua and Honduras in the Caribbean Sea, Nicaragua v Honduras*, ICJ Reports 2007, available at http://www.icj-cij.org/docket/files/120/14075.pdf at para 174.

23 *Sovereignty over Pulau Ligitan and Pulau Sipadan (Indonesia/Malaysia)*, ICJ Reports 2002, p 625, at p 682, para 134.

24 Judge Huber, *Island of Palmas Case*, 2 RIAA 829 at p 839.

25 *Island of Palmas Case*, 2 RIAA 829 at p 867.

26 *Fisheries Case*, Judgment of December 18 1951, ICJ Reports 1951, p 116, at p 133.

subject to governmental authorisation and therefore the International Court of Justice held that they constituted public works and constituted *effectivités*, thus supporting Honduran sovereignty over the islands in dispute.[27]

5. Maritime delimitation and provisional arrangements

5.1 The Convention

The Convention sets out principles based on equidistance (in the case of the territorial sea) and equitable solutions (in the case of the exclusive economic zone and continental shelf). Pursuant to Article 15 of the Convention, where the coasts of two states are opposite or adjacent to each other, except where agreed otherwise, neither is entitled to extend its territorial sea "beyond the median line every point of which is equidistant from the nearest points on the baselines from which the breadth of the territorial seas of each of the two States is measured". This does not apply where it is necessary by reason of historic title or other special circumstances to delimit the territorial seas of the two states in a way which is at variance with this requirement.

According to Articles 74 and 83 of the Convention, the delimitation of the exclusive economic zone and continental shelf between states with opposite or adjacent coasts must "be effected by agreement on the basis of international law ... in order to achieve an equitable solution". The Convention thus requires delimitation by reference to principles of international law. What constitutes an equitable solution and the development of the jurisprudence by the International Court of Justice and international tribunals is discussed further below. If no agreement can be reached within a reasonable period of time, the parties should refer the matter to dispute resolution.

5.2 Exceptions to the equidistance rule

The equidistance rule is the general starting point for a maritime delimitation and "has a certain intrinsic value because of its scientific character and the relative ease with which it can be applied".[28] However, the rule can be departed from to take into account historic title or special circumstances (not just to correct an equidistant line), in the case of the territorial sea, or in pursuit of equitable solutions, in the case of the exclusive economic zone and continental shelf.

The International Court of Justice will not apply the equidistance rule where it cannot identify baselines, since it will not be possible to delineate a provisional equidistance line. This was the situation in the *Nicaragua–Honduras* case, where the International Court of Justice confirmed that the bisector method is a viable substitute method in certain circumstances where equidistance is not possible or appropriate.[29] In the *Gulf of Maine* case, the International Court of Justice chose to follow the bisector method rather than the equidistance rule.[30] The bisector method is a geometrical approach which the International Court of Justice has used to give

27 Above at note 22, at para 204.
28 *Nicaragua v Honduras* case, above at note 22, at para 272.
29 *Ibid.*
30 *Delimitation of the Maritime Boundary in the Gulf of Maine Area*, Judgment, ICJ Reports 1984, at p 246.

effect to equitable solutions. It seeks to approximate the relevant coastal relationships on the basis of the macro-geography of a coastline as represented by a line drawn between two points on the coast.

5.3 Provisional measures and duty of good faith

Articles 74(3) and 83(3) of the Convention expressly provide that, pending agreement on delimitation, the states concerned, in a spirit of understanding and cooperation, must, without prejudice to the final delimitation:

- Make every effort to enter into provisional arrangements of a practical nature. It is generally accepted that this can include joint development agreements for hydrocarbon exploitation in contested maritime boundary areas.

  According to the tribunal in the *Guyana v Suriname* arbitration, this obligation is designed to promote interim regimes and practical measures to provide for provisional utilisation of disputed areas and "constitutes an implicit acknowledgment of the importance of avoiding the suspension of economic development in a disputed maritime area, as long as such activities do not affect the reaching of a final agreement" and "imposes on the Parties a duty to negotiate in good faith".[31]

  Joint development zones define an area where two or more states claim rights and have agreed a framework for cooperation to develop and share natural resources in that area. The geographical scope of the area may be expressly limited to the area connected with the resources or may extend to broader marine areas. Joint development zones provide a positive interim solution pending delimitation of a maritime boundary, permitting both states to proceed with, and benefit from, exploitation of resources in a disputed area. The arrangements for cooperation are set out in a joint development agreement which may range from a simple structure for cooperation to a more complex scheme for administration and revenue sharing. Often a joint commission is established to administer the zone and facilitate development and the states agree a framework for settlement of disputes. Joint development agreements are usually a temporary solution and are limited in time. As a treaty, they are binding as a matter of customary international law and must be performed in good faith.[32] A joint development zone can be distinguished from unitisation of a single discovery which straddles a delimited boundary and is not reflected in treaty arrangements between states.

  Joint development zones often demand complex administration, with potentially conflicting legal, financial, contractual and operational issues. They have therefore only been used in a relatively limited number of cases, although there have been an increasing number of such agreements in recent years.[33] It is also essential that joint development agreements clearly stipulate that they do not determine any questions of sovereign rights over all or any

---

31 *Guyana v Suriname* arbitration, above at note 7, at paras 460 and 461.

32 Vienna Convention on the Law of Treaties, Article 26.

33 See Peter D Cameron, "The Rules of Engagement: Developing Cross-border Petroleum Deposits in the North Sea and the Caribbean", 55 *ICLQ* 559 (2006).

portion of the joint development zone and are without prejudice to the positions of the respective states with respect to the delimitation.

The exploitation of resources under the banner of a joint development zone has been proactively encouraged by the International Court of Justice and arbitral tribunals, which recognise that provisional arrangements of a practical nature are important tools in achieving the objectives of the Convention. Indeed, the International Court of Justice has gone beyond expecting joint development agreements merely to be used as a provisional measure. For example, in the *North Sea Continental Shelf* cases, the International Court of Justice stated that where there are overlapping areas and the parties fail to agree the delimitation, these should be resolved "by an equal division of the overlapping areas, or by agreements for joint exploitation, the latter solution appearing particularly appropriate when it is a question of preserving the unity of a deposit"[34] in order to secure "the most efficient exploitation or the apportionment of the products extracted".[35] This was reinforced in the *Eritrea v Yemen* arbitration, where the arbitral tribunal concluded that, in the case of exploitation of resources that straddle maritime boundaries, "Eritrea and Yemen should give every consideration to the shared or joint or unitised exploitation of any such resources".[36]

- During the transitional period, the reaching of the final agreement should not be jeopardised or hampered. In the *Guyana v Suriname* arbitration, the tribunal clarified that whilst this requirement is an important aspect in the Convention's objective of strengthening peace and friendly relations between nations and settling disputes peaceably, the obligations are not intended to preclude all activities in a disputed maritime area.[37]

6. Equitable solutions

The starting point of the legal process adopted consistently by the International Court of Justice is to consider the meaning of 'delimitation'. This was set out by the International Court of Justice in the *North Sea Continental Shelf* cases, where it stated that delimitation is "a process which involves establishing the boundaries of an area already, in principle, appertaining to the coastal State and not the determination *de novo* of such an area. Delimitation in an equitable manner is ... not the same thing as awarding a just and equitable share of a previously undelimited area, even though in a number of cases the results may be comparable, or even identical."[38] The mission of the International Court of Justice was further elaborated in the *Jan Mayen* case, where the International Court of Justice stated that its task was to define the boundary line between the areas under the maritime jurisdiction of two states and that the sharing out of the area was the consequence of delimitation, not vice versa.[39]

---

34 Above at note 20, at p 52, para 99.
35 *Ibid* at p 52, para 97.
36 Second Award, above at note 6, at para 86.
37 *Guyana v Suriname* arbitration, above at note 7, at para 465.
38 *North Sea Continental Shelf*, above at note 20, at p 22, para 18.
39 *Maritime Delimitation in the Area between Greenland and Jan Mayen*, Judgment, ICJ Reports 1993, p 38, at p 67, para 64.

In applying this process of delimitation, however, the International Court of Justice has identified a number of relevant principles which can be taken into account when determining maritime boundaries. It has been argued that these broad principles afford the International Court of Justice "considerable freedom to choose both the relevant principles and relevant factors, circumstances or criteria ... taking account of some, such as geographic configuration of the coast and the presence of islands, and rejecting others, such as the local economic, security or political aspects, though these sometimes enter into the verification process; proportionality and non-encroachment are regarded as safeguarding these interests as well as other equities".[40] On the other hand, the International Court of Justice has stated that its task is "to apply equitable principles as part of international law, and to balance up the various considerations which it regards as relevant in order to produce an equitable result. Whilst it is clear no rigid results exist as to the exact weight to be attached to each element in the case, this is very far from being an exercise of discretion or conciliation; nor is it an operation of distributive justice."[41] In this regard, the jurisprudence of the International Court of Justice and international tribunals has gradually clarified the principles of equidistance and equitable solutions and how they are applied. Although there is still scope for discretion, the application of the applicable rules and principles at least appears to have developed a more consistent pattern in recent judgments and awards.

According to the jurisprudence of the International Court of Justice, the first step in delimitation (subject to possible exceptions set out below) is to ascertain the equidistance line. "The equidistance line is the line every point of which is equidistant from the nearest points on the baselines from which the breadth of the territorial seas of each of the two States is measured. It can only be drawn when the baselines are known."[42] Once the equidistance line is identified, the International Court of Justice can then examine whether there are circumstances to depart from that line to achieve an equitable solution. This approach has recognised that equidistance can be applied not only in delimiting the territorial sea, but also in delimiting the exclusive economic zone and the continental shelf, albeit with provision for special circumstances in accordance with Articles 74 and 83 of the Convention. For example, in the *Qatar v Bahrain* case, the International Court of Justice stated that for the delimitation of the maritime zones beyond the 12-mile zone it will "first provisionally draw an equidistance line and then consider whether there are circumstances which must lead to an adjustment of that line".[43]

There is, however, substantial jurisprudence over what justifies an adjustment of the equidistance line and what is equitable. For delimitation to be equitable, account must be taken of the relevant circumstances of the case. A number of factors have been considered by the International Court of Justice since 1958 (under the Geneva Conventions and the more recent interpretation of the Convention as well as general state practice). It has been argued, however, that the determination to achieve an

40 Gerald Blake, *Maritime Boundaries and Ocean Resources*, Helm Ltd, 1987, at pp 33 to 34.
41 *Continental Shelf (Tunisia/Libyan Arab Jamahiriya)*, Judgment, ICJ Reports 1982, p 18, at p 60, para 71.
42 *Qatar v Bahrain* case, above at note 21, at p 94, para 177.
43 *Ibid* at p 111, para 230.

equitable result must be applied cautiously,[44] although the recent body of evolving jurisprudence emanating from the International Court of Justice appears to offer greater certainty than the general principles set out in the Convention, which were ultimately the result of political compromise. A clearer body of customary international law is slowly evolving.

Some of the more common relevant circumstances taken into account by the International Court of Justice in determining equitable solutions are set out below. The circumstances of oil and gas resources and related conduct are considered in the following section. Relevant circumstances operate within the framework of equitable principles, rather than being a self-sufficient factor in delimitation.[45]

6.1 Geography

"States have increasingly attributed weight to geographical circumstances such as coastal configurations, the lengths of coasts, and location and importance of islands."[46] It is therefore unsurprising that in maritime delimitation, the geography of the coastal situation can be taken into account, with a view to achieving "an equal distribution of the areas where the maritime projections of the coasts of the States between which delimitation is to be effected converge and overlap".[47] This factor has also been applied to take into account the general configuration of the coasts and any unusual features,[48] disparity of coastal lengths and general consistency with land-based boundaries.

The concept of equal distribution is based on the principle of proportionality, which seeks to achieve a reasonable degree of proportionality between the continental shelf and the coastline of the states concerned.[49] Used in isolation, the equidistance rule may leave out of the calculation appreciable lengths of coast and afford undue influence to others. In accordance with proportionality, in the *Libya v Malta* case, the International Court of Justice held that "coasts which are broadly comparable ought not to be treated differently because of a technical quirk of a particular method of tracing the course of a boundary line".[50] Proportionality is, however, subject to the equitable solution test and therefore it is within the discretion of the International Court of Justice to determine what is reasonable. In the *Libya v Malta* case, the International Court of Justice adjusted the equidistance line as a result of the disparity in lengths of the relevant coastlines.

The presence of islands makes maritime delimitation more complex. While a territorial sea, contiguous zone, exclusive economic zone and continental shelf attach to islands, islands are not always fully considered in delimiting maritime boundaries, since "the equitableness of an equidistance line depends on whether the

---

44 The concept of equitable principles is a dangerous one if applied loosely, given its high degree of abstraction. See L Herman, "The Court Giveth and the Court Taketh Away: an analysis of the Tunisia – Libya Continental Shelf Case", 33 *ICLQ* 825 (1984). at p 842.

45 Malcolm D Evans, "Maritime Delimitation and Expanding Categories of Relevant Circumstances", 40 *ICLQ* 1 (1991), at p 3.

46 Gerard J Tanja, *The Legal Determination of International Maritime Boundaries*, TMC Asser Instituut, 1990, at p 307.

47 *Gulf of Maine* case, above at note 30, at p 327, para 195.

48 *North Sea Continental Shelf* cases, above at note 20, at p 54, para 101.

49 *Ibid.*

50 *Libya v Malta* case, above at note 19, at p 44, para 56.

precaution is taken of eliminating the disproportionate effect of certain 'islets, rocks and minor coastal projections'...".[51] Thus, as with geographical features, the equidistance line may be subject to adjustment or may not be applied where it would not be equitable to do so.

6.2 Geology

The equidistance rule which applies to the territorial sea under Article 15 of the Convention is subject to exceptions "where it is necessary by reason of historic title or special circumstances". The International Court of Justice confirmed in the *Nicaragua–Honduras* case that such special circumstances may include "geomorphological problems".[52]

Moreover, the International Court of Justice has stated that one of the factors which should be considered in the negotiation process of delimiting the continental shelf between states is "the physical and geological structure, and natural resources, of the continental shelf areas involved".[53] However, the role of geology has increasingly been of limited importance in determining equitable solutions in delimiting the continental shelf.

In the *North Sea Continental Shelf* cases, the International Court of Justice declared that boundary delimitation should leave each state as large an area as possible of the shelf constituting a natural prolongation of its land territory into the sea without encroaching on similar prolongation of the other state, although this is generally not relevant where states are less than 400 nautical miles apart. This was recognised in the *Libya v Malta* case, where the International Court of Justice stated that whatever the geological characteristics of the corresponding seabed and subsoil, there is no reason to ascribe any role to geological or geophysical factors within that distance either in verifying the legal title of the states concerned or in proceeding to delimitation as between their claims. It went on to clarify that "where verification of the validity of title is concerned, since, at least insofar as those areas are situated at a distance of under 200 miles from the coasts in question, title depends solely on the distance from the coasts of the claimant States of any areas of sea-bed claimed by way of continental shelf, and the geological or geomorphological characteristics of those areas are completely immaterial".[54]

6.3 Other relevant circumstances

There are a number of other relevant circumstances which the International Court of Justice has taken into account, including defence and security interests, navigational interests and conservation and management of living resources. The International Court of Justice has also taken into account historical factors, observing that the *uti possidetis* principle may in certain circumstances play a role in a maritime delimitation, for example in relation to historic bays and territorial seas.[55]

---

51 *Ibid* at p 48, para 64.
52 Above at note 22, at para 291.
53 *North Sea Continental Shelf* cases, above at note 20, at p 54, para 101.
54 *Libya v Malta* case, above at note 19, at p 35, para 39.
55 *Nicaragua v Honduras* case, above at note 22, at para 232.

On the other hand, the International Court of Justice does not generally attach any weight to socio-economic circumstances, including disparities in wealth, as a relevant factor in determining equitable delimitation. The International Court of Justice has stated that these are unpredictable variables[56] and "neither the rules determining the validity of legal entitlement to the continental shelf, nor those concerning delimitation between neighbouring countries, leave room for any considerations of economic development of the States in question".[57]

7. Hydrocarbon resources and delimitation

> *"Oil is an ambiguous factor in the security equation: it triggers higher levels of regional expansionism and international interventionism, but oil revenues can also play a moderating role in many regional conflicts and encourage 'national' integration at home."*[58]

The discovery of oil and gas increases the strategic and economic importance of territorial delimitation. The presence of hydrocarbons has also promoted maritime delimitation, for example in the Persian Gulf, where oil exploration "was the catalyst for much of the rapid progress made towards finalising the political map of Arabia during the 1990s".[59] States have inherent rights to exploit natural resources within their continental shelf. These are exclusive rights, since whether the coastal state exploits such resources or not is irrelevant; but no one else may do so without its express consent.[60] Likewise, the granting of concessions or licensing of oil and gas-related activities by a state does not prejudice its sovereign rights over the delimitation of its territory or that of the neighbouring state bordering such concession or licence area.

Nevertheless, oil and gas activities in themselves are not determining factors in delimiting a maritime boundary and there is no requirement to respect any limits which are set out under a concession or licensing agreement. In the *Guyana v Suriname* arbitration, the tribunal rejected the argument put forward by Guyana that the conduct of the parties granting oil concessions should determine the final location of the boundary line, holding that "the cases reveal a marked reluctance of international courts and tribunals to accord significance to the oil practice of the parties in the determination of the delimitation line".[61]

Whilst discoveries of oil and gas may heighten the need to delimit a boundary and/or settle any dispute between neighbouring states, where a state has granted concessions or licensed oil and gas activities beyond the equidistance line, such

---

56 See, for example, the *Tunisia v Libya* case, above at note 41, and the *Guinea v Guinea-Bissau* case, above at note 6.

57 *Libya v Malta* case, above at note 19, at p 41, at para 50.

58 Ghassan Salamé, "Assessing Alternative Future Arrangements for Regional Security", in Geoffrey Kemp and Janice Gross Stein (ed), *Powder Keg in the Middle East: the Struggle for Gulf Security*, Rowman & Littlefield, 1995, pp 65 to 86, at p 74.

59 Richard N Schofield, "Border Disputes in the Gulf: Past, Present, and Future", in Gary G Sick and Lawrence G Potter (eds), *The Persian Gulf at the Millennium: Essays in Politics, Economy, Security and Religion*, Macmillan, 1997, pp 127 to 165, at p 134.

60 Article 77, the Convention; *North Sea Continental Shelf* cases, above at note 20, at p 22, para 19.

61 *Guyana v Suriname* arbitration, above at note 7, at para 390.

concessions or licensing are only relevant if they are further to an agreement between the two states concerned: "it is clear that neither concessions unilaterally granted nor exploration activity unilaterally undertaken by either of the interested States with respect to the disputed areas can be creative of new rights or deprive the other State of any rights to which in law it may be entitled ...".[62] In addition, such agreement must be an express agreement between the states concerned. In the *Cameroon v Nigeria* case, the International Court of Justice held that:

> *"... although the existence of an express or tacit agreement between the parties on the siting of their respective oil concessions may indicate a consensus on the maritime areas to which they are entitled, oil concessions and oil wells are not in themselves to be considered as relevant circumstances justifying the adjustment or shifting of the provisional delimitation line. Only if they are based on express or tacit agreement between the parties may they be taken into account."*[63]

Furthermore, there must be compelling evidence of such a tacit legal agreement, since:

> *"... establishment of a permanent maritime boundary is a matter of grave importance and agreement is not easily to be presumed. A de facto line might in certain circumstances correspond to the existence of an agreed legal boundary or might be more in the nature of a provisional line or of a line for a specific, limited purpose, such as sharing a scarce resource. Even if there had been a provisional line found convenient for a period of time, this is to be distinguished from an international boundary."*[64]

In the *Indonesia v Malaysia* case, the International Court of Justice considered that the limits set out in the concessions did not constitute tacit agreement and "may have been simply the manifestation of the caution exercised by the Parties in granting their concessions. This caution was all the more natural ... because negotiations were to commence soon afterwards between Indonesia and Malaysia with a view to delimiting the continental shelf."[65] In addition, conditions in the concessions and lack of publicity deprived concessions of impacting on the delimitation in the *Malaysia v Singapore* case, where the International Court of Justice stated that "[G]iven the territorial limits and qualifications in the concession and the lack of publicity of the coordinates, the Court does not consider that weight can be given to the concession."[66]

Where there is tacit agreement, the International Court of Justice has taken into account the granting of oil concessions when considering the parties' conduct. In the *Tunisia–Libya* case, the International Court of Justice stated that "a de facto line ... was the result of the manner in which both Parties initially granted concessions for offshore exploration and exploitation of oil and gas. This line of adjoining concessions, which was tacitly respected for a number of years ... does appear to the

---

62 Aegean Sea Continental Shelf, Interim Protection, Order of September 11 1976, ICJ Reports 1976, p 3, at p 10, para 29.

63 *Land and Maritime Boundary between Cameroon and Nigeria (Cameroon v Nigeria: Equatorial Guinea intervening)*, Judgment, ICJ Reports 2002, p 303, at p 447, at para 304.

64 *Nicaragua v Honduras* case, above at note 22, at para 253.

65 *Indonesia v Malaysia* case, above at note 23, at p 664, para 79.

66 *Sovereignty over Pedra Branca/Pulau Batu Puteh, Middle Rocks and South Ledge (Malaysia v Singapore)*, ICJ Reports 2008, available at http://www.icj-cij.org/docket/files/130/14492.pdf, at para 253.

Court to constitute a circumstance of great relevance for the delimitation."[67]

8. Interests of oil and gas companies

Throughout the world, numerous boundaries between states remain unresolved, including regions where oil and gas reserves are of prime importance. This does not necessarily equate to numerous territorial disputes, since the states involved may not have commenced the delimitation process. However, in areas where there are abundant hydrocarbon resources neighbouring or straddling an undefined or disputed boundary, oil and gas companies will need to make a full evaluation of the risks involved in advance of committing their resources and commercial reputations. Whilst it is not possible to predict with certainty how a boundary may be delimited or what the outcome of a dispute may be, various safeguards can be considered by oil and gas companies in order to mitigate the very real economic and commercial risks of operating in disputed waters.

8.1 Due diligence

The first step for an oil and gas company being granted a concession or awarded licensing rights is to check the status of the contract area. Where a contract area lies within 200 nautical miles of a neighbouring state, this indicates that there is at least a potential for competing claims.

A state's right to grant rights over its hydrocarbon resources can only be exercised within its own boundaries. Therefore, if there is a determination that all or part of the contract area does not lie within the boundaries of the host state, this could lead to the concessionaire/licence holder losing rights in so far as the rights do not lie in an area which is within the boundaries of the host state.

The ramifications are, however, broader than a mere loss of rights, since the neighbouring state which exercises sovereignty over an excluded contract area could demand that any activities be discontinued and/or impose penalties against a company which has been illegally operating in its territory. The fact that the activities were authorised by the host state will not protect a company from action by the neighbouring state in such circumstances. For this reason, it is not only necessary to examine the applicable laws of the host state, but where there is uncertainty over the jurisdiction of the contract area, the potentially applicable laws of any relevant neighbouring states should also be assessed.

Where there is a determination that all or part of the contract area does not lie within the boundaries of the host state, the company could also be in breach of its concession/licensing agreement with the host state, in the absence of provisions granting relief from targets and contractual obligations in such a scenario. It is thus critical that the status of the territory within which the contract area lies be established at the outset.

If the contract area belongs to the host state and this is confirmed by way of an undisputed treaty, judgment or arbitral award, then this should provide a degree of legal certainty and comfort going forward. However, if the contract falls within an

67 *Tunisia v Libya* case, above at note 41, at p 71, para 96.

area which has not yet been delimited and/or potentially neighbours or crosses a disputed boundary, this will necessitate a more detailed assessment of the risks and uncertainties involved as a result of the geographical scope of the contract area being potentially uncertain.

If there is a dispute between the host state and a neighbouring state with a competing claim over all or part of the territory constituting the contract area, an assessment must be made of the potential for settling the dispute, taking into account the political relations between the states concerned, the legal principles that may be applied (bearing in mind that whilst the International Court of Justice generally commences any delimitation by applying the equidistance line, the application of 'equitable solutions' may give rise to a number of possible outcomes) and the technical difficulties which may be involved in delimiting the boundary in question. If the matter has been referred to an arbitral tribunal, the International Court of Justice or other judicial body, this could indicate that it will take a long time to resolve the dispute; such disputes are generally protracted.

8.2 Contractual safeguards

In addition to general legal and technical due diligence, oil and gas companies should to the extent possible include safeguards in the relevant contract, whether it is a concession agreement, production sharing contract or licensing agreement. These safeguards should aim to protect the company against the adverse consequences of the contract area falling within a disputed area or of an unfavourable determination that all or part of the contract area does not lie within the boundaries of the host state. Although host state governments may be reluctant to include additional provisions to protect companies, where there is doubt as to the territorial scope of the contract area, companies should seek to negotiate safeguards such as the following:

- If there is a territorial or boundary dispute which involves the contract area, there should be no breach of the contract by the company and the host state should not apply any penalties. This could be included as part of a *force majeure* or compensation event mechanism in the contract, or as a separate relief clause.
- If it is determined that all or part of the contract area does not lie within the boundaries of the host state, the contract should include an indemnity by the host state indemnifying the company for any losses due to such circumstances.
- The company's obligations, in so far as they are affected or put at risk by a boundary determination, should be suspended until the matter is resolved. The contract should remain in full force until the boundary dispute is finally resolved.

8.3 Activities in disputed waters

Where a boundary is disputed, the *Guyana v Suriname* arbitration has set out the parameters within which oil- and gas-related activities may be carried out. The tribunal found that "[I]n the context of activities surrounding hydrocarbon exploration and exploitation, two classes of activities in disputed waters are therefore permissible. The first comprises activities undertaken by the parties pursuant to provisional arrangements of a practical nature. The second class is composed of acts which, although unilateral, would not have the effect of jeopardizing or hampering the reaching of a final agreement on the delimitation of the maritime boundary."[68] The tribunal went on to explain that unilateral acts which do not physically change the marine environment generally fall into the second class, but anything involving a physical change may only be undertaken pursuant to an agreement; a party to a dispute should not "undertake any unilateral activity that might affect the other party's rights in a permanent manner".[69]

As a result, where a company is operating in disputed waters, according to the *Guyana v Suriname* arbitration it should only carry on activities which do not involve physical change, such as seismic operations. If a company goes beyond this and carries on exploration activities, there is a risk that it would be in breach of international law, since exploration of oil and gas reserves falls within activities which involve physical change in the seabed or subsoil.

Oil and gas companies are therefore not only subject to the laws and regulations of the host state and the terms and conditions of their contracts, but they will also have to bear in mind that if they are operating in disputed waters, certain activities may not be permitted as a matter of international law, in accordance with the requirements set out in the *Guyana v Suriname* arbitration.

8.4 Prohibition of the use of force

If a company does find itself operating in a disputed area, the claimant neighbouring state should not use force against the company, since this would be in breach of international law. In the *Guyana v Suriname* case, the tribunal found that the expulsion by Suriname from the disputed area of the commercial oil rig and drill ship, which were operating further to a concession granted by Guyana for oil exploration in the disputed area, constituted a threat of the use of force in breach of the Convention, the UN Charter and general international law, and also threatened international peace and security, jeopardising the potential for reaching agreement on delimitation.[70]

8.5 Contracting with both states

Oil and gas companies can consider the possibility of contracting with both the original host state and the claimant neighbouring state. In practice, however, this is often not a realistic option, since each state may believe it has a legitimate claim to the whole contract area and there may also be political objections, particularly if the states do not have friendly relations. Given the financial stakes involved and the potential loss of revenue from a reduced contract area, states may be reluctant to be part of such an arrangement.

---

68 Above at note 7, at para 466.
69 Above at note 7, at paras 467 and 470.
70 Above at note 7, at paras 484 and 488(2).

8.6 Agreed boundary

Even where there is an agreed boundary, the development of hydrocarbon resources on either side of the boundary will be subject to differing domestic legal regimes and procedures applicable to their exploration and exploitation. The problem is exacerbated where there is a common reservoir. Technical problems can arise in apportioning the reserves and there is a risk that operations on one side of a boundary can have a negative impact on the reserves on the other side of the boundary. Procedures for unitising reserves have thus been adopted in many cases where such problems arise.

8.7 Assistance to the host state government

Finally, in this context, oil and gas companies can assist a host state government in understanding the legal complexities, commercial issues, economic analysis and technical problems. International oil and gas companies may be in a better position to provide information and data which may be helpful in delimiting a boundary and/or resolving a dispute. Companies with international resources and technical expertise can be of positive assistance, although the host state government will ultimately be the decision-making authority on the strategy it decides to pursue in relation to its boundaries.

9. Conclusions

The pressure to discover and exploit hydrocarbon resources is intensifying with an increasingly energy-hungry world. This will lead to a greater likelihood of resources being exploited in areas where boundaries have yet to be delimited and/or are disputed. The mix of hydrocarbon resources coupled with an undelimited or disputed boundary offers the potential for toxic disputes in the future.

Where there is a dispute, it may not be possible to predict the outcome and timing for resolving that dispute, since a single rule or method may not be applicable. Although the equidistance line is generally the starting point, it is subject to extensive uncertainties which arise in the 'equitable solutions' language used in the Convention and by the International Court of Justice and international tribunals, and in some cases the equidistance rule may simply not be an appropriate solution. However, although it may not be possible to eliminate uncertainty, it is at least possible to minimise that uncertainty. Oil and gas companies seeking an interest in a potential contract area where the boundaries have not been delimited or are in dispute should mitigate the risks involved by carrying out careful due diligence, working proactively with the host state government and seeking the appropriate contractual safeguards. In so doing, oil and gas companies should be able to make an informed assessment of the risks involved and reduce the potential for a toxic mix.

Licences, concessions, production sharing agreements and service contracts

Jubilee Easo
Ashurst LLP

1. Introduction

All hydrocarbon resources in the soil and the subsoil, in interior waters and in the territorial sea, on the continental shelf and in the exclusive economic zone are typically the province of the state. However, it is often the case that states with significant hydrocarbon resources do not have easy access to risk capital and lack the technical expertise to explore and develop the hydrocarbon resources located in their territory. In these cases, the task of finding and extracting oil and gas is delegated to an international (and in some cases domestic) oil company (IOC) which possesses the expertise and financial resources to undertake the task. The relationship between the state and the IOC must then be regulated by some type of legal instrument or contractual framework which specifies the rights and obligations of each party. This chapter discusses the four most important regimes developed to govern such a relationship: the licence, the concession, the production sharing agreement (PSA) and the service contract.

At the heart of each of these regimes is the desire to address the tensions inherent in the relationship between the state and the IOC. Broadly speaking, these tensions can be divided into two categories: the allocation of risk between the parties and the provision of incentives to the IOC to accomplish the state's objectives.

The upstream petroleum sector is faced with physical, commercial and political risks at every stage of the exploration and production process. While those risks are no different in nature to those that arise in other economic spheres, the oil and gas sector is distinctive in terms of the significant investment required for the exploration and production of oil and gas and the large uncertainty often surrounding the ability to profit from such investment. Prior to attempting to extract hydrocarbons from the subsoil, seismic exploration and exploratory drilling must be carried out, and sufficient reserves must be found to make the project commercially viable. Unfortunately, more often than not, a commercial discovery will not occur, in which case it will not be possible to recover the exploration costs. Even if a commercial discovery is declared, significant uncertainty affects the actual cost at which the hydrocarbons can be extracted, developed and produced. History is witness to the dramatic fluctuations in the international price of hydrocarbons. The high cost of extraction and production and the fluctuations in the price of hydrocarbons together translate into risk with respect to the profitability of the venture.

Generally, under every prevailing upstream licence/contractual regime, it is the IOC that shoulders the brunt of the exploration risks. However, the regimes are very different in how they define ownership of the hydrocarbons and the legal nature of the instrument granting rights to the IOC. The four upstream regimes are also quite different in how quickly the exploration costs can be recovered by the IOC at the production stage, and in the ways in which they allocate the other risks between the state party and the IOC.

Under both licences and concessions, all hydrocarbons produced belong to the IOC, whereas under both PSAs and service contracts, it is the state that owns the hydrocarbons produced with a portion of these hydrocarbons being allocated by the state to the IOC as payment for the risks taken and services rendered. In addition to ownership, the licence and concession regimes allocate most of the exploration risk to the IOC, whereas under the PSA and (especially) the service contract arrangements the state retains a relatively larger portion of the risk associated with the commercialisation of any discovery.

What type of regime a state chooses will depend on its own capabilities, the extent of competition among IOCs, the size of the risk at each stage of the production process and the requirements of its constitution. The state will naturally be more keen to bear the exploration risks arising from less uncertain fields, while delegating to the IOC the more significant risks associated with speculative fields. A typical example of this is Brazil, where the finance minister made a case for a move from a concession system to a PSA system following significant deep-water discoveries in 2007. The concession system, he argued, worked for the state party when it was not clear whether and how much oil was present but "now there is no longer any risk, we know the oil is there, so the picture has changed".

Under all four upstream regimes, a source of risk that an IOC entering into a relationship with a state party cannot ignore is the fact that the IOC's counterparty is a sovereign state and can, therefore, use a number of legal and regulatory instruments to expropriate *de facto* entire fields or blocks, or reduce the revenue received by the IOC from such fields or blocks. The state party can, for example, decide to change the laws retrospectively, increase taxation or refuse to issue export permits.

Historically, sovereign risk is perceived to be higher the more profitable the venture becomes for the IOC, either because any resource- or field-related uncertainties have been resolved favourably, or because the IOC has managed to negotiate favourable conditions in the contractual arrangements. For example, following the positive oil price shock in 1973, the Indonesian government realised that, under the then existing PSAs, the IOCs were earning substantial profits. As a result, the Indonesian government introduced new economic terms – reworked in its favour – applicable to both future PSAs and, importantly, to existing PSAs. This, to some extent, is unsurprising. When the proceeds received by IOCs turn out to be substantial, governments will tend to feel that the state's wealth is being unfairly appropriated by the IOCs. In such circumstances, the political and/or reputational consequences of appearing as an unreliable business partner will seem comparatively lower for the host government. From the perspective of the IOC, the existence of sovereign risk can lead to a Catch-22 situation, in which it is invited to bear the potential downside inherent in the exploration and production of hydrocarbons but, equally, it takes the risk that the upside may not be as significant as it first expected.

While a certain amount of sovereign risk is unavoidable, there are contractual and legal provisions aimed at limiting its extent. Regardless of the upstream licence/contractual regime governing the relationship, the IOC will want to ensure that stabilisation provisions provide a certain amount of protection against future opportunistic behaviour by its sovereign counterparty.

The second objective of the licence/contractual arrangement between state and IOC is the provision of adequate incentives for both parties, but especially for the latter. It is clear that an IOC will not be adequately motivated to explore a field efficiently unless it is entitled to an accepted level of benefit from a discovery. Different regimes deal with this issue in different ways, but the key economic factors from the IOC's perspective are the fiscal terms and the minimum work commitments imposed on it. The work commitments represent the minimum level of financial commitment on the part of the IOC, and the fiscal terms represent the revenues that the IOC will be able to earn from production in the event of a discovery. The level of royalty, taxation and profit sharing imposed by the state will determine whether a field, which is a technical success, is also a commercial success for the IOC.

It is often also the case that the state party is interested in accomplishing certain objectives from the business relationship with the IOC which are not strictly related to the maximisation of the proceeds from the extraction of hydrocarbons. These objectives may include some or all of: the transfer of technology from the IOC to the host government, earning foreign exchange, the promotion of direct and indirect local employment, and the retention of a certain percentage of hydrocarbons for the local market. These objectives may conflict with the interests of the IOC and will need to be included in the contractual arrangement if the IOC is to be motivated to achieve them. Of course, these secondary objectives may come at a cost, as they may limit the ability of the IOC to carry on its main activity in the most economically efficient manner. Each of the regimes discussed below can, in principle, incorporate clauses addressing these secondary objectives. However, regimes such as the PSA or the service contract where the state is more directly involved in the extraction process tend to allow the state to pursue those objectives more effectively.

2. Licence regime

A licence (referred to in some countries as a lease) is essentially a permission granted by a state to an IOC to exploit a certain geographical area in return for a fee or a royalty. All hydrocarbons are owned by the state *in situ*, but ownership of any extracted hydrocarbons transfers to the IOC at the well-head. Therefore, the licence grants the licensee a proprietary right over the hydrocarbons at such point and any profits obtained by the IOC from sale of the hydrocarbons are taxed by the state. The licensing regime is a relatively free market regime, under which the IOC bears most of the risk and enjoys a significant share of the benefits and is allowed to pursue its interests with relative freedom, subject to environmental, timing and other constraints imposed by the terms and conditions of the licence. The United

Kingdom, Canada, Norway and, more recently, Russia are the main countries using a licensing regime to grant access to their hydrocarbon resources.

The conditions of the licence are usually reflected in parliamentary legislation. Notwithstanding this fact, in most countries, licences are considered contractual instruments rather than regulatory instruments. This has important legal consequences for the licensee: contractual relationships cannot generally be amended unilaterally, whereas regulatory instruments are subject to unilateral amendment by the state. In the United Kingdom, the relationship between the licensee and the state is generally regarded as a contractual one, albeit with a strong regulatory flavour in the sense that a considerable degree of discretion remains with the state.

2.1 Licensing in the United Kingdom

In the United Kingdom, the authority which grants exploration and extraction licences is the Department of Energy and Climate Change (DECC) (Petroleum Act 1998). The licence takes the form of a deed under which the licensee is bound to observe the conditions of the licence. Secondary legislation contains these conditions (known as model clauses), governing issues such as the grant of rights, implementation of development plans, working methods, measurements and work programmes and the relinquishment of a certain proportion of the licence area. The actual terms vary across licensing rounds and depend partly on the assessment of the expected environmental impact of the extraction activities. Instead of royalties, UK licences currently require the payment of an annual charge (also known as a rental).

DECC currently issues two types of offshore licence: the exploration licence and the production licence. An exploration licence allows the licensee to carry out seismic surveys in a particular area and to undertake shallow drilling. Offshore exploration licences are usually granted for a period of three years, with the possibility of extension for a further three years.

Under a UK production licence, an IOC has the exclusive right both to explore for and exploit hydrocarbons in the geographical area covered by the licence. Separate consents are required prior to drilling and development. Three different types of production licences are issued, depending on the characteristics of the particular fields. Traditional licences – the most common type – apply to well-known, not-too-deep areas and applicants with proven technical and financial capabilities. 'Promote' licences are designed to enable smaller companies to obtain a production licence before proving those capabilities – the IOC is required to pay only 10% of the traditional fee in the first two years and is able to bypass some of the more stringent licensing requirements, thus allowing new players to join the search for hydrocarbons more easily. Lastly, 'frontier' licences are intended to encourage exploration in areas that are remote or in deep water. The IOC is required to pay only 10% of the traditional rate, but then has to relinquish 75% of the licensed area after the initial exploration. The onshore licensing regime is similar to the offshore licensing regime.

Currently, three types of taxes apply to hydrocarbon activities in the United Kingdom:

- *The ring-fence corporation tax*: With some modifications (in relation to capital allowances and losses), this is the normal UK corporation tax with the exception of a ring-fence and a 100% first-year allowance for almost all capital expenditure. The purpose of the ring-fence is to prevent taxable profits from hydrocarbon extraction being reduced by losses from other activities or by excessive interest payments. However, losses from ring-fenced activities can be relieved against profits from non-ring-fenced activities (as well as against ring-fenced income) provided that, but for the existence of the ring-fence, the non-ring-fenced and ring-fenced activities would comprise a single trade.
- *Supplementary charge*: Since April 2002, there has been an additional charge on a company's ring-fenced profits, without deducting costs of debt finance. The supplementary charge is currently 20%, bringing the effective tax rate on ring-fenced activities to 50%.
- *Petroleum revenue tax*: This is a field-based tax applicable to profits arising from the exploitation of hydrocarbon fields for which development consent was given before March 15 1993. Profits for petroleum revenue purposes are based on the excess of the proceeds from the disposal of oil from the field over that field's expenditure. The current rate is 50% and it is charged prior to corporation tax and is deductible for the purposes of calculating the ring-fence corporation tax and the supplementary charge.

The tax regime which applies to any UK hydrocarbon field depends on the date on which development consent was received, because:

- fields which received development consent before March 16 1993 are subject to the petroleum revenue tax, the ring-fence corporation tax and the supplementary charge; and
- fields which received development consent on or after March 16 1993 are subject only to the ring-fence corporation tax and the supplementary charge.

2.2 Licensing in Norway

In Norway, the Petroleum Act of November 29 1996 provides the legal framework for the licensing system which regulates petroleum activities. The Ministry of Petroleum and Energy is the body with the authority to award licences. In each licensing round, and following applications, the ministry allocates each licence to an individual IOC or group of IOCs. An operator of the consortium, responsible for carrying out the day-to-day activities under the terms of the licence, is then appointed by the ministry. IOCs are currently only awarded an area for which they have submitted complete plans.

Each production licence provides exclusive rights for exploration and exploitation of hydrocarbons in the relevant geographical area and includes terms and conditions supplementing those of the Petroleum Act. The production licence is awarded for an initial exploration period of up to ten years. Certain minimum exploratory activities, including seismic surveys and/or shallow drilling, must be carried out during this initial period. Following exploitation, the licensees can only retain areas in which they plan to start production. A licensee, who has fulfilled the work commitment and the conditions otherwise applicable to the individual production licence may demand that the licence be extended after the expiry of the initial period. The extension period is stipulated in the licence and generally may be up to 30 years (although in some cases it may be up to 50 years).

Currently, the taxation regime includes the ordinary Norwegian corporation tax of 28%, plus a special tax of 50%. In respect of both taxes, consolidation between fields is permitted. In order to shield the normal return from the special tax, an extra deduction, the uplift, is allowed in the calculation base for special tax. This amounts to 30% of the investments (7.5% per annum for four years from the year the investment is made). Other important taxes linked to petroleum activities are the carbon dioxide tax and area fee. The carbon dioxide tax rate in 2007 was Nkr0.8 per litre of petroleum or standard cubic metre of gas. The area fees accrue on all production licences after the expiry of the initial period.

The Norwegian government can directly participate in the proceeds arising from oil and gas fields under the State's Direct Financial Interest (SDFI). The state participation is decided at the time at which licences are awarded and it varies from field to field, according to the state's preferences. Once the relevant participation is decided, the state behaves like any other company, paying its share of costs and participating proportionately in the production proceeds. This arrangement allows the state to adjust the amount of risk that it wishes to undertake while maintaining a licensing regime.

2.3 Licensing in Russia

In Russia, there are two key pieces of legislation that govern oil and gas exploration and production: the Law on Subsoil Resources of February 21 1992 (the Subsoil Law) and the Federal Law on Production Sharing Agreements of December 30 1995, as amended (the PSA Law). The PSA Law sets forth the legal framework for Russian and foreign investment in the exploration and production of mineral resources under PSAs. However, following unfavourable amendments to the PSA Law in 2003, very few PSAs have been concluded under the PSA Law because of the difficult procedures involved. It is therefore unlikely to be the regime of choice for investment in the Russian oil and gas sector. Under the Subsoil Law, exploration for and production of hydrocarbons can be performed only by the holder(s) of an exploration and/or production licence. Exploration and production licences are awarded, following a tender or auction, by the Federal Agency for Subsoil Use (Rosnedra), Russia's licensing authority. Exploration licences are awarded for a maximum of five years (onshore) and ten years (offshore). Production licences may be awarded without a tender or auction, following a commercial discovery under an existing exploration licence. Production licences are usually awarded for 20 years, but may be extended.

The current taxation regime that is applicable to licensees under the Subsoil Law includes:

- the typical taxes that are applicable to all companies (profit taxes, VAT, property tax, payroll-related taxes and certain minor regional taxes);
- a subsoil-role payment, which may take different forms such as a licence

issuance fee, a one-off fee for the use of the subsoil, a fee for the grant of subsoil rights or a fee for geological information; and

- a mineral extraction tax on oil at the rate of Rb419 per tonne of extracted oil, multiplied by a coefficient calculated under a formula based on world prices and the maturity of the fields.

A different tax regime applies to IOCs operating under a PSA.

3. Concession regime

In the early twentieth century the concession regime was the most common framework by which IOCs acquired the right to explore and produce hydrocarbons on what very often were large portions of the host government's territory. The term 'concession' describes a relationship between a state and an IOC under which the state concedes sovereign control over its hydrocarbon resources. These old-style concessions were usually very favourable to the IOC; the state granted to the IOC absolute authority over the territory and surrendered to the IOC the title to all the hydrocarbons *in situ*. Furthermore, the concessions were granted for relatively long periods of time, during which the terms of the concession were often preserved and the state had very little say on how the area was developed and how the recovered hydrocarbons were disposed of. For example, in the 1920s a consortium of British and French companies and the Iraq Petroleum Company signed three concession contracts with the ruler of Iraq, King Faisal. The concessions were for approximately 75 years and collectively granted the Iraq Petroleum Company rights to all of the hydrocarbons in the entire country.

Under the old concession regime, the IOC would pay an initial consideration, similar to the modern-day signature bonus, and an annual rent that was independent of the results of the exploration and production activities. These old-style concessions allocated all risks (and rewards) to the IOC. While this may have seemed like an effective way of allocating incentives to explore and extract hydrocarbons in a cost-efficient manner, the host governments did not generally provide the IOCs with incentives to achieve any other objectives, such as those relating to the environmental and wider development objectives.

The post-1950s concessions are significantly different with respect to ownership of hydrocarbons. The state has permanent sovereignty over the hydrocarbons within its territory and the concessions grant an IOC a legal title to the hydrocarbons, but only once recovered at the well-head. As with licences, the concessionaires have proprietary rights over the concession areas. In addition, the modern concessions are for shorter periods of time and the concession areas are limited to smaller geographical areas that may be required to be relinquished depending on the work programme and budget. The IOC takes most of the exploration risks and the state generally derives all its revenues from royalties, income taxes and other similar payments.

The concession will typically take the form of a concession agreement which will contain the terms and conditions on which the concession is granted. The agreement will create a mini-legal system applicable only to the concessionaire and will cover a range of regulatory matters such as the right to import and export goods, work permits, foreign exchange, health and safety, taxation, planning and environmental issues. In the past, it was likely that the concession agreement would have been directly negotiated with the IOC. Nowadays it is more likely that their terms, and the conditions on which they are granted, will be regulated. For example, standard terms may be laid down by legislation (the Libyan Petroleum Law of 1955 is an early example of this). Further, these standard terms may be circulated among interested oil companies on a take-it-or-leave-it basis. In other words, there may be little or no room for negotiation – instead, the risks posed to the IOC (including political risk) would need to be reflected in the bid price.

Whether concession agreements are contractual or regulatory instruments has been a disputed issue. The question was considered in the *Aramco*[1] and *Texaco*[2] oil arbitrations, in which it was held that concession agreements are not mere administrative instruments capable of unilateral amendment by the state. In both these cases, it was held that interference with these contractual rights would amount to expropriation, for which compensation would be payable by the state.

Concessions are in practice similar to licences, except that they are more commonly used in developing countries that have an underdeveloped or unstable legal system. Unlike in the case of licences, in concessions the state is very often likely to impose obligations on the IOC regarding local employment, training and technology transfer as well as provide sovereign assurance to the IOC by way of state support arrangements.

3.1 The concession regime in Brazil

In Brazil, concessions to exploration and production blocks have been granted competitively since 1995 when the Petrobras monopoly was dismantled. Following the enactment of the Petroleum Law in 1997, the National Petroleum Agency became responsible for issuing tenders to grant concessions to domestic and foreign companies. The tenders are open to any company meeting the technical, economic and legal requirements. The concessionaires are entitled to all oil and gas produced, subject to taxes and other government reciepts. The government take includes a signature bonus (the minimum amount is established in a public notice tender); royalties of 10% over gross production (or 5% in exploration and production blocks with extreme geological risks); a special participation fee, with variable percentages applied to the net revenue of high-productivity fields; and an annual rental fee assessed per square kilometre. Onshore producers are subject to an extra royalty of 0.5% of production (paid directly to the relevant landowner).

While this concession system is the regime currently in place in Brazil, the 2007 deepwater offshore discoveries may change the legal arrangement in due course. Important authorities, including Brazil's current finance minister, Guido Mantego, have expressed the wish to move away from the concession system and into a PSA regime under which Petrobras would represent the state in all Brazilian oil and gas

1 (1963) 27 ILR 117.
2 (1977) 53 ILR 389.

fields. This is predictable: a decrease in the exploration risks has resulted in a willingness on the part of the state to take more of this exploration risk and enjoy more of the production benefits.

4. Production sharing agreement

A production sharing agreement (PSA) is a contractual relationship between an IOC and the state, authorising the IOC to explore for and exploit oil and gas in a defined area and for a defined period. The state, as the owner of the hydrocarbons, hires the IOC as a contractor for the conduct of exploration and production work in exchange for an entitlement on the part of the IOC to a stipulated share of revenues from the hydrocarbons produced as compensation for the risks taken and services rendered.

The fundamental legal difference between a PSA and a licence is that the relationship between the IOC and the state under a PSA is that of a contractor or service provider. Under a PSA, the state always remains the owner of the resources in the ground – although the contract establishes the agreed compensation that the IOC will receive for services rendered, part or all of which will be in hydrocarbon revenues. The IOC will therefore have a contractual right to be delivered a portion of the hydrocarbon production which becomes available (usually after treatment and processing) at the point of transfer. In other words, the PSA is a service contract with payment in kind. While in practice this arrangement provides the state with the same share of the hydrocarbons extracted that the tax and royalty regime would allocate, maintaining formal ownership of the hydrocarbons has been an important factor for countries keen on protecting their sovereignty over their national resources. This aspect appealed to the growing nationalist cultures of host states in the post-colonial era.

A PSA often provided countries with a more extensive contractual environment in which to tailor the agreed conditions to the specific circumstances of the field, the IOC, the business environment and other factors. The PSA's terms may be confined to petroleum exploration, development and production or it may cover a range of other issues such as the right to import and export goods, work permits, foreign exchange, health and safety, taxation, planning and environmental issues. In this way, the PSA, like the concession, can be used to plug gaps in the overarching regulatory system, which, from the point of view of legal certainty, can be particularly useful (to both the state and the IOC) where the legal system of the state is less advanced.

The key document will be the PSA itself. The parties to the PSA will usually be the state (acting through the relevant ministry or government official), the state oil company (which will take delivery of the state's share of production) and the IOC. A 'licence' may be built into the PSA or granted separately. The rights of the IOC under the PSA are designed to be contractual, rather than proprietary. The issues typically dealt with in a PSA include the following:

- *Definition of the geographical area which the PSA covers and the term of the PSA.* The term is typically split into an exploration phase (usually lasting around ten years over two or more phases) and a production phase if a commercial discovery is made (usually lasting around 20 years), with compulsory partial relinquishments after each exploration phase by which any non-exploited acreage is surrendered back to the host state.

- *Specification of who is the operator in charge of operations.* This is generally the IOC; and if the contractor under the PSA is a consortium of IOCs, then one of them is designated as the operator. In some countries, once a commercial discovery is made, the state party has the option to take over the role of the operator (eg, in China), or to operate jointly with the IOC through a joint venture company (eg, in Egypt).
- *Prescription of minimum work and expenditure commitments.* Given that only a small number of exploration efforts actually lead to a commercial discovery, the work commitment and financial obligations are crucial negotiation factors as they define the extent of the exploration risk. Equally crucial is the definition of commerciality and who determines whether a field is economically viable or not. While some PSAs allow the IOC to decide whether a development is commercial, it is common for the state to have a significant say in determining commerciality.
- *The state's option to participate in the venture.* This, however, does not imply that the state will share in the exploration costs and risks. Usually, the IOC carries the state, which means that the IOC bears all the exploration costs and, if the field is declared commercial, the state has the option to participate in the production revenues.
- *The division of the hydrocarbons produced.* This critical division essentially depends on the relative bargaining power of the state party and the IOC, which is determined by issues such as the strength of the competition among IOCs, the field risks of the exploration and production, the characteristics of the field and so on. In general, however, the process of splitting the hydrocarbon produced goes along the following lines:
  - An initial share (around 10% to 15%) is set aside as royalty hydrocarbons.
  - A share of the remaining hydrocarbons is recovered by the IOC as cost hydrocarbons (ie, to compensate the IOC for the costs it incurred during exploration and production). The speed at which the IOC can recover its costs is an important issue – the quicker the cost recovery the less is the chance that the hydrocarbons will run out before the IOC has recovered its exploration costs.
  - The taxes are often discharged by the state party, but in some PSAs the IOC is subject to the income tax laws of the host state.
  - The remaining hydrocarbons are regarded as 'profit hydrocarbons', to be divided between the parties to the PSA. The percentage corresponding to the state party could be independent of the volumes of hydrocarbons produced. However, it is often the case that the percentage due to the state increases with the amount of hydrocarbons produced. The logic, from the state's perspective, is that once the IOC has obtained a reasonable return on its investment, as much as possible of the upside should go to benefit the state.
- *Any obligation on the IOC by the state to sell hydrocarbons domestically.* While

some PSAs specify that a certain percentage of the production has to be made available for the domestic market, others give the state a more general option to require a sale of up to 100% of the IOC's profit hydrocarbons should the domestic market require this.

- *A stabilisation clause.* This is intended to protect the IOC from the possibility that the state might alter laws or taxes, thereby changing the IOC's return from the development. Even when such clauses exist, an extra issue is the extent to which they are enforceable against the host state.
- *The mechanisms by which the state will monitor that both its primary and its secondary objectives are accomplished.* Supervision or management of operations by the state is usually achieved through a management committee. This management committee will approve investments, annual work programmes and budgets and any declaration of commercial discovery.
- *Ownership of assets.* Typically, all movable and fixed assets acquired by the IOC for the operations immediately become the property of the state party, while the IOC only retains the use of such assets for operations and the right to recover purchase cost out of cost hydrocarbons. As a result, IOCs usually use subcontractors for their drilling and other operations and, where possible, lease rather than purchase equipment and installations.

4.1 Production sharing in Russia

Russia represents a good example of many of the issues surrounding the practical evolution of the PSA regimes, including initial enthusiasm on the part of the state for embracing a PSA regime in order to encourage investment, followed by the state's dissatisfaction with the PSA regime due to the unsatisfactory nature of profit sharing in the actual PSAs during a period of unprecedentedly high energy prices and, finally, the taking of steps by the state to recapture control over its hydrocarbons.

A PSA regime, allowing production sharing with the IOC, was established in Russia in parallel with the licensing regime in order to encourage foreign investment in geographically isolated and technologically complex hydrocarbon projects. Three large PSA projects, Sakhalin I, Sakhalin II and Kharyaga, followed. These three rounds were signed at a time at which the IOCs had a strong position in the negotiations. As a result, the conditions included were favourable to the IOCs. Against a backdrop of increasing energy prices, the Russian government became dissatisfied with existing PSA projects. This led to a series of amendments to the PSA Law in 2003 which, in effect, forced potential PSA operators either to switch to the licensing regime under the Subsoil Law or abandon the projects altogether. Though Sakhalin I, Sakhalin II and Kharyaga were made exempt from this regime change, in 2006 when Shell, the operator of Sakhalin II, announced that project costs would increase, the Russian government withheld its approval. Subsequently, the state renegotiated the Sakhalin II PSA and ultimately took a 51% stake in the field.

5. Service contract

The service contract is a regime under which the host state at all points retains full ownership of all the hydrocarbons being produced on its soil and the IOC performs the exploration and production work as a service to the state. They have been adopted in countries with strong elements of nationalism, including those in which the constitution actually prohibits foreign control or ownership of natural resources, such as Saudi Arabia, Kuwait and Iran. These countries usually have substantial capital at their disposal, but seek the technical expertise of IOCs to carry out the exploration and production activities.

In a *risk service contract*, the IOC is responsible for the capital expenditure and management of exploration and development and all exploration is undertaken at the IOC's own risk, which means that, unless hydrocarbons are found in sufficient quantities, the IOC will not be compensated. If oil can be produced in commercial quantities, the capital expenditure and operating costs incurred are treated as a loan by the IOC to the state, which may be recovered (plus interest) from the state in the following ways:

- Payments made by the state may be in cash (usually out of the proceeds of oil sales). The cash compensation will include reimbursement of capital expenditure and operating costs and a fixed sum per unit of production. The risks associated with fluctuations in oil price are therefore borne by the state, not the IOC.
- The IOC may be entitled to a share of the market value of production recovered for a fixed number of years, with an option to convert that sum into hydrocarbons if it wishes (in which case the arrangements will be very similar, in effect, to a PSA).
- The IOC may be appointed agent for the state for the purposes of marketing and sales of petroleum, in which case it will be entitled to retain a certain percentage of sales proceeds in reimbursement of the loan, together with a nominal commission.

In a *pure services contract*, all exploration and production risks and rewards are retained by the state. The IOC is contracted to perform certain services (eg consulting, engineering, construction, operational, managerial services and so on), as defined by the agreement, in return for a fee. The IOC is a mere contractor, working under the supervision of the state, and it has no legal or beneficial interest in the enterprise itself. This category of contracts includes management contracts (eg, contracts for management services, start-up and operational assistance and so on) and turnkey contracts (under which the contractor will be responsible for the construction and commissioning of a whole facility). Occasionally, the IOC may be given the right to buy back a proportion of production from the state, under separate sales arrangements.

5.1 Service contracts in Iran

In Iran, the constitution prohibits the granting of concessions to foreign companies involved in hydrocarbon extraction. As a result, all exploration and extraction of hydrocarbons is conducted by the Ministry of Petroleum and the National Iranian Oil Company (NIOC). Indirect foreign participation is, however, allowed under a buy-back scheme, which is essentially a risk service contract.

Under an Iranian buyback contract, the IOC will fund all investment costs and implement exploration and/or production operations on behalf of NIOC as per an agreed scope of work. In return, the IOC will receive remuneration for advances on these investment funds, operating costs, related bank charges with interest and the negotiated rate of return through NIOC's allocation of production. The remuneration will be from the sale of petroleum up to a maximum of 60% of production under a long-term export oil sale agreement. The sale agreement will continue until the contractor has fully offset its petroleum costs and the remuneration. The IOC is usually committed to a development period of two to three years and a remuneration period of five to eight years.

6 Conclusion

This chapter has outlined the two main tensions arising in the relationship between an IOC and the state when they join forces to exploit and produce hydrocarbons. The actual choice of the contractual arrangement used to deal with these tensions varies significantly across countries and across time. Important determinants in this respect have been the rise and fall of oil prices, the significance of the oil and gas discoveries actually made and the degree of nationalism exerted by the host state.

Looking ahead, it seems safe to predict that governments and IOCs will continue to innovate in the search for new contractual instruments to govern their relationships more effectively. In this respect it is likely that a change in circumstances (as in the case of Brazil) or disappointment with the outcomes of a previously chosen regime (as in the case of Russia) will provide the trigger leading to these innovations.

Upstream joint ventures – bidding and operating agreements

Charez Golvala
Chadbourne & Parke LLP

1. Introduction

Joint bidding agreements and joint operating agreements are classic features of the oil and gas industry, borne of a commercial need to work together in challenging and costly physical, regulatory and economic environments. As a microcosm of the way in which the oil industry works, they provide a fascinating insight into both the issues addressed in the agreements themselves and the practical, day-to-day management of operations and relationships that are governed by the agreements.

This chapter will explore, in brief, the objectives, structure and some details of joint bidding agreements and joint operating agreements. Whilst it takes as its starting point the international and UK standard forms for a joint operating agreement, the issues and provisions are common to joint operating agreements around the world and this chapter will seek to highlight some particular variations that one is likely to encounter. Similarly, these forms of joint venture agreements are applicable whatever the form in which hydrocarbon rights are granted (whether by licence, concession or production sharing arrangement). (For convenience, this chapter refers to a 'licence' or 'hydrocarbon rights' to encompass a wide range of ways in which the right to explore for and get petroleum can be granted, and to 'licensing' whatever the form of grant may be.)

Joint bidding agreements and joint operating agreements have many features in common. Joint bidding agreements are most commonly found in regions where a consortium of bidders needs to apply to an authority for the issue of hydrocarbon rights. Joint operating agreements are the basic form of organisation for groups of oil and gas companies doing business in the industry around the world. Both forms of joint venture agreement aim to share risks, liabilities and financial commitments between participants and to establish the rights, responsibilities and operational objectives of the group.

2. Joint bidding agreements

Applications for grants of the right to explore for and get petroleum take place in a number of different ways around the world. The United Kingdom awards licences through offering acreage in UK waters to companies in regular licensing rounds. Other countries announce that competing bids may be received for the granting of hydrocarbon rights for a period of time, and yet other countries allow oil and gas companies to negotiate ad hoc for a licence, concession, or production sharing agreement. Whatever the form in which the hydrocarbon rights are awarded, where more than one company joins together to seek the award of such rights, it is common for them to enter into an agreement governing their relationship during the application period. Such agreements are commonly referred to as joint bidding agreements.

In grouping together joint venture participants, different strengths and areas of expertise are sought in order to make a successful bidding team. Technical capability and, if possible, specific technical knowledge of the area for which the group is bidding is an advantage. The financial ability to develop the project is an essential requirement, but the commercial acumen and contacts to exploit the opportunity are also desirable. The softer skills of good connections with the host government and a good track record in the same location can be equally important to the success of the joint venture group. Of course, not all participants will have all of the characteristics in equal measure, and understanding what each player brings to the team is essential for developing the joint bidding agreement.

2.1 Prior to joint bidding agreements

In many cases, there are several steps before a joint bidding agreement is drafted, during which the parties assess and discuss what each of them can offer the venture. Any exchange of confidential information should be made under the terms of a confidentiality agreement. Negotiation of a confidentiality agreement can be remarkably contentious where the underlying data is of real value and unique to one party. Although data exchange has become less important in developed petroleum provinces where large, accessible, data libraries have been created, elsewhere in the world one co-venturer's entry into the group may rely exclusively on having a technical edge through ownership of data. In any event, a confidentiality agreement can help deal with what obligations of non-disclosure and return of information should apply if the bid does not go ahead.

Another document that commonly precedes a joint bidding agreement is an agreement that creates an area of mutual interest. The area of mutual interest agreement signifies broad alignment between different companies, expressing a desire to work together in the event that the area becomes available for development. Area of mutual interest agreements may be entered into for a variety of reasons, including because the area concerned is within a company's strategic objectives or just in its back yard, or as part of long-running or developing relationships within the industry. Area of mutual interest agreements can vary from loose statements of principle to rights of first refusal or exclusivity when acreage comes up for licensing. There may be several areas of mutual interest agreements between different parties, relating to different and/or overlapping areas (which may not be identical to the area for which hydrocarbon rights are being offered) and containing a variety of terms. Checking which areas of mutual interest relate to the bid area, and negotiating between the parties to those agreements to create the bidding group, involves great skill in preserving commercial relationships whilst still forming the ideal bidding group.

2.2 The joint bidding agreement

The joint bidding agreement is itself a precursor to a joint operating agreement and shares several of the same features. Focused on the bid, it nonetheless sets out the basic terms of any subsequent joint operating agreement that would be entered into upon a successful award of hydrocarbon rights. Indeed, in some cases, no joint operating agreement is finalised and operations proceed on the basis of the joint bidding agreement. Depending on the objectives of the group, the time available and the inclination of the parties, a joint bidding agreement can be more or less detailed and cover all or only some of the issues that the eventual joint operating agreement will need to deal with. It is worth bearing in mind that joint operating agreements frequently take a long time to agree, leaving the joint bidding agreement as the only governing document under which the participants will operate, at least in the early years of development. The amount of detail in a joint bidding agreement is often determined by the parties' more or less realistic assessment of the needs of the joint venture during this period.

The joint bidding agreement's primary job is to set out the terms on which the parties will make their bid for the hydrocarbon rights. It will need to delineate the area and type of rights being applied for (often also called an area of mutual interest) and the timetable and actions required to prepare and submit the bid. The duration of a joint bidding agreement is governed by the circumstances of the grant of hydrocarbon rights and usually terminates:

- on notification that the application has been unsuccessful;
- upon an award of the same acreage to a third party;
- if no bid has been submitted by the end of the application period; or
- where the bid is successful, on execution of a joint operating agreement.

A joint bidding agreement will usually also prohibit the parties from making any application for hydrocarbon rights within the specified acreage separately from the group and may contain warranties that the bid area does not conflict with existing areas of mutual interest and other relationships.

Within the joint venture, each participant will wish to be liable only for a set percentage of the costs of the bid and the operation and in turn will be entitled to the same percentage, generally, of the acreage won and the petroleum extracted. (It is not impossible for a joint bidding agreement to deal with a carried interest, under which one party is responsible for a lower percentage or the costs but receives a higher percentage of the petroleum, perhaps in return for particularly relevant knowledge or connections.) The parties will usually intend that these percentage interests will be the same for the subsequent joint operating agreement, but a joint bidding agreement needs to provide for circumstances in which one or more participants drop out of the group or even in which the group needs to be enlarged or reduced in order to win the bid. The percentage interests will also heavily influence the management of the joint venture, with each party having a share of the vote equal to its participating interest. There is usually a lot of debate before agreement is reached on which decisions require unanimity (such as the decision to apply for the interest) and the voting threshold applicable to other decisions.

The principal function of the joint bidding agreement is to prepare the application for hydrocarbon rights and decide between the various terms for the bid that may be proposed by the participants. Each of the parties will contribute to this process; and the inevitable conflict arising from their different strengths and perspectives, whilst being exactly why the bidding group was formed, will need to be managed. Of course, the day-to-day management of the technical evaluation meetings is in the hands of the parties' representatives, but the joint bidding agreement can contribute to the ultimate resolution of any differences by setting the standards against which competing proposals are measured and, ultimately, their voting thresholds.

The joint bidding agreement needs to be tailored to the application process for which it will be used and since these vary around the world, suitable proposals and factors for evaluating them will differ accordingly. Some examples would include: how closely the bid complies with the terms governing the application; the financial cost of the proposals; their technical feasibility for the group; and which overall proposal is most likely to succeed in winning the bid.

Once the preferred bid is voted through by the participants, most joint bidding agreements will provide for a period during which any party that does not wish to proceed can withdraw from the group. That party's interest will either be absorbed by the remaining parties or some of them (pro rata to their interests), or a new party acceptable to the co-venturers will need to be found. To enable a new party to join the group, the joint bidding agreement will have to deal with: the approval of the new party by the existing parties (usually requiring unanimous approval); the financial terms on which the new party joins, including whether it is responsible for a share of past costs of the group; and the mechanism by which the new party accedes to the joint bidding agreement. The withdrawing party will commonly be bound not to make a competing bid for the same acreage or to participate in the same application process, if the choice of acreage could be altered, whether on its own or with another group. It will also be obliged to return or not use shared data and to treat the terms of the bid as confidential.

As mentioned above, the joint bidding agreement should provide enough terms that it can be used to operate the development in the early stages whilst a fully-termed joint operating agreement is being negotiated. A joint bidding agreement may tackle in outline:

- the thresholds for approval of expenditure;
- a short-form accounting procedure;
- the effect of failure to meet financial commitments;
- the terms on which the operator can be removed;
- basic terms for withdrawal, pre-emption and non-consent;
- the consequences of *force majeure*; and
- the treatment of data derived from joint operations.

These issues will be dealt with in more detail in the next section below on joint operating agreements. The level of detail in the joint bidding agreement will be driven by the participants' estimate of how quickly the acreage will be developed, the nature of the working relationship between the parties and how quickly they think a joint operating agreement can be agreed.

Joint bidding agreements are a useful tool in creating and managing the bidding process. Although a bid could conceivably be made without a governing agreement, the commitment in time and money involved in making the bid justifies investing some more time and money in setting out the terms governing the new relationship in reasonable detail. Whilst the joint bidding agreement cannot substitute for good relations between the parties, it can help smooth out the process and provide a framework from which a, hopefully, successful bid will emerge.

3. Joint operating agreements

Joint operating agreements are one of the characteristic elements of the oil and gas industry, having evolved unique techniques for dealing with the issues arising in upstream operations. A joint venture agreement by ancestry, the joint operating agreement has several interesting and novel mutations that are bespoke to the industry. The practical, day-to-day management of an oilfield is reflected in the joint operating agreement; it is a living contract, kept close to hand on the shelves of the technical, financial and operational teams as well as the legal department. Joint operating agreements also play a significant role in mergers and acquisitions and major litigation in the industry. If (or when) the oil and gas industry is no more, a close examination of joint operating agreements from around the world would provide an archaeologist with a perfect fossil record of the way in which the industry worked.

The joint operating agreement is one half of a pair of documents from which a company's hydrocarbon rights are derived and is inextricably linked to, and influenced by, the way in which rights to obtain petroleum are granted. In nearly all circumstances, except where purely private land ownership and the rule of capture applies, a government will grant some species of legal right to 'explore for and get' petroleum (to use the old formula from the United Kingdom). Where more than one company is granted such rights over the same area, the grant will impose joint and several liability on the parties; for example, under a production sharing agreement the co-venturers are often referred to in the singular, as 'Contractor'. Of course, the nature of the co-venture is to allocate risk and reward between the parties and, therefore, the first job of a joint operating agreement is to separate that joint liability into percentage interest shares in the venture. Such a separation works between the participants and not against the grantor of the hydrocarbon rights, but the law or instrument under which the hydrocarbon rights are awarded may require that the joint operating agreement be approved by the granting authority because of that fundamental attempt to separate the interests of the participants into discrete parts. Third parties may also take action against those members of the group that they consider to have the deepest pockets and, therefore, a joint operating agreement will also contain cross-indemnities between participants under which each party agrees to hold the others harmless against all liabilities to the extent of their percentage interest.

Joint operating agreements are designed to last for the life of the field, during exploration, appraisal and development. Amendments, though not rare, are less common than might be expected for a document with a 30-year lifespan. Joint operating agreements used not to deal with abandonment of operations in detail, though this is more common now as the industry adapts to end-of-life and short-life fields. Joint operating agreements vary in how much they deal with the sale of production, depending on the environment in which they are to operate, and are not usually the best place to tackle matters such as unitisation, onshore developments, transportation or processing. This chapter will focus on the key features of the joint operating agreement, but there is far more to say about each of them than can be dealt with here and taking time to read a couple of such agreements in depth (including the model forms put out by the AIPN and the UK Oil and Gas Industry Association) will assist when it comes to working with joint operating agreements in practice.

3.1 Controlling the operator

A joint operating agreement creates a contractual, unincorporated joint venture, which is expressly not a partnership, though there are examples of joint operating agreement-type provisions being included in shareholders' agreements for incorporated entities. As you would expect from its title, the control of operations is a major part of the agreement. One party is appointed as 'operator' with the role of carrying out the joint operations, representing the joint venture to government and third parties, and managing the internal affairs of the group, including meetings and accounting. The operator performs these roles on the basis that it takes no additional risk and obtains no additional reward for the role (ie, over and above its percentage interest share). An operator will be an agent of the other participants and is usually considered to have a fiduciary duty towards its co-venturers. The nature of that duty and the consequences of breach have been extensively debated and litigated. The joint operating agreement will set the standard to which the operator should perform as that of a 'reasonable and prudent' operator and will usually define it by reference to what other operators would do in similar circumstances. This industry benchmarking has variously been described as a 'soft' or 'high' standard depending on the exact terms used and the circumstances of the breach. However, because the operator functions on a not-for-profit basis, the joint operating agreement will provide that it is only liable when guilty of wilful misconduct or for failure to maintain insurances required by the venture. 'Wilful misconduct' is another term that is carefully negotiated and defined in the joint operating agreement; it usually includes intentional or reckless acts and the debate will focus on whether to extend the definition to include gross negligence (which is not a term that has a settled meaning under English law) and what degree of foresight or seniority of management is required before wilful misconduct will have been established.

Given this limited liability, many pages are devoted to the control of the operator and of expenditure. The joint operating agreement will set up an operating committee with representatives from all participants and delineate which matters have to be considered at the operating committee and which have been delegated to the operator. The operating committee will usually create (and a joint operating agreement will provide for) various sub-committees in which a lot of the hard work of operating the venture is done. Voting at the operating committee and in sub-committees will be by percentage interests and therefore establishing the aggregate percentage interest required to agree a proposal (the passmark) will be hotly negotiated in the group. It is worth noting that passmarks are usually described as the 'affirmative vote' of a party and therefore abstentions or absences count against the proposal. Passmarks may be different for separate phases of operations and decisions such as relinquishment of the licence, dismissal of the operator or surrender of parts of the acreage may require higher passmarks or even unanimity. Joint operating agreements vary significantly in the complexity of their voting arrangements, particularly with regard to techniques for avoiding a deadlock; for example, the passmark may be lowered if a proposal is repeatedly brought back to a committee.

The other way in which an operator can be supervised is through the control of expenditure, which is achieved in a number of different ways. An annual work programme and a budget for it will be agreed, consisting of both capital and operating items. The period for which the programme applies will differ depending on whether the field is in the exploration, appraisal, development or production phase and on the regulatory framework with which the participants have to comply. During the exploration phase, the parties may only be willing to commit to an annual programme and provisions will be necessary to deal with circumstances in which the minimum requirements of the licence are not met. In contrast, during the development phase, plans will be required for the duration of the development, not least because approval of the development plan by the regulating authorities is usually required. Appraisal, on the other hand, is mostly an iterative process, requiring the programme to be revisited several times during the appraisal process. Production is relatively straightforward and the work programme and budget can be reviewed on an annual basis.

In addition to the process of agreeing and reviewing the work programme and the overall budget, the operating committee will reserve the right to approve expenditure within the budget of more than a specified figure or type. This use of authorisations for expenditure enables non-operators to review and control the operator's implementation of the work programme and budget. The operator will normally retain discretion in implementing the work programme within the overall budget; however, non-operators will not want the operator's discretion to be unfettered. Of course, the authorisation-for-expenditure procedure is open to abuse, with non-operators blocking plans that are within the overall agreed programme and budget for unconnected reasons. The categories and amounts of expenditure for which an authorisation is required, the circumstances in which an objection is deemed genuine, and the passmark applicable for approval, provide fertile grounds for negotiation and gaming.

As a further control over expenditure, the operator is usually required to observe set procedures with regard to contracting for certain types of work, including a competitive tendering process, restrictions on using affiliates and, possibly, other limitations on the choice of contractor. Requirements for local content, minimum environmental and health and safety standards and other matters may lead to an approved list of contractors. While the operator will want to maximise its ability to get on and operate the field, other parties (including the governmental regulatory agency) may want to ensure that they are protected against not merely bad operations but poor operations. In practice, dissatisfaction with the performance of contractors is a common source of tension between operator and non-operator. It is, of course, impossible for a joint operating agreement to predict and deal with all the scenarios that can arise, particularly as the relationship between oil companies and service providers changes over time. For example, building global relationships and taking a measure of risk has been a key theme over the last few years, whereas, recently, the scarcity of contracting resources has assumed dominance. As contracting parties change their identity and create new joint ventures with companies that may not, previously, have been acceptable, even an approved list of contractors will not always assist.

Access to information and a right to audit accounting information is crucial in order that non-operators can police the conduct of operations. An accounting procedure normally forms a significant part of the joint operating agreement and establishes the nature and categorisation of expenditure charged to the joint account. Given the level of detail involved in this section of the joint operating agreement and the input provided by accounting teams on the ground in each co-venturer, drafting the accounting procedure can take a significant amount of time. But this time will be repaid in the everyday use to which this section is put. Critical areas include the scope of general and administrative costs (including overheads borne by the operator and potentially by its parent company); the amount of contingency to be built into budgets; the extent to which information should be provided to non-operators; and the frequency and terms on which the accounting records can be audited.

3.2 Exceptions to the joint venture

Whilst in principle the parties to a joint operating agreement have agreed to participate in the development of the field in accordance with the decisions made jointly between them, the interests of the parties will usually diverge sufficiently at some point that joint operating agreements will normally contain rights not to participate in joint activities ('non-consent'), or to undertake activities in smaller groups ('sole risk'). Whereas parties might initially have been willing to do everything together, their understanding of the field, its risks and costs, and their own position (economically, commercially or in circumstances where they have been acquired) may have changed over time. Parties with smaller interests may not wish to fund larger commitments than they expected (or than their new owners would like) and larger participants may wish to press ahead with more costly or risky development, even though they do not achieve the passmark for joint action. As mirror images of each other, these provisions can be complex and, because they run contrary to the basic premise of the joint operating agreement, the consequences of non-consent or sole risk need to be set out in detail.

Non-consent is usually not permitted for mandatory obligations under the licence and may be limited to other types of projects. If at a later date a non-consenting party wishes to rejoin that part of the venture, it will normally have to buy its way back in by picking up its share of the cost, commonly together with some sort of time-based additional charge. Sole risk clauses are also limited to certain types of projects depending on the phase of development of the field overall. The operator will usually operate a sole risk project, particularly if joint property is used, and there will be provisions to ensure that joint operations take priority. As with non-consent, there will be penalties for rejoining the venture at a later time, commonly based on a multiple of the original cost. Buying back into the venture at a multiple effectively represents a risk premium to the sole risk parties which can be paid from cash or production or a mixture of both. Finally, provisions for dealing with the sole risk area when liaising with regulators and third parties will be included in the joint operating agreement.

Sole risk and non-consent provisions are not universal in joint operating agreements and in practice are often used as a means of leverage in negotiation rather than for the practical operation of the field. They are useful as a hedge against changing circumstances but need to be carefully reviewed so that, if used in practice, they do not create more harm than good.

3.3 Leaving the joint venture – withdrawal and default

There are normally three ways in which a party can leave a joint operating agreement. A party may choose to transfer its interest, withdraw from the joint venture completely or, in circumstances where a party is in default of its obligations, compulsorily forfeit its interest in the joint operating agreement. Forfeiture is the ultimate price paid for failure to contribute a percentage interest share of the cost of the joint venture. The consequences of default usually escalate over time, beginning with the party losing all rights under the joint operating agreement a period of time after the default has occurred. For as long as the default continues, a party in default will not receive information, be entitled to attend and vote at joint operating agreement meetings or take its share of petroleum. A defaulting party will have the right to make good its default within a period of time and will usually have to pay interest (sometimes at a high rate) on the amount overdue. If the default continues for a further specified period, the defaulting party may be obliged to forfeit its interest under the joint operating agreement and transfer that interest to its co-venturers.

If one party is in default, the other parties to the joint operating agreement will be required to pay the sums in default, each in the proportion that its percentage interest bears to the total of the non-defaulting parties' percentage interests. Any failure to pay these additional sums is normally treated as a default itself. Upon a defaulting party forfeiting its rights, co-venturers will have the right to acquire the defaulter's interest in the proportion that their percentage interests bear to the total percentage interests of those parties exercising their right to acquire. Those parties continuing with the joint venture are unlikely to want to take up the withdrawing participant's interests if those interests are subject to an encumbrance (such as net production interests or overriding royalties) and may wish to renegotiate other aspects of the joint operating agreement in order to make the venture more attractive to them. In circumstances where other parties do not wish to take up the defaulting party's interest, the joint venture normally dissolves and the licence will have to be relinquished because, in effect, parties have realised that the venture is no longer worth continuing.

One practical difficulty with forfeiture is that the defaulting party or parties should also lose its interest under the licence, and creating an enforceable mechanism for this under the joint operating agreement can be challenging. The mechanism by which parties give up their hydrocarbon rights will need to be tied into the terms on which those rights were granted. A joint operating agreement may provide for the defaulting party to be deemed to have withdrawn from the licence and provide for the other parties to act on its behalf to enforce this. In addition, the clause will need to make provision for executing transfer documents by the defaulting party, who is unlikely to wish to cooperate at that stage.

A party may decide even without defaulting on its obligations that it wishes to withdraw from the joint venture and the licence. In these circumstances, other parties will be entitled to take up the leaving party's interests, in proportion to their percentage interests as for default. Participants may be restricted from withdrawing from the joint venture before mandatory obligations under the licence have been fulfilled or during the final critical periods of negotiation for an extension or renewal with the licensing authority. Again, the relationship with the terms of the licence needs to be dealt with in the joint operating agreement so that the two agreements march step in step.

When a party is in default and forfeits its interest, or when it chooses to withdraw from the venture, its liability for abandoning and decommissioning operations will remain and the joint operating agreement should provide for this. Whilst this is unlikely to be an issue during the productive life of a field, as production begins to decline the temptation increases for parties to withdraw before facing abandonment obligations, and every company will have its own view of when its interest becomes uneconomic. However, decommissioning liabilities are often hard to forecast significantly far in advance and even then the margin of error is considerable. It will often prove impossible to determine or agree a sufficiently certain figure for the departing party to provide security for its abandonment obligations, and the continuing parties will have to rely on the covenants and indemnity contained in the joint operating agreement. Consequently, as mentioned in subsection 3.5(b) below on abandonment, it is essential that detailed provisions governing security for the costs of decommissioning are negotiated far enough ahead of the point at which a field becomes uneconomic for any party, so that the party does not pre-empt its abandonment obligations crystallising by withdrawing early from the venture.

One legal point that should be borne in mind is that it has been argued that the provisions for remedying a default, including forfeiture of an interest, may constitute a penalty under English law and, therefore, be unenforceable. Whilst most of the English law on the subject of penalties does not deal with exactly similar circumstances, the general principle remains that an obligation to pay a sum of money or to forfeit property the value of which is significantly in excess of the loss suffered may be considered unconscionable. Of course, the special circumstances of a joint operating agreement and, in particular, the risk to operations of a default and the significant additional cost to other parties in bearing their proportionate share of the default are powerful arguments against this general rule. For the remedy of forfeiture to work, the value of the defaulting party's interest (either from current or anticipated production) must exceed the amount in default and that lays the ground for a claim that the forfeiture is unlawful. On balance, however, because the forfeiture provisions apply to all participants and the agreed return for the risk of contributing to the venture is the reward of a percentage interest, the forfeiture provisions are likely to be seen not as a one-sided penalty to ensure performance but as legitimate protection for all parties' interests.

3.4 Leaving the joint venture – transfers and pre-emption

A party's interest under a joint operating agreement and licence will constitute an asset which is transferable to a third party and, therefore, joint operating agreements regulate the terms on which, and the circumstances in which, such transfers may be permitted. Where the parties have spent a long time choosing their co-venturers, negotiating the terms of a joint operating agreement and working together over the life of the field, control over the terms on which a party leaves and, in particular, the identity of the new joiner to the joint venture is crucial. There are a number of common provisions in a joint operating agreement that deal with transfers, and these can be divided into permitted transfers and rights of pre-emption.

(a) Permitted transfers

All joint operating agreements require that the continuing parties consent to the identity of the proposed purchaser of an interest. Very often consent is qualified by an obligation on the other parties to be reasonable, or a more detailed statement saying that consent may only be refused on grounds of the financial and technical capability of the proposed transferee. (English case law has held that, in the absence of a more detailed provision, "consent not to be unreasonably withheld" means having regard to whether the proposed transferee is financially and technically competent to perform the relevant obligations in similar circumstances.) It is worth noting that this provision requires the consent of each co-venturer (the passmark does not apply) and will usually require sufficient information on the proposed transferee to be provided. Particularly with field developments entering a phase of significant expenditure or getting close to being abandoned, the ability of the new venturer to pay its percentage interest share of the costs may lead the continuing parties to request some form of financial security before agreeing to a transfer.

There are several other usual provisions for a permitted transfer. The transfer must be of an 'undivided' interest, which means that a party may not transfer a subset of its rights and obligations under the joint operating agreement (this does not prohibit the sale of part of the percentage interest). Normally seen as a stand-alone provision, but conceptually operating as an exception to the foregoing rule, a party is permitted to assign rights under the joint operating agreement as security for financing. Some joint operating agreements will limit the minimum percentage interest that a party may own and, therefore, restrict the part of a percentage interest that may be transferred such that neither the transferor nor the transferee may hold less than the minimum percentage interest following the transfer.

Finally, transfers to affiliates are usually permitted without restriction, provided the transferor remains secondarily liable for the performance of obligations under the joint operating agreement. There is usually a supplementary provision requiring reassignment to the original party if the affiliate is no longer part of the same group as the original party. Taken together, these provisions ensure that a participant does not transfer the interest into a shell company that cannot play a full part in the joint operating agreement (although it is possible for special purpose vehicles to hold the interest with the financial and technical contributions being made by an affiliate) and prevent a subsequent sale of a new affiliate out of the group, thereby circumventing the restriction on assignment.

(b) *Pre-emption rights*

Many joint operating agreements provide co-venturers with the right to pre-empt the sale of an interest in the venture to a third party. While parties need their hydrocarbon assets to be tradable, selling out of the venture runs the risk of breaking up the original cohesiveness of the group. Although highly contentious, pre-emption rights can actually be seen as a compromise; they allow a party to sell its interest but still preserve the culture of the joint venture by preventing an unacceptable third party from joining the group. In practice, pre-emption rights can inhibit the saleability of hydrocarbon assets, because potential purchasers will be put off by the prospect of having their deal swiped from under their noses after months of hard and costly work. The industry continues to be split over the desirability of pre-emption rights; the UK government has indicated since its twentieth licensing round in 2002 that it would exercise its right not to approve a joint operating agreement if it contains pre-emption rights. However, there are (and will continue to be) plenty of joint operating agreements with pre-emption rights and the issues that they throw up for acquisitions and disposals in the industry will keep lawyers and negotiators entertained for years to come.

Pre-emption clauses in joint operating agreements vary significantly in their complexity. A broad conceptual distinction can be made between clauses that provide only for rights of first refusal or first offer and those that contain true rights of pre-emption. A right of first offer will usually allow co-venturers a period of time in which to consider whether and when to make an offer for the interest being sold. The selling party may, of course, not accept such an offer, believing that it will find a better price from a third party; however, rights of first refusal often go on to state that no sale may be made to a third party for less than the highest offer made by a co-venturer.

If rights of first refusal are a relatively soft protection, a fully termed pre-emption clause is much more aggressive and gives co-venturers the right to acquire the interest on the same terms as have been negotiated with a third party. The period of time allowed for considering whether to pre-empt can be lengthy (90 to 180 days is not unusual), which, even if no co-venturer exercises its rights to pre-empt, provides a significant disincentive to a potential purchaser. In addition, provisions governing when that time period commences and what information must be provided to co-venturers may have a significant effect on the sales process. Many pre-emption clauses are unclear as to whether an agreement in principle, a reasonably detailed term sheet, or a fully-termed agreement needs to be in place before the offer is circulated to co-venturers.

The other main complexity in drafting and interpreting pre-emption provisions arises in considering the obligation to match the offer. Where the offer is a cash price, matching its terms is not difficult; however, it is not uncommon to see purchasers structure their deal to create a so-called 'unmatchable' offer by including other assets (whether oil fields or oil paintings) in the price. The object is to defeat the pre-emption rights by arguing that no co-venturer can pre-empt the offer because it cannot provide the same consideration. Some more canny pre-emption provisions provide that a cash equivalent must be stated by the selling co-venturer or can be determined (by an expert or ultimately by the courts) if the offer includes non-cash consideration.

Further difficulties arise where a co-venturer is selling several assets covered by more than one joint operating agreement, some of which contain pre-emption rights and some of which do not. In these circumstances it has been argued that the package deal is unmatchable, although this argument is threatened if the sale and purchase agreement negotiated with the third party allocates separate values to each asset (which is sometimes required for tax purposes). Although untested, it is also possible to argue that the pre-emption rights under a single joint operating agreement could be read to mean that the offer consists of purchasing the other assets in the package deal (particularly, if they involve assumption of liabilities) and, therefore, that the entire package deal may be pre-empted.

3.5 Other common provisions

(a) Lifting and disposal

The joint operating agreement gives each party the right to take ownership of and dispose of a percentage interest share of the petroleum won from the operations (which under the licence would be owned jointly by the group). In addition to the right to 'lift' a percentage interest share of hydrocarbons, there will be a corresponding obligation to do so. The commercial, financial and technical commitments involved mean that a failure to lift has serious consequences for other parties. No one is allowed to use the reservoir to store their own production. Production not lifted will be deemed not to have been produced and will, therefore, form part of the reserves and be available for lifting in the future by all parties. The joint operating agreement will commonly oblige the parties to agree detailed provisions governing lifting at the appropriate time in a separate agreement; these are rarely fully-termed at the exploration stage. Detailed provisions relating to over-lifting and under-lifting will also be tackled in the lifting agreement.

Joint operating agreements where the parties expect to find gas will contain analogous provisions, but the most economic method for production of the gas usually cannot be determined when the joint operating agreement is being drafted and, therefore, detailed provisions dealing with the transportation and processing of gas will be left for later. In addition, joint operating agreements written for use where the hydrocarbon rights are granted by a production sharing contract will typically contain provisions relating to the disposal of oil and gas which are tailored to the allocation of cost oil and profit oil under that agreement.

(b) Abandonment and decommissioning

Joint operating agreements do not usually go into great detail about the abandonment and decommissioning of operations, other than to mention that the parties will remain responsible for their percentage interest share of the costs involved. However, as assets enter into late life and for extended field life projects, more detailed abandonment provisions become necessary and it is common for a separate abandonment agreement to be drawn up. Abandonment agreements regulate when, what and how much financial security for abandonment costs is to be provided and are dealt with in more detail in the final chapter of this book. Abandonment agreements are written to continue to bind parties who are no longer co-venturers, unless their decommissioning obligations (including any abandonment agreement) have been transferred to acceptable buyers. Entry into an abandonment security agreement can form part of the terms on which co-venturers consent to a party exiting the group.

For joint operating agreements where it is known or expected that the life of the field may be short, however, some greater detail on the principles of the abandonment agreement, or the time at which it must be negotiated, may be included in the joint operating agreement. As noted above, many joint operating agreement groups run the risk that parties will exit the joint venture prior to their abandonment obligations crystallising and prior to any security being required for future decommissioning liabilities.

(c) Data

Joint operating agreements often contain provisions dealing with the terms on which data acquired during operations may be accessed, exchanged with third parties, or even sold. Geological and geophysical data are valuable assets of the joint operating agreement group and acquiring data which relates to the licence or surrounding area will be a significant cost. All parties to the joint operating agreement are entitled to receive copies of data acquired by the joint venture. Even if they own or intend to acquire data separately which overlaps with data sought by the joint venture, co-venturers are not permitted to prevent the acquisition of data by the group. The terms on which traded data may be acquired may limit its disclosure to co-venturers and, consequently, the fact that one party has such data may not obviate the need for the joint operating agreement group as a whole to acquire that data.

(d) Force majeure

Joint operating agreements will also contain provisions relating to *force majeure*. The definition of *force majeure* is now fairly well settled and tends not to require lengthy negotiation. Generally, it is now accepted that failure to pay (except in a general banking crisis) is not *force majeure*, though careful drafting of what sort of labour disputes are *force majeure* is still required. More thought will be required on which obligations should be relieved and after what period of *force majeure*, and some effort should be made to synchronise the *force majeure* provisions with those of the licensing regime and any known financing requirements.

4 Conclusions

Sandy Shaw (for many years the respected head of upstream legal and commercial at LASMO) made the analogy between marriage and the joint operating agreement, saying that the parties agree "to have and to hold in accordance with the terms of the joint operating agreement until termination, withdrawal, assignment or default do us part". Like marriages between people of different cultures and backgrounds, joint operating agreements differ somewhat around the world, though the fundamentals remain the same. In emerging markets you might find secondment and skills-transfer provisions or reserved rights for the national oil company. In developed provinces most joint operating agreements will have a string of novations, trust deeds, area of mutual interest agreements and other documents bobbing along in their wake. You may find that the concepts of the unincorporated joint venture created by the joint operating agreement are adapted to fit into a shareholders' agreement for the creation of a special purpose vehicle for undertaking an oil and gas project. Whatever the flavour of the joint operating agreement, its concepts of cooperation and control are common to regulating oil and gas operations around the world. If in the distant future, archaeologists find a civilisation in the fossilised remains of joint operating agreements, for so long as the oil and gas industry remains alive, the joint operating agreement will be the double-helix of its DNA.

Unitisation and unitisation agreements

Danielle Beggs
Justyna Bremen
Denton Wilde Sapte LLP

1. Introduction

This chapter gives an introduction to the concept of unitisation and an overview of the commercial issues involved. It does not attempt to provide a comprehensive review of the legal regimes underlying national and international unitisation arrangements, because these are described in detail in other works and are beyond the scope of this chapter.

2. Why unitisation is necessary

An oil or gas field may underlie more than one, even several, adjacent licence or concession areas which are often held by different licensees or concession holders. In the absence of any special arrangements, the producers in each licence or concession area will undertake their own separate petroleum production activities in respect of the portion of the field which underlies their own particular concession area.

This is particularly the case in jurisdictions where the rule (or law) of capture applies. This rule provides that a producer who extracts petroleum from its portion of a cross-concession area field will not be legally liable to account to the producers from any adjacent concession area for the extracted petroleum. Under this rule, this is so even where it could be proved that the extracted petroleum originates from a part of the field which lies in the adjacent licence area, so long as the extracting well does not trespass onto the adjacent licence area.

The practical consequence of this rule is that the producers in each licence area will compete to extract the most petroleum from the common field for their own exclusive benefit. This competition between the different producer groups could result in an unnecessary and wasteful duplication of production facilities and often means that a particular field might not be exploited in the most efficient manner, nor to the fullest extent possible. This may ultimately reduce the amount of petroleum recovered from the common field. The most cited illustration of this issue was the situation in a number of states in the United States in the early years of the industry, where the law of capture meant that very large numbers of wells were drilled very close together.

To overcome these problems the different producers of adjacent licence areas may decide jointly to develop common fields as single units to maximise efficient production from the common field. It is also in the national interest for a country's petroleum reserves to be developed in a way that enhances the total amount of petroleum recovered from each field. For that reason, in many jurisdictions the relevant petroleum authority may have powers to compel producers to develop a field as a single unit.

'Unitisation' is the term used to describe this process, where the producers agree jointly to develop a particular field as a single unit, in accordance with the geophysical boundaries of the actual field rather than the artificial boundaries of the individual concession areas, determined at the time the licence or concession award was made.

Unitisation can apply to several adjacent concession areas in one country (eg, in the United Kingdom, the Britannia gas field). It can also apply to cross-border fields if there is intergovernmental agreement on this issue (eg, in the United Kingdom and Holland, the UK/Dutch Markham Gas Field).

Unitisations are becoming increasingly common. There are a number of reasons for this. As oil and gas areas mature, exploration blocks become smaller, making it more likely that two or more licences may relate to one field. At the same time, geophysical studies are become more sophisticated, leading to earlier identification of common fields. Governments are also taking a more proactive role in managing their oil and gas resources and are encouraging or directing producers to unitise common fields.

A unitisation and unit operating agreement (in this chapter referred to as a unitisation agreement) is the principal agreement negotiated and entered into by the producers to regulate the basis upon which the unitisation will take place, and the way in which the unitised field will be operated between the unitising producers.

In the United States and Canada, it is typical for producers to enter into two separate agreements – a unit agreement and a unit operating agreement. The unit agreements deals with the creation of the unit (ie, to set out the parties' respective interests in the unit, in terms of the sharing of costs and production, and the appointment of a unit operator). The unit operating agreement, on the other hand, then deals with how operations will be carried out on a day-to-day basis.[1] Outside the US and Canadian context, however, it is standard for parties to enter into a single unitisation agreement, dealing with both creation of the unit and unit operations.

In some cases, before the producers in a field decide to enter into a unitisation agreement, they will first enter into a pre-unitisation agreement in order to set out the terms upon which the parties may carry out any joint appraisal drilling and evaluation of the field. Such an agreement may provide for the way the cost of the appraisal studies is shared between the parties. This may need to be adjusted once it is determined how production in the field will be split between the parties (ie, once the parties' unit equities are determined, as discussed below).

3. Unitisation distinguished from other arrangements

Sometimes a decision is made by licensees to develop separate fields as one, for greater efficiency and pooling of resources. Such arrangements, often referred to as 'pooling', must be distinguished from unitisation. Pooling is an established part of US oil and

---

1 See para 4.2 of "International Unitization of Oil and Gas Fields: the Legal Framework of International Law, National Laws, and Private Contracts", Association of International Petroleum Negotiators (AIPN).

gas law and industry practice, and has been described as "the joining together of small tracts or portions of tracts for the purpose of having sufficient acreage to receive a well drilling permit under the relevant state or local spacing laws and regulations, and for the purpose of sharing production by interest owners in such a pooled unit".[2] The important distinction between pooling and unitisation is that the basis of unitisation is the fact that there is a single geological formation underlying the licensees' individual interests. This is not the case with pooling.

4. Examples of the legal framework for unitisation

Unitisation rules were first developed in the United States to deal with the race by oil producers to drill multiple wells, as described above. This has been followed by other countries. A major issue for any legislation dealing with unitisation is that while the relevant petroleum authority may direct producers to unitise their operations, ultimately the individual producers must be able to negotiate the commercial arrangements that strike a balance between their individual commercial interests and the benefits of unitisation.

The legal regime applicable to unitisation in the United Kingdom is discussed here by way of illustration. It is not certain whether or not the law of capture as it applies to petroleum is part of English law; there has been no case law directly on point, nor an express statement of the UK government's position. Some commentators have expressed the view that the law of capture is likely to be part of UK oil and gas law.[3] However, since the Petroleum Act 1934 and consistently since then, the secretary of state has been granted powers to impose schemes to unitise production between licence holders if he/she considers it to be in the national interest to secure maximum recovery of petroleum and in order to avoid unnecessary competitive drilling. Currently, clause 27[4] of the model clauses for seaward production licences gives the secretary of state the power to give licensees notice requiring them to prepare a development scheme for the development of the petroleum field as a unit. Importantly, the secretary of state also has the power to develop such a scheme on behalf of the licensees if they fail to do so.

The provisions of the model clauses are supplemented by the guidance notes issued by the Department of Energy and Climate Change (DECC), which set out DECC's practice in relation to unitisation. The guidance notes specify that licensees should discuss their plans with their neighbouring licensees at an early stage and propose an agreed field development programme. The guidance notes also say that the proposal "could be either a unitised development or other commercial arrangement", so long it allows "an optimum Field Development Programme and demonstrate[s] that there would be no risk of unnecessary competitive drilling".[5] According to the guidance notes, licensees may make representations to DECC about

---

2 See paragraph 1.02 of *The Law of Pooling and Unitization*, Bruce M Kramer and Patrick H Martin (3rd Edition), looseleaf updated to October 2008, Matthew Bender.

3 See paragraph 1-723 and 3-811 of *United Kingdom Oil and Gas Law*, Daintith and Willoughby (3rd Edition), Sweet & Maxwell, 1984.

4 See Schedule 1 of the Petroleum Licensing (Production) (Seaward Areas) Regulations 2008/225.

5 See paragraph 2.5.1 of DECC's guidance notes on procedures for regulating offshore oil and gas field developments.

why they do not think the field in question should be unitised. However, the guidance notes also state that "the Secretary of State will not necessarily refuse to grant development consent to a particular group of Licensees who have not concluded an agreement with the Licensees of an adjacent block on the basis that they have not concluded a unitisation agreement", and that "the Department's acceptance or rejection of any Field Development Programme will, therefore, be on the basis of whether or not it is an optimum development in terms of maximising the economic recovery of oil and gas". This makes it clear that DECC will only interfere in so far as unitisation will have a bearing on the total amount of petroleum recovered from the field. DECC does not consider that its role is to deal with any potential disputes or inequities between licence holders' groups in relation to how much petroleum the respective groups are able to extract from the underlying field.

5. Cross-border unitisation

As mentioned above, petroleum fields may also cross international boundaries. The issues involved in the international context are more complex, because for unitisation to take place agreement needs to be reached not just between the different concession or licence holders, but also with the countries involved. It is usual for the respective governments to enter into a treaty or other intergovernmental agreement in order to deal with unitisation of the particular field. Sometimes cross-border unitisation is a way for resolving a maritime boundary dispute.[6]

One example of a cross-border unitisation is the Markham Field. The United Kingdom and the Netherlands entered into the UK/Dutch Markham Gas Field Treaty on May 26 1992. The treaty provides that the exploitation of the Markham Field Reservoirs is to be undertaken in an integrated manner, and each government must ensure compliance by the Markham licensees with the terms of the treaty. In particular, each government is obliged to require its respective groups of Markham licensees to conclude "licensees' agreements" to regulate the exploitation, in accordance with the treaty, of the Markham Field Reservoirs. The licensees' agreements require the approval of both governments. Under the treaty, production may not commence until a development plan for the effective exploitation of the Markham Field Reservoirs, which has been submitted by the unit operator and contains a programme and plans agreed in accordance with the licensees agreement', has been approved by the two governments.

The UK government has also entered into treaties with Norway[7] in relation to a number of fields.

On April 4 2005, the United Kingdom and Norway signed a new treaty on cross-border cooperation between the two countries in relation to offshore oil and gas resources (the "Framework Agreement between the Government of the United Kingdom of Great Britain and Northern Ireland and the Government of the Kingdom of Norway concerning Cross-boundary Petroleum Co-operation"). The principal

---

6 The Greater Sunrise gas field in the Timor Gap is one example.

7 The two governments entered into treaties relating to the exploitation of, and the offtake of petroleum from, each of the Frigg, Statfjord and Murchison fields.

objective of the treaty is to facilitate all future cross-border projects in the North Sea, and to avoid the need for individual treaties, such as the ones mentioned above, to be negotiated for future cross-border oil and gas projects. Chapter 3 of the treaty deals specifically with unitisation of transboundary reservoirs and provides a good example of the process followed for international unitisations. It provides for a process where the two governments will agree, after consultation with the licensees, that a particular field should be exploited as a single unit. Provision is made for the licensees to enter into a "Licensees' Agreement" (ie, a unitisation agreement), which is then to be approved by both governments. The unitisation agreement is to provide for such matters as the apportionment of the reserves as between the licensees of each state. If there is a dispute between the two governments relating to issues such as the apportionment of reserves, then the matter is to be referred to expert determination in accordance with the procedure set out in Annexure D of the treaty. The unit operator appointed by the licensees needs to be approved by both governments. Before production can commence, the unit operator would need to submit for approval by both governments a development plan for the exploitation of the reservoir.

A treaty such as the one discussed above is only binding on the governments, not the licensees. Accordingly, there needs to be specific provision dealing with international unitisation in the national laws of the countries involved. This is required so that once an intergovernmental agreement is reached, the respective governments can direct their licensees to cooperate with each other as per the agreement reached. In the United Kingdom, model clause 28[8] gives the secretary of state power to give directions to licensees about the "manner in which the rights conferred by [the] licence shall be exercised" where he/she is "satisfied that any strata in the Licensed Area or any part thereof form part of an Oil Field, other parts whereof are in an area … [outside the United Kingdom], and the Minister is satisfied that it is expedient that the Oil Field should be worked and developed as a unit in co-operation by the Licensee and all other persons having an interest in any part of the Oil Field".

6. Unitisation and other contractual arrangements

In addition to considering the national and international laws relevant to their unitisation arrangements, licensees also need to be mindful of the impact of the unitisation on other contractual arrangements. In particular, the joint operating agreements (JOAs) entered into between the individual groups of licensees will still remain in force, to govern the relationship between the licensees *inter se*. So in effect the joint operating agreement and the unitisation agreement will exist side by side. However, the unitisation agreement will usually provide that its terms will prevail over the joint operating agreement to the extent of any inconsistencies.

Where joint operating agreement operations commenced before the unitisation takes place, there may be issues that need to be dealt with for a smooth transition from joint operating agreement operations to unit operations. In particular, the

8 See Schedule 1 of the Petroleum Licensing (Production) (Seaward Areas) Regulations 2008/225.

unitisation agreement will need to deal with issues such as the transfer of certain contracts to the unit operator, and the deeming of any work that has already commenced to be now carried on under the control of the unit operator.

The provisions of any other contracts that may be affected by the unitisation also need to be considered. For example, it may be that when operations were first commenced and various project and financing agreements were entered into by the licensees, the unitisation was not contemplated. If a subsequent unitisation is decided upon, or indeed forced upon the licensees, then it is likely that the licensees will need to obtain approvals from their financiers and other counterparties, depending on the terms of the financing and other project documents.

Often unitisation takes place at the host government's behest and involves close cooperation with the government. However, it goes without saying that if the decision to unitise is made at the initiative of the parties themselves, then all relevant consents from the relevant government authority (DECC in the United Kingdom) will still need to be obtained by the licensees.

7. Typical issues dealt with in a unitisation agreement

7.1 Overview

A unitisation agreement will set out the principles governing the conduct of operations within the unitised area that have been agreed between two or more licence groups. In many ways it is similar to a joint operating agreement, although there are important differences stemming from the fact that even though joint operations will be undertaken, the different groups of licensees ultimately hold different hydrocarbon interests. This discussion of the content of a typical unitisation will focus on unitisation agreements which are not cross-border. The reason for this is that a cross-border unitisation agreement is likely to contain similar provisions to a standard unitisation agreement, as well as dealing with complex issues relating to the interface between the different legal regimes applying in the countries involved. It is difficult to generalise about these issues, but they are briefly discussed at the end of this chapter.

The only industry model form of unitisation contract known to the authors is the AIPN Model Form International Unitization and Unit Operating Agreement.[9]

A typical unitisation agreement is likely to contain clauses dealing with the following issues:

- an expression of an intention by the licensees to operate the field as a unit;
- the percentage interest to be held by each group of licensees in the unit, and possibly provision for a redetermination of that interest;
- the appointment of a unit operator and an operating committee;
- rights and duties of the unit operator;
- voting and decision making;

9 The word 'international' in the context of this model agreement is used to mean that the agreement is intended to be used internationally, in different jurisdictions; not that the agreement is intended to deal with cross-border unitisation issues.

- expenditure and budgeting;
- ownership and disposal of the petroleum produced;
- sole risk operations and non-unit operations;
- decommissioning; and
- default, assignment and termination.

Below we have set out a more detailed discussion of some of these issues.

7.2 Creation of a new unit

The primary function of a unitisation agreement is to create a new unit out of individual licence or concession areas held by various producers. The terminology used will vary according to the agreement in question, but generally the agreement will provide for the parties to undertake 'unit operations' in relation to the 'unit area', being the total area of the parties' respective licences, without regard to the boundary lines between the licences.

The portion of the field area covered by one licence area is often referred to as the 'tract' owned by the relevant licensees.

All the rights, liabilities and obligations of the parties under the agreement will be in proportion to their 'unit equity' (often referred to as the 'tract participation'), which will be set out in the agreement. Often the parties' rights, liabilities and obligations are expressed to be several in proportion to their unit equities, rather than joint and several.

7.3 Unitised substances

The agreement will typically refer to all the hydrocarbons produced as a result of the unit operations as 'unitised substances', and this will include crude oil and/or gas. There may be instances where both crude oil and gas are present in the field, but only one is subject to unit operations – for instance, if crude oil is only found in one part of the field, attributable to only one licensee group. However, this is not typical.

7.4 Determination of tract participations/unit equity

Where a number of parties decide to conduct exploration and production activities in a standard JOA-type situation, their respective interests in the joint venture will be agreed at the outset, usually according to their financial contribution to the venture, and will not change unless one or more of the parties decide to sell the whole of part of their interest in the venture. In a unitisation, however, the situation is more complicated. This is because the two (or more) groups of licensees need to determine what interest each group will have in the unit. This is one of the most significant differences between a unitisation agreement and a joint operating agreement. Each group of licensees will wish its unit equity to be based on the percentage of total hydrocarbons in that portion of the field which actually underlies its tract. The interest held by each individual party will then be that proportion of the unit equity that the party is entitled to under that group's joint operating agreement. So for example, if group A has a participating interest of 60%, and group A is made up of four licensees, each holding a 25% interest, then each of those licensees will ultimately be entitled to 15% of the hydrocarbons produced.

Unit equity is important because it determines each party's entitlement to the hydrocarbons produced (the unit substances), the money each party is expected to contribute, and each party's voting rights.

There are many different methods for calculating the volumes of hydrocarbons in the field at the time the unitisation agreement is entered into. This is a technical issue discussed in detail in other publications,[10] but for the purposes of this chapter it should be noted that this is an important issue that will be the subject of detailed negotiations between the parties. Once the licensee groups' participating interests have been calculated, there may be instances where the parties wish further to adjust the interests. For example, if one group of licensees were to have undertaken extensive work before unitisation took place, the parties may decide that those licensees will be compensated by an increased interest, rather than a cash payment. Any such adjustments will need to be documented in the agreement (most likely in one of the annexures which set out how various calculations and determinations are made). Because the participating interest is used to calculate not only what proportion of hydrocarbons the parties will receive but also the amount of money to be contributed towards works going forward, it is important for any such adjustments to be carefully considered in the context of the whole unitisation agreement.

7.5 Redeterminations

A calculation of the amount of hydrocarbons attributable to each tract can only ever be a very good estimate until such time as those hydrocarbons are extracted. For this reason, the agreement will often make provision for the unit equities to be adjusted during the term of the agreement, when more accurate information is available. This adjustment mechanism is referred to as a 'redetermination' and is one of the most complicated issues in unitisations.

A redermination provision needs to deal with the following:

- *The trigger for a redetermination* – this could include providing for redeterminations to take place at certain regular intervals during the term of the agreement; upon a certain volume of hydrocarbons being produced; or by one party making a case for it. Care should be taken to ensure there is some limit on this procedure being triggered, as it can be a lengthy and expensive process to deal with.
- *Timing* – it is usual to limit redeterminations to the first few years of production. It should be possible for the parties to get a more accurate assessment of the field quite soon after more extensive drilling has taken place. Importantly, it would not be practical for a redetermination of the quantity of hydrocarbons each party is entitled to lift to take place towards the end of the life of the field.
- *The redetermination procedure to be followed* – the operating committee (see below) will usually be in charge of undertaking the redetermination procedure, although provision may also be made for a separate

10 See paragraph 1-743 of *United Kingdom Oil and Gas Law* (see n 3 above) for a detailed discussion of the most common methods of calculation.

'redetermination committee'. Often the terms of reference for the redetermination will be included as an exhibit to the agreement. These terms of reference would be expected to be based on the procedure that was followed to work out the original determination of unit equities.

- *Consequences of the redetermination* – a redetermination of the unit equity affects all the rights and obligations that the parties have under the agreement, from the beginning. Accordingly, the agreement should then provide for adjustment of any hydrocarbons that have already been lifted by the parties before the redetermination. The financial investments made by the parties, which are in proportion to their interests, will also need to be adjusted. This is often done by giving the parties with the new, larger interest the right to take an even greater proportion of the hydrocarbons going forward. These additional rights would be designed to compensate those parties for the entitlements they should have received before the redetermination. Such a calculation is quite complex, because it also needs to take account of the larger expenditure such a party should have made. Typically (and this is the case under the AIPN model agreement), no compensation will be given to parties for the fact that the market price of the hydrocarbons may have changed.
- *Government consent* – the redetermination may need to be subject to consent from the relevant regulatory authority, depending on the legal regime for petroleum applicable to the unitisation.
- *Dispute resolution* – ideally the parties should be able to agree to amend the unit equities they hold, but provision needs to be made for what will happen if agreement cannot be reached. Typically, the matter will be referred for determination by an expert. The agreement may employ different tactics to ensure that any disputes as to redetermination are resolved quickly. One cited example is the so-called 'pendulum' procedure, under which an expert is only able to adopt the position of one of the parties. This is designed to encourage the parties to be reasonable in the positions they take.[11] The expert would be unlikely to adopt the position of a party who takes an extreme view, if the position of the other party is more reasonable.

Because redeterminations can give rise to such complex legal and practical problems, there have been some unitisations where the parties have elected not to provide for a redetermination of their original unit equities.

7.6 Adjustments to the unit area

Just as the licensee groups' participation unit equities can only be estimates based on seismic data, as well as perhaps some appraisal wells, the extent of the unit area (that is, the field underlying the licences held by the licensee groups) can also only be estimated at the time the unitisation agreement is entered into. A change in the area will usually mean that there will be a change in the licensee groups' participating

11 See paragraph 1-743 of *United Kingdom Oil and Gas Law* (see n 3 above).

interests, and so this will usually be tied into the redetermination clause (if there is one). The AIPN model agreement provides for changes in the unit area and any necessary redeterminations.

It may be that, as drilling progresses, it turns out that the field underlies areas which are outside the licence areas already held by the licensees. It may even be that a third party is the holder of a licence which overlaps the field area. Bringing additional licence areas and/or third parties into the unitisation poses such a significant change to the agreement that it would necessarily involve a complete renegotiation of the agreement. This scenario is unlikely to be dealt with in a typical unitisation agreement.

7.7 Unit operator

Similarly to a joint operating agreement, a unitisation agreement will provide for the appointment of a unit operator to have overall responsibility for all unit operations.

The rights and duties of the unit operator under the agreement may include:

- a general duty to carry out all operations in accordance with good industry practice, in accordance with all relevant laws and consents, and in accordance with the requirements of the licences/concessions;
- a duty to follow the directions of the operating committee (see below);
- a right to employ sub-contractors to carry out work or services relating to unit operations on the basis that the unit operator remains responsible for the unit operations and liable for acts and omissions of such agents and contractors;
- a duty to pay and discharge all costs and expenses incurred by the unit operator and keep accounts in accordance with the accounting procedure set out in the agreement;
- a duty to prepare programmes and budgets, implement such programmes, and provide the other parties with reports, data and information concerning the unit operations; and
- a duty to obtain all governmental consents and comply with any governmental directions relating to the unitisation and unit operations.

7.8 Operating committee and decision making

The agreement will also provide for an operating committee, to supervise the unit operator's activities. The operating committee will generally be made up of representatives from each party. Although a unitisation agreement is between two (or more) groups of licensees, the agreement will usually give each individual party voting rights. Each party's voting rights are determined by the extent of its tract participation interest (unit equity). To ensure that there is no excessive dominance by one group, it is common to provide that some, if not all, decisions must be supported by at least one licensee from each group.

7.9 Sole risk operations

As with sole risk operations under a joint operating agreement, sole risk operations under a unitisation agreement involve a party undertaking drilling work at its own risk and cost. It will generally be provided that such operations may be conducted by a party, but only with prior approval of the operating committee. At the core of a unitisation agreement is the intent that the field should be operated as a unit for the benefit of all the parties. Accordingly, approval for sole risk operations may only be given where the operations will not prejudice unit operations. The agreement may provide that if the sole risk operations lead to a discovery and the operating committee decides that further work is appropriate, then all further work will be undertaken by the unit operator. The party that undertook the sole risk operations would then be reimbursed for the cost of the work it had undertaken. All hydrocarbons recovered will form part of the unit substances divided between all the unit parties.

7.10 Non-unit operations

A typical unitisation agreement will also deal with non-unit operations (ie, any operations which are not unit operations or sole risk operations). This usually describes any operations which are undertaken by a party or licence group within its licence area, but outside the unit area. The agreement may allow parties to use unit facilities/property for non-unit operations. This right is usually subject to some limitations. As with sole risk operations, non-unit operations must not prejudice any unit operations. Additionally, unit facilities can only be used for this purpose if there is spare capacity.

There are a number of different approaches to how such operations may be treated by the parties in the unitisation agreement. The AIPN model agreement, for example, provides for a number of different options. For instance, the non-unit operations may be carried out by the unit operator, or by the operator for the relevant group of licensees (ie, the operator under the relevant joint operating agreement). Naturally, such operations are at the relevant parties' own cost and risk. Usually the parties will not be charged for using the unit facilities/equipment, but there may be some circumstances where a fee will be payable (most commonly if the parties use the facilities more than had been allocated to them according to their unit equity).

7.11 Disposal of hydrocarbons produced

The agreement will typically provide that each party will be free to dispose of its share of hydrocarbons produced as a result of the unit operations. The agreement will provide that regardless of which portion of the field the hydrocarbons actually came from, the hydrocarbons owned by the licensees shall be deemed to have been produced from that licensee's tract and attributed to that licensee's licence interest. Depending on the legal regime applicable, this may be important for the purposes of tax law and any other laws which require the hydrocarbons to be attributed to a particular licence interest.

The AIPN model agreement sets out a detailed procedure dealing separately with the disposal of crude oil and gas. How this is dealt with by parties to a particular unitisation will depend on what hydrocarbons the parties anticipate will be produced, and what arrangements for their lifting are in place at the time the agreement is entered into.

7.12 Decommissioning

A unitisation agreement will typically provide that the costs of decommissioning (abandonment) will be borne in proportion to each party's unit equity. The parties' actual decommissioning obligations will be determined by the relevant petroleum legislation.

7.13 Assignment

An assignment of interest under a unitisation agreement by a party must be tied to assignment of interest under the relevant joint operating agreements and the licence or concession interests held by that party. As with assignments under a joint operating agreement, a unitisation agreement is likely to include provision for pre-emption rights, giving the other parties the opportunity to buy the interest being disposed of. The AIPN model form agreement does not provide for pre-emption rights, on the basis that any pre-emption rights set out in the relevant joint operating agreements will apply. This is on the basis that limiting pre-emption rights to only within each licensee group will prevent disturbing the voting balance between the different licensee groups.

7.14 Other provisions

A unitisation agreement will also contain other provisions of the type found in a joint operating agreement, including dispute resolution, what constitutes an event of default, termination, dispute resolution, the accounting procedure, confidentiality and intellectual property.

8. Cross-border unitisation agreements

As mentioned above, cross-border unitisation agreements need to deal with additional issues arising from the fact the unit operations are in effect being undertaken pursuant to two (or more) separate legal regimes, and supervised by at least two different government authorities. Some of the more complex issues may include the following:

- *Governing law and dispute resolution* – as in any international agreement, this may be a point of contention between the parties. Because national interests are also involved, the governing law and forum for determining disputes may be decided upon by the governments. One example of an international dispute resolution clause is for the dispute to be referred to the relevant government for determination, and if the governments decide that the dispute in question is not one which should be decided by them, the matter will then be referred to international arbitration.
- *Work programmes* – all work programmes are likely to need the approval of both governments.
- *Decommissioning* – decommissioning is an increasingly important issue and any decommissioning plan will need to comply with the regulatory regime of both countries.
- *Redeterminations* – in cross-border unitisations, the governments involved will want to maximise the amount of petroleum which can be attributed to their

> group of licensees. Accordingly, they will take an interest in the initial calculation of the unit equities, as well as any redeterminations. In terms of the unitisation agreement this may mean that any redeterminations or adjustments cannot be made without close government involvement and approval. The unitisation agreement may also give the governments the right to call for a redetermination.

Ultimately, the terms of a cross-border unitisation agreement will reflect the commercial arrangements of the parties, in the same way that a standard unitisation agreement does. This will be superimposed with provisions that reflect the governments' interests in preserving their fair share of the reserves, as provided for in the relevant intergovernmental agreement.

Financing upstream developments

Nicholas Ross-McCall
Huw Thomas
Ashurst LLP

1. Introduction

The broad upward trend in petroleum prices over the last few years (with the notable exception of the last months of 2008) has made many marginal oil and gas discoveries commercially viable development projects and justified further development of producing fields. Smaller players look to international commercial banks with specialist project finance or reserve-based lending (RBL) teams to supply a significant part of the funding for such projects. The focus of this chapter is therefore on international commercial bank financing, the prominent form (for borrowers which cannot raise bank debt off the strength of their balance sheets) being the borrowing base facility (BBF). The chapter will focus further on oil and gas assets in the UK continental shelf (UKCS) which, together with the US Gulf Coast, has been one of the main basins where reserve-based financing techniques have been used to date, but it will also look to other locations where such techniques are being utilised, or are likely to be utilised in future.

2. Background

2.1 Strong appetite for debt

In recent years there has been a strong appetite among new-entrant independent oil and gas companies for debt financing to fund the development and acquisition of upstream assets. There have also been rapid developments in the types and locations of transactions financed, the choice of debt options and the terms on which the debt is made available. At the same time projects have become in some ways riskier from the point of view of lenders, which has probably led to an increase in pricing of senior debt and a lower limit on the amount of traditional senior debt which banks are able to provide. This has in turn led to the development of multi-source financing structures, including venture capital, convertible bonds and mezzanine debt.

2.2 Development of market from single asset financings to borrowing base facilities

During the early years of the UK continental shelf industry in the 1970s and 1980s, the development of assets was either financed on balance sheet by the majors or, where debt was financed by smaller players, it involved financing a single asset on a project-finance basis. Projects were not, with the benefit of hindsight, particularly risky financing propositions because fields were large, loans were based on conservative reserves figures (leaving substantial cushions of reserves), sponsors were generally large companies and abandonment was a distant prospect. As the North Sea basin matured, that type of financing largely became inappropriate for the smaller fields which were then being developed. As long ago as the early 1990s financing a portfolio of assets by way of a borrowing base facility began to become established in the UK market as a more feasible and less cumbersome approach. Funding a portfolio of assets is attractive to lenders as it de-risks the asset base; a deterioration in reserves at one field may be offset by upside from another.

2.3 Continued appeal of the classic borrowing base facility

The borrowing base facility remains popular with borrowers today primarily because of the flexibility and relatively favourable pricing that it provides. It enables borrowers to raise financing based on the value of their assets, generally in the United Kingdom on a P50 basis for producing assets and on a P90 basis for development assets (see Section 3.3). In the US market, account is generally only ever taken of P90 reserves. But that is at least partially balanced out as UK banks make their calculations based on post-tax cash flows, whereas the US market looks at pre-tax cash flows. Borrowing base facilities are also attractive in that the facility is revolving (ie repaid amounts can be re-borrowed) and will often permit expenditure for general corporate purposes, so that the funds do not always have to be spent on the assets supporting the financing. The net present value (NPV) of future cash flows projected to be generated by the assets being financed is of central importance in setting the amount of debt available. Assuming the net present value is adequate to support the financing, the rest of the representation and covenant package is relatively light compared to what would be found in a full-blown project financing.

3. Basic principles of reserve-based lending

3.1 Cash-flow financing

The riskier a project, the more suitable it is for equity financing as opposed to debt financing. Debt providers will only lend to projects with a sufficiently low risk profile and clear cash flows to justify their expected fixed returns, whereas borrowers have a higher and uncapped potential return on their equity contributions with a greater appetite for risk. Borrowers can use hedging arrangements to underpin the cash flows upon which a project depends, including hedging interest rates, currency exchange rates or commodity prices, to make the financing more attractive to lenders.

Debt financing is dependent on stable cash flows and traditionally is not appropriate for exploration and appraisal projects. With debt providers being keen to secure relationships with new market entrants at an early stage in their business cycle, in recent years pre-development assets have become capable of being debt financed.

3.2 Calculation of net present values and related projections

RBL transactions essentially involve financiers lending against the net present value of future cash flows projected to be generated from independently audited oil and gas reserves of included fields. Calculation of the net present value and key financial ratios is achieved using an audited computer model to produce a projection through to the end of the life of the loan and beyond. The inputs for the model include certain assumptions. Usually, lenders provide economic assumptions (eg, interest rates and forward-curve petroleum prices) and the borrower provides technical assumptions (eg, capital expenditures, operating expenditures, decommissioning costs and reserves figures). The net present value is calculated by taking the projections of gross proceeds for each future period (usually six months) and then deducting projected capex, opex, taxes (in the United Kingdom but not in the United States) etc for such period and discounting the remaining amounts at a fixed rate of discount, usually comparable to the interest rate payable on the loan.

This initial projection is then redetermined periodically throughout the life of the facility, usually every six months, to ensure that the lenders have comfort that the borrowings under the facility are covered by expected cash flows from the relevant fields. The reserves figures used in the computer model are usually taken from an annual independent reserves report and a semi-annual update from the borrower's in-house engineers.

3.3 Borrowing base amount

The borrowing base amount is the term used to describe the maximum amount permitted to be drawn under the facility at any particular time, which must in any case be within the limit based on the total commitments of the lenders at that time. The borrowing base amount is based on the net present value of cash flow, taking account of – as stated above – P50 or P90 reserves, divided by a denominator which is usually 1.5.

P90 (or P1) and P50 (or P2) are shorthand for proved reserves and proved and probable reserves respectively. Typical definitions are thus:

- *P90* means those quantities of petroleum which have a 90% or greater probability of being recovered from the included fields (determined in accordance with the guidelines of the Society of Petroleum Engineers); and
- *P50* means those quantities of petroleum which have a 50% or greater probability of being recovered from the included fields (determined in accordance with the guidelines of the Society of Petroleum Engineers).

Of course, there is no absolute certainty that the projected cash flows will be achieved. Economically recoverable reserves may be less, or expenditure may be higher than expected – for example if the geology of a field is more complex than anticipated, increasing the costs of development.

The borrowing base amount can be increased through commodity hedging, if the borrower enters hedging contracts ensuring a price above the deck used by lenders in their projection.

3.4 Ratios

A cover ratio is a forecast of the financial viability of a project which is redetermined on a running basis in projections.

Three key ratios in a classical project financing are the debt-to-equity ratio, debt service cover ratio (DSCR) and loan life cover ratio (LLCR). The first is not much used in borrowing base facility documentation, but it will underpin a project's economics and the size of the lenders' commitments.

A debt service cover ratio is used by lenders to gain comfort that the borrower will have funds available to make its debt repayments on a current basis. It is the ratio of net revenue before payment of financing costs during a certain period and the financing costs due to be repaid during that period. In reserve-based lending transactions the debt service cover ratio is usually determined on a projected rather than a historical basis. Uses of the ratio (for which targets for the ratio will typically range from 1.0 to 1.3) include as a condition precedent to first drawdown, as a trigger for an event of default, as a device to vary the interest rate, as a distribution block, as a tool to determine whether insurance proceeds must be applied in prepayment, as a drawstop preventing further utilisation of the facility, and as a further limit on the borrowing base amount.

A loan life cover ratio is the ratio of the net present value at a relevant calculation date of future projected revenue during the life of the facility and the amount of principal debt outstanding on that calculation date. It has the same range of uses as a debt service cover ratio.

Often there is no loan life cover ratio in a borrowing base facility, supposedly because loans are not being matched against the net present value of a single asset. With the portfolio approach, there is a spread of assets which may change over time so the non-inclusion of loan life cover ratio is agreed by lenders to meet borrowers' requirements for increased leverage, justified by this de-risking of the loan.

In a borrowing base facility, the project life cover ratio (PLCR) is usually the key ratio, as banks focus more on the life of the assets rather than that of the debt. It is the ratio of the net present value at a relevant calculation date of future projected revenue during the life of a project to the principal debt outstanding on that calculation date.

The project life cover ratio assists lenders in ascertaining the cushion available if the loan is not paid by the final maturity date. For additional protection, banks prescribe the date on which a certain amount (typically 20% to 25%) of the original reserves of the included fields remain, as a longstop date for repayment of the loans. This is known as the reserve tail date and protects the banks from relying on speculative future recovery from the end of the life of the fields, allowing them to take a more robust approach towards abandonment costs. The theory used to be that decommissioning costs would be matched by revenue arising after the reserve tail date, but this may no longer hold true for UK deals (see Section 6.7).

Some borrowing base facilities incorporate features from corporate-style loans, with looser controls over the borrower group in exchange for corporate lending ratios, such as a current ratio and a total borrowings to EBITDA (earnings before interest, tax, depreciation and amortisation) ratio.

3.5 Control of borrowing base asset cash flows

Control over cash flows in reserve-based lending transactions is achieved using secured bank accounts through which all receipts relating to the relevant assets will pass. Under an agreed cash waterfall, withdrawals may only be permitted to meet expenditures set out in the latest cash-flow projection (or to a set percentage over and above such figures, say 10%) and, subject to additional restrictions, surpluses after payment of finance costs and funding of any other relevant project accounts can be paid out as dividends and used for general corporate purposes.

Additional accounts might include cash lock-up accounts, to which all free cash must be transferred in the event of certain cover ratios being breached, and a debt service reserve account to which funds representing a certain period of debt service (typically two to six months) must be kept at all times.

4. Types of facility

4.1 Sources of funds

International commercial banks are by far the largest providers of project and reserve-based finance. Other sources include the bond market, specialist investment institutions providing high-yield subordinated finance, and multilateral institutions such as the International Finance Corporation or the European Investment Bank.

4.2 Single-asset financing

As we have seen, originally independent oil and gas companies commonly used a single-asset project financing structure to fund their share of capital expenditure in respect of a field. The approach of lenders was conservative in that:

- when calculating the net present value of the borrower's share of production for the purposes of determining the loan amount and the cover ratios, they would look only at P90 reserves, even for producing assets;
- in addition to a project life cover ratio, the loan agreement would include a loan life cover ratio and a reserve tail date; and
- they required a full security package, including specific fixed security over the borrower's interest in the relevant licence, the joint operating agreement (JOA), EPC contracts, marketing agreements, transportation agreements and other project documents, possibly also with lender direct agreements.

This approach is still appropriate for financing large, single assets outside the UK continental shelf. A number of factors drove a move in the United Kingdom from these single-asset project financings to a portfolio or borrowing base structure, including:

- the assets under development in the UK continental shelf are smaller now (originally perhaps 100 million barrels or greater but now more like 10 to 30 million barrels);
- technology risk has increased, with a greater reliance on enhanced recovery techniques to extract petroleum and yet also reliance on ageing infrastructure;
- the field life remaining of the assets being financed has become shorter (down to perhaps five years now as against 20 years at the high point of UK continental shelf discoveries), with decommissioning now a key issue;

- where the lenders see the risks as having increased, they will want to charge a commensurately higher margin and fees; and
- the single-asset approach is not cost-effective for raising a relatively small amount of debt, given the expense of putting together a quite complex and extensive finance document package.

4.3 Borrowing base facilities with portfolio of producing assets

For the reasons described above, single-asset project financings have become unattractive for lenders and borrowers in the UK continental shelf and other mature basins around the world, with the borrowing base facility now prevalent. Key features include the following:

- There is a pooling of assets, perhaps some in development and some in production. The borrower has the flexibility to bring new assets into the portfolio (albeit subject to bank approval) and to dispose of assets from the portfolio (again subject to bank approval and repayment of a portion of the loan by reference to the net present value of the disposed asset).
- Calculation of the loan amount and ratios is by reference to the net present value of (probably) P50 reserves for producing assets and P90 reserves for development assets until they have been in production for a certain period. The maximum facility amount at any time is the lower of the lenders' commitments and the borrowing base amount (see Section 3.3).
- There is usually no loan life cover ratio.
- There is a relatively light security package, including only perhaps a charge over accounts and share pledges and maybe, in jurisdictions which recognise the concept, a floating charge over the assets of the borrower.

The portfolio approach of the borrowing base facility mitigates the risk of problems with one asset affecting the ability of the borrower to service the loan and permits a large enough loan to be raised with simple enough documentation, so as to make the exercise economic. In essence, a borrowing base facility seeks to match the amount of money lent to the net present value of future income from the portfolio of assets. If, for example, a new projection is produced on the basis of a lower oil price or the reserves are revised downwards, the borrowing base shrinks and the borrower will be required to prepay the loans to the extent that the outstandings exceed the revised borrowing base amount. In recent years, borrowing base facilities have been made available to small and mid-sized independents acquiring assets being divested by larger oil companies. As there is no strong parent company behind such a borrower, these have been secured by way of a floating charge. Some commentators regard borrowing base facilities as thinly disguised corporate loans to sub-investment-grade companies, and the defensive security as a means to justify the extra risk before credit committees. Whilst there may be some truth in this, in the authors' view the protection that the lenders receive through careful modelling and controls over the borrowing base cash flows provides legitimate differentiation for borrowing base facilities as against corporate facilities.

4.4 Other features of borrowing base facilities

Other features of borrowing base facilities may include those set out next:

- As the borrowing base amount is recalculated periodically during the life of the facility (see Section 3.2), it will be a revolving facility (as opposed to a term loan), but usually with the lenders' commitment reduced on six-monthly reduction dates. On a reduction date, the loan will need to be paid down to the lower of:
  - the reduced commitment amount; and
  - the borrowing base amount, but possibly only to the extent that the borrower has available free cash flow (as a nod to limited recourse project financing techniques).
- A letter of credit facility might be included for the purposes of providing security for the borrower's obligations in respect of decommissioning liabilities.
- Secured collection accounts might be set up into which all project revenues are received and out of which payments are to be made in the order set out in an agreed cash waterfall.
- Requirements for hedging petroleum prices in respect of a certain proportion of projected production might exist. In times of strong petroleum prices, borrowers have been largely successful in resisting specific requirements, such that there is only a high-level agreed hedging policy in the documentation.

4.5 Senior stretch

Occasionally, senior debt in a borrowing base facility will be divided into base senior and senior stretch (or conforming and non-conforming) tranches, the stretch tranche being lent against a higher percentage of the net present value, with the excess being in effect the size of the stretch tranche. A higher margin will apply. Usually only lenders with in-house technical skills tend to be able to lend over and above the base senior debt, as they have the know-how to assess which assets can support the extra debt.

4.6 Hybrid borrowing base facility/project financing for development assets

The classical borrowing base facility is based on a portfolio of mainly producing assets, with net present values attributed to development assets possibly composing a relatively small part of the total borrowing base net present value. This is fine for a company with significant producing assets, but what if the company's portfolio still largely consists of development assets?

As the market has developed, banks have been willing to finance such portfolios using a hybrid project finance and borrowing base structure. Key features of such a hybrid facility may include the following:

- *Strict control over facility drawdowns with a project finance style of accounts structure.* Drawdowns may only be allowed for expenditures within the projection approved by the majority lenders and when regular testing demonstrates that the borrower has sufficient funding available to it from committed sources to achieve completion on key development assets.

Distributions and application of funds to general corporate purposes may only be permitted once such completion is achieved.

- *Tests for such completion being clearly defined and met to the satisfaction of the lenders* before the relevant assets are counted as producing, with the critical move from consideration of P90 reserves to P50 reserves in the calculation of the net present value.

4.7 Pre-development bridge financing

What are the debt options for a company whose portfolio consists only of assets which have been successfully appraised but as yet do not have final development plan (FDP) approval? The company may have already exhausted the equity markets. At the time of writing, the London Stock Exchange's Alternative Investment Market (AIM), popular with start-up oil and gas companies, is a less readily available source of equity than it has been. This has resulted in companies turning to lenders willing to make available short-term bridge financing, the bridge to be taken out by way of a borrowing base facility at such time as the borrower has sufficient borrowing base capacity under standard net present value calculations.

Lenders providing such bridges need to be satisfied that everything is in place to ensure the borrower will be able to bring its pre-development assets to final development plan approval, and then onwards into production, at sufficient levels and within the right timeframe to enable a refinancing within a satisfactorily short period, typically 12 to 18 months. Examples include in the case of oil to be produced from an inland location, lenders being assured that it will be feasible to transport that oil to market, or in the case of a gas field, if regulatory approval is required for the gas to be sold into a domestic market, lenders being assured that there no reason why such approval will not be forthcoming. A bridge financing should be relatively quick and easy to complete, but a thorough due-diligence exercise will need to be undertaken to satisfy the lenders on the refinancing risk. The terms of the bridge loan will encourage refinancing prior to the full term, for example a periodic step-up in the interest rate.

4.8 UDABs

A recent development on the bridge facility has been the undeveloped asset backed facility/pre-sanction facility (UDAB) which provides bridge financing for pre-development assets, but on a conveyor-belt principle. A structure is established whereby assets are approved as UDAB assets when the lenders are satisfied, as described above, that they qualify for bridge financing. As and when the UDAB assets reach final development plan approval, they are moved out of the UDAB facility and into a borrowing base facility, with an appropriate portion of the UDAB facility being repaid. During the life of the UDAB facility, further assets can be put forward by the borrower for approval by the lenders for inclusion as UDAB assets, to move along the conveyor belt in a similar manner. The available amount under the UDAB facility is calculated in a highly conservative manner, with the lenders having a wide discretion as to determination of the reserves and net present values attributable to those assets. Only a few US dollars per barrel value will be attributed to such reserves on a probabilistic or contingent basis.

The market for UDABs has dried up at the time of writing (ie late 2008) and it may be some time before banks feel comfortable again lending against pre-development assets.

4.9 UDAB with borrowing base facility

Depending on circumstances, it may make sense partially to mitigate the refinancing risk inherent in a UDAB facility by putting in place a borrowing base facility at the same time as the UDAB facility, the borrowing base facility standing ready to receive new assets (subject to the assets meeting specified acceptance conditions and majority bank approval) as they come off the UDAB facility conveyor belt. Alternatively, the UDAB facility may be put in place before the borrowing base facility, so saving the borrower commitment fees but increasing the refinancing risk.

4.10 Junior debt

In addition to senior stretch tranches (Section 4.5) borrowers may supplement their senior debt with junior debt, typically on similar terms albeit with subordination to the senior debt on repayment and on enforcement of security and a higher margin.

4.11 Second lien

In the United States and Canada, second lien lending (also known as tranche B lending) has emerged in the last ten years or so and more recently spread to the United Kingdom and the rest of Europe, although this new market is effectively closed at the time of writing. Second lien loans are seen as a response to a pricing gap in the capital structure that previously existed between senior debt and mezzanine/junior financing. Second lien debt is 'lien subordinated' only, as opposed to 'debt subordinated' mezzanine debt. This means a second lien lender is only required to turn over to the senior lenders proceeds from the enforcement of shared security rather than from any source, including any before the enforcement of security. Other common features are a longer maturity than the senior debt, a bullet repayment or limited amortisation and no equity kicker.

In the US market, there are real advantages to the lenders from a bankruptcy law perspective in structuring the security rights in this way. In the United Kingdom this is really a distinction without a difference, so second lien debt is seen by some as an excuse for borrowers to replace classic mezzanine debt and its equity element with a pure subordinated debt tranche, albeit at similar pricing.

4.12 Convertible bonds

Some independents have incorporated the issuance of convertible bonds as a key part of their capitalisation. The bonds may be listed or, more commonly for smaller companies, privately placed. They are typically issued by a finance vehicle subsidiary with the benefit of a guarantee of, and convertible into the equity of, the parent company. An advantage is that investors view such bonds as quasi equity, so the covenant package tends to be rather light and should not interfere with the ability of the group to raise senior debt at operating company level.

4.13 Quasi bond alternative

A further possible funding source for borrowers at an early stage of development has been a quasi bond promoted by investment banks, including a short-maturity term loan arranged, but not underwritten, by an investment bank with a group of non-bank lenders, including hedge funds. The loan is advanced in a single tranche at financial close, giving the borrower the comfort of having the funds in its account, but comes with higher interest rate margins and arrangement fees, albeit no commitment fee. However, the market for this product is again effectively closed at the time of writing.

Borrowers considering such a bond need to weigh up what happens if developments do not go to plan. It may not be as easy to obtain consent from a group of non-bank lenders for a waiver or extension as it would be if dealing with just one bank or a fairly small syndicate of commercial banks. On the other hand, given that at least some of the non-bank lenders may be shareholders in the borrower, they may have an added incentive to keep the business moving forward. Bridge and UDAB facilities are more common than these quasi bonds, and lender involvement at this stage in a borrower's development may provide an additional welcome form of discipline.

4.14 Inter-creditor issues, subordination and UK administration

An inter-creditor agreement will be required if funds are being provided from multiple sources which are not structurally subordinated. It will typically cover which categories of lenders have to agree before any one group can accelerate any debt, take enforcement action and whether or not any group has a veto over a proposed exercise of discretion under other loan documentation with different lenders, and it will contain provisions on the sharing of recoveries and subordination.

Subordination of debt is principally relevant where a borrower is insolvent, so it must be effective on an insolvency. There are different methods to achieve subordination in the United Kingdom (not all necessarily effective in other jurisdictions). Turnover subordination occurs where junior lenders hold any proceeds they receive from the borrower on trust for the senior lenders. Contractual subordination occurs where junior lenders are only entitled to be paid after the senior debt is paid in full and can be complete or spinning (where interest only can be paid until a default). Structural subordination occurs where junior debt is borrowed at a higher level than senior debt in the structure of the borrower group. Convertible bonds are typically structurally subordinated.

The security regime in the United Kingdom currently balances the law in favour of an administrator and away from an administrative receiver. In English law an administrator acts for all of a company's creditors and tries to continue to run a company as a going concern, whereas an administrative receiver acts in the interests of the security holders which appoint it. Receivers may run the business as a going concern, but are not required to do so.

Administration is seen by lenders as an inferior remedy, because when an administration order is made, enforcement of security and the institution or continuation of any legal process against the company without the permission of the court or the consent of an administrator is not allowed. Lenders are now only entitled to appoint an administrative receiver in certain specified situations, none of which is likely to be applicable in the context of a borrowing base facility, although some may be in the context of a single-asset project financing style of transaction. This is due in part to the fact that North Sea projects have not included step-in rights for lenders.

5. Borrower group structures

5.1 Choice of structure

A key issue when contemplating a reserve-based lending transaction is where the assets to be financed are located in the group structure, and which companies within the group are to be borrowers and guarantors under the facility. This is easy enough in the case of a single asset financing which may be undertaken in a special purpose company, as is typical in a classic project financing, but for a borrowing base facility the assets are likely to be held by a number of field companies, at least some of which will own non-borrowing base assets – for example, exploration assets.

5.2 Whole group

In a whole group financing, every company in the group is a party to the loan documentation, providing cross guarantees and security. This structure tends to be appropriate for relatively small companies with a significant proportion of development assets, where the lenders might expect the whole group to stand behind the financing. Or it may be appropriate for larger companies with a wide portfolio of assets which want to achieve more beneficial borrowing terms more akin to a corporate facility.

5.3 Borrowing base group

The limited borrowing base group approach is used where the parent only wants a certain sub-group in the corporate structure to be party to the loan documentation, and in this respect the loan takes on a project finance flavour, with typically no or only limited recourse to the parent or other parts of the group.

5.4 Non-recourse subsidiaries

The concept of non-recourse subsidiaries is used where there are companies located in the group structure such that they would otherwise fall to be obligors under the finance documents, but which the parent wants to exclude from the reach of the facility so that it can carry out (and finance) other projects independently within such companies. Restrictions would be imposed under the finance documents which insulate the obligors under the finance documents from the creditors of the non-recourse subsidiaries and limit the dealings of the obligors with the non-recourse subsidiaries.

6. Bankability and due diligence

6.1 Bankability issues

Bankability is an art, not a science; and as the requirements of borrowers have changed, so the market's view of what is a bankable structure has shifted to accommodate, so far as possible, those requirements. In the UK market the acute need to boost the borrowing capacity for smaller companies has led to structural modifications. For instance to maximise the amount of cash flows taken account of in the projections, an add-back of say six-months' worth of budgeted capex in the past may now be extended into 12 months' add-back; or a balloon repayment at maturity may be acceptable so long as the cover ratios imply that a refinancing at maturity will be feasible. The art is for an arranging bank to put together a deal which gives the borrower what it needs but where any changes from the previous norm can be justified to ensure that the financing is still readily saleable in the bank market.

The lenders will need to be able to rely on a legal due diligence report prepared in respect of the assets being financed. This may involve commissioning a new due diligence report or, updating an existing due diligence report (with a letter of reliance) which may have been prepared in connection with a listing of the company or the acquisition of those assets.

6.2 Licences/production sharing contracts/concessions

Lenders will focus on establishing title to the assets, and will seek comfort that the terms of any licenses, production sharing contracts or concession agreements are sufficiently robust, free of restrictions on granting security over the assets and free from hair-trigger defaults leading to counterparty termination rights. The due diligence report may also typically report on term, consideration, relinquishment, work obligations and profit sharing under production sharing contracts.

6.3 Joint operating agreements

In the North Sea, with its regime of licences and joint operating agreements, the focus for lenders is on assignment clauses. Usually, assignment by way of security is permitted provided such security is expressly subordinated to the rights of the counterparties to the joint operating agreement. The due diligence report may also typically report on operatorship, insurance, work programmes, voting, default and termination, and decommissioning security.

6.4 Offtake/sales contracts

Lenders will focus on how secure are the cash flows for petroleum sales, and again on restrictions on creating security.

6.5 Public international law issues/treaties

Where an oil or gas field straddles a maritime boundary between two sovereign states (eg the UK and Norway in the North Sea), then recourse may have to be had to relevant treaties governing the border. In some cases the countries may have agreed a general process on how to unitise the field. In other cases, the borrower may be proceeding to exploit the field from one side of the boundary without a unitisation, but in compliance with the relevant treaty by, for example, only drilling further than the minimum distance from the border specified. In the latter case, lenders will need to make an assessment of the risk of a dispute arising which may interfere with the development of, and production from, the field.

6.6 Environmental issues

The Equator Principles are frequently invoked as a condition precedent and/or covenant requirement in borrowing base facilities, although there is some debate over whether they technically apply to portfolio financings with more than one asset. They seek to regulate the approach of financial institutions to environmental issues and are a voluntary code of conduct; however, most commercial banks active in the reserve-based lending market have agreed to abide by them. They are in effect a recognition that lenders are able to influence the environmental aspects of a project. They are substantially based on World Bank/IFC policies and apply to projects with a total capital cost of more than $10 million.

The Equator Principles divide projects into three categories based on their likely environmental impact and, depending on categorisation, an environmental impact assessment (EIA) may be required. The environmental impact assessment examines potential negative and positive environmental impacts and recommends measures to prevent, minimise, or compensate for them and to improve environmental performance. Affected groups including indigenous people and local NGOs must be consulted as part of the process and the final report must be published. In addition, an environmental management plan (EMP) may be required, which must draw on the conclusions of the environmental impact assessment and address mitigation, action plans, monitoring, management of risk, and time schedules.

Lenders may impose documentary requirements such as proof of compliance with the environmental management plan and may require an independent environmental expert to be appointed to report on compliances.

6.7 Decommissioning

In certain petroleum basins, particularly in the UK continental shelf, the costs of decommissioning has become a major issue on debt financings, especially acquisition financing given that vendors, co-venturers or governmental authorities may require security to be given by new parties to the licence or production sharing contract.

The decommissioning of UK oil and gas assets is primarily governed by the Petroleum Act 1998. Section 29 entitles the Department for Business, Enterprise and Regulatory Reform (BERR – previously the Department for Trade and Industry, but whose relevant functions are in future to be carried out by the new Department of Energy and Climate Change (DECC)) to serve notice on all parties then associated with an asset, requiring them to submit a decommissioning programme for approval and implement it. Under Section 34, BERR/DECC can also require a wider group, including recalling any former Section 29 holders or associated companies of Section 29 holders, to share the responsibility. As past licensees can be brought back to share liability for decommissioning, the regime appears tough, but the politically unacceptable alternative is that the cost could fall on the taxpayer. The regime has become a serious barrier to asset trading in the UK continental shelf despite initiatives to encourage new entrants, such as 'fallow field' and 'promote' licences. Many commentators believe the regime is unjustified, as the costs of securitisation to the UK continental shelf industry is far greater than any potential default liabilities which might arise in relation to decommissioning costs.

Lenders, larger co-venturers and BERR/DECC all take a cautious approach on the level of security to be provided in respect of decommissioning costs. Purchasers and smaller co-venturers take the opposite view, as the costs of providing security result in a substantial liability on their balance sheets, limiting their ability to borrow funds. This conflict has led to development of a standard-form template decommissioning security agreement or decommissioning cost provision deed (DCPD) as a fair starting point for negotiation. Options for security include cash, letters of credit (LCs), bonds and guarantees. The level of security needed is typically the net present value of estimated decommissioning costs multiplied by a risk factor (minimum 1.5), all divided by the net present value of revenues from the field (typically post tax) to the end of its economic life.

Issuing letters of credit is becoming riskier for lenders because acquiring companies tend to be less financially robust, the letters of credit are being used to cover increasingly mature or smaller fields, and the average value of the letters of credit is increasing in line with abandonment costs.

A problem is that due to the potential annual redetermination process by BERR/DECC as to decommissioning costs for a particular field, lenders may be requested to post a letter of credit greater than that for which they have approval if the size of the abandonment liability under the decommissioning cost provision deed goes up. Conversely, if the redetermined commissioning cost goes down, the borrower may be over collateralising. A partial solution is to document a base case cash collateralisation build-up requirement based on agreed ratios. If the borrower generates cash flow in excess of that required in any period to cash-collateralise the letter of credit, it may borrow the excess as a loan subject to the facility's other requirements. If, conversely, cash flow reduces in any period to below that required, repayment of the loan is accelerated to achieve the target ratios. This structure, whilst a solution, is inefficient as it requires a large cash build-up over time to ensure there is full cash collateralisation of the letter of credit.

Getting the balance right between the lenders, borrowers and BERR/DECC's interest is crucial as acquisition deals are being done, or potentially done, on more marginal fields where costs are finely balanced.

7. Security

7.1 Lenders' asset-level security concerns

The main objectives when considering a security package are to trump unsecured creditors, protect assets from actions by unsecured creditors and confer control of the company on a default. Often security is only taken defensively as enforcement in practice may be unrealistic, particularly over oil and gas fields where governmental consents to any sales or transfer will invariably be required.

In a classic project financing, lenders' concerns include ensuring that effective security can be taken over project contracts and that the key project contracts remain in place in one form or another if and when lenders enforce their security. To meet the first concern the contracts should be capable of being charged or assigned by way of security and any necessary consents obtained. In a borrowing base facility structure, lenders may be more relaxed and may be prepared to close a financing on the basis of no security being taken over certain project agreements or an undertaking from the borrower to use reasonable endeavours to obtain any necessary counterparty consent for the granting of security. To meet the second concern, it is necessary to examine termination clauses in the underlying contracts. Typically, they entitle the counterparty to terminate if the project company is not solvent, if any security it gives is enforced or if another party obtains control of its shares. Hence, lenders ask to have these provisions amended or to have direct agreements with the relevant counterparty. In a borrowing base facility structure, again lenders tend to be more relaxed and will usually be prepared to live with the existing provisions.

Cross-guarantees and security given by English companies are now likely to be of little use for lenders in appointing an administrative receiver (Section 4.14). Banks have been willing to live with this, perhaps emphasising the point that their principal protection is through the operation of the borrowing base amount concept, which limits total borrowings.

7.2 Other types of security

In addition to asset-level security, lenders will take security over:

- the project accounts, which will be located in a jurisdiction where appropriate security rights exist;
- shares in the companies within the borrower group so that lenders can step in at this level, regardless of whether they have effective asset-level security; and
- the borrower's insurances (Section 9).

As we have seen, in borrowing base facilities, a light touch is typically taken by lenders and little, or only defensive, security may be taken at the asset level. In many jurisdictions it is not possible, or at least difficult, to take security over the licence, production sharing contract or concession. Borrowing base facility lenders will generally accept this position, so long as they have adequate security over the shares of the companies in the borrower group, project accounts and insurance proceeds.

7.3 The UK open permission

Petroleum assets in the UK continental shelf are managed by way of a licence-based regime with joint operating agreements entered into by the parties to a licence. The terms of the licences prevent the granting of security except with the consent of the secretary of state, who in the past gave individual formal written consents to the creation of security over licence interests. However, in recent years this cumbersome process has been replaced by an open permission, which is a general consent by the appropriate UK secretary of state to the creation of security over licences, with certain notification conditions. The consent is stated to cover crystallisation of a floating charge into a fixed charge. The more modern joint operating agreements expressly contemplate and allow assignments by way of security, although previous versions often do not. Under the borrowing base facility structure, usually only a floating charge will typically be taken over the licence interest and the borrower's interest under the joint operating agreement.

The limitations with securing a company's interest in a UK continental shelf licence are that it only covers an interest in the licence, not petroleum in the field. Direct agreements with the government are not typically entered into by participants in the UK continental shelf, lenders instead being comfortable with the history of the government's involvement. Under the licence conditions, the secretary of state may revoke a licence if a receiver or administrator is appointed in relation to a licensee. Therefore, his/her consent would be required for any transfer or sale of a licence interest on an enforcement of security. Whether the co-licensee's consent would also be required would depend on the provisions of the joint operating agreement's assignment clause. Co-licensees may also have pre-emption rights under the joint operating agreements which apply in such circumstances.

Given these qualifications, UK continental shelf licence security is often only defensive in that it can prevent others dealing with assets, not giving effective control over the assets on enforcement.

7.4 Other jurisdictions

A floating charge is a common-law concept only available for lenders in countries which have inherited an English-law-based legal regime. Given that, in the future, many of the jurisdictions playing host to reserve-based financings will be civil law based, it will not always be possible to create floating security over the assets. Lenders would ideally like to see 'equivalent' security, involving taking security in some form over the licence interests, contracts and other assets. In many jurisdictions this may be difficult or impossible and a cost–benefit analysis will be required to decide whether it is worthwhile or practicable to take such asset security.

For example, in Norway the market view is generally that asset-level security is not worth taking because of the difficulty of obtaining consents and adjusting the finance documentation so that enforcement can only be taken on a Norwegian asset-related default. In the Netherlands there is debate over whether even defensive security can be taken without breaking the relevant licence terms.

8. Documentation

8.1 Typical package

Before full loan documentation is drafted, a borrower will execute a mandate letter with the lead arrangers, setting out rights and obligations which apply prior to execution of definitive finance documentation and attaching a term sheet. Arrangers are appointed on a sole (or joint in the case of multiple arrangers) and exclusive basis and are obliged to underwrite the debt subject to conditions including no material adverse change, agreement of full documentation, no competing financing by the borrower, satisfaction of due diligence, no breach by the borrower of the mandate letter and credit approval. At the time of writing, 'club' deals have become prevalent, whereby arranging banks will assemble a small club of banks to sign up to the definitive finance documents, without any bank assuming a prior underwriting commitment.

The definitive finance documentation package will include principally the facility agreement, security documents, a security trust deed and (if required) an intercreditor agreement and an accounts agreement.

The principal document is the facility agreement, which will include the following:

- *Representations and warranties* – these serve a different purpose from in a commercial contract such as a sale and purchase agreement. Lenders are not interested in suing for damages for breach, but rather want to force disclosure, and allow them to call a default on breach and force borrowers to the renegotiating table.
- *Covenants* – in classical project finance documentation these are extensive and are designed to give a contractual vote to the banks in relation to the basic management of the company. In terms of weight and tightness of covenant package, borrowing base facilities range from much less restrictive corporate-finance-style restrictions, to a package closer to a project financing for a hybrid borrowing base/project finance deal.
- *Events of default* – the banks view events of default as the ability to be heard in the management of the project if things go wrong, rather than an opportunity to get their money back instantly. They force the borrower to come to the negotiating table. Some bankers have been heard to take the view that it is not a bad thing if at any point in time the lenders can point to a default by way of technicality under a facility agreement, but of course borrowers' counsel will make every effort to ensure that only genuine issues trigger an event of default.

8.2 Loan Market Association documentation

Since the publication by the Loan Market Association (LMA) in the United Kingdom of a template English-law syndicated loan agreement for investment grade borrowers, the time taken agreeing mechanical and standard provisions of credit agreements has been greatly reduced. Although borrowing base facility borrowers are unlikely to be of investment grade, LMA documentation is still used in the upstream oil and gas financing market as a basis for negotiations.

8.3 Market flex

In a bond issue, underwriters pre-sell the bonds before they are prepared to sign the underwriting agreement themselves. If there is a market *force majeure* event after the underwriters have signed the underwriting agreement, or there is a material adverse change in the issuer's financial condition or the project, the underwriters are not obliged to subscribe.

The bank market reaches the same end result through market flex provisions in mandate letters. These allow changes to key financial terms should syndication prove more difficult than expected, to ensure a successful syndication. In the reserve based lending market, before the onset of the 2008 credit crunch, although a market flex provision would typically have been included in mandate letters, it was often restricted to only a right to change pricing, and then perhaps subject to a cap. Since then it has become fairly standard for full market flex provisions to apply. As noted above, at the time of writing club deals have largely supplanted syndicated transactions.

9. Insurance

9.1 Types required

Insurance typically required by lenders on upstream oil and gas financings during the operating phase follow a fairly standard 'energy package', which may incorporate: property all risks, operator's extra expense, comprehensive general liability, builder's risk, marine hull, protection and indemnity, directors' and officers' liability and all other insurances required by local legislation or the project agreements.

Lenders may request delay in start-up and business interruption insurance, but borrowers are likely to push back on such requirements due to the expense. Depending on the jurisdiction, lenders may request political risk insurance to cover expropriation, non-convertibility of local currencies into hard currencies, and breach of contract by a governmental authority or public body. Again, this may well be resisted by borrowers on grounds of cost.

The operator of a field would typically take out the energy package insurance on behalf of the joint venturers, and the lenders will be satisfied with this arrangement.

9.2 Recognising the lenders' interests

In the case of insurances taken out by the borrower, the lenders will require the security trustee on behalf of the lenders to be adequately noted as, for example, co-insured and loss payee on property damage types of insurances and additional insured on liability-type insurances. In the case of insurances taken out by the operator on behalf of the joint venturers, the lenders will accept that this notation is probably not practicable.

9.3 Brokers' letters

A typical condition precedent to the initial utilisation under a borrowing base facility is provision of a letter from the insurance brokers of the borrower confirming, at the minimum: the level of cover; that the insurances required by the facility agreement are in place and effective; that all premiums have been paid; and that the notations recognising the interests of the security trustee as required by the facility agreement have been endorsed on the policies.

Brokers should be able to provide such a letter, though it may require negotiations as to the exact wording used.

9.4 Cut-through

Where local law requires that all or part of the insurances are taken up by local insurance companies, invariably lenders require that such risks be reinsured in a major foreign insurance market because the local providers may not be bankable. A contract whereby the lenders can cut through the local insurance policy to the reinsurer is typically given, but will normally be ineffective on the insolvency of the local insurer and it is necessary for the borrower and also the banks either to have an assignment of the reinsurance policy from the local insurer or else a direct agreement with the local insurer and foreign reinsurer, whereby the foreign reinsurer would pay the borrower/banks direct. Cut-through arrangements in certain jurisdictions, including Thailand, leave a risk that if the local insurer becomes insolvent, the reinsurer may also be faced with a claim from a liquidator and have to pay twice. Borrowing base facility lenders will look at all the circumstances and may take a more relaxed view than project finance lenders.

10. Acquisition finance

The use of the borrowing base facility as an acquisition financing tool is now well established and, with many acquisition transactions being managed as auctions, the borrowing base facility, particularly with the addition of stretch and junior tranches, is well suited to maximising the debt available to the borrower. In the United Kingdom in particular, where many of the assets being purchased are nearing maturity, a consideration will be that, if they are successful, bidders are likely to be required to post substantial letters of credit to back the standard indemnity required by vendors in respect of decommissioning liabilities (Section 6.7). This reduces the amount of cash which would otherwise be available to make the acquisition.

11. Security over operating entities

In the scenario of the transformational acquisition undertaken by a previously small independent oil and gas company, the principal value will be found in the target assets. To avoid pre-emption and other contract and licence transfer issues and also perhaps for tax reasons, the acquisition will typically involve a share purchase of one or more asset-holding target companies. The lenders will want the target companies to give security over their assets in conjunction with a cross-guarantee covering any group borrowings under the facility which, in certain jurisdictions, is restricted by laws relating to corporate benefit, financial assistance and reduction of net assets. In the United Kingdom, the giving of financial assistance by a private target company to an acquirer for the purposes of assisting the acquisition of the target's shares is (post October 2008) no longer prohibited. Corporate benefit issues would still be relevant, but it should be fairly straightforward to demonstrate adequate corporate benefit for a subsidiary in securing the obligations of its parent.

11.1 Public company bid financing

At the time of writing, conditions look ripe for consolidation among the numerous smaller independents which are listed on junior exchanges such as AIM and the TSX Venture Exchange in Toronto. As a consequence, there may be more listed company takeovers and a drive to follow a wider market trend in taking some of these companies private, in each case possibly funded with acquisition financing debt. There are additional risks involved in this type of deal, as compared with funding purely private company acquisitions. A key factor in UK public company bids is the lack of conditionality that the lenders can place on the availability of funds, once the offer has been announced. Although the offer will invariably be made subject to numerous conditions, including no material adverse change in the target's business, in practice the UK Takeover Panel will not allow bidders to rely on them. Similarly, the bid financing facility agreement will contain some events of default, but in practice – other than in the case of insolvency of the acquirer's acquisition vehicle (which is unlikely, given that it will be a newco) and illegality – the banks would be required to fund through a default. This may be unfamiliar territory for oil and gas banks which are not existing players in the public company acquisition financing market.

11.2 Limited diligence on public company deal

An associated issue on a public company acquisition is the relative lack of ability, particularly on a hostile bid, to undertake due diligence over and above publicly available information. This may be adequate to allow the acquirers and their bankers to make a proper assessment of what debt structure the business will support, but it may be more challenging to use only such publicly available information to build the sophisticated and well-grounded computer model used by oil and gas banks on borrowing base facilities. Having said that, if the target assets in question are in mature basins, they may have been financed several times over in the past, so banks who are active in the market will have a good understanding of them.

12. Refinancings

12.1 Why refinance before maturity?

Project financings of petroleum assets are usually conservative, with caution being shown in at least four places: first, banks tend to lend against proven rather than probable reserves; secondly, they apply a reserve tail date and ignore the last 25% or so of reserves; thirdly, lenders will not lend against the full value of such reserves but apply a project life cover ratio test and typically lend only 67% or so of the net present value; and, fourthly, lenders adopt conservative views in their internal price decks for future oil prices.

So there are often good reasons for borrowers to refinance existing debt, even if prepayment fees are incurred. Margins tend to be expensive for project financings pre-completion. Even if lenders agree to decrease margins post-completion, depending upon performance, the reductions will probably not be as great as those that might be available were the completed project taken to market. Covenant packages will also be less restrictive post-completion and refinancings can unlock value early for shareholders.

Refinancings are therefore certainly attractive on single-asset project financings, but also to an extent in the case of borrowing base facilities, where during the life of the facility borrowing base assets may move from the development phase to the production phase. Terms may be built into the facility to recognise the de-risking of the assets as this change occurs – including relevant reserves for the projections moving from P90 to P50 and a step down in the margin when key assets reach production. But as with the single-asset project financing, it may still be more advantageous for the borrower to seek a refinancing, particularly because the classic borrowing base facility includes a step down in commitments on six-monthly reduction dates, even with the onset of the credit crunch and the tightening in credit terms.

Some borrowers are, at the time of writing, struggling to refinance their debt due to the global liquidity crisis.

12.2 Special factors on refinancings

Special factors to consider on a refinancing include the timing mechanics for repayment of the existing indebtedness, the release of existing security and closure of existing bank accounts. There is a technical chicken-and-egg problem in that existing security cannot be released until the existing debt is repaid, but this can only be done from the proceeds of the new debt, which cannot technically be drawn while existing debt and security is in place. The usual solution is for the new lender to permit a utilisation request to be submitted on being satisfied that the existing indebtedness will be repaid and existing security released upon the first utilisation under the new facility being made. A funds flow deed is sometimes used to clarify payment mechanics.

Consideration should be given when amending existing agreements or guarantees as to whether a new guarantee is required. As material variations of the principal contracts can discharge guarantees unless consent is given to the variation by the guarantor, material variations are generally done in practice with contemporaneous consent from all of the guarantors.

13. International market

13.1 London and Paris as centres

It is probably fair to say that London is now established as the premier international centre for upstream oil and gas financing, though Paris is also home to several strong banking teams. The UK-based oil and gas banks are no longer focused just on the UK continental shelf – they are financing deals much further afield. Hand in hand with that is the fact that there are now many independent oil and gas companies headquartered in London which have activities around the world. A strong consulting and advisory community has grown up to support the deals.

13.2 International growth

The growth in international activities of independent companies has seen banks becoming involved in financing upstream developments in a wider variety of newer jurisdictions, from West Africa, to Russia, to South East Asia and to the Middle East (the Middle East being new ground for smaller independent oil and gas companies). The borrowing base facility is a flexible piece of technology and can quite readily be adapted for different jurisdictions, including licence or production sharing contract regimes, common law or civil law regimes, and less developed or mature oil and gas territories. The borrowing base facility structure allows for producing assets in a mature territory to be placed in a borrowing base portfolio with more risky development assets from a newer territory.

Certain countries in the Middle East, such as Oman and Egypt, already offer potential for borrowing-base-style lending. Despite the tight grip of the national oil companies in many parts of the Middle East, as fields mature there may be openings for independent oil and gas companies to be allowed in to operate assets that the big players may consider not worthwhile, as has happened in the UK continental shelf and more recently in Indonesia. Such companies are likely to use debt financing to fund their activities.

West Africa presents fertile ground for reserve-based financings, including large-scale developments in Nigeria and Ghana. In Russia there is significant activity among smaller to mid-size independents which have successfully raised debt financing. In any of these or other territories where political risks are deemed to be higher than the norm, the lending criteria and terms for such deals may be commensurately more conservative, but this should not prevent deals from being successfully closed on the right terms.

14. Conclusion

The business of financing upstream activities is dynamic, with debt providers and their advisers adapting rapidly to the changing requirements of independent companies, enabling them to exploit the many new opportunities which are arising around the world. Being able to adapt tried and tested tools to new market conditions and new territories is where the exciting challenges lie for oil and gas financing specialists. The continued evolution of the borrowing base facility and more recently the emergence of the UDAB facility as ways of catering to the wider needs of independents is a testament to this innovation. With setbacks arising out of the global credit crisis and volatility in oil and gas prices, it looks certain that this evolution will continue, perhaps in the short term at least with a tendency towards more conservative structures.

This chapter has shown how upstream financing involves the combined disciplines of project finance, corporate finance and acquisition finance being applied across numerous jurisdictions with the involvement of a wide range of players. All these factors combine to make the upstream oil and gas financing sector a fascinating area of practice.

Bibliography

Mills, S and Bousfield, C, "Horses for Courses" (2004) and "Smart Money" (2006). *Project Finance Magazine.*

Stevens, W, "Impact of the Decomissioning Cost Provision Deed on Financing Structures", a presentation (2008).

Vintner, G (with contributions from Gareth Price), *Project Finance – A Legal Guide* (3rd edition) (Sweet and Maxwell Ltd, 2006).

Wils, J and Neilson, E (Editors) *The Technical and Legal Guide to the UK Oil and Gas Industry* (Aberlour Press, 2007).

Wood, P, *Project Finance, Securitisations, Subordinated Debt* (2nd edition) (Sweet & Maxwell Ltd, 2007).

Transboundary[1] pipeline development and risk mitigation

William E Browning
Infrastructure Development Partnership LLP
Thomas J Dimitroff
Oil and Gas Consultant

1. Introduction

Dislocations in global supply and demand for oil and gas are becoming increasingly marked. In the first quarter of 2007, the three largest consuming markets (North America, Europe and Asia-Pacific) accounted for consumption of 64% of all oil and gas while, possessing only 11% of global reserves.[2] The IEA estimates that the world is likely to continue its heavy reliance upon hydrocarbons over the coming decades and that the aforementioned dislocations are likely to grow more acute, notwithstanding recent price retreats.[3] With remaining lower-cost hydrocarbon reserves increasingly concentrated in the Middle East, the Former Soviet Union (FSU) and the Arctic Region, the distances from producing fields to markets will increase, thereby requiring the construction and operation of additional oil and gas pipelines from source to markets including export terminal facilities for storage, loading and onward shipment via oil and liquefied natural gas (LNG) tankers. According to the "2008 International Pipeline Construction Report" of the *Oil & Gas Journal*, 77,314 miles of oil and gas pipelines are now either on planning and negotiation tables or under construction. ("Much of the interest in beginning long-planned projects is expected to be driven by higher energy prices, growing energy consumption in developing nations and the strong outlook for LNG's role in developing gas markets.") Significantly, as distances from producing fields to consuming markets increase, so will the frequency with which large-scale pipeline developments straddle international boundaries.

Following the nationalisations and subsequent oil price shocks of the 1970s, many large private-sector oil and gas companies were forced to diversify their search for reserves away from OPEC countries and towards newer locations. Concurrently, the Former Soviet Union began to diversify its oil and natural gas production and delivery away from exclusively internal use and towards export options, initially

1 'Transboundary' is intended to include the international law concept of transit and transit pipelines (ie, the transportation of energy products and materials from one state through the territory of a second (or multiple states) for onward delivery to another state for consumption or further refinement).
2 See *BP Statistical Review of World Energy 2008*.
3 See *International Energy Agency World Energy Outlook 2009*.

through Eastern Europe to markets in the European Union.[4] Throughout much of the late 1980s and 1990s, the large-scale oil and gas pipelines that were developed to bring this new production to markets were largely contained within single countries or political and legal blocks.[5]

With the collapse of the Former Soviet Union and the opening of emerging markets to private sector investment in the mid to late 1990s, pipeline developers were presented with the task of constructing and operating trans-boundary pipelines across jurisdictions that lacked international and domestic precedent, or which were saddled with nascent or anachronistic legal regimes. Given the scale of capital investment required and the relatively low price of oil, the range of risks which developers were aware of at that time was focused largely on political, legal, fiscal and regulatory risks to investment. Against the backdrop of the current supply–demand dislocations referred to above, the recent collapse of the global financial markets (and the price of oil), the increasing awareness of project impacts on people, communities and the environment, the medium to longer-term concerns with security of supply and climate change, there is an enhanced realisation that the scope for risk that lawyers now need to be aware of in advising clients on trans-boundary pipeline developments is becoming much broader.

The development of the Baku–Tbilisi–Ceyhan (BTC) oil pipeline emerged precisely at a time when the true breadth of potential risks posed to complex trans-boundary pipeline developments was beginning to be understood. With Baku–Tbilisi–Ceyhan, the range of risks started to move beyond the direct risks posed to the project by governments, to a broader assessment of risks that included indirect hard and soft compliance risks resulting from project impacts on the environment, people and communities and on the host state's macro-economy. Together these direct and indirect risks have taken on increasing resonance over the last decade, particularly with civil society organisations[6] and socially responsible investors, which have applied increasing pressure on international financing institutions and publicly traded oil and gas companies. Given that a systemic lack of transparency (in conjunction with insufficient regulatory oversight) appears to lie at the heart of the recent global financial crises, the case for re-regulation of private sector activities within the OECD as well as within 'emerging' markets will only grow in strength, and with this, so will the panoply of new compliance and additional risks posed to future large-scale investment activities including pipeline developments.

Any credible attempt to deal with the many risks and legal considerations facing developers of trans-boundary oil and gas pipeline projects would require a book in itself. We have, therefore, chosen to focus this chapter more narrowly on identifying

---

4 Note that for purposes of this chapter, we do not consider pipelines developed within the context of the European Union as trans-boundary pipelines, as they are subject to the common directives of the European Union.

5 While rare before the 1980s, transboundary pipelines have a relatively long history. For example, note the original Baku–Batumi oil pipeline (1897) and the long-distance oil transit pipelines that provided export of Iraqi oil from the Kirkuk field (Northern Iraq) to British-mandated Palestine and to French mandated Lebanon and Syria during the 1930s.

6 We have chosen to use the term 'civil society organisations' rather than non-governmental organisations (NGOs) to capture more accurately the wide array of voluntary, civic, social, not-for-profit and non-governmental organisations that form the basis of a well-functioning democratic society.

key risks posed to future pipeline developments and the various practical considerations, including an understanding of the relevant stakeholders and the drivers informing their concerns, that together will enable lawyers to devise tools to allocate, manage and mitigate these risks. Accordingly, we have attempted to examine these risks by using the BTC oil pipeline development as a point of reference throughout this chapter. Section 2 of the chapter will focus on the identification of areas of concern and interest which sovereign states have in enabling the development, construction and operation of trans-boundary infrastructure projects across their territory and which transcend commercial interests. Section 3 will set the scene with an overview of the BTC project. Section 4 will use the Baku–Tbilisi–Ceyhan lens to survey nine categories of direct and indirect risks which we have identified, including:

- fiscal and commercial;
- investment protection;
- governmental and political;
- financing;
- environmental and social;
- reputation;
- construction;
- security; and
- operations.

Section 5 will conclude by identifying briefly some of the likely future trends in trans-boundary oil and gas pipelines.

2. Concerns of sovereign states in transboundary pipeline developments

Regardless of whether a transboundary pipeline development is supported by private sector investment, it will always retain overriding interests that are unique to sovereign states. While the private sector will be concerned primarily with effective risk mitigation (in order to underpin large-scale, long-term investment), the interests of producing, transit and consuming states will not be limited to risk mitigation and the rate of return on the infrastructure investment itself. In the first instance, these interests include the revenue generated from the production and sale of the resource (benefiting primarily the producing country). However, there are at least four additional areas of interests that legal advisors should bear in mind and which are identified below.

2.1 Geopolitical and regional interests

Oil and gas remain strategic commodities, due to the vital role energy plays in the global macro-economy. Accordingly, the sovereign interests involved in the development, construction and operation of large-scale and long-term trans-boundary oil and gas pipelines will also transcend the supply interests of the states themselves, as the energy resource is often delivered to markets beyond those of the host states themselves.[7] Moreover, transboundary oil and gas pipelines will also have

7 An obvious and recent example here is the transit of Russian gas to European markets through the Ukraine.

an indirect impact upon neighbouring states that do not directly benefit from either the pipelines or the energy materials transported through the pipelines.[8] In this regard, the mutual interdependency created among the host states necessitates forms of international cooperation and integration that may bind the states in key areas such as mutual security, with obvious potential implications for neighbouring states.

2.2 Security of supply and other national interests

States, regardless of their position in the 'value chain' (ie, as recipient of rent from the production and sale of upstream resources, transit taxes, or, in the case of gas, as downstream offtaker), will have broad national strategic interests. In particular, the physical security of infrastructure will have security of supply implications for neighbouring states and may, therefore, require direct military, intelligence and other forms of cooperation among other states (and international organisations) with larger and more global interests.[9] Finally, in the case of a state that depends on the infrastructure for secure supplies of energy for its domestic needs (in particular its needs for natural gas), the security of the infrastructure will also take on a national security interest.

2.3 Fiscal terms

The fiscal terms which sovereign states apply in taxing (and applying other fees, duties and charges to) the construction and operation of transboundary pipelines is fundamental to the long-term sustainability and underlying economics of the project. The difficulty with evaluating the appropriate fiscal terms to be negotiated with a host state is that views on what is appropriate will inevitably change over time. For example, as oil prices rise, the monetary benefits to the producing state will rise dramatically but the transit fees being collected by transit states will typically remain the same. Nevertheless, the producing state's reliance upon the transit state for export will ensure that the latter will retain leverage over the former's ability to monetise its energy resources. Consequently, an enduring temptation will remain for transit states to expect an adjustment in fiscal terms proportional to the windfall benefits accruing to the producing state as a result of higher oil prices.[10]

2.4 Local impacts with local and potentially international consequences

Finally, the construction and operation of onshore pipelines will inevitably have a direct, immediate and potentially lasting impact upon people, communities, the environment and, depending upon the scale of the project, the macro-economy. These impacts must be properly taken into account and must not be traded against commercial risks. Indeed, this is perhaps one of the most difficult areas for a lawyer adequately to anticipate and address, as it involves taking appropriate account of the

---

8 Consider the strategic implications that Baku–Tbilisi–Ceyhan has upon Azerbaijan's relations with Armenia, Russia and Iran (none of which had any direct interest or involvement in the construction of BTC or in the oil now shipped through BTC to world markets).

9 See US EUCOM efforts in this regard at www.ndu.edu/inss/Press/jfq_pages/editions/i43/20%20JFQ43%20Wald.pdf.

10 Prof John Stevens refers to this as the problem of the 'obsolescing bargain' – see "The Coming Oil Supply Crunch", a Chatham House report, 2008.

interests of a multiplicity of parties who may not be directly involved in any of the project arrangements. Moreover, where trans-boundary pipeline developments are undertaken in jurisdictions with laws and standards that are not sufficiently developed to protect against these impacts, a variety of international stakeholders may introduce new areas of risk of which project developers and their legal advisors need to be increasingly aware.[11] These concerns will be addressed within the context of the various risks analysed in Section 4 below.

3. The Baku–Tbilisi–Ceyhan (BTC) oil pipeline and the development of the IGA and HGA framework

The development of trans-boundary oil and gas pipelines and related infrastructure is perhaps nowhere more critical than in the Caspian Sea Region. The various oil and gas basins in the Caspian Sea Region containing large-scale proven and probable reserves[12] are located at a point where various geopolitical fault lines converge.[13] Hydrocarbons produced from fields located in these basins must traverse vast distances,[14] through jurisdictions with transitional legal and regulatory frameworks and through territories that contain an abundance of technical, social and environmental challenges before reaching international downstream markets. The Baku-Tbilisi-Ceyhan oil pipeline and the South Caucuses Pipeline (a trans-boundary gas pipeline running in parallel) are the only large-scale pipelines now operating that enable the export of hydrocarbons produced from the Caspian Sea Region to international markets while avoiding Russian Federation territory. The BTC oil pipeline traverses 1,764km of onshore territory across three jurisdictions (the Republic of Azerbaijan, Georgia and the Republic of Turkey) to deliver more than one million barrels per day of crude oil produced from the Azeri–Chirag–Guneshli offshore oil fields in the Azerbaijan sector of the Caspian Sea to Ceyhan on the Turkish Mediterranean coast.

The development, construction and operation of the BTC pipeline across the three transit jurisdictions in bald reliance upon the existing legal, fiscal and regulatory frameworks would have materially affected Baku–Tbilisi–Ceyhan in at

---

11 An emerging body of tort law, sometimes referred to as foreign direct liability (FDL), identifies new forms of civil liability resulting from claims brought in the courts of a developed (OECD) country for an activity undertaken by a multinational company (MNE) in a developing country. For example, foreign direct liability may result where a multinational company operates in a state knowing that the state does not respect the rule of law (eg, international human rights norms) and the host state breaches a fundamental norm of international law in connection with furthering the activities undertaken by the multinational company. However, there are trends suggesting that foreign direct liability claims may not be limited to human rights claims, but may also extend to breaches of health, safety and environmental standards prevailing in the multinational company's home state but not adhered to by the multinational company in the developing host state.

12 The Republic of Kazakhstan alone is reported to have in excess of 40 billion barrels of proven developed and undeveloped oil reserves and probable reserves estimated to be as high as 100 billion barrels. The Republics of Azerbaijan and Turkmenistan add another 25 billion barrels of oil equivalent in proven oil and gas reserves, with the totals for probable reserves for the Caspian Region exceeding 150 billion barrels of oil and oil equivalent (see IEA).

13 Central Asia borders China, the Russian Federation and the Middle East and the US Government has asserted a strong interest in maintaining an east–west energy corridor for Central Asian hydrocarbons that avoids Russian Federation and Iranian territories.

14 Export routes for crude oil and natural gas must traverse considerable distances from each of the Caspian littoral states via rail or pipelines through Russian Federation territory to the Black Sea and Europe via pipeline across the length of Kazakhstan to China, via tank ship to Iran and pipeline to the Persian Gulf, or via the various pipeline and rail options from Azerbaijan, including BTC.

least three important ways. First, reliance on the existing frameworks would simply not have supported the commitment of large-scale foreign direct investment (planned to be $15 billion upstream and $4 billion midstream) for the construction of BTC,[15] due to high levels of perceived political, legal, fiscal and regulatory risks. Second, reliance on the existing frameworks would have posed significant challenges to the application of health, safety, environment, security, social and other international standards beginning to be demanded by international financial institutions and the oil and gas companies. Finally, even if each of the transit jurisdictions had sufficiently mature legal, regulatory and fiscal frameworks to support the necessary large-scale investment, the development of the BTC pipeline would have been impeded by the absence of a mechanism to bind the three jurisdictions together in support of the project and to ensure the harmonised application of construction, operational and project impact standards and the appropriate fiscal treatment of the BTC project company and BTC shippers.

The initial risk mitigation efforts of the Baku–Tbilisi–Ceyhan lawyers focused largely on crafting instruments to manage political, legal, fiscal and regulatory risks by using an intergovernmental and host government agreement structure (IGAs and HGAs). In order to ensure that all three jurisdictions formally demonstrated their support for the BTC pipeline, a treaty-level IGA was entered into among the three transit governments. In addition, in light of the challenges posed to the investment and to the ability of the developers to implement standards satisfactory to multilateral lending institutions, the lawyers advising Baku–Tbilisi–Ceyhan also drafted individual investment protection agreements (ie, host government agreements) that were entered into between the project development company (BTC Co) and each of the three governments. This intergovernmental and host government agreement structure was designed to provide an umbrella to protect investment in Baku–Tbilisi–Ceyhan against government-sourced risks by shielding the underlying commercial structure and transportation arrangements over the life of the project.

While the early BTC development efforts were subject to external criticism by civil society organisations,[16] the states themselves were prepared to adapt the applicable legal regime to accommodate the commercial and export-related needs of the private sector players involved. Accordingly, the intergovernmental and host government agreement structure served both to jump-start a traditionally long-lead infrastructure project and to provide a form of risk mitigation which, at the time, was sufficient to support major infrastructure investment. Ironically, the intergovernmental and host government agreement structure also enabled a sufficiently flexible structure within which a much broader range of risks could ultimately be accommodated. The nature of the eventual structure will be examined within the context of the individual risk areas considered below (see Section 4.2).

15 Taking into account Shah Deniz ($3 billion upstream) and the South Caucuses Pipeline ($1.3 billion), the total investment required for the combined projects (upstream and midstream) was in excess of $23 billion.

16 See Friends of the Earth Campaign (www.foe.org/camps/intl/institutions/bakuceyhan); see also, "Human Rights on the Line", a report issued by Amnesty International on the BTC Pipeline (www.amnestyusa.org /business/btc_pipeline.html); and World Wildlife Fund (www.foe.co.uk/resource/ media_briefing/ how_public_money_funds_oil.pdf).

4. Nine key areas of risk

Over the last few years, there has been an increasing awareness that sovereign states (through wholly state-owned entities), as opposed to the private sector, control the overwhelming majority of oil and gas reserves. Accordingly, we see a strong trend for states to take the lead in the development, construction and operation of future trans-boundary pipeline developments. Nevertheless, we believe that the private sector will retain a key role in the majority of these projects by contributing investment, unparalleled access to downstream marketing and distribution, project management, technology and knowledge of how to implement complex and sustainable projects outside home jurisdictions. In any event, regardless of whether state or private-sector investors take the lead on future projects, the array of risks posed to these new developments will grow. Moreover, these increasing risks will not discriminate between the public and private sectors. Therefore, regardless of mitigation techniques, nine fundamental areas of risk in any transborder pipeline will remain and each will be examined below through the lens of Baku–Tbilisi–Ceyhan.

4.1 Commercial

Baku–Tbilisi–Ceyhan is an excellent example of a commercially viable midstream development supported by a world-class upstream resource, creating a compelling private-sector investment opportunity. As a basic premise, pipeline developments must be robust commercially both on a standalone basis (ie, as revenue-generating businesses in their own right) and as a tool implemented to monetise the resource base underpinning the project.[17] We have seen a tendency on the part of states occasionally to promote projects that may have arguable local and regional benefits, but that simply cannot achieve success given the dearth of supply or the existence of competing, established pipeline or other export possibilities.[18] Pipelines of any significant scale will likely have a monopolistic feature that will be the bedrock of their success; therefore, in regions that host alternative transportation and transit possibilities, the likely success of large-scale greenfield pipeline developments that lack a clear revenue steam whether through a dedicated supply source or take-or-pay or ship-or-pay commitments from creditable shippers is questionable.[19]

In terms of other key commercial issues, the structuring of business models for transboundary pipelines is tending to move away from the purely private-sector 'producer' pipeline model. Increasingly, investor/developers will be required to

---

17 Note that while Baku–Tbilisi–Ceyhan is an example of a pipeline which is underpinned by a particular supply source (the Azeri–Chirag–Guneshli oil field in the Azerbaijan sector of the Caspian Sea), there are numerous examples of commercial pipelines that are not necessarily tied to a single field or supply source – for example, the planned Burgas-Alexandropolous oil pipeline (which will bypass the Turkish Straits). In this regard, note that the commercial viability of an oil or gas pipeline can be underpinned by take-or-pay or ship-or-pay commitments from creditworthy shippers (rather than a multiple-field commitment as in the case of BTC).

18 For example, consider the Odessa–Brody oil pipeline and the associated Samartia Consortium.

19 For example, producer pipelines are particularly suspect in the context of the European Union's competition directives and regulations, which appear to provide for few exceptions that would exempt a producer pipeline from the strictures of third-party access and tariff regulation. See Directive 2003/55/EC of the European Parliament and Council of June 26 2003 concerning common rules for the internal market in natural gas.

accommodate state interests not only in terms of equity participation but also in terms of governance and control, third-party access and related capacity rights issues, local content and other specific commercial issues.[20]

Nevertheless, key producers will remain at the forefront of any successful development and their willingness to participate on an equity basis will ultimately depend on the integrated commercial terms of the proposed project. While the desire to attract this type of investor (ie, one that brings the vital upstream link) will be strong, the desire of a host country (regardless of whether it is a producer, transit or consuming state) to enhance the rent it receives from the pipeline and its users will also be strong. Although this commercial tension existed during the BTC negotiations, the overriding concern to tailor the commercial terms to fit the perceived risk profile and ensure that the project would be implemented was a governor in the economic rent arena. The shift in today's investment environment from states in effect nurturing transborder projects to instead driving them forces a shift in focus on fiscal terms. The higher the state investment in the midstream asset, the more the focus will shift from transit taxes or fees to capacity usage fees, or tariff. In any event, there will be a balance that will attract investors and volumes to the pipeline over alternative investments or export routes respectively, but the focus will be more on achieving that balance than on incentivising investors to commit money and volumes.

A final aspect of the overall midstream commercial envelope (and perhaps more a matter of negotiation leverage) lies in the interplay between a project's commercial and fiscal underpinnings and the potential for a successful project financing. As the negotiation of the base project documentation goes forward, it should remain foremost in the minds of the investor/developers that banks will closely scrutinise the commercial viability of the project. A project's failure to achieve commerciality when measured against what might appear to be strained sensitivities could well result in the project's failure to be bankable. If the availability of external debt is a driver, then so is bankability; and it is a direct influence on the commercial and fiscal terms. While there are a great number of things that go into an overall bankability analysis (some of which will be discussed in the financing risk section below), the experience of BTC demonstrates that fundamental economics (ie, commerciality) is, and will remain, a core value for investors as well as banks.

4.2 Investment protection

From the standpoint of investment protection, there are at least two critical components to creating and most importantly maintaining a favourable investment

20 In this regard, liability allocation will most likely shift very much to a causation-based scheme and away from more traditional oilfield risk-allocation schemes. In the case of BTC, a liability scheme was applied that reflected the investors' perceived development risk and thus looked to the host governments to shoulder greater risks of matters considered to be beyond the control of the investors, as well as those that could conceivably result in overly onerous damages. Such a shift away from a contracted risk allocation scheme to a causation-based structure is yet another indication of the era of states needing to incentivise investment, where states are driving development. For the practitioner, a liability allocation scheme that applies a causation-based approach is more in line with market attitudes in the industry in general, but it will continue to give concern to the extent that issues of determining liability as between a host country (regardless of the role in the development) and a private sector party are difficult and generally do not favour the private sector side.

environment for a transboundary pipeline development: (i) certainty and predictability in how the legal regime is applied in practice; and (ii) the ability for project developers to ensure that the development will be constructed and operated in accordance with high (international) standards. The former component lies near the heart of the rule of law and ensures in practice that opportunities for direct, indirect and creeping expropriation through rent-seeking behaviour by the state are minimised. The latter ensures that applicable standards meet the internal compliance requirements of the developers, the legal and regulatory requirements of the host states, as well as any extraterritorial requirements that may be applied by the developer's home states, and the overall corporate responsibility expectations of domestic and international civil society activists.[21]

In the case of Baku–Tbilisi–Ceyhan, two of the state jurisdictions had recently emerged from the Former Soviet Union with insufficiently developed legal, fiscal and regulatory frameworks to support a project of the scale and complexity of BTC. The thinking among the BTC lawyers (given the pace of upstream development, as well as the magnitude of the resource and capital costs to develop it), was that the organic development of the rule of law in Azerbaijan and Georgia would be slow at best, and more likely erratic and conflicting. Project timing and security concerns, therefore, dictated an approach that ultimately resulted in ratification of the intergovernmental agreement (a public international law treaty) by all three host countries. This effectively enshrined into overriding domestic and binding international law not only the intergovernmental agreement but also the host government agreements, as well as the $1.3 billion Lump Sum Turnkey Agreement for the construction of the portion of Baku–Tbilisi–Ceyhan within the territory of the Republic of Turkey and the associated treasury guaranty.[22] It was a novel approach to take an intergovernmental agreement and the associated host government agreement structure to this level, but it created a project-specific prevailing legal regime (PLR) that enabled significant, real-time investment and it also created conditions where agreed high standards could be implemented with relative certainty and predictability. The common wisdom in the post-BTC world is that replicating this approach would be very difficult given the degree to which national legislation has now developed within the principal producing and potential transit countries.[23]

---

21 For example, the OECD Guidelines for Multinational Companies apply investment and operational standards to multinational companies [organised or headquartered] in an OECD country relating to their activities in non-OECD (developing) countries (see www.oecd.org/daf/investment/guidelines). Although compliance with the OECD Guidelines is voluntary, they also provide for a quasi-adjudicative process that enables *inter alia* civil society organisations to have standing to challenge where a violation is alleged. See also the United Nations Global Compact www.unglobalcompact.org and the Equator Principles – a framework for banks to manage environmental and social issues in project financing (see www.equator-principles.com/principles.shtml).

22 For a comprehensive explanation of the prevailing legal regime for BTC, see the Citizen's Guide to BTC, http://www.bp.com/genericarticle.do?categoryld=9006628&contentld=7013498).

23 While the use of intergovernmental and host governmental agreements to support trans-boundary pipeline developments is becoming much more common (eg, the Energy Charter Secretariat has recently published its second edition of its Model Agreements www.energycharter.org), the use of a project-specific prevailing legal regime (such as that employed in support of Baku–Tbilisi–Ceyhan), is unlikely to be replicated.

An important, albeit controversial, aspect of the Baku–Tbilisi–Ceyhan prevailing legal regime was its 'economic equilibrium' (or stability) guarantee. After the governments had executed and ratified the Baku–Tbilisi–Ceyhan intergovernmental and host government agreements in 2000, civil society organisations took exception to the apparently wide-ranging application of the prevailing legal regime's guarantee of stability which included 'stabilising' laws and regulations governing health, safety and the environment, as well taxes and other fiscal legislation. Civil society organisations alleged that the stability guarantee abridged the human rights of local communities that might be impacted by Baku–Tbilisi–Ceyhan, as the stability guarantee would have a "chilling effect" on the project states' willingness to regulate the project's compliance with health, safety and environmental standards.[24] Faced with either reopening a ratified set of arrangements, or risking the derailment of the financing of Baku–Tbilisi–Ceyhan, the BTC lawyers devised the BTC Human Rights Undertaking (effectively a deed poll). This estopped the project from asserting its rights under the intergovernmental and host government agreements in circumstances where human rights would be violated.[25] The project also entered into a number of unprecedented additional instruments, which specifically addressed impacts on people, communities and the environment. The net impact of these various additions to the prevailing legal regime was to limit the application of the stability guarantee to the fiscal components of the project. In this way, Baku–Tbilisi–Ceyhan has led the way towards setting current international best practice in the industry.[26]

4.3 Governmental and political risk

Closely related to the more generic topic of investment protection is that of governmental or political risk. The mitigation scheme for this category of risk is largely the same as above, but with the distinction that political risk focuses exclusively on what a host country can do (or cannot do) to upset the base bargain originally entered into to support the investment. For Baku–Tbilisi–Ceyhan, the primary political-risk mitigation tool is the intergovernmental and host government agreement structure (ie, the documents that gave the prevailing legal regime its force in international and domestic law). As discussed above, a robust prevailing legal regime undertaking similar to Baku–Tbilisi–Ceyhan seems an unlikely trend going forward; however, with the exception of the most sophisticated jurisdictions, there will probably be a need for some form of direct investment agreement forming a contractual basis for recovery against an offending government. In many jurisdictions, there are bilateral investment protection treaties and direct investment

---

24 See www.amnesty.org.uk/article_print.asp?ArticleID=2408.

25 The BTC Human Rights Undertaking in fact goes much further and ensures that the project states *inter alia* have the ability to enforce more stringent health, safety and environmental standards and that locally impacted communities have appropriate access to justice within the local courts to bring grievances against BTC Co. It is worth noting that the BTC Human Rights Undertaking is the first instance in which a multinational company has undertaken directly to a government a legally binding obligation to adhere to international human rights standards.

26 See "Stabilization Clauses and Human Rights", a research project conducted for the International Finance Corporation and the United Nations Special Representative to the Secretary General on Business and Human Rights, March 11 2008.

laws of general application in place to provide some protection against political risk. Additionally, it is a commonly held belief that multilateral financing agencies bring with them a 'halo' effect that provides additional political risk mitigation.

The Baku–Tbilisi–Ceyhan approach created a project-specific prevailing legal regime (ie, a legal regime applicable only to the BTC project) in which the states ensured *inter alia* freedom of transit and investment protection, and harmonised application of technical, environmental, social and safety standards (including a threshold that such standards were no less stringent than applicable EU standards) across all jurisdictions. The host government agreements between the project investors and each transit host country further elaborated the standards and clarified investment protection, setting down applicable practical issues such as permissions, land acquisition, liability, foreign currency regulations, environmental strategy and so forth. In addition, the Baku–Tbilisi–Ceyhan prevailing legal regime anticipated the subsequent addition of other related agreements that went even further to give clear guidance on international best practice for health, safety, security, labour and human rights.[27] The Baku–Tbilisi–Ceyhan prevailing legal regime represents perhaps the most sophisticated articulation of this concept, providing a large measure of investment protection whilst remaining dynamic and evolving together with the standards and practices upon which it is based.

4.4 Financing

As stated above, raising significant third-party debt in connection with a project financing can bring with it the additional benefits of risk mitigation. Specifically, a significant project financing may bring new geographically unrelated 'stakeholders' to the project. To the extent that the relevant host countries are sensitised to their reputations, international financing will provide a form of additional risk mitigation. An international project financing involving multilateral and bilateral agencies will add additional dimensions to this form of risk mitigation. However, there is a note of caution to be struck: once the financing is in place, the borrower's ability to use its lenders on more routine matters of state performance is limited. Thus, the utilisation of a financing as a risk mitigation technique should be viewed as part of an overall strategy and not as an end in itself (ie, using lenders to influence a host country is a one-off option and is, therefore, a measure of last resort).

Other positive features of a project financing will depend on the financial wherewithal of the proposed investors. Several of the Baku–Tbilisi–Ceyhan investors required financing in order to participate, including the State Oil Company of the Azerbaijan Republic (SOCAR). Indeed, securing the meaningful participation of SOCAR was a primary driver for the remaining BTC investors. This approach ensured that Azerbaijan (the producing host state) had meaningful cash at risk as a further buffer against untoward state action or inaction. At the same time, this also eliminated any possibility of a 'carry' of the state's interest until a pre-agreed payback point. Notwithstanding the recent fall in commodity prices, it remains less likely

27 See *inter alia* the BTC Human Rights Undertaking, the BTC Joint Statement and the BTC Security Protocols for Azerbaijan and Georgia (subsites.bp.com/caspian/citizens%20guide%20final.pdf).

that a state would today be unable to participate for lack of readily available funds. Nevertheless, if a financing does facilitate state participation, then it should seriously be considered.

In terms of continuing risk mitigation, a financing will bring with it an important external stamp of approval, although it is worth noting that this imprimatur can also be achieved in other ways. For example, Baku–Tbilisi–Ceyhan created its own independent panel (the Caspian Development Advisory Panel) in order continually to review and challenge all aspects of the project from origination through construction and operation and to make public its findings as well as BTC's responses to such challenges. While the Baku–Tbilisi–Ceyhan financing exercise may be more than most developers would care to undertake, a financing will also bring with it public challenge and scrutiny. This mandated form of transparency is another critical component to building an effective overall risk-mitigation strategy into a trans-boundary project. If every major aspect of a project and its implementation is available in the public domain, then the opportunity for a state to go off on a destructive tangent is tempered.

Assuming that there is flexibility in funding and recognising that there are definite yet often subtle and difficult-to-trigger advantages embedded in a major project financing, investors (and their advisers) should look carefully at the countervailing burdens. Project financings are invariably costly, not only in terms of external advisers and consultants on both sides of the table during the negotiation and arrangement phase, but also in respect of the significant ongoing costs in terms of monitoring and general bank and agency oversight after financial close. In the case of the Baku–Tbilisi–Ceyhan financing, 208 agreements with 78 parties and 17,000 signatures were generated. On a forward basis, the project is to a degree constrained in certain decisions that project personnel would normally think to be the responsibility of the relevant implementation teams. This fact can give rise to a perception of loss of control among project personnel. All these factors should be considered against the very laudable project goals of government and other investor participation – external international approval and oversight, resulting political risk mitigation and fundamental transparency.

4.5 Environmental and social impacts

Onshore pipeline developments – especially those which are proximate to communities, agricultural production or environmentally sensitive areas – have impacts which must be carefully identified, assessed (internally and independently) to a very high standard and minimised. In the absence of a coherent set of environmental standards or processes for administering standards, Baku–Tbilisi–Ceyhan prescribed its own set of standards ("no less stringent than the health, safety and environmental standards applicable within the European Union from time-to-time"[28]) and a process strategy which was set forth in each of the host government agreements.

The strategy, process and resulting environmental and social impact assessments

28 See Article IV of the BTC Intergovernmental Agreement.

(ESIAs) were required to be produced by internationally recognised consultancies and were world class.[29] The disclosure package consisted of 11,000 pages, which were translated into four languages and uploaded to the Baku–Tbilisi–Ceyhan website, with each document subject to extensive public question-and-answer sessions and further documented in published matrices. Twenty-three hard copies of the environmental and social impact assessment were placed in various key public (and publicised) venues around the world. The environmental and social impact assessment process was further and significantly augmented by the anticipated requirements of the presumed lending institutions, most notably the World Bank/International Finance Corporation (IFC) and the European Bank for Reconstruction and Development (EBRD). In terms of environmental compliance, Baku–Tbilisi–Ceyhan agreed post-financing to be subject to external monitoring – initially on a quarterly basis and later on an annual basis – to ensure compliance with the contractually mandated environmental and social action plan (ESAP), a comprehensive set of commitments by the project to its lenders. Each referenced resulting report is made public.[30] In addition, on the social side, specialised twice-yearly monitoring ensured compliance with the contractually mandated social and resettlement action plan (SRAP). Dedicated support for ongoing monitoring well exceeds the initial environmental and social impact assessment requirements.

For extractive industries, and associated sectors such as pipeline infrastructure, environmental issues can be a real or perceived Achilles heel. This is a critical risk that must be recognised and in one or more forms be precisely and effectively managed. As with other developments in the post-BTC era, states (and local communities) have awakened to the very public nature of environmental issues and their ability to affect not only public opinion but also to attract capital investment in country, as well as debt. In terms of local and international reaction, environmental issues resonate and can have lasting and negative impacts.[31] For projects oriented towards the extractive industry, management of environmental issues is delicate and often only surfaces in the negative (ie, 'bad' behaviour is publicly exposed, but scrupulous environmental compliance and other related successes are not generally publicly recognised). Thus, the necessary objective is to put in place an environmental compliance strategy that is robust and can effectively respond to external challenge.

As a risk mitigant, the Baku–Tbilisi–Ceyhan environmental standards and processes are unparalleled in their rigour, but a legitimate question may be asked as to whether this degree of rigour is realistic or applicable to every development. Therefore, states have taken account of international trends, standards and models for environmental analysis and ultimately compliance, and have adapted legislation accordingly. While in many jurisdictions, this somewhat new state attitude to

29 ["The BTC Project] will bring significant revenue along with high transparency, business and environmental standards to Azerbaijan and Georgia, combined with prospects for sustainable economic development" EBRD Press Release November 11 2003.

30 See http://www.caspiandevelopmentandexport.com/ASP/PD_BTC.asp.

31 For example, note the deep-seated and enduring problems that international companies operating in the Niger Delta have faced as a result of failing adequately to engage with local communities in the appropriate mitigation of the local environmental and social impacts of their activities.

environmental compliance arguably appears disingenuous when compared with past practice, the new paradigm in emerging economies is solidly in support of compliance with international environmental standards. It would appear that in the post-BTC development world, practitioners are probably confined to a close analysis of applicable local and national legislation and regulation prior to development and/or financing, and then a determination as to the ability to achieve robust compliance. If there are valid reasons why compliance would be questionable (all the while maintaining compliance with international standards), then there may be scope for modifying environmental requirements in the applicable host government agreement. Note that this would also require an in-depth analysis to determine where such modifying host government agreement sits in the legal hierarchy of the relevant country. (See the discussion above relating to prevailing legal regimes.)

4.6 Reputational risk and civil society organisations

With Baku–Tbilisi–Ceyhan, the project financing highlighted the importance of managing – and having specific commercial accountability for monitoring and enhancing – the reputation of both the project and the sponsoring companies. Quite early in the BTC financing negotiation process, it became apparent that the rising importance of civil society organisations (both local and international) and their influence over various project stakeholders (not least potential lenders) called for a new model for managing the relationship between reputational risk and commercial objectives. As stated above, any infrastructure project (particularly onshore pipeline projects), will inevitably impact on local communities and the environment and will, therefore, involve an interaction between the underlying business and potentially thousands of affected people and communities. This gives rise to reputational risk (and potentially to legal and regulatory risks).[32] Even in the absence of a project financing, this link will continue to prove more significant in a world which demands increasing accountability from the private sector.[33] Layering in a project financing that involves multinational companies further complicates the issues, as finance decision makers tend to be driven primarily by political not economic considerations and thus, like politicians, are very sensitive to the risks associated with negative reputation. The amplification of reputational risk by civil society organisations is very real. Failure to manage this aspect of a transborder project can certainly undermine a financing at any point during the process, and perhaps the entire project if the investors lose their nerve.

There is no single civil society organisation that focuses specifically on energy infrastructure projects. Some are committed to impeding future oil and gas projects and cannot be brought onside under any circumstances; some hope to influence positive outcomes; and others are prepared to participate in the implementation of

32 Note the Green Alternative claim brought against Baku–Tbilisi–Ceyhan and BP in the Georgian courts. Note also the claim brought before the European Court on Human Rights by the Kurdish Human Rights Project.

33 In addition, as transnational state oil and gas companies continue their investment trend (particularly in the developing world), they will be subject to increasing scrutiny by international civil society organisations, and eventually to international and local legal and regulatory requirements.

'soft' objectives (eg, social investment). It may be helpful, for example, contractually to involve human rights organisations in the context of community and environmental investment programmes (CIP, EIP). In the case of Baku–Tbilisi–Ceyhan, the different priorities, aims, tactics and impacts of the various groups were analysed and required different strategies and techniques of management. A practitioner's focus should be to anticipate and manage the commercial and operational impact of criticism, to assess and manage stakeholder (eg, investor, lender, contractor, host government, local community, civil society) exposure, and perhaps to negotiate with the aim of concrete positive outcomes – but never with the expectation of approval.

Project finance brings with it a high degree of international visibility, third-party scrutiny and potential behaviour modification, to the extent that host countries wish to maintain the approval of international financing institutions and international commercial banks. Community investment, on the other hand, brings in-country visibility and an important level of buy-in for the project within the communities affected by the project. Specifically, sustainable community investment programmes identify project impacts both positive (job creation) and negative (disabling land from traditional use). They attempt to channel investments into areas that help local communities to take advantage of positive impacts (eg, education and training) and to mitigate negative impacts (eg, by deploying construction crews and equipment to install access roads and irrigation systems).

Baku–Tbilisi–Ceyhan employed a successful process which built internal staff confidence, effectively managed questions and answers, simplified routine communication, developed consistent messages, was committed to quality administration (distribution lists, document dispersal and so on), and noted the value of spending quality time with two to three credible, global civil society organisations. In addition, community investment proved to be an important key. The Community Investment Program (CIP) budget was $25 million during the construction phase and supported working with 82 communities in Azerbaijan, 72 communities in Georgia and 300 communities in Turkey. The CIP targeted income and employment creation, infrastructure, health and sanitation, capacity building and agriculture. The money has continued to grow, with the original investment having been further leveraged with external funds.

The standards set by Baku–Tbilisi–Ceyhan are arguably those by which project stakeholders (local communities, investors, lenders and host governments) will measure future projects. Sensitivity around reputational risk and the power of civil society organisations will be a factor in all future development, and the successful projects will require a dedicated, focused programme to identify the specific risks and to put in place a multi-faceted engagement plan. Not every project will have the promotional resources (financial and human) available to Baku–Tbilisi–Ceyhan. However, the Baku–Tbilisi–Ceyhan example contains elements of a plan that may be applied successfully by any transboundary pipeline development company – hands-on identification and a dedicated, targeted management of risks. In this way, it is possible to turn this area of risk into a positive and to showcase the regional benefits of a given project.

4.7 Construction

Construction risk is probably the easiest to understand. This is the risk that has shifted least since Baku–Tbilisi–Ceyhan construction was commenced and completed. As a transboundary project, Baku–Tbilisi–Ceyhan utilised BP as a common operator and construction manager across the pipeline. In Turkey, BP sat at a level above BOTAS, effectively the in-Turkey construction manager.[34] In support of the construction manager's role, the project must insist on the deployment of reputable well-qualified construction contractors throughout the project. Note that projects of this scale, magnitude and length bring multiple coordinated contractors to bear and the complexities of managing the construction under these circumstances cannot be overestimated (nor the cost of getting this element wrong in terms of sheer monetary cost, schedule impact and erosion of reputation). Pipeline developments stretch over a vast, potentially disconnected area and, therefore, the provision of hands-on regional leadership is critical.

Further, the IGA and HGA (host government structure) works well to create common environmental and technical standards. Similarly, supporting activities such as human rights training and monitoring are implemented very consistently throughout the entire 1,764-kilometre project. While any construction project of this magnitude (at one point during construction it was the largest non-military infrastructure project in the world, employing 25,000 people) is challenging, harmonisation of standards and practices is critical to successful realisation of the project. With agreement to harmonisation of standards, this should not be a difficult hurdle to overcome. In addition, obvious but nevertheless important issues such as favourable route selection are key to a successful construction strategy. Intergovernmental oversight and engagement through the treaty-mandated BTC Implementation Commission also proved to be a useful tool for addressing cross-border issues affecting construction.[35]

In summary, the Baku–Tbilisi–Ceyhan project relied on strong experienced leadership in the manager's role and in the multiple construction roles. The host government agreement structure provided a harmonised technical environment which was rigorously followed. Lastly, where the need arose, the intergovernmental agreement provided a forum for the governments to come to the table to address any differences affecting construction. This formula should be applicable irrespective of later development trends regarding projects currently being contemplated.

4.8 Security risks

The topic of security risks is best understood as a category of risk that relates holistically to the broader array of risks already addressed. Due to the international (and sometimes geopolitical) importance of transboundary oil and gas pipelines, their security is important not only from the commercial perspective (ie, prevention

---

34 BOTAS is the wholly Turkish stated-owned oil and gas pipeline company that functioned as the lump-sum turnkey construction project management company and its subsidiary, BOTAS International, Ltd, now functions as the physical operator of Baku–Tbilisi–Ceyhan within the territory of the Republic of Turkey.

35 See Article VI of the Baku–Tbilisi–Ceyhan intergovernmental agreement.

of revenue disruption), but also from a local supply and physical and national security perspective.[36] Some developing country jurisdictions lack the manpower, resource and training to provide adequate physical security. Others place such a high degree of emphasis on physical security that other risks are created for local communities and pipeline owners and operators. In the case of Baku–Tbilisi–Ceyhan, both dimensions of government security were encountered and required careful management.

The Baku–Tbilisi–Ceyhan pipeline was constructed and now operates through a geopolitically fluid part of the world proximate to actual conflicts zones (eg, South Ossetia in Georgia, the Kurdish region of south-eastern Turkey and Nagorno Karabakh, and the frozen conflict zone between Azerbaijan and Armenia). In the case of Georgia, and to a certain extent Azerbaijan, government security services were inexperienced in providing adequate security to the pipeline. In the case of Turkey, government security providers are highly skilled and trained, but have a legacy (particularly among international human-rights civil society organisations) that raised concerns. Accordingly, what began to be understood in the context of Baku–Tbilisi–Ceyhan security was that the pipeline owners and operators needed to pay increasing attention not only to security risks posed to the pipeline but also to the risks which the security measures (and other project impacts such as environmental impacts, treatment of local landowners and ethnic groups, employment practices and delivery of tangible benefits to local communities) themselves posed. These risks can in turn exacerbate physical security risks to a pipeline project and are, therefore, best understood holistically. They can also give rise to areas of legal liability if not adequately understood and managed.[37]

When considering the management of security risks, lawyers are well advised to pay careful attention to the Voluntary Principles on Security and Human Rights.[38] In the case of Baku–Tbilisi–Ceyhan, considerable attention was paid to security and human rights risks both by civil society organisations and by the international financing institutions. Accordingly, the BTC lawyers took steps to have the Voluntary Principles on Security and Human Rights formally incorporated into the prevailing legal regime via a Turkish-government-sponsored intergovernmental agreement, known as the Security Protocol. In addition BP, as operator of Baku–Tbilisi–Ceyhan, formally entered into detailed security protocols with the governments of Georgia and the Azerbaijan Republic to ensure that a broad spectrum of security risks were appropriately and periodically monitored and analysed. The Baku–Tbilisi–Ceyhan project ensures, through both internal and independent external monitoring processes, that its interface with public and private security providers takes careful account of the project's impacts on people, communities and

36 Indeed, the Russian military action in South Ossetia and in the territory of Georgia (within close proximity to both the Baku–Tbilisi–Ceyhan, South Caucuses Gas Pipeline and Western Export Route Pipelines) in August 2008 were actions with geopolitical significance.

37 The US Alien Tort Claims Act has given rise to more than 60 civil actions against multinational companies for their actions in developing countries. The most frequent ground for such actions is the alleged complicity of the multinational company in the perpetration of human rights abuses against local community members impacted by a project, and abused by government security forces.

38 See www.voluntaryprinciples.org.

the environment and is taking steps to minimise these impacts with a view to reducing overall security risks.

4.9 Operations

As operations are the final (and longest) phase of any project, they also represent perhaps the key risk that will determine the success and long-term sustainability of any transboundary pipeline project. Many of the risks cited above remain throughout the life of a project, ebbing and flowing depending on the relevant stage of the project, the focus of activities at any given point, the state of the local economy, the political environment including regional dynamics, and a variety of other factors as they exist from time to time. Assuming the risks set out above have been adequately managed, what defines the sustainability of the project over its life?

The key areas ultimately determining sustainability are commercial and technical longevity and managing local impacts over the life of the project. As regards the fiscal and commercial risks noted above, which focus on the near-term feasibility of a project, a long-term view of the integrated commerciality of a project must be carefully planned, initially established and maintained. If circumstances change dramatically, there must be a recognition that sustainability risk has commensurately increased. This may need to be promptly acknowledged and addressed. Alternatively, it may be an issue over which a 'watching brief' is established. In any event, close scrutiny must be maintained over the original commercial trade and its effect on stakeholders over time. If the deal remains profitable for stakeholders across the investment and there is no significant change in the circumstances of those parties, then the chances are good that the project will remain commercially stable throughout its anticipated life. Technically, sustainability depends on solid, international-standard operations. With Baku–Tbilisi–Ceyhan, BP is the nominated operator and brings with it a wealth of applicable experience and trained resource. Its expertise, coupled with a robust nationalisation programme, should underpin successful operations and long-term maintenance.

Finally, environmental and social impacts that have been carefully identified and sensitively managed during the development and construction phase of a project must also be treated with continuing care in order to ensure long-term sustainability. Baku–Tbilisi–Ceyhan is fairly typical in the array of risks it attracts as a significant transborder infrastructure development. Further, the project developers were innovative in responding to those risks in an era not nearly as developed as that faced by today's infrastructure developers. Thus, Baku–Tbilisi–Ceyhan's identification of risks and mitigation techniques remains valid, but should be carefully examined through a lens informed by developments over the past decade. The risks cited above also remain valid (and there are undoubtedly further variations on those elaborated above), but today's developer or investor will be faced with empowered emerging states who will not only be full participants in, but also drivers of, the development process and will have initiated their own local or national solutions to those risks. Investors and those advising them will be required to be creative in dealing with perceived risks, and in some instances may be required to accept risk that in the BTC negotiation era was considered unacceptable.

5. Conclusions

With the current global economic downturn (and the dramatic fall in demand for oil and, therefore, oil prices), it would be natural to assume that there will be a slowdown in capital expenditure for upstream developments and associated infrastructure, including transboundary oil and gas pipelines. However, most upstream resources are now controlled by states and not the private sector, and we can assume that states will continue to forge access to markets for oil and gas. Indeed, without counter-cyclical investment, the chances that oil prices might well rebound and exceed the recent peaks reached in July 2008 are high. Accordingly, we would anticipate that transboundary pipeline developments will continue and that we will see still further developments by state companies in other jurisdictions, sometimes in partnership with other states, and frequently in partnership with the private sector. As these novel forms of partnership develop, the risks examined in this chapter will continue to change, and the degree of international and domestic regulation of these activities will evolve and become more comprehensive.

Liquefied natural gas

Erin Dyer
Daniel Reinbott
Melanie Williams
Ashurst LLP

---

1. Introduction

Where a party holds an entitlement to develop natural gas reserves, it may commercialise such reserves in various ways. Typically, these include transporting the natural gas to an adjacent market via a pipeline, implementing a gas-to-liquids conversion project, using the natural gas as a feedstock for a local power-generation or petrochemicals project or developing a liquefied natural gas export project. As most of the world's natural gas reserves are located in areas having insufficient domestic demand, many host countries are turning to liquefied natural gas (LNG) projects to monetise these otherwise stranded gas reserves. This chapter provides an introduction to LNG and outlines recent developments in the LNG sector.

2. What is LNG?

LNG is natural gas which has been condensed into a liquid. Natural gas can be transformed into a liquid state by the application of pressure or extreme cooling or a combination of both. Due to the hazards associated with the application of extreme pressure, the LNG industry adopts a cooling process which operates at atmospheric pressure. LNG is predominantly methane, with small proportions of ethane, propane, butane and pentanes. The resulting liquid is chemically inert in respect of most substances and will not burn or explode. At ambient temperatures LNG boils away leaving no residue, and any LNG which transforms into gaseous state is about half the density of air and consequently rises and disperses. The transformation of methane gas into liquefied methane yields a volume reduction of approximately 600 to one. This super-cooled liquid can be stored cryogenically in insulated tanks constructed of special steel (as normal steel cannot withstand the low temperature of LNG) or aluminium, which can then be installed on ocean-going vessels for transportation.

3.1 The LNG industry

3.1 Gas reserves[1]

As at the end of 2007, the world's proved reserves of natural gas were estimated at 6,263.34 trillion cubic feet, with nearly one quarter of those reserves located in the Russian Federation (24.5%), and 41.3% located in the Middle East. Only 8.9% of the

---

1 Reserves statistics from BP, *Statistical Review of World Energy*, June 2008, p 22.

world's gas reserves occur in OECD countries. The reserves-to-production ratios indicate that, at current levels of production, the Russian Federation's reserves will last for the next 73.5 years, and that Iran and Qatar each have reserves for more than 100 years.

3.2 Global LNG trade

The world's first regular LNG trade commenced with Algerian exports to the United Kingdom in the 1960s. In the 1970s, Indonesia commenced LNG exports to Japan and South Korea. Since then, the LNG trade has evolved from distinct regional markets in the Atlantic and Pacific basins towards a more global trade:

- On the supply side, there have been many new entrants – including Australia, Malaysia, Nigeria, Qatar and Trinidad & Tobago. In 2007, Qatar was the largest exporter of LNG, followed by Malaysia and Indonesia; and
- Currently, Japan and Korea predominate as importers of LNG, accounting for 39.3% and 15.2% respectively of total imports in 2007, with import volumes also going to the United States and Europe.[2] The increasing energy requirements of China and India will be of future significance to the global LNG trade.

3.3 Supply–demand equation

The International Energy Agency (IEA) estimates that from 2006 to 2011 global gas demand will increase to 113 trillion cubic feet. This is equivalent to growth of 2.4% per year. The IEA also notes the plateauing of gas production in OECD countries, yet the increasing OECD import dependence on gas, particularly with strong OECD investment in gas-fired power stations.

The LNG supply–demand equation is somewhat unbalanced at present. There is strong demand for LNG, yet tight LNG supply due mainly to a bottleneck in the development of liquefaction capacity. The tight supply situation is unlikely to be significantly eased by the new liquefaction projects coming on stream in the near term as most of the volumes are already committed (see table below).

Anticipated commercial operation date	Project	Capacity (million tonnes per annum)	Location
3Q 2008	Qatargas II (first train)[3]	7.8mtpa	Qatar
4Q 2008	North West Shelf Train 5	4.4mtpa	Australia
Early 2009	Sakhalin II (two trains)	9.6mtpa	Russia
Early 2009	Tangguh (two trains)	7.6mtpa	Indonesia
Early 2009	Yemen LNG	6.7mtpa	Yemen
1H 2010	Peru LNG	4.4mtpa	Peru
Late 2010	Pluto LNG (first train)	4.8mtpa	Australia

2 BP, *Statistical Review of World Energy*, June 2008, p 30.
3 Inclusive of this train, Qatar plans to increase its current output of approximately 31 million tonnes per annum (mtpa) to 77mtpa by 2012.

In addition, delays in final investment decisions (FID) (due largely to escalating construction costs and, in some cases, political uncertainty) mean further constraints on future LNG supplies.[4] Industry analysts appear undecided as to whether the supply tightness (and consequent price pressure) may be eased by the proposed development of further LNG projects, including:

- in Angola, and the Olokoka LNG project (OK LNG) in Nigeria, estimated for start-up in 2012; and
- in Papua New Guinea, Russia, Brass LNG in Nigeria, Greater Sunrise in the Timor Sea and Browse, Gorgon, Wheatstone and Scarborough off north-west Australia, all estimated for start-up around 2014 to 2015.

3.4 Political risk

The geographical location of gas reserves leads to many LNG projects being situated in areas of high political risk. The development of LNG projects in areas such as Nigeria, Papua New Guinea, Russia and Yemen requires sponsors to manage significant risk on LNG projects. However, the capacity to do this is not without limits. Total and the Shell–Repsol–YPF joint venture announced suspensions of final investment decisions in respect of their respective LNG projects in Iran, citing high political risks and political pressure.

Another factor relevant to the high political risk of many LNG projects is increasing resource nationalism by host governments, particularly in the context of high commodity prices and pressure to achieve the best possible returns on the nation's resources. There are numerous examples, including the recent further reopening of LNG prices under long-term contracts for LNG supply from the Indonesian Tangguh project, and the decision of foreign sponsors to proceed with the Sakhalin II LNG project in Russia, despite the dilution of their interests as a result of Gazprom becoming a majority participant.

Even in seemingly low political risk environments, such as the United States and Australia, LNG projects are affected by political considerations. The difficulty in obtaining local approvals for LNG import terminals in certain areas of the United States is well known and the development of further LNG projects in north-western Australia has been hampered by the difficulty in obtaining regulatory approval for sites for the onshore facilities.

As the natural gas market underlying LNG diversifies, so too do its interests align. The Gas Exporting Countries Forum (GECF) is an informally structured group of the world's largest natural gas exporters which, between them, are estimated to control up to 60% of global proved and provable gas reserves and approximately 50% of current global gas exports. Indications in early 2008 were that some natural gas exporters, notably Russia and Iran, had mooted further cooperation between the GECF members in the areas of gas pricing, infrastructure and consumer relations. Such cooperation was regarded by some commentators as tantamount to the formation of a 'gas OPEC'. Given the sensitivity surrounding LNG pricing and the increasing roles of national oil companies and host governments in some GECF

4 For example, no new liquefaction projects were sanctioned in 2008.

members, any suggestion of cartel activity is likely to cause concern amongst parties seeking to develop LNG projects or those relying on LNG imports.

4. LNG value chain

4.1 Introduction

The LNG 'value chain' is a process continuum by which natural gas is produced, transformed into LNG, transported from where it is produced to where it is needed and consumed once it has been restored into its gaseous state as regasified LNG. The value chain lends itself to divisions between the 'upstream' (being natural gas production, transportation and liquefaction), the 'midstream' (being LNG sales and shipping) and the 'downstream' (being LNG regasification and regasified LNG storage and downstream transportation). The following diagram illustrates the LNG value chain.

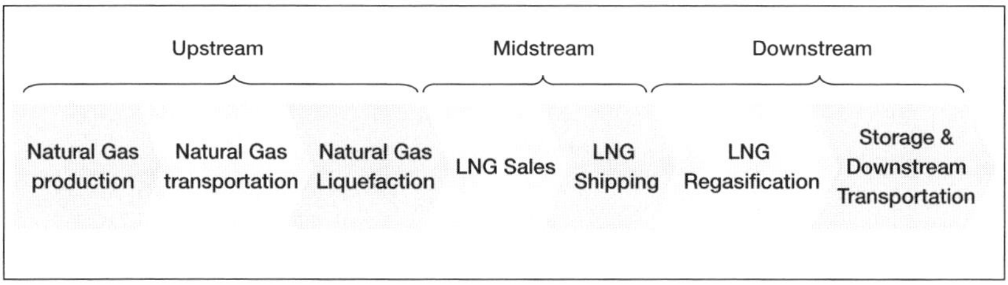

4.2 Natural gas production

A party may hold an entitlement to develop natural gas reserves in a variety of ways. It may hold its entitlement through a bilateral contract between the host government (commonly known as a production sharing contract, concession or licence), or under a statute (eg, in Australia). Regardless of the form which the entitlement takes, it will usually contain a risk-sharing mechanism whereby the private sector contractor bears the upfront risk associated with exploration and development of the field in return for a potential profit-share from production once it commences. In addition to the risk-sharing mechanism, many production sharing contracts and concessions contain a requirement for the contractor to remit a portion of its production to the domestic market. Whilst much has been made of uncertain domestic requirements in emerging markets, notably Indonesia and Nigeria, contractors in more mature markets such as Australia must also grapple with requirements to make a share of production available domestically at below-market prices.

In order to monetise natural gas reserves, the field or block must be developed. Development of a field with a view to producing LNG is no different from developing a standard natural gas field. Wells are drilled and appraised, water and other impurities removed and processed natural gas is then transported by pipeline to a nearby liquefaction plant.

In an unintegrated LNG project which is not based on a tolling model, the LNG project company will need to enter into one or more natural gas sales agreements with natural gas suppliers in order to procure the supply of natural gas to the LNG project. It is the gas suppliers, some of whom may be affiliates of the LNG project company, who will be parties to a production sharing or other concession contract and who are involved in the exploration and production of natural gas.

4.3 Liquefaction

The liquefaction plant is the second of three large infrastructure projects involved in the LNG business. After production, natural gas is transported by pipeline to a liquefaction plant. Liquefaction is the most complex and capital-intensive component of the LNG value chain, and involves super cooling the natural gas to approximately –160°C, at which point it condenses into a liquid. The liquefaction process occurs in units, commonly referred to as 'trains', and during the process impurities such as nitrogen, oxygen, carbon dioxide and water are stripped out of the natural gas. Approximately 10% of the natural gas received by a liquefaction plant is consumed for its own operations.

The liquefaction link in the value chain may be performed by the gas producers as part of an integrated natural-gas-to-LNG operation, or by an independent third-party liquefaction entity under a tolling arrangement. The table below sets out details of existing, and proposed liquefaction plants, along with those presently under construction (including the plants detailed above).

Region	**Existing***	**Under construction***	**Proposed***
Asia	9	2	7
Europe	1	1	1
Middle East and Africa	21	7	8
The Americas	4	1	2
Total	35	11	18

Source: Petroleum Economist LNG Data Centre 2008
**Status defined as follows:*
Existing – Plant is currently built and producing LNG for the market.
Under construction – Plant has had all the necessary approvals and has started construction.
Proposed – Any one of the following: plant has received all necessary approvals but has not started construction; plant has received approval from local or national government; plant has received firm financial backing; or plant has had heads of agreement or letter of intent to deliver LNG to a third party.

After constructing the first liquefaction train, a liquefaction facility operator is often able to add additional trains (and thus increase production capacity) at a lower incremental cost. Significant unit-cost reductions resulting from economies of scale have led liquefaction plant operators such as QatarGas to upsize their facilities. The 'megatrains' presently under construction and proposed by QatarGas are the largest in the world, with each having the capacity to produce 7.8mtpa of LNG. However, the *Petroleum Economist* notes that unit-cost reductions in the liquefaction process achieved by economies of scale through increasing train size, along with improved design and increased competition, appear to have come to a halt.[5]

Once the liquefaction process is complete, LNG is loaded onto an LNG ship at the loading port for transportation to the buyer.

4.4 LNG sales, and LNG sale and purchase agreements

LNG is generally sold or traded in accordance with LNG sale and purchase agreements (LNG SPAs). In the context of an LNG project, LNG produced at the liquefaction plant is usually sold by the project company or the sponsors who are involved in the development of that project. LNG purchasers are typically utility companies which require natural gas for their own operations (eg, power generation) or which supply natural gas to end users in their domestic market. The emergence of a more liquid LNG spot market in recent years, especially in the Atlantic basin, has also encouraged LNG cargoes to be marketed and traded on an entrepreneurial basis including, in some cases, by entities who are not directly involved in the production of LNG or the utilisation of natural gas.

As the revenue generated by LNG sales underpins the cash flows of an LNG project, LNG sale and purchase agreements are largely considered to be the most important of the contracts for an LNG project from both a contractual and financing perspective. Accordingly, substantial time and resources are usually devoted to LNG marketing and the negotiation of the terms and conditions of an LNG sale and purchase agreement, particularly the key terms of price and quantity.

LNG SPAs contain many of the terms and conditions that are common in other energy offtake contracts, such as those used for crude oil and natural gas. However, the unique nature of LNG, LNG trading and transportation and the LNG industry requires many terms and condition in LNG sale and purchase agreements to be tailored to meet these specific needs. As a detailed analysis of the terms and conditions of LNG sale and purchase agreements is beyond the scope of this chapter, the following is an overview of certain of the key terms and conditions of LNG sale and purchase agreements.

(a) Term and delivery period

Due to the high initial investment cost and the capital intensive nature of LNG projects, LNG producers and their lenders prefer the sale of LNG to be contracted on a long-term basis. LNG sale and purchase agreements are therefore typically long-term contracts which may have a delivery period of 20 years or more.

In the case of LNG which is to be supplied from a greenfield LNG project, or to a greenfield regasification terminal, the delivery period of the LNG sale and purchase agreement will usually commence on the date of commencement of commercial operations of the relevant facilities, which is achieved following a period of commissioning of those facilities. The delivery period is often capable of extension

5 The Petroleum Economist, *Encyclopedia of LNG*, 2005, p 9.

for a limited period (eg, up to 365 days) to permit the offtake of make-up or *force majeure* restoration quantities.

(b) ***Natural gas sources, designation and priority of reserves***

As part of the management of upstream supply risks, LNG purchasers usually require that LNG sellers produce LNG only from natural gas which is sourced from designated gas fields or gas reservoirs. In addition, LNG sellers are typically required to provide regular information to the purchasers (eg, on an annual basis) with respect to the remaining proved and probable gas reserves of the relevant gas fields or reservoirs. Such information may be in the form of reserves certificates issued by a reputable petroleum engineer. However, in cases where the reserves of the designated field or reservoir are considered particularly marginal, LNG purchasers may also require additional information with respect to the relevant fields or reservoirs, such as natural gas production history and forecasts or, in exceptional circumstances, 3D seismic data. LNG sale and purchase agreements will also typically include procedures for the addition, whether voluntary or compulsory, of other gas fields or reservoirs by the LNG sellers.

As part of the designation of gas reserves, LNG sale and purchase agreements may also require that the seller not enter into future agreements for the supply of LNG to third parties unless there are sufficient proved and probable reserves remaining in the designated fields or reservoirs, as verified by the most recent reserves certification. This is to ensure the seller is able to satisfy its contractual commitments to both the existing and proposed LNG purchasers. It is not common practice for LNG sellers to dedicate the reserves of specified gas fields or reservoirs to the supply under the relevant LNG sale and purchase agreement. Dedication of reserves imposes a contractual limit on the LNG sellers' ability to monetise gas reserves and may also limit the seller's ability to negotiate the terms for the sale of additional quantities of LNG, given the captive nature of the reserves. LNG sale and purchase agreements may also establish a priority regime, as between other LNG purchasers of the seller, which provides for the allocation of available cargoes in the case of shortfalls in the supply of LNG during a contract year.

(c) ***Quantity, build-up and flexibility***

The quantity of LNG to be made available by the seller and taken by the purchaser in each contract year during the delivery period is often referred to as the annual contract quantity (ACQ) and is generally expressed in MMBtus (million British Thermal Units). In the case of greenfield facilities, the annual contract quantity may be lower in the initial contract years of the delivery period (subject to design capabilities of the facilities) to allow for the gradual build-up in the capacity of the LNG plant or the LNG regasification facilities to which LNG cargoes are to be delivered. A build-up in the ACQ may also be relevant where LNG is to be delivered into a new market, in order to accommodate the downstream market's ability to absorb natural gas in the form of regasified LNG that is priced by reference to international price benchmarks. The timing and number of cargoes of LNG to be made available and taken during a contract year is typically set out in an annual programme which is agreed between the parties. In the case of greenfield facilities, a commissioning programme is usually also separately agreed between the parties in order to provide for the delivery of commissioning cargoes during the commissioning period.

LNG SPAs typically permit the LNG purchaser to exercise some degree of downward and upward flexibility with respect to the applicable annual contract quantity for a contract year. The exercise of such upward or downward flexibility by the LNG purchaser is usually subject to an overall cumulative cap during the delivery period or over a specified number of contract years. As LNG is transported in specially designed vessels, LNG sale and purchase agreements usually also permit the annual contract quantity to be rounded up or down at the end of a particular contract year to allow for the LNG purchaser to take LNG quantities which are equal to a whole cargo. If the annual contract quantity is adjusted in a contract year by a round-up or round-down quantity, the annual contract quantity in the immediately succeeding year is then often reduced (in the case of a round-up in the previous year) or increased (in the case of a round-down in the previous year).

(d) Take or pay and make-up

LNG SPAs typically require the purchaser to take and pay for a quantity of LNG during a contract year which is equal to the adjusted annual contract quantity, or to pay for such part of the adjusted annual contract quantity which is not taken by the purchaser during the relevant contract year (ie, the annual quantity deficiency). The adjusted annual contract quantity for a contract year is typically calculated by adding upward flexibility quantities exercised by the purchaser and any restoration quantities to the annual contract quantity for the contract year, and then deducting any downward flexibility quantities exercised by the purchaser and any quantities of LNG which were not made available for delivery by the seller, or taken by the purchaser, due to the seller's default, events of *force majeure* and other agreed matters. It is usual for the LNG purchaser's take-or-pay obligation to apply only during the delivery period and not during the commissioning period.

If an LNG purchaser is required to pay for an annual quantity deficiency in a particular contract year, the LNG purchaser is typically entitled to take a quantity of LNG in future contract years, up to the amount of the aggregate annual quantity deficiency, either at no charge or at a reduced charge, once it has taken the annual contract quantity or adjusted annual contract quantity for those contract years. In this regard, an LNG purchaser's obligation to pay a take-or-pay amount to the LNG seller may be contrasted with an obligation to pay liquidated damages, as the purchaser's payment of a take-or-pay amount is effectively a prepayment for the right to take additional quantities or LNG in the future.

The LNG purchaser's right to take such quantities of LNG in the future is often referred to as 'make-up' and may be subject to certain conditions, such as the time period in which the LNG purchaser is entitled to exercise its make-up rights and the limits on the quantity of LNG which may be taken as make-up. LNG purchasers may also be required to pay a make-up price for make-up quantities taken if the LNG price at the time the make-up quantities are taken is higher than the LNG price used to determine the take-or-pay amount which was initially paid by the LNG purchaser. As mentioned above, the term of the delivery period under an LNG sale and purchase agreement may be extended for a limited time to permit the LNG purchaser to take any make-up balance outstanding at the end of the initial term.

(e) ***Purchaser's remedy for seller's shortfall***

LNG sale and purchase agreements typically require the LNG seller to make available a minimum quantity of LNG to the LNG purchaser in each contract year. This minimum quantity is often calculated by reference to the applicable annual contract quantity after making allowances for amounts not made available by the seller due to *force majeure*, reasons attributable to the LNG purchaser or regasification terminal operator and other agreed matters. If the LNG seller does not make available the required quantity of LNG during each contract year, the LNG sale and purchase agreement may require the LNG seller to pay liquidated damages (often calculated as the product of the shortfall quantity and a fixed percentage of the average contract price applicable during the relevant contract year) to the LNG purchaser, or the purchaser may be entitled to other remedies, such as a discount on future quantities of LNG delivered. It is common for any liquidated damages to be subject to an annual and/or aggregate cap.

(f) ***Price***

As with all offtake contracts, pricing is one of the key commercial provisions in an LNG sale and purchase agreement. LNG pricing is usually based on crude oil or natural gas price indices, although the choice of index will be subject to negotiation and is invariably dependent upon the market into which the LNG is being delivered, given that the basis for calculating the price of natural gas varies from market to market. If natural gas is traded in a market on the basis of a gas price index (eg, where there is a liquid natural gas market due to domestic production of natural gas or importation by gas pipeline), the pricing formula for LNG to be imported into that market will almost always involve a reference to the applicable domestic gas price index or indices. In markets where there is no domestic natural gas price index or significant competing supply of natural gas, the price of LNG delivered into such markets is typically indexed to the price of other competing energy sources, such as crude oil. By way of example, the price of LNG delivered into Japan is usually determined by reference to the Japanese Crude Cocktail (JCC), whereas the price of LNG delivered into the continental United States of America is often determined by reference to Henry Hub natural gas prices (although this may vary depending upon the proximity of the relevant LNG receiving terminal to other gas-trading hubs) and LNG delivered into the United Kingdom increasingly involves some level of price indexation to the National Balancing Point natural gas price.

Given the recent high oil price environment, LNG sellers are increasingly reluctant to agree to a cap or ceiling in the pricing formula. As a compromise, LNG sellers may agree to a reduced slope in the pricing formula above a certain oil or natural gas price (depending upon the price index). Similarly, whilst an LNG price floor may assist in the bankability of an LNG project, by reducing price risk at low oil or gas prices, LNG buyers may not be willing agree to a price floor and may instead be willing to agree to a higher price slope up to a specified index price. These changes in the slope of the LNG price curve are often referred to in the LNG industry as 'kink points' and result in some price formulas creating a so-called 'J-curve' or 'S-curve'.

(g) ***Price review***

As LNG sale and purchase agreements are typically long-term contracts, some such LNG agreements contain a price review clause or mechanism. Whilst there is no market standard price review clause for LNG sale and purchase agreements, such provisions typically stipulate some or all of the following:

- the circumstances which trigger a price review;
- the frequency in which a price review may occur;
- the elements of the LNG price which may be subject to review;
- factors to be considered in renegotiating the LNG price; and
- the procedure for redetermining the LNG price and resolving any disputes as to the applicable LNG price.

(h) ***Delivery point, destination flexibility and diversion***

The location of the delivery point at which the LNG seller is required to make LNG available to the purchaser will depend upon the shipping arrangements agreed by the parties. Where the LNG seller undertakes to arrange for the shipping of the LNG, the delivery point will usually be at the receiving point at the designated LNG regasification terminal or terminals. In certain cases, LNG sale and purchase agreements (eg, from certain Middle Eastern countries) may provide for the production and transportation of LNG by the LNG seller and the delivery of regasified LNG (ie, natural gas) to the purchaser after receipt from the regasification import terminal. Where the LNG purchaser undertakes to arrange for the shipping of the LNG, the delivery point will usually be at the loading port which is adjacent to the LNG terminal.

LNG sale and purchase agreements may permit LNG purchasers to nominate in advance the LNG terminal (typically from a list of agreed terminals) at which a specific cargo is to be delivered. Such destination flexibility (see below for further discussion) gives LNG purchasers flexibility to manage their gas supply portfolios. The price applicable to such cargoes may vary depending upon the destination. Some LNG sale and purchase agreements also provide the LNG seller with the right to divert certain LNG cargoes from the LNG purchaser to the seller's other purchasers, enabling LNG sellers to supply to markets which offer higher LNG prices. Diversion rights are usually subject to certain limitations, including a limitation on the number of cargoes in each contract year and the payment of nominal compensation to the LNG purchaser. In recent years, numerous cargoes contracted into the US market have been diverted to the Asian market where LNG prices have been markedly higher than US domestic gas prices.

(i) Transportation and loading or unloading

Regardless of which party takes responsibility for arranging for the transportation of LNG, LNG sale and purchase agreements typically contain detailed provisions with respect to the required specification of LNG ships, the facilities at the loading or unloading port (as the case may be) and the procedures for the delivery of LNG cargoes, such as notice of readiness, lay time and demurrage.

(j) Force majeure

The events of *force majeure* which excuse the affected party to an LNG sale and purchase agreement from performing certain of its obligations are generally similar to those contained in other offtake agreements. However, given the importance of the functioning of the entire LNG value chain in the processing, transportation and delivery of LNG, it is common for the events of *force majeure* in LNG sale and purchase agreements specifically to include certain upstream events, such as loss or failure of designated gas reservoirs, delays in completion of upstream facilities and gas pipeline constraints, events affecting the liquefaction plant, including delays in completion and accidental damage to the LNG facilities, and certain downstream events, such as delays in LNG shipping or regasification terminal constraints.

(k) Consistency with upstream natural gas supply agreements

As discussed above, where the LNG project company does not have an entitlement to natural gas, it will need to enter into one or more natural gas sales agreements (gas supply agreements) with natural gas suppliers.

These gas supply agreements usually follow a similar format to LNG sale and purchase agreements and contain many of the main commercial and legal terms which are found in such LNG agreements. However, one of the key aspects of these gas supply agreements is that they provide for a transfer of title and risk in the natural gas supplied from upstream gas suppliers to the LNG project company at the delivery point (usually at the receiving flange at the liquefaction plant).

This transfer in title and risk, as well as the back-to-back nature of the gas supply agreements with the LNG sale and purchase agreements may raise potential issues with respect to the risk allocation between the natural gas suppliers (gas sellers) and the LNG project company (gas purchaser). If the rights, remedies, duties and obligations of the LNG project company (as gas purchaser) under the gas sales agreements are not back to back with the rights, remedies, duties and obligations of the LNG purchasers under the LNG sale and purchase agreements, the LNG project company will assume the risks that are associated with the mismatch in the relevant terms and conditions. Depending on their nature and extent, such mismatches may expose the LNG project company to commercial, financial, legal and technical risks and may adversely affect the bankability of the LNG project if project financing is to be relied upon. For this reason, at the inception of the project, the gas sales agreements and the LNG sale and purchase agreements should be negotiated in parallel, so as to facilitate consistency in terms of risk allocation and, to the extent feasible, to achieve back-to-back terms and conditions between the supply and offtake arrangements.

4.5 Shipping

Transportation of LNG from the liquefaction plant to the regasification terminal is the largest variable cost in the LNG value chain, with the fluctuation based principally on the size and number of vessels required to service a long-term LNG contract. The current LNG vessel fleet is estimated to stand in the region of 260 vessels and is expected to continue its historically rapid expansion until at least 2010, with 2008 statistics continuing this trend (see table below).

LNG fleet	Number	Capacity (million m^3)
Current fleet	284	38.698
Order book	93	16.505
New orders (2008)	6	0.981
Deliveries (2008)	39	7.066

Source: LNG OneWorld with data compiled by Drewry Shipping Consultants

The largest vessels currently transporting LNG are the Q-Flex (which has a capacity of between 210,000 and 217,000 cubic metres) and its larger stable-mate the Q-Max (which has a capacity of between 263,000 and 266,000 cubic metres). Conventional LNG vessels have a capacity of 135,000 to 152,000 cubic metres. The larger vessels have the technology to complete the liquefaction process onboard in a more cost-effective manner than the onshore liquefaction plant, and to reliquefy boil-off LNG. In addition the larger vessels are more fuel efficient than conventional LNG vessels. However, only a limited number of ports can receive these behemoths and many regasification terminals are presently upgrading their ports in order to receive these vessels.

LNG buyers and sellers will determine the responsibility for LNG shipping amongst themselves, or may elect to have an independent third-party transport the LNG. The long-term time charter remains the most common shipping arrangement.

4.6 Regasification facilities, storage and downstream transportation

Compared with liquefaction plants, regasification terminals are comparatively simple installations. In general, LNG ships are berthed at the regasification terminal and the LNG is unloaded from the LNG ship, regasified by the terminal and stored or distributed to customers. Similarly to liquefaction plants, regasification terminals may be operated by the upstream entity (ie, the LNG seller) (eg, the South Hook terminal at Milford Haven in Wales), or by an independent third party under a tolling arrangement (as is the case particularly in the United States but also in the United Kingdom and in the proposed Singapore LNG regasification terminal).

The table below sets out details of existing and proposed regasification terminals, along with those presently under construction.

Region	Existing*	Under construction*	Proposed*
Asia	33	7	18
Europe	16	9	10
Middle East and Africa	0	0	0
The Americas	9	11	25
Total	58	27	53

Source: Petroleum Economist LNG Data Centre 2008
**Status defined as follows:*
Existing – terminal is currently built and receiving LNG from the market.
Under construction – terminal has had all the necessary approvals and has started construction.
Proposed – any one of the following: terminal has received all necessary approvals but has not started construction; terminal has received approval from local or national government; terminal has received firm financial backing; terminal has had heads of agreement or letter of intent to receive LNG from a third party; a US onshore terminal has received approval from FERC; a US offshore terminal has received approval from the United States Coast Guard (USCG) and the Maritime Administration (MARAD).

Despite the impeccable safety record of the LNG industry, public opposition remains a significant barrier to the development of regasification terminals in close proximity to populated areas (eg, Shell's Broadwater LNG off Long Island, New York, and BP's Crown Landing in New Jersey). However, the lack of public appetite for the construction of new regasification terminals in the United States generally is not the only factor detracting from its attractiveness as a market. Existing regasification terminals on the US East Coast and the Gulf of Mexico have been operating with spare capacity due to US domestic gas prices which are insufficiently high to attract cargoes bound for the higher-priced Asian and European markets. Whilst global demand for LNG remains high and with major consumers (eg, China) indicating willingness to pay market prices, absent increased prices in the US domestic gas market, spare capacity in US regasification terminals is likely to continue.

Once the LNG has been regasified, it is transported (usually by pipeline) to the gas transmission or distribution network or directly to large industrial customers – for example, power plants. Transportation of the regasified LNG may be undertaken by the regasification terminal operator or by the LNG seller or LNG buyer (where these parties are not the same party), and will be undertaken pursuant to a separate (typically) arm's-length gas transportation contract. It will be important for the gas transporter to back-to-back its arrangements with the applicable LNG supply agreement to the extent that it is able to maximise its protection from take-or-pay liabilities from end-users.

5. Financing of LNG projects

5.1 Why project finance?

As the LNG industry has evolved, so too has the specialist financing of LNG projects. The key concern of project finance lenders is the cash flows of the project available to service the debt throughout the life of the loan. In many ways the cash flows generated by a traditional LNG project are suitable to project financing, as the cash flows derive from long-term, high-volume, take-or-pay LNG sale and purchase agreements with minimal flexibility, and with creditworthy offtakers. It is also typical that the sponsors provide credit support (such as completion guarantees or debt service undertakings) during the construction of the project, known as completion support. In addition, the interests of sponsors and lenders in ensuring successful integration of the LNG value chain are aligned.

A sponsor may choose to finance an LNG project for various reasons. These include high capital costs, mitigation of political risk (often a key driver), and, in the case of committed long-term offtake, project economics which support a high level of gearing. In addition, where one of the sponsors is less creditworthy, its partners may prefer to participate in a project financing rather than carry the weaker credit. Finally, a successful project financing allocates the risks associated with each part of the LNG value chain through appropriate contracts and other risk mitigants such as insurance. This process will involve management time and attention and transaction costs, including the engagement of various experts. Although onerous, the rigour associated with obtaining project financing may also provide a useful discipline to the project, and some additional comfort to the management of the sponsors.

The involvement of lenders will invariably mean constraints on operations. Given the economies of scale associated with LNG projects, key concerns for sponsors will be its ability to expand the project and to fund that expansion.

5.2 Benchmark LNG financing – the Qatari model

The Qatari model for financing LNG projects is regarded as the industry benchmark, with aggressive terms and record pricing, progressively refined over a series of financings of both the Qatargas and RasGas projects located at Ras Laffan Industrial City in Qatar. The US$7.6 billion Qatargas II project financing achieved a number of firsts, as:

- the largest ever energy financing;
- the first LNG project to be financed across the LNG value chain, from gas production from the North field offshore from Qatar through transporting the gas to market in the United Kingdom;
- a technology first, with the two 7.8mtpa megatrains; and
- financing on the basis of all sales going into the UK market, the lenders effectively accepting UK gas market risk.

The model was further refined in the Qatargas 3 financing of more than US$4 billion, again an integrated financing across the LNG value chain. The Qatargas 3 financing was also significant due to the lenders' acceptance of US market risk (ie, Henry Hub pricing), another first, and the introduction of export credit agencies in addition to commercial bank lenders. The final financing in the Qatargas series was the US$4.225 billion Qatargas 4 financing, which again saw further improvements in pricing and terms. Of particular note was lenders' acceptance of a certain amount of flexibility for LNG sales.

Following commencement of production, the RasGas 2 and 3 projects successfully accessed the US capital markets for funding, as part of a US$10 billion funding programme, which further diversified the funding sources.

5.3 Recent LNG financings

Despite the credit crunch, multi-billion dollar LNG financings have recently closed in the high political risk areas of Peru, Russia and Yemen. This is a firm indication of lender appetite for LNG risk, and commentary indicates that high political risk will not in itself preclude the financing of Nigerian LNG projects. The US$5.3 billion Sakhalin II financing in particular is an interesting case study of the ability of an LNG project to obtain financing despite significant pressure over environmental and social concerns, the doubling of project development costs and the forced introduction of Gazprom. The project was also fortunate to be located close to Japan, which will take substantial volumes of LNG from the project, enabling it further to diversify its sources of energy supply, and which explains the high Japanese component in the lending consortium.

5.4 Future challenges for sponsors and lenders in financing LNG

Lenders have accepted the risks on traditional LNG project financing, premised on committed long-term offtake volumes with minimal contractual flexibility, sponsor completion support and proven LNG technology. As the LNG industry evolves, particularly as to contractual flexibility on sales, the emerging spot market and new LNG technologies, sponsors and lenders alike will face new challenges in the financing of LNG projects.

6. Current issues in LNG

6.1 Destination flexibility

While there are a number of liquefaction projects scheduled to come onstream in the coming years as noted above, global demand for LNG is significantly outstripping supply. Furthermore, recent developments in shipping technology (including, in particular, on-board liquefaction technology and the development of Q-Max and Q-Flex ships) and higher gas prices in downstream markets have made LNG competitive over longer distances. As a result, European gas markets must compete for LNG supply on both long- and short-term bases with gas markets in North America and Asia-Pacific, which are priced using different indices. US LNG contracts are often benchmarked against the Henry Hub price, whereas European contracts are generally linked to heavy fuel oil prices and gas oil prices, and many Asian contracts are based on a basket of crude grades, commonly referred to as the Japanese Crude Cocktail (JCC), which are adjusted on a monthly basis.

Increasingly, long-term LNG contracts are moving away from the traditional conservative point-to-point sales (whereby trades have been from a single nominated loading port to a single nominated unloading port) and embracing destination flexibility, on both the seller's side and the buyer's side. From a seller's perspective negotiated destination flexibility provides an opportunity to take advantage of more favourable prices in other markets, and from a buyer's perspective to mitigate the impact of the imposition of a strict take-or-pay regime. Sellers and buyers will usually share in any cost-savings which result from such diversion.

Aside from negotiated restrictions on each party's ability to divert cargoes, competition laws may also have an impact. The European Union, for example, prohibits contracting parties from agreeing to limit the destinations which a cargo may be diverted to where the destination is within the European Union. Lenders may also curtail a party's flexibility to divert a particular cargo as many LNG projects are financed on the basis of the creditworthiness of a particular buyer, or maturity or depth, or a particular market. Prohibitive shipping costs will also be a relevant consideration in any proposed diversion.

6.2 Trading

LNG trading typically entails the buying and selling of LNG other than on a long-term, high-volume, take-or-pay basis. Notwithstanding this historical position, concurrently with the significant growth in the global LNG market, spot and short-term markets have developed. These appear likely to continue to grow both absolutely and as a percentage of global LNG traded due to the continued rise of aggregators and an increasing liquidity generated in part by an increasing number of market entrants. Established portfolios of liquefaction, shipping and regasification assets provide aggregators (principally international oil companies) with the contractual flexibility to take advantage of opportunities arising due to seasonal fluctuations in demand or increased profitability of a particular market. The aggregator model has historically been more prevalent in the Atlantic and Mediterranean Basin than in the longer-established Asian market. However, recently the Singapore LNG regasification project has also adopted an aggregator model.

(a) Spot sales

Increasing market liquidity, greater demand for LNG, surplus regasification terminal capacity, uncommitted vessels and increasingly flexible contracts have facilitated the emergence of a spot LNG market which has grown from virtually zero before 1990 to 1% of the total LNG trade in 1992, 8% in 2002, approximately 11% in 2006 and is forecast by the IEA to increase to 20% of LNG sales in the near term.[6] Algeria, Oman, Qatar, Trinidad and Tobago and the United Arab Emirates (principally Abu Dhabi) are among the leading global short-term sellers, whilst the United States, Spain, South Korea and France are major short-term importers. Whilst not strictly a spot market – it operates on a weeks- or months-ahead basis – spot or short-term contract cargoes may alleviate the impacts of scheduling mismatches between liquefaction facilities and regasification facilities or the effects of a short-term event of *force majeure*.

6 International Energy Agency, "Towards a Global Gas Market", *Natural Gas Market Overview*, 2006.

Like any commodity not committed to a customer, spot LNG will typically flow to where the highest price is on any given day. Spot or short-term (up to about one year) trades may be effected by way of a bespoke contract or by a standardised master sales agreement which sets out the general terms and conditions, supplemented by a short-form confirmation for each trade. The risk allocation between the parties in a spot or short-term contract generally mirrors that in a long-term LNG contract; however, many usually contentious provisions such as price and price-review, take-or-pay and termination may be simplified due to the truncated (or one-off) nature of the sale.

Despite their recent preponderance, spot and short-term sales are unlikely to overtake long-term contracted sales due to the capital-intensive nature of the LNG industry, which is explored above. In addition, as buyers are increasingly willing to pay higher prices to secure supply for their regasification facilities and seemingly insatiable domestic markets, capacity which may once have been 'spot' is being contracted for on a long-term basis.

(b) ***Swaps***

Swaps, as the name suggests, occur where two buyers or two sellers agree to swap cargoes. Swaps may be based on a geographic proximity (ie, where each sale involves a considerable distance and therefore associated cost) or scheduling mismatch rationale. For example, where seller 1 and buyer 2 are geographically more proximate than seller 1 is to buyer 1, and vice versa in respect of seller 2 and buyer 1, the parties may agree that it is more efficient (both in terms of time and cost) for each seller to sell its LNG cargo(es) to the other's original buyer (and the converse). A scheduling mismatch may occur due to delays in commissioning of the seller's liquefaction or the buyer's regasification facilities which will eventually be the subject of a long-term contract, or due to scheduled or unscheduled maintenance on either LNG facility. In the case of a scheduling mismatch, the upside of any swap may be the saving of each buyer's take-or-pay liability under its long-term contract.

Any swap will usually require the consent of the relevant counterparties, and how any cost savings or upside will be shared amongst the parties will be a matter for negotiation between the four parties. Determining any cost savings will require a consideration of the risk allocation regime in each underlying contract, and where a party is asked to take a greater risk than envisaged in the original contract, expediency and certainty usually dictate that the parties agree a fixed-sum adjustment (eg, through a reduction in cargo price) rather than haggle over the actual quantum of any upside. At the same time as settling the commercial terms of any swap, the parties will need to verify the compatibility of each party's onshore infrastructure and vessels.

(c) ***Arbitrage***

The global LNG market is not yet fully liquid and, as noted above, divergences in LNG prices in the US, European and Asian–Pacific markets create arbitrage opportunities for LNG buyers and sellers to redirect a cargo to a market offering a higher price. The Atlantic Basin is the most susceptible to price arbitrage as it has the highest proportion of flexible capacity. The proximity of the Middle East, one of the world's largest LNG exporters, to both the Atlantic and Pacific Basins further fosters price arbitrage, as exporters in the Middle East retain the flexibility to ship cargoes into either market at similar cost and have visibility as to pricing in both markets.

6.3 Third-party access to LNG facilities

(a) *European Union*

The EU legislation which establishes a third-party access regime for LNG facilities is the 2003 Gas Directive.[7] EU member states must in principle ensure that regulated, non-discriminatory third-party access is provided to liquefaction and regasification terminals, as well as to transmission and distribution systems. The third-party access rules applicable to regasification facilities include granting access to ancillary facilities and temporary storage necessary for the regasification process and subsequent delivery to the transmission system. The 2003 Gas Directive also provides for non-discriminatory third-party access to standalone gas storage facilities.

An exemption from the third-party access regime is available to major new gas infrastructure, including LNG terminals, provided that certain criteria are met. The exemption regime aims to strike a balance between incentivising investment and facilitating competition. The majority of European regasification terminals currently being developed have obtained exemptions from the third-party access regime. The South Hook, Dragon, and Isle of Grain in the United Kingdom regasification terminals have obtained an exemption for all of their respective regasification capacity, whereas in other cases, for example the various Italian models, 80% of the regasification capacity is reserved for the sponsors with the remaining 20% being offered to third-party users.

Given the strategic importance of LNG to Europe and consequently of investments in LNG terminals, the European Commission proposes that there should be legally binding guidelines in respect of how third-party access to LNG terminals will operate where it applies. However, these proposals are yet to have their first reading before the European Parliament.

(b) *United States*

New US LNG facilities are not required to offer capacity to third-party users. Although LNG facility operators need not be concerned with third-party access to the LNG facility itself, third-party access may be an issue in respect of the downstream pipeline interconnecting the LNG facility with the gas distribution system.

Prior to the 2002 FERC order in respect of the Hackberry LNG Terminal,[8] LNG facilities in the United States were subject to a third-party access requirement to make capacity available to third-party users during an 'open season' (similar to the third-party open-access regime applicable to pipelines), on terms and conditions

---

7 Directive 2003/55/EC of the European Parliament and of the Council Concerning Common Rules for the Internal Market in Natural Gas.

8 Hackberry LNG Terminal, LLC, 101 FERC § 61.294 (2002).

covering *inter alia* tariffs regulated by FERC. The 2002 order abolished this open-access requirement and also removed the previous requirement that the LNG facility operator publish all capacity contracts which it had entered into in respect of the LNG facility. This position was partially codified in the Energy Policy Act 2005.

The Marine Transportation Security Act 2002 governs offshore LNG facilities in the United States and, similarly to the 2002 FERC order and the Energy Policy Act 2005, provides that LNG facility operators need not provide open third-party access to their facilities nor be subject to regulated terms and conditions or tariffs. With an expected increase in LNG import dependence, this light-touch approach to regulation should serve to encourage new investment into the US LNG sector.

(c) Australia

Unlike the United States, where many LNG facilities have traditionally been underutilised, LNG facilities in Australia suffer from a distinct lack of spare capacity. Accordingly, common arguments advanced in favour of third-party access (including a need to achieve full and efficient utilisation of a facility) have not tended to be persuasive in the Australian context. However, for projects presently under development or in the pre-feasibility stage, for example the second train of Pluto LNG or the Browse LNG project, issues regarding third-party access are more likely to arise as levels of spare capacity increase. Early indications are that the Australian government is looking at overhauling the third-party access rules applicable to export infrastructure. However, it is unclear how or whether this will impact upon new LNG projects in Australia.

6.4 Increasing engineering, procurement and construction (EPC) costs and labour shortages

The LNG industry is not immune from the global trend of increasing costs for raw materials (especially steel) and construction, together with labour shortages. An extreme example is the blowout in development costs for the Sakhalin II project in Russia from less than US$10 billion to more than US$20 billion. Both greenfield and expansion LNG projects are experiencing delays due to these factors. Given the tight LNG supply and the LNG project pipeline over the coming years, the demand for contractor services will only continue. It has been observed that contractors may need to change their contract models to best meet this demand. LNG project sponsors will also need to look to innovative solutions to manage these risks, such as modular construction[9] and multi-currency tenders, in order to place foreign exchange risk with the party best equipped to manage it.

A recent example of innovation is the strategy used for the development of the Qatargas 3 and Qatargas 4 onshore and offshore assets. These two projects are being jointly developed by an integrated team to capture cost, technology and labour synergies, with each onshore train being developed under a single EPC contract with a Chiyoda–Technip joint venture.

---

9 As was seen in the construction of the fifth LNG train of the North West Shelf project.

6.5 New technologies

The slow pace of development of LNG projects, and high commodity prices, means that new technologies are being seriously canvassed, such as the use of coal bed methane to supply LNG plants and floating liquefaction facilities and storage and regasification facilities.

(a) *Coal bed methane[10] (CBM) to LNG*

As the natural gases stored in coal beds or coal seams typically have a higher concentration of methane than conventional natural gas (often more than 95%), and usually do not contain hydrogen sulphide or other sulphur components, coal bed methane represents an alternative to conventional natural gas as a feedstock in the production of LNG.

Coal bed methane is a form of natural gas, generated during the process of coalification (the progressive conversion of plant materials to coal), that attaches to coal surfaces and coal fractures and is held in place by hydraulic pressure. Coal bed methane is typically produced by removing the water from a coal bed (a process referred to as dewatering), which depressurises the coal bed and eventually causes the methane stored on the coal surfaces to separate from the coal. The methane then flows through the fractures and cleats which exist in the coal bed, before being extracted by gas production wells. The production of coal bed methane occurs as the water is continually removed from the coal bed. The process of dewatering and depressurisation may need to be conducted for some time (potentially as long as three or four years, or more) before the realisation of stable commercial coal bed methane production.

At the time of writing, a number of LNG projects have been proposed in Queensland, Australia,[11] in an attempt to monetise the substantial coal bed methane reserves which exist in the Bowen and Surat basins of central and south-east Queensland, and to market these reserves to the higher-value international LNG market. The Queensland projects have received much international attention and have attracted participation and significant investment from major international LNG players including BG, Shell, Petronas and Sojitz, who will separately partner with Australian-based energy companies including Santos, Queensland Gas Company and Arrow Energy. The initial design capacities of these projects is varied, ranging from 0.5mpta to 1mpta to 3mpta to 4mpta, with expansion plans for some projects of between 10mpta and 12mtpa having been suggested.[12]

The development and production of coal bed methane differs in a number of

---

10 Coal bed methane is also referred to as coal seam methane or coal seam gas.

11 The coal bed methane produced as part of these projects is intended to be piped (over 400km in some cases) from the inland coal fields to the central coast port of Gladstone where the LNG terminals are proposed to be built. Given the close proximity of the proposed sites for certain of these projects, there may be potential for the sharing of infrastructure and facilities between the different projects.

12 In contrast to the projects mentioned above, another coal bed methane to LNG project has been proposed in Queensland by Liquegas Energy, a subsidiary of the Norwegian-based AGR Group, which intends to market LNG from a 100 tonne per day plant, to be transported by road to industrial and power generators in Queensland and New South Wales.

respects from the development and production of conventional natural gas. Certain of these differences will need to be carefully considered in structuring the technical, commercial, contractual and financial aspects of coal bed methane to LNG projects, including the following:

- *Initial estimation and establishment of recoverable coal bed methane reserves:* as coal thickness, permeability and coal bed methane content may vary significantly throughout a coal bed or coal seam, the estimation and establishment of the recoverable coal bed methane reserves typically requires more intensive appraisal drilling and sampling from the various appraisal wells in order to reduce uncertainty. Sufficient uncommitted proved and probable gas reserves usually form the cornerstone of an LNG project and LNG project developers, LNG purchasers and project financiers will need to pay particular attention to the nature and level of recoverable reserves which are available for a coal-bed methane-to-LNG project. Given the risk and uncertainty involved in estimating and recovering coal bed methane reserves, and the absence of precedent coal-bed methane-to-LNG projects, project counterparties are likely to place increased reliance on proved (P1) reserves when assessing the sufficiency of available reserves.
- *Continuing development and ongoing production analysis:* once production of coal bed methane commences, additional development drilling is normally required and the number of coal bed methane wells increases over time in order to build up or retain coal bed methane production levels. In addition, regular production analysis throughout the term of a coal-bed methane-to-LNG project is likely to be required (particularly by lenders and LNG buyers) in order to assess the level of the remaining commercially recoverable coal bed methane reserves.
- *CBM production profile:* in contrast to the production of conventional natural gas, which peaks initially and declines relatively steeply thereafter, coal bed methane production normally increases to a stable production rate before gradually declining over a longer period of production. The coal bed methane production profile will be a key consideration in determining the design and optimum capacity of the liquefaction facilities and when negotiating the annual contract quantities and build-up periods in LNG sale and purchase agreements.[13]
- *Capital investment and risk:* capital investment for a coal bed methane project is typically higher and more uncertain during the development and production of coal bed methane, than during the exploration phase of the coal bed methane project, as additional development and wells are required to build up and maintain coal bed methane production. The financing plan for a coal-bed methane-to-LNG project will need to provide for the necessary

13 One other interesting aspect of coal bed methane production is that once the coal bed has been dewatered and the coal bed methane flow has begun, it is generally not feasible to stop the production of coal bed methane (eg, it may require water to be injected in the coal bed, which would then need to be pumped out again to resume production) and coal bed methane may need to be flared if there is constraint in the midstream or downstream facilities.

capital that will be required during these phases, as well as allowing for sufficient contingency to address potential delays and cost overruns. Whilst capital expenditure may be relatively higher during the production phase of a coal bed methane project, when compared to a conventional natural gas project, these higher levels of expenditure often coincide with relatively stable coal bed methane production levels over the life of the project.

(b) ***Floating LNG***

Strong advances have been made in the technology for floating storage and regasification units (FSRU) for LNG, with the recent completion of the first floating storage and regasification units for use offshore from Brazil. Recent press also reports proposals for FSRU technology to be used offshore from Dubai, China (Guangdong), Italy and South Africa. However, floating LNG liquefaction technology is not yet considered proven, though advances are being made. Shell recently issued a tender for the construction of a 3.5 million tonnes per annum floating LNG liquefaction facility, noting that floating LNG systems use less energy to cool gas and negate the need for costly pipelines. Floating LNG liquefaction technology is also likely to facilitate the development of smaller, stranded gas reserves (perhaps as low as 0.5 trillion cubic feet), which would not otherwise justify the expenditure for an onshore liquefaction plant and associated infrastructure. Other advantages for both floating liquefaction and regasification include mitigation of political risk (due to the offshore location), fewer onshore regulatory issues (including social and environmental concerns) and shorter lead times for project development. Challenges for the technologies include being able to withstand extreme offshore conditions (particularly in respect of loading and unloading), increased safety concerns and logistical issues associated with the offshore location and constraints on expansion of the project.

6.6 Climate change and LNG projects

Using common energy distribution and conversion technologies, the lifecycle emissions from LNG are about 50% to 60% of conventional fossil fuels based on export from Australia to customers in Japan. In an era of climate change concerns, this should mean a preference for LNG as an energy source on a global basis. Interestingly, the recent Australian government announcement, following its ratification of the Kyoto protocol, of a proposed emissions trading scheme has drawn howls of protest from many oil and gas companies (bearing in mind that at least A$60 billion is proposed to be invested in Australian LNG projects!). In brief, the complaint is that the scheme fails to recognise that LNG usually replaces more greenhouse-intensive fuels in its export destinations. It remains to be seen how this tension will be resolved.

Bibliography

Argus Global LNG Monthly, Volume IV, Issue 7, July 2008.

Argus Global LNG Monthly, Volume IV, Issue 8, August 2008.

Atkins, B, "Coal Bed Methane – From Resource to Reserves", *Focus* (Gaffney, Cline & Associates), Issue No 34, October 2003.

BP, *Statistical Review of World Energy*, June 2008.

Bros, T, "Global LNG Overview Points way to Changing Market Fundamentals", *LNG Journal* (accessed July 31 2008).

Cobley, B, "Floating LNG Production – a Chasm Waiting to be Filled", *Infrastructure* Journal, October 10 2007.

Griffin, P (Consulting Editor), *Liquefied Natural Gas: The Law and Business of LNG*, Globe Law and Business, 2006.

Haines, L (editor), "Opportunities in Coalbed Methane", *Oil and Gas Investor*, December 2002.

LNG Unlimited, Issues No 86, 87 and 88, August 2008.

[NC], "Queensland's Coal Seam Gas Industry Continues to Brighten" *Queensland Government Mining Journal*, March 2008, pp 40 to 47.

PricewaterhouseCoopers, *Value and Growth in the Liquefied Natural Gas Market*, 2007.

Project Finance Magazine, June and July/August 2008 editions.

Total, *Liquefied Natural Gas* (available at http://www.total.com/static/en/medias/topic449/Total_2004_en_LNG.pdf).

Gas sale and purchase agreements

Daniel O'Neill
Ashurst LLP

1. Introduction

A gas sales agreement (GSA) is an agreement pursuant to which a party (the seller) agrees to sell and deliver natural gas (gas) to another party (the buyer) at a designated delivery point.

In linking the upstream production or supply of gas with the downstream consumption or onwards supply of gas, the GSA will often be the most important agreement in a gas commercialisation project and will be central to the project's economics and overall success. Most of the other project agreements will usually be developed around the terms of the GSA.

There are different types of GSAs, and some of the key distinguishing characteristics are as follows:

- *Means of bringing gas to market:* the means by which gas is transported and brought to market will have a significant bearing on the nature and terms of the gas sales arrangements. In broad terms, commercial quantities of gas can be bought and sold in the form of:
  - pipeline gas;
  - liquefied natural gas;[1]
  - liquefied petroleum gas; or
  - compressed natural gas.

  As pipeline gas constitutes the majority of traded gas, the focus of this chapter will be upon GSAs in the context of pipeline gas rather than liquefied natural gas, liquefied petroleum gas and/or compressed natural gas sale and purchase arrangements (although some of the issues discussed below will be equally applicable in the context of liquefied natural gas, liquefied petroleum gas and compressed natural gas sale and purchase arrangements).
- *Responsibility for pipeline transportation:* whether the buyer is responsible for the pipeline transportation of the gas from its point of upstream production or supply to the buyer's gas-receiving facilities (sometimes referred to as an 'FOB' deal), or the seller is responsible for such transportation (sometimes referred to as a 'CIF/delivered' deal) – which in a greenfield gas commercialisation project will involve the construction of the pipeline and associated infrastructure – is likely to have a impact on the approach of the

1 Refer to the previous chapter for a detailed discussion of liquefied natural gas.

seller and the buyer to risk allocation under the GSA.[2]

- *Depletion and term-supply contracts:* GSAs are often categorised as depletion contracts or term-supply contracts. Under a depletion contract, the seller dedicates all gas capable of being economically produced from a particular field or fields for supply to the buyer. The duration of the contract and the quantities of gas supplied under it will be dependent upon the production profile of the dedicated field(s).[3] Under a term-supply contract, the seller commits to delivering agreed contractual quantities of gas for a specified period of time, often without reference to the source of the gas. Some 'hybrid' GSAs exhibit characteristics of both depletion contracts and term-supply contracts.[4] Depletion contracts tend to be more common in new or developing gas markets. As a gas market matures and liberalises, the concerns of sellers and buyers shift from market risk and security of supply to ensuring flexibility and diversification in gas supplies and markets, and this is usually accompanied by a shift from depletion contracts towards term-supply contracts. As term-supply contracts are more common, the focus of this chapter will be on term-supply GSAs.
- *Long-term, short-term and spot arrangements:* because of the significant upfront capital costs associated with gas commercialisation projects, gas producers and their lenders have historically insisted upon long-term offtake commitments supported by robust take-or-pay obligations to ensure that gas producers/sellers receive a minimum guaranteed cash flow to underpin their capital investment and/or debt service obligations. Accordingly, the majority of GSAs have tended to be long-term, bespoke contracts with a duration often exceeding 20 years. As a gas market matures and liberalises, this will usually be accompanied by a proliferation of gas infrastructure and capacity availability, with the consequence being that the duration of GSAs tends to become shorter (with the final evolution being spot trading on standardised terms) as sellers and buyers seek to preserve gas marketing and supply flexibility. However, the majority of gas continues to be traded under bespoke, long-term arrangements and therefore the focus of this chapter will be on long-term GSAs.

2. Parties

Given the long-term nature of gas commercialisation projects, both the seller and buyer will be concerned as to the identity of its counterparty and its ability to

---

2 The terms 'FOB', being the acronym for 'free-on-board', and 'CIF/delivered' (with 'CIF' being the acronym for 'cost-insurance-freight') are shipping terms which have been adopted by the petroleum industry to connote the allocation of risk and responsibility for pipeline transportation between the seller and buyer of pipeline gas.

3 Depletion contracts will also usually afford the seller with *force majeure* relief for reserves shortfall or reservoir failure and a right to terminate the agreement when it is no longer economic for the seller to continue to produce gas.

4 An example of a hybrid GSA would be a term-supply contract which also imposes certain reserve commitments and obligations on the seller, such as an obligation on the seller periodically to provide to the buyer reserve certificates demonstrating that the proven, or proven and probable, reserves within a designated source are sufficient to meet the seller's total remaining gas supply obligations under the GSA, together with restrictions on the seller's ability to dispose of gas from that designated source to third parties without the buyer's prior approval.

perform its obligations for the duration of the GSA.[5] Further, because the identity of the counterparty will have been an important factor in a party's decision to embark on the gas commercialisation project, that party will wish to limit its counterparty's ability to exit the project through the inclusion of stringent transfer restrictions.

2.1 Collateral support

As the buyer's principal obligation will be the payment of money, the seller will want to ensure that the buyer is a creditworthy entity capable of meeting its payment obligations for the duration of the GSA. If the seller has concerns as to the buyer's creditworthiness, the seller may insist on the provision of collateral support by the buyer, usually in the form of a parent-company guarantee and/or a revolving letter of credit or bank guarantee to cover short-term liquidity concerns. A seller may also insist on having the right to request the provision of collateral support by the buyer if the buyer (or the guarantor, as the case may be) is subject to a change in financial circumstances.[6]

Given that the seller's principal obligation under the GSA will be the supply of gas, it is generally less common for a buyer to insist on collateral support from the seller.[7]

2.2 Multiple sellers and/or buyers

Although a GSA may be a bilateral arrangement between a single seller and a single buyer, in some circumstances there may be multiple sellers and/or multiple buyers to the gas sales arrangements. This will often be the case if the gas is being sold from its point of production, as upstream gas developments are generally undertaken by a number of seller parties in joint venture due to the high cost and risk involved in exploring for and producing gas.

Where multiple sellers are selling gas to a single buyer, the sellers will usually prefer that the GSA be expressed as taking effect as a separate agreement between each of the individual sellers and the buyer, with each seller being severally liable for the performance of its obligations under the GSA to the extent of its proportionate share of the total gas quantities to be supplied.[8] Although the separate agreement

---

5 For example, depending on the structure of the gas commercialisation project, the buyer will wish to ensure that the seller has the right to produce and sell gas, and has title to the gas at the point of sale. Some of these issues may be addressed by way of representations and warranties (see Section 18 below).

6 What constitutes a change in financial circumstances of the buyer (or the guarantor, as the case may be) triggering the right of the seller to request the provision of collateral support may be the subject of considerable negotiation. Common trigger events based on objective criteria may include a deterioration in the buyer's credit rating, or the buyer's financial statements revealing negative earnings or negative cash flow from operations, or a total debt to tangible assets exceeding an agreed ratio.

7 A buyer may insist on collateral support in certain circumstances – for example, if the seller entity is a special purpose vehicle of limited financial standing and/or is acting in the capacity of gas aggregator and is not itself the entity having title or long-term access to gas reserves underpinning the GSA.

8 If such a structure is contemplated, the GSA will also usually need to provide (i) that gas to be supplied by the sellers under their separate agreements will be supplied in a common stream, with each seller having been deemed to have supplied its proportionate share of gas within that common stream, (ii) for one of the sellers to be appointed as the sellers' representative to discharge certain obligations arising under the GSA on behalf of each of the sellers under their separate agreements, including all nomination and notification requirements, and (iii) that a default by one seller shall not constitute a default by the other sellers, nor shall it release the other sellers or the buyer from the performance of their respective obligations under the GSA.

between each seller and the buyer may be documented in a single agreement, this will usually be expressed as being for the parties' convenience such that it does not undermine the fundamental principle of separate agreements and several liability of each of the sellers.

The buyer, however, may not wish to be exposed to the sellers' several liability and may insist on a single agreement with the sellers being joint and severally liable for the performance of the sellers' obligations under the GSA.[9]

Similar issues to those discussed above in the context of multiple sellers would also need to be considered in the context of a GSA providing for multiple buyers.

3. Term and effectiveness

Depending on the circumstances of the particular project, the term of a GSA may comprise a number of distinct periods during which different rights and obligations will apply. By way of example, the term of a GSA may comprise the following periods delineated by particular milestones or occurrences:

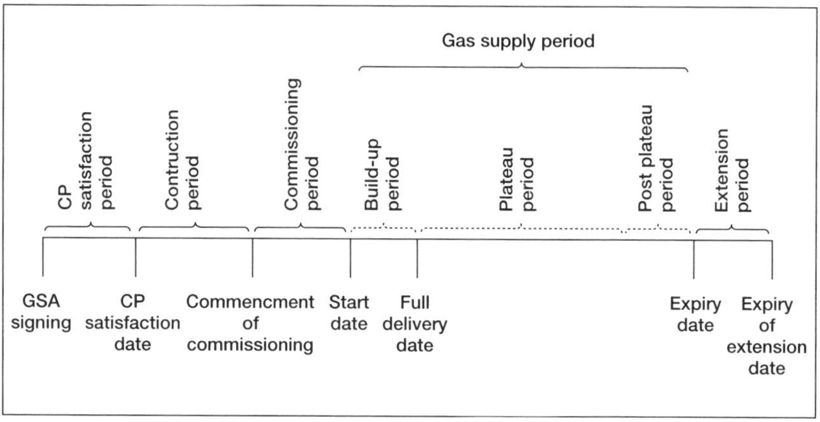

Although the term of the GSA will commence upon signing, if the GSA is expressed as being subject to the satisfaction of conditions precedent, then some but not all of the rights and obligations under the GSA will become binding with effect from signing.[10]

9 Apart from joint liability of multiple sellers being commercially more attractive to a single buyer, practically the multiple seller separate agreement and several liability approach can give rise to complexities and concerns from a buyer's perspective. Because the gas will be supplied in a common stream, it may be difficult for a buyer to determine which individual seller was liable for a particular default. Further, because the sellers will usually insist on the inclusion of a provision that default by one seller shall not constitute a default by the other sellers, the sellers will usually resist any attempt by the buyer to include a provision to the effect that any seller default under the GSA shall be apportioned pro rata in accordance with the sellers' respective proportionate shares, as the sellers may regard this as undermining the principle of several liability.

10 Those provisions coming into force upon signing would typically include the definitions and interpretation provisions, the conditions precedent, the dispute resolution provision, confidentiality obligations and other boilerplate provisions.

3.1 Conditions precedent

The inclusion of conditions precedent will enable the parties to commit to the terms of the GSA while deferring the performance of substantive obligations relating to the supply and offtake of gas and capital investment, until such time as certain matters fundamental to the ability of the parties to be able to perform the GSA have been adequately addressed.

While the conditions precedent will need to be tailored to the particular circumstances of the project, conditions precedent commonly seen in GSAs include:

- obtaining all necessary government approvals necessary for the performance of the agreement;
- entry by the applicable parties into, and/or coming into effect of, other key project agreements;[11] and
- entry into, or first drawdown under, any third-party financing arrangements.

To avoid uncertainty as to the effectiveness of the GSA, it is important that only those conditions precedent which are genuinely necessary for the parties to be able to proceed with the gas commercialisation project be included.

Upon satisfaction (or waiver) of each of the conditions precedent, the GSA will become unconditional and certain rights and obligations of the parties will come into effect. This will usually be the time when the parties will be obliged to make their respective capital investments in the gas commercialisation project and commence the construction of the project facilities.

3.2 Start date

The parties will generally be obliged to have completed the construction of their respective facilities and be ready to supply or receive gas on or before a particular date (the start date). The start date will, therefore, usually be the date on which the seller is first obliged to deliver gas to the buyer in accordance with the buyer's proper nominations, and it will also be the date on and from which the seller will be liable for shortfall for a failure to deliver a properly nominated quantity of gas to the buyer, and the buyer will be subject to take-or-pay (discussed below).

Although the parties may agree a fixed start date at the time of entering into the GSA, more commonly they will defer the determination of the start date until a later time during the term, when the construction of the project facilities is well advanced and the parties are in a better position to judge and mutually agree an appropriate state date. This is normally achieved through a 'window' start date mechanism, pursuant to which the parties periodically agree on window periods (usually of several weeks or months in duration) within which the start date will occur, with those window periods gradually narrowing as the construction phase progresses and with the parties finally agreeing on a start date falling within the final window period. The window mechanism removes a significant degree of the uncertainty

---

11 Examples may include (i) gas transportation arrangements where pipeline transportation of the gas will be carried out by an entity other than the seller or buyer, (ii) governmental agreements supporting the project, and (iii) EPC contracts relating to the construction of project infrastructure.

associated with having to predict the start date so far in advance of the completion of the construction of the project facilities, and enables the parties better to coordinate and synchronise their respective project timetables so as to minimise potential liabilities associated with late start-up and unwanted facilities downtime.

3.3 Late start

If a party (the 'late start party') is not ready to deliver or receive gas on and from the start date and the delay is not excused under the GSA (eg, pursuant to *force majeure*), then in the absence of provisions to the contrary a late start seller would be liable for full shortfall gas liabilities, or a late start buyer would be liable for full take-or-pay liabilities, on and from the start date.

As the imposition of full liabilities on the seller or buyer on and from the start date may be considered unduly onerous at such a formative stage of the gas commercialisation project, the parties may provide for reduced shortfall gas and take-or-pay liabilities to apply for an initial period following the start date to lessen the severity of the application of those liability regimes.[12]

3.4 Commissioning and performance testing

As the commissioning of a party's facilities will usually require the cooperation of its counterparty either to deliver or take gas, the GSA will generally prescribe a mechanism pursuant to which the parties are to agree procedures for the coordination and synchronisation of the commissioning of their respective facilities ('commissioning procedures').

Commissioning will typically occur over a number of days or weeks immediately prior to the start date ('commissioning period'). During the commissioning period, the parties will be under a reasonable endeavours obligation to either deliver or take gas, with neither the seller nor the buyer being subject to shortfall gas or take-or-pay liabilities for any failure to deliver or take gas during this period.

The price which the buyer is obliged to pay for commissioning gas may be a contentious issue in the GSA negotiations. Whereas the buyer may argue that a price discount should apply to commissioning gas on the basis that such gas is not supplied on a firm basis and therefore has a reduced economic value to the buyer, the seller may argue that the full contract price should apply to commissioning gas, particularly if the buyer is able to utilise the gas for its intended commercial purpose.

The GSA may also provide for performance tests to be conducted in respect of the parties' respective facilities prior to the start date in order for each party to satisfy its counterparty that its facilities are capable of fully discharging its gas supply or offtake obligations under the GSA.

3.5 Gas supply period

The gas supply period is the period during which the seller is under a firm obligation

---

12 For example, a GSA may provide that a late start party has a grace period of 30 days following the start date during which it will not be liable for shortfall gas or take-or-pay (as the case may be), following which 50% of the applicable liabilities shall apply for any further period of late start up to 30 days and thereafter full shortfall gas and take-or-pay liabilities shall apply.

to deliver gas to the buyer in accordance with the buyer's proper nominations, and the buyer is obliged to take and pay for, or pay for if not taken, a minimum contractual quantity of gas as reflected in the take-or-pay obligation.

Under a term-supply contract, the gas supply period will normally commence on the start date and end on an anniversary of the start date (eg, on the twentieth or twenty-fifth anniversary of the start date).

The gas supply period may itself be divided into several sub-periods, including (i) a 'build-up' period, during which the quantities of gas to be supplied will gradually increase as the gas production comes on-stream (ii) a 'plateau' period, which will run for the majority of the gas supply period and during which the full contractual quantities obligations will apply, and (iii) a 'post-plateau' or 'tail-off' period, during which the quantities of gas to be supplied may gradually reduce. While term-supply contracts may not provide for a build-up and/or post-plateau period, depletion contracts will typically provide for a build-up period, plateau period and post-plateau period to reflect the changing production profile of the dedicated field(s) over the term of the GSA.

3.6 Term extensions

The GSA may provide for the gas supply period to be automatically extended in certain circumstances, including where outstanding make-up gas or shortfall gas quantities exist at the expiry of the gas supply period, or to enable the delivery of quantities of gas not able to be delivered during the initial gas supply period due to *force majeure*. Other than in these circumstances, the right to extend the gas supply period will generally be subject to the mutual agreement of the parties.

4. Sale, purchase and delivery

4.1 Sale and purchase

Most GSAs will contain a brief provision reciting the parties' principal obligations, often to the effect that the seller shall sell and make available to the buyer at the delivery point, and the buyer agrees to take and pay for, or pay for if not taken, gas in accordance with the terms of the GSA.

4.2 Delivery point

The seller will be obliged to make gas available to the buyer at an agreed delivery point (delivery point), the specific coordinates for which will usually be annexed to the GSA.

All risk and title in, and liability[13] for, the gas will generally pass from the seller to the buyer at the delivery point.

4.3 Delivery pressure and control of gas flow

Given that the rate at which gas flows from the seller's facilities into the buyer's

13 A qualification to this provision may be in respect of certain off-specification gas liabilities of the seller arising downstream of delivery point.

facilities at the delivery point may be influenced by the pressure maintained by the parties in their respective facilities immediately upstream and downstream of the delivery point, the GSA will usually oblige both the seller and the buyer to maintain pressure in their facilities within a specified pressure range. Gas-flow rates may also be controlled by a valve located at the delivery point, and in those circumstances the GSA should stipulate which party is to have control over the valve.[14]

5. Gas reserves

5.1 Reserve assurances

Unlike in a depletion contract, where the dedication of gas reserves by the seller in favour of the buyer is a key component of the GSA, in a term-supply contract the seller will generally resist giving assurances to the buyer in relation to its gas reserves, often arguing that the shortfall gas remedy affords the buyer with adequate comfort that the seller is prepared to stand behind its gas supply obligations. The buyer, however, may argue that the shortfall gas remedy alone does not provide the buyer with adequate comfort that the seller has sufficient gas reserves to meet its supply obligations for the full term of the GSA, and it may insist on the seller providing reserve assurances.

Where the seller is prepared to provide reserve assurances in favour of the buyer, those assurances may consist of:

- an undertaking from the seller that gas to be supplied to the buyer under the GSA is to be derived from a designated source, and that the designated source contains sufficient gas reserves to enable the seller to meet its gas supply obligations for the full term of the GSA;
- the buyer having the right to seek a periodic re-certification of the gas reserves within the designated source to confirm that there are sufficient remaining reserves for the seller to meet its total remaining gas supply obligations under the GSA; and/or
- an undertaking from the seller that it will not supply gas from the designated source to any third party without the buyer's prior consent (although the seller may object to such an undertaking on the basis that this would effectively amount to a dedication of reserves akin to a depletion, rather than a term-supply, contract).

5.2 Seller's reservations

Irrespective of whether the seller provides reserve assurances in favour of the buyer, the seller will want the GSA to include certain express reservations aimed at preserving the seller's operational and/or marketing discretion and flexibility. Examples of seller's reservations commonly seen in GSAs include:

- the right of the seller to supply gas derived from sources other than those

14 Typically, the seller will have control of the valve as otherwise the buyer would be able to exert too much control over the gas-flow rate and could therefore influence and impede the seller's ability to discharge its obligations under the GSA.

designated in the GSA to the buyer, subject to such gas complying with the specification;

- the seller not being obliged to purchase alternative fuel from any third party in the event of unavailability of gas or insufficiency of reserves (and hence limiting its exposure for non-performance to shortfall gas liabilities); and
- the right to use gas from the designated sources in petroleum operations, including as fuel gas in the seller's facilities, as well as the right to flare gas.

6. Quantities

Together with the gas-pricing provisions, the quantities provisions will often be the most contentious in a GSA negotiation. As well as defining the scope of the seller's principal obligations under the GSA, the quantities provisions will have a significant bearing on the risk allocation between the parties and the overall project economics.

The key tension that arises between the seller and the buyer in the negotiation of the quantities provisions is the degree of quantities flexibility to be afforded to the buyer and how the cost of building in such flexibility is to be apportioned between the parties. A buyer will wish to ensure that the quantities provisions afford it as much flexibility as possible to enable it to manage downstream demand through the GSA, while at the same time minimising its corresponding take-or-pay obligations. The seller, on the other hand, will wish to restrict the level of quantities flexibility afforded to the buyer, or to ensure that the cost of building in quantities flexibility into the GSA at the buyer's request is passed on to the buyer, while at the same time seeking to minimise its own potential liability for gas supply failures.

6.1 Contract quantities

The quantities provisions will generally be formulated on the basis of agreed contractual quantities of gas that are to be supplied within specified time periods (expressed in either volumetric or calorific terms). These contractual quantities will form the basis of the seller's gas supply obligations and the buyer's take-or-pay commitment.

(a) Daily contract quantity

The daily contract quantity (or DCQ) will usually constitute the daily quantity of gas which the seller is obliged to deliver to the buyer on each day during the term of the GSA. Typically, the daily contract quantity will represent the average, rather than the maximum, daily quantity of gas which the seller is obliged to make available to the buyer.

(b) Annual contract quantity

The annual contract quantity (or ACQ) will usually constitute the annual quantity of gas which the seller is obliged to deliver to the buyer under the GSA in a given year, and may serve as an annual cap on the seller's total gas supply obligation for the year.

Depending on how the gas sales arrangements are structured (in particular, the take-or-pay obligations), typically either the daily contract quantity or the annual contract quantity will serve as the base contractual quantity obligation around which the other quantities provisions will be formulated.[15]

(c) *Maximum daily contract quantity*

Although in some GSAs the seller may only be obliged to deliver gas to the buyer up to the daily contract quantity on any given day, most GSAs will afford the buyer with a degree of flexibility to nominate quantities of gas in excess of the daily contract quantity up to a certain limit (referred to as the maximum daily contract quantity (or MDCQ), which will typically be expressed as a percentage over and above the daily contract quantity, for example 110% of the daily contract quantity). The maximum daily contract quantity will oblige the seller to deliver to the buyer a properly nominated quantity of gas equal to the maximum daily contract quantity on any given day during the term of the GSA,[16] failing which the seller will be liable to be a buyer for shortfall gas.

Although most GSAs will provide for a maximum daily contract quantity, the apportionment of the incremental cost associated with building such upwards quantities flexibility into the GSA between the seller and the buyer will often be a contentious issue in the GSA negotiations.[17]

6.2 Excess gas

If the buyer requires gas in excess of the maximum daily contract quantity (or daily contract quantity, as the case may be) on a given day ('excess gas'), typically the seller will only be under a reasonable endeavours obligation to supply such excess gas.

Whether a price premium should apply to quantities of excess gas delivered by the seller to the buyer will depend on, among other things, the circumstances of the particular gas market. For example, a seller wanting to capture a greater share of the gas market may seek to incentivise the buyer to take excess gas by not charging a price premium (or even offering a price discount in respect of excess gas quantities), whereas in a high-demand or gas-constrained market the seller may insist on a price

---

15 If the annual contract quantity is the contractual quantity upon which the quantities provisions are to be formulated, then the daily contract quantity may be determined by reference to the annual contract quantity (ie, the annual contract quantity divided by the number of days in the applicable contract year to arrive at the daily contract quantity). Conversely, if the daily contract quantity is the contractual quantity upon which the quantities provisions are to be formulated, the annual contract quantity may be determined by direct reference to the daily contract quantity (ie, the daily contract quantity multiplied by the number of days in the applicable contract year to arrive at the annual contract quantity).

16 This will be subject to any other quantities limitations that may apply under the GSA, for example any annual quantities cap.

17 Unless the seller is adequately compensated through the gas price in providing the buyer with upwards quantities flexibility through the maximum daily contract quantity, the maximum daily contract quantity may represent a significant burden for the seller. Given that the imposition of a maximum daily contract quantity means the seller must be able to deliver that quantity on any day during the term of GSA, the seller will be obliged to make additional investments in its gas production and/or its facilities. However, the seller's guaranteed minimum revenue stream will not increase proportionately despite the seller making those additional investments, because ordinarily the take-or-pay obligation will still be determined by reference to the daily contract quantity (or annual contract quantity), and not the maximum daily contract quantity. Therefore, if the buyer only nominates the maximum daily contract quantity occasionally, meaning the additional capacity built in by the seller is rarely utilised by the buyer, the seller may not recover its capital and operating costs and/or receive a return on its investment in making that additional capacity available.

premium applying in respect of excess gas quantities.[18]

7. Take-or-pay, carry forward and make-up

7.1 Take-or-pay

The purpose of a take-or-pay obligation is to provide the seller with a periodic guaranteed minimum cash flow from the gas commercialisation project irrespective of whether the buyer takes the quantities of gas for which it has contracted.

Under a take-or-pay obligation, the buyer is obliged to take and pay for, or to pay for if not taken, a minimum quantity of gas within a specified period of time (typically a month, a quarter or a year). The take-or-pay obligation will be expressed as a percentage of an adjusted contract quantity of gas. For example, if a GSA imposes an annual take-or-pay obligation on the buyer, the buyer will be obliged to take and pay for, or pay for if not taken, a certain percentage of the annual contract quantity as adjusted downwards to take account of certain quantities of gas not able to be taken by the buyer other than due to the buyer's own fault ('take-or-pay quantity'), such that if during a year the buyer has not taken a quantity of gas equal to or greater than the take-or-pay quantity, then the buyer will be obliged to pay to the seller the difference between the take-or-pay quantity and the quantity of gas.[19]

There are a number of important components of a take-or-pay obligation which, when taken together, will determine the relative robustness of the obligation, as set out next.

(a) Take-or-pay level/percentage

The percentage of the applicable contractual quantity at which the take-or-pay level is set will have the greatest impact on the robustness of the take-or-pay obligation. A seller will negotiate for the highest take-or-pay percentage as is commercially achievable in order to increase its guaranteed minimum cash flow, whereas the buyer will prefer that the take-or-pay percentage be set as low as possible to minimise the circumstances where it is obliged to pay for gas which it has not taken.[20]

(b) Frequency of application of take-or-pay

The frequency of the application of the take-or-pay obligation will also have an important bearing on the robustness of the obligation. For the seller, the more frequently that the take-or-pay obligation can be imposed on the buyer (eg, monthly or quarterly rather than annually) the greater the protection afforded to the seller's guaranteed minimum cash flow. The buyer, on the other hand, would prefer an

---

18 In including excess gas provisions in the GSA, the parties will also need to consider whether the seller should be liable for shortfall gas in circumstances where it has given a firm commitment to deliver excess gas to the buyer and subsequently fails to do so. Similarly, the parties should also make clear whether or not excess gas quantities should be taken into account for the purposes of take-or-pay.

19 It is recommended that the seller obtains legal advice to confirm that the take-or-pay provisions will be enforceable under the governing law of the GSA, as in some jurisdictions there may be some uncertainty in this regard (eg, take-or-pay provisions may in some jurisdictions be unenforceable on the grounds of being a penalty).

20 By way of guidance, typical take-or-pay percentages in long-term GSAs would range between 75% and 90%.

annual take-or-pay obligation to afford it with more time and flexibility in which to manage offtake fluctuations and therefore reduce the likelihood of it incurring take-or-pay liabilities.

(c) *Adjustments*

The GSA will typically provide for certain downward adjustments to be made to the contractual quantity by reference to which the take-or-pay quantity is determined. Those downward adjustments broadly reflect those circumstances where the buyer was not able to take quantities of gas due to no fault of its own, therefore ensuring that the take-or-pay quantity is not artificially inflated to the benefit of the seller. For example, in a GSA providing for annual take-or-pay, the take-or-pay quantity will be the product of the adjusted annual contract quantity multiplied by the applicable take-or-pay percentage. Standard adjustments for the purposes of calculating the applicable take-or-pay quantity include:

- *force majeure:* quantities of gas which the seller was unable to supply or which the buyer was unable to take due to an event of *force majeure;*
- *shortfall gas:* quantities of gas which the seller has failed to deliver in accordance with a buyer's proper nomination;[21]
- *carry-forward quantities:* discussed in Section 7.2 below; and
- *maintenance:* quantities of gas which were not delivered by the seller or not taken by the buyer on account of the seller or buyer undertaking scheduled facilities maintenance in accordance with the provisions of the GSA.

7.2 Carry forward

The GSA may provide that where the buyer takes a quantity of gas over and above the applicable take-or-pay quantity or an alternative quantity threshold (eg, the daily contract quantity), the buyer will accrue 'carry-forward credits' in respect of those gas quantities exceeding the applicable threshold. The carry-forward credits may then be set-off against future take-or-pay obligations of the buyer with the effect of lowering the take-or-pay quantity in those subsequent periods and reducing the buyer's liability for take-or-pay.[22]

Although the buyer may assume that carry-forward rights are synonymous with the imposition of a take-or-pay obligation, the seller may resist the inclusion of carry-forward rights, particularly if the buyer wishes to set the carry-forward threshold at the take-or-pay level. In those circumstances, the seller may argue that the buyer should not be rewarded for having taken a quantity of gas over and above the take-

---

21 This would encompass quantities of off-specification gas unknowingly taken by the buyer which are to be treated as having not been delivered, therefore constituting shortfall gas.

22 As a simplified example, if in a GSA providing for 80% annual take-or-pay the buyer takes a quantity of gas equivalent to 90% of the adjusted annual contract quantity in a year, the buyer will accrue carry-forward credits equivalent to 10% of the adjusted annual contract quantity. If in the following year the buyer was to take a quantity of gas equivalent to only 70% of the adjusted annual contract quantity, meaning at the end of the year it was liable to pay the seller for a quantity of gas equivalent to 10% of the adjusted annual contract quantity pursuant to the take-or-pay obligation, the buyer could offset its accrued carry-forward credits against that take-or-pay liability, meaning it would not be obliged to make any take-or-pay payment to the seller in respect of that year notwithstanding that it did not take the take-or-pay quantity.

or-pay quantity when the terms of the GSA and the investments made by the seller thereunder will have been predicated principally on the basis of the daily contract quantity or annual contract quantity, and not the take-or-pay quantity.[23]

If the seller is prepared to accept the inclusion of carry-forward rights, it may insist on those rights being subject to certain limitations.[24]

7.3 Make-up gas

Where the buyer is obliged to pay for gas not taken pursuant to the take-or-pay obligation ('make-up gas'), the buyer will usually be entitled to nominate and receive those quantities of make-up gas at a subsequent time during the term of the GSA.

Having already paid for the gas, the buyer may be entitled to receive make-up gas quantities at no additional charge, although some GSAs may provide for certain adjustment payments to be made at the time the buyer takes the make-up gas to account for differences in price and/or calorific value between when the take-or-pay obligation was incurred and when the make-up gas is actually taken.

The seller will not wish for the buyer to have unrestricted make-up rights and will usually seek to impose limitations on the buyer's ability to recoup make-up gas, including:

- *Time limit:* because make-up rights give rise to an element of cash-flow uncertainty for the seller, the seller will generally wish for the buyer to exercise its make-up rights within a reasonable period of time following the accrual of such rights, failing which the make-up rights shall be deemed to have been forfeited by the buyer. The forfeiture of make-up rights by the buyer will also result in a significant commercial benefit for the seller as it would have received payment for gas which it never had to supply to the buyer. Accordingly, it is in the seller's interest to ensure that the time period within which the buyer is to exercise make-up gas rights is as short as possible.[25]
- *Make-up gas threshold:* to ensure that the buyer's make-up gas rights do not significantly erode the seller's cash-flow position, the seller may argue that the buyer shall only be entitled to recoup make-up gas once it has nominated and taken a minimum quantity of gas (eg, the daily contract quantity or the daily equivalent of the take-or-pay quantity). If the buyer accepts such a

---

23 A seller may also argue that carry-forward rights introduce an element of cash-flow uncertainty for the seller and therefore undermine the principal purpose of the take-or-pay obligation.

24 Limitations on carry-forward rights commonly seen in long-term GSAs include: (i) carry-forward credits accruing only in respect of gas quantities taken by the buyer over and above the applicable contract quantity (eg, either the daily contract quantity or the annual contract quantity), rather than the take-or-pay quantity; (ii) the buyer being obliged to exercise carry-forward rights against future take-or-pay obligations within a specified period of time following the carry-forward credits accruing, where time limits on exercising carry-forward rights typically seen in long-term GSAs typically range between two and five years; and (iii) to prevent the buyer from accruing carry-forward credits over an extended period and applying those credits on a one-off basis causing disruption to the seller's cash flow, the buyer's right to exercise carry-forward credits may be subject to an annual volumetric cap. For example, the GSA may provide that the buyer is not entitled to utilise carry-forward credits exceeding 5% of the adjusted annual contract quantity in any given year.

25 By way of guidance, in long-term GSAs time limits on exercising make-up gas rights often range between two and five years.

limitation, it will need to be careful to ensure that there is adequate scope and flexibility with the quantities provisions to enable the buyer to exercise its make-up gas rights in an effective manner.

- *Annual cap:* to prevent the buyer from 'stockpiling' make-up gas rights over an extended period and exercising those rights on a one-off basis causing a significant disruption to the seller's cash flow, the buyer's right to nominate make-up gas may be subject to an annual cap.[26]

The GSA will also need to prescribe what is to occur in relation to outstanding make-up gas existing upon expiry or termination of the GSA. The seller may argue that such outstanding make-up gas should be extinguished, whereas the buyer will argue that it should be entitled to receive the benefit or value of such accrued make-up gas rights notwithstanding the expiry or termination of the GSA. The GSA may therefore provide for (i) a term extension to enable any outstanding make-up gas to be delivered by the seller to the buyer, (ii) outstanding make-up gas to be monetised and paid to the buyer,[27] or (iii) the seller to discharge the outstanding make-up gas by delivering to the buyer alternative fuel equivalent in value to the unrecovered make-up gas.[28]

8. Shortfall

Where the seller has failed to deliver a properly nominated quantity[29] of gas to the buyer and the seller's failure is not otherwise excused under the GSA, the seller will usually be liable to the buyer in respect of that shortfall quantity of gas (with the quantities of gas not delivered being referred to as 'shortfall gas').

8.1 Remedies

Most GSAs will provide for an express remedy in favour of the buyer for shortfall gas rather than leaving occurrences of shortfall to be addressed under the general dispute resolution provisions in the GSA (which would be administratively burdensome, time consuming and costly for both parties). In broad terms, a GSA will usually prescribe either an actual loss remedy or liquidated damages in respect of shortfall gas.

An actual loss remedy will generally oblige the seller to compensate the buyer for the buyer's actual and direct loss incurred as a result of the seller's shortfall, subject to certain limits on the liability of the seller. To be entitled to compensation under an actual-loss shortfall gas remedy, the buyer will usually be obliged to provide the

---

26 For example, the GSA may provide that in any contract year the buyer is not entitled to receive a quantity of make-up gas in excess of 5% of the annual contract quantity.

27 This will usually involve the seller refunding the buyer the earlier amounts paid by the buyer in respect of the take-or-pay obligation.

28 Other make-up gas issues that the parties may also wish to clarify in the GSA include whether the seller's failure to deliver make-up gas should give rise to shortfall gas liabilities, and how excess gas and make-up gas nominations are to be reconciled. The GSA should also make clear whether carry-forward credits should accrue in relation to make-up gas nominated by the buyer (usually this is not the case). The GSA will also usually stipulate that make-up gas is to be taken on a first-in-first-out basis.

29 An under-delivery of gas by the seller will only constitute shortfall to the extent that it relates to a properly nominated quantity of gas, and the buyer will usually not be entitled to be compensated under the applicable shortfall gas remedy in respect of under-deliveries relating to gas quantities that were not properly nominated by the buyer in accordance with the nominations regime.

seller with reasonable evidence of the buyer's loss to substantiate its claim for compensation. While an actual-loss remedy has the benefit of matching the compensation payable by the seller with the buyer's actual-loss, actual loss shortfall gas remedies tend not to be favoured by parties to a GSA due to the burden associated with the buyer having to demonstrate and quantify its actual loss on each occasion of shortfall and the potential uncertainty surrounding the extent of seller's liability and the success of the buyer's claim.

A shortfall gas liquidated damages remedy, on the other hand, provides the parties with a greater degree of certainty, both in terms of the level of compensation afforded to the buyer and the extent of the seller's liability for non-performance. Shortfall gas liquidated damages are typically formulated on the basis of a price discount ('shortfall gas price discount') applying to a quantity of gas equivalent to the shortfall gas quantity to be delivered by the seller to the buyer at a subsequent point during the term (typically in the following month). To ensure that the remedy is upheld as liquidated damages, the GSA will normally prescribe that the shortfall gas price discount constitutes a genuine pre-estimate of the buyer's loss arising from the shortfall and that the buyer waives any defence as to the validity of such liquidated damages on the grounds that such liquidated damages are void as a penalty.[30]

A buyer will wish for a seller's liability for shortfall gas to crystallise as frequently as possible (eg, on a daily basis) to ensure that the remedy is sufficiently robust to discourage the seller from not performing, whereas the seller will prefer that liability for shortfall be assessed over a longer period (eg, on a monthly basis) to afford the seller with greater flexibility to even out under-deliveries and minimise its shortfall gas liabilities.

Unless the seller's failure to deliver gas falls within one of the recognised exceptions (discussed below) the seller's liability under the shortfall gas liquidated damages remedy will usually be absolute, so that the seller will be obliged to compensate the buyer without the buyer having to demonstrate actual loss.[31]

To prevent the buyer from challenging the adequacy of the shortfall gas remedy and/or bringing an alternative claim, as well as ensuring that the shortfall gas remedy operates as an effective cap on the seller's liability for non-performance, the seller should always ensure that the GSA provides that the shortfall gas remedy constitutes the buyer's sole and exclusive remedy in respect of the seller's non-performance, and for the buyer to indemnify the seller in respect of any claims brought against the seller in respect of such non-performance (including in respect of claims brought by third parties, including the buyer's end-users).

30 Such provisions are common to GSAs governed by English law. Although the shortfall gas price discount will typically be expressed as being a genuine pre-estimate of the buyer's loss arising as a consequence of shortfall, the discount will often be arrived at purely as a matter of commercial negotiation, with each party seeking to achieve the best commercial outcome (ie, the lowest possible price discount in the case of the seller, and the highest possible price discount in the case of the buyer).

31 A buyer may argue that where shortfall occurs as a result of the seller's wilful misconduct (eg, where the seller knowingly shortfalls the buyer to sell such gas to another customer on more favourable economic terms), then the shortfall gas remedy should not apply and the buyer should be entitled to bring a claim against the seller for its actual loss, meaning the seller would not have the benefit of the limitation on liability afforded by the shortfall gas remedy.

8.2 Exclusions form shortfall

Not all instances where the seller delivers less than a properly nominated quantity of gas to the buyer will constitute shortfall. Common examples of exclusions from shortfall include:

- *gas not taken by the buyer:* gas made available by the seller at the delivery point in accordance with the buyer's proper nomination, but not taken by the buyer;
- *force majeure:* where the seller's failure to deliver gas is attributable to an event of *force majeure* affecting the seller or the buyer;
- *buyer's acts or omissions:* quantities of gas not able to be delivered due to acts or omissions of the buyer;
- *delivery tolerance:* if the GSA provides for a delivery tolerance, then an under-delivery of gas which is within the delivery tolerance will usually not constitute shortfall;
- *commissioning gas:* most GSAs provide that quantities of gas which the seller fails to deliver during the commissioning period will not constitute shortfall;
- *off-specification gas:* if the GSA prescribes a separate remedy in relation to the delivery of off-specification gas (eg, an off-specification gas price discount), then such off-specification gas will be excluded from shortfall; and
- *make-up gas and excess gas:* the seller will usually insist on the failure to deliver make-up gas and/or excess gas being excluded from shortfall.

8.3 Outstanding shortfall gas entitlements on expiry or termination

The GSA will need to prescribe what is to occur in relation to outstanding shortfall gas entitlements of the buyer existing upon expiry or termination of the GSA. The seller may argue that such entitlements should be extinguished, whereas the buyer will argue that the entitlements are accrued rights which should be exercisable by the buyer, notwithstanding the expiry or termination of the GSA. The GSA may therefore provide for a term extension to enable any outstanding shortfall gas to be delivered by the seller to the buyer, or for the buyer's unrecovered shortfall gas entitlement to be monetised and paid to the buyer.

9. Quality

Gas supplied by the seller to the buyer under the GSA will need to comply with an agreed quality specification (the specification). If the gas made available by the seller to the buyer does not comply with the specification at the delivery point, such gas will be classified as off-specification gas and the GSA will generally prescribe certain rights and remedies in favour of the buyer in relation to such off-specification gas quantities.

9.1 Buyer has prior notice of off-specification gas

The seller will usually be obliged to monitor continuously the quality of gas prior to its delivery to the buyer. If the seller detects the presence of off-specification gas prior to delivery, the seller will be obliged to notify the buyer of the off-specification gas, including providing details of the extent to which the gas does not comply with the specification. The buyer will then have a specified period of time (typically a number of hours) within which to elect to either accept or reject the off-specification gas.

If the buyer wishes to reject the off-specification gas, the buyer will usually be obliged to notify the seller within a specified period of time following notification from the seller of the existence of off-specification gas. If the buyer fails to notify the seller of the buyer's rejection within the applicable timeframe, the buyer may be deemed to have accepted the off-specification gas (although the buyer may prefer such off-specification gas quantities to be deemed rejected). If the buyer rejects the off-specification gas in accordance with the requirements of the GSA, the seller will generally be deemed to have failed to have delivered a properly nominated quantity of gas corresponding to the off-specification gas quantity, and the buyer shall be compensated for its loss through the shortfall gas remedy.

If the buyer elects to accept (or is deemed to have accepted) the off-specification gas, the seller may argue that such acceptance implies that the buyer is able to utilise the gas for its intended purpose and therefore the buyer should not be entitled to any compensation in relation to such quantities. The buyer, on the other hand, may argue that notwithstanding its acceptance of off-specification gas the buyer may nevertheless incur loss in respect of those quantities entitling the buyer to some form of compensation from the seller.[32] As it will usually be in the seller's interest for the buyer to accept off-specification gas (rather than the buyer rejecting those quantities, resulting in the seller being liable to the buyer for shortfall gas), the GSA may provide for a price discount to apply in relation to off-specification gas quantities knowingly accepted by the buyer to compensate the buyer for any loss associated with the off-specification gas, as well as incentivising the buyer to take such off-specification gas quantities.

9.2 Off-specification gas taken unknowingly

Circumstances may arise when off-specification gas is delivered by the seller to the buyer prior to the buyer receiving notice from the seller of the existence of such off-specification gas. As the buyer was not afforded the opportunity to either accept or reject such off-specification gas, the GSA will usually oblige the seller to assume a greater degree of liability in respect of those off-specification quantities unknowingly taken by the buyer.

The seller will usually be obliged to indemnify the buyer for actual direct and foreseeable loss incurred by the buyer as a result of unknowingly taking off-specification gas, although the seller may seek to confine the scope of the indemnity to specific items of loss or otherwise limit its liability.[33] The GSA may also provide that the buyer shall not be obliged to pay for any quantities of off-specification gas taken unknowingly, with the shortfall gas remedy applying in respect of those off-specification gas quantities. Alternatively, the GSA may prescribe that the buyer shall be entitled to liquidated damages in the form of a price discount to apply to off-

32 For example, in having to treat the gas to bring it back into compliance with specification, facilities clean-up costs and/or resultant liabilities under downstream contracts attributable to the gas being off-specification and/or delay.

33 The seller may wish to limit the indemnity to physical damage caused to buyer's facilities by the off-specification gas and clean-up or gas treatment costs. The seller may also seek to limit its liability by reference to a monetary cap.

specification gas quantities unknowingly taken by the buyer.

As with the shortfall gas remedy, the seller will wish to ensure that any off-specification gas remedy provided for in the GSA is expressed as being the buyer's sole and exclusive remedy in respect of the seller's breach (with the buyer indemnifying the seller in respect of any claims brought against the seller in respect of such breach, including claims brought by third parties, such as the buyer's end-users), and that any off-specification gas price discount remedy is expressed as constituting liquidated damages and genuine pre-estimate of the buyer's loss, with the buyer waiving any defence as to the validity of such remedy on the grounds that such liquidated damages are void as a penalty.

10. Price

The gas price terms will often be regarded as the most important commercial provisions in the GSA and will have a significant bearing on the other GSA terms. For example, a lower gas price may mean the buyer is prepared to assume a greater degree of risk elsewhere in the GSA, including less quantities flexibility. Conversely, a higher gas price may mean that the seller is willing to provide greater quantities flexibility to the buyer and/or to accept a less onerous take-or-pay obligation.

Although the seller and the buyer will each seek to achieve the best commercial outcome in the gas price negotiations, certain fundamental objectives will generally apply. The seller will be concerned to ensure that the gas price enables it to recover its capital and operating costs associated with its upstream and midstream projects and facilities, as well as receive a reasonable return on its investment. The buyer, on the other hand, will be primarily concerned to ensure that the gas price remains competitive with the price of competing fuels for the duration of the GSA.

The gas price will usually be expressed in terms of calorific value (either British thermal units or joules).

10.1 Determination of the gas price and indexation

In developed gas markets where traded gas prices are reported, the gas price may be determined wholly or partly by reference to those reported gas prices.[34]

However, in less developed gas markets where there are no reported prices for traded gas, the gas price will usually be calculated by reference to an agreed base price which is periodically indexed by reference to an agreed formula.

The purpose of the indexation formula is to ensure that the base price retains parity with the prevailing market conditions. Commonly, the formula may refer to a number of fuels quoted on international exchanges,[35] with each index within the formula being given a relative weighting. Which indices are to be included in the

---

34 Examples would include Henry Hub in the United States, and the National Balancing Point in the United Kingdom.

35 In some markets, crude oil has historically been regarded as being the alternative fuel to gas and therefore the gas price may be indexed to a single or basket of regional crudes. In other markets, however, it may be more appropriate for the indexation formula to reference refined oil products such as light sulphur fuel oil or heavy sulphur fuel oil as the alternative fuel for gas, particularly if the buyer is purchasing gas for power generation purposes. The indexation formula may also build in an inflation component, or may refer to other competing energy sources (eg, coal).

formula and the relative weighting to be afforded to each index will often be the subject of lengthy negotiation. However, each party will be equally concerned to ensure that the indexation formula will be responsive to changes in market conditions in a balanced and reasonable manner.

Although the indices included in the gas price formula will change daily, the gas price will usually be calculated in accordance with the formula on a less frequent basis (eg, at the beginning of each contract year, quarter or month)[36] with the resultant gas price applying for the duration of the applicable time period.[37]

While indexation will ensure that the gas price reflects changes in market conditions, it will by no means be perfect and the parties may wish to insulate themselves from the volatility of the market by including a price floor below which the gas price cannot fall, and/or a price ceiling which the gas price cannot exceed.

10.2 Price review clauses

Although the gas price formula will ensure, to a large extent, that the gas price reflects changes in market conditions, circumstances may arise when a party considers that the formula no longer adequately reflects or caters for changes in market conditions to such an extent that the divergence between the gas price and the market price means it is no longer economic or commercial for that party to continue to sell or buy gas at the price calculated in accordance with the gas price formula.

To cater for this situation, some GSAs may provide for a right of either party periodically to request a review of the gas price. Price review clauses, and similar provisions which contemplate an adjustment to the price such as 'hardship' clauses or 'most favoured nation' provisions, come in a wide variety of forms but will usually stipulate (i) the frequency with which a party may request a price review, (ii) the information to be taken into account in carrying out the price review, (iii) the procedures for conducting the price review and (iv) the consequences if the parties are unable to agree upon a revised gas price (typically reference to an independent expert for determination).

Although including a price review provision may seem sensible to the parties at the time of entering into a long-term GSA, because the provision seeks to afford the parties the right to renegotiate the most important commercial term of the contract such provisions are sometimes prone to abuse by the parties. The parties should therefore give detailed consideration to the precise circumstances in which a party is

---

36 Although calculating the gas price in accordance with the gas price formula on a more frequent basis will help ensure that the gas price reflects more accurately changes in market conditions, this needs to be balanced against the continuity of the gas-pricing arrangements and the administrative burden associated with having continuously to recalculate the gas price.

37 If the parties disagree on the calculation of the gas price, the GSA will usually provide that either party may refer the matter to an independent expert for determination. Further, where an index included in the gas price formula is temporarily unavailable or has been published in an erroneous form, the GSA may prescribe a mechanism for a provisional price to be agreed between the parties during the interim and for subsequent adjustment payments to be made once the actual or corrected figures have been published or become available. Similarly, where an index included in the gas price formula permanently ceases to be quoted, or if there is a material change in the underlying basis upon which the index is quoted, the GSA may prescribe a mechanism for agreeing a replacement index, failing which either party may have the right to refer the matter to an independent expert for determination.

to have the right to reopen negotiations on the gas price, and they should ensure that any price review provision that is included in the GSA is carefully drafted to avoid any uncertainty as to when the provision is intended to apply.

11. Nominations, undertake and overtake

Although the parties will have agreed the contractual quantities of gas which the seller shall be obliged to deliver to the buyer (discussed in Section 6 above), the buyer's day-to-day requirements will usually differ from the agreed contractual quantities. Accordingly, the GSA will usually provide for detailed procedures pursuant to which the buyer gives advance notice to the seller of its future requirements for gas.

11.1 Nominations

Under a typical nominations regime, the buyer will notify the seller in advance of its requirements for gas in respect of each nomination period (usually an hour) for the forthcoming day. The buyer will need to notify the seller of its forward nominations by a particular time each day, failing which the buyer will usually be deemed to have made certain nominations.[38] These nominations will constitute firm or 'proper' nominations and will be fixed for the purposes of the GSA. The seller will therefore be obliged to deliver gas in accordance with those proper nominations, failing which the seller may be in shortfall. The GSA will also normally provide that nominations are to be given in good faith.[39]

The buyer will usually be mindful of ensuring that the nominations regime is sufficiently flexible to accommodate its downstream demand requirements. The seller, on the other hand, will be concerned to ensure that the nominations regime is manageable within the operational limits of its upstream gas production and/or midstream facilities.

11.2 Limitations

The GSA will also prescribe limits within which a buyer's nominations must fall. Those limitations will need to reflect the limits on the seller's gas production or supply, as well as the physical and operational limitations of the seller's upstream and midstream facilities. Ordinarily, the seller's aggregate nominations for a day will not be able to exceed the maximum daily contract quantity (or the daily contract quantity, as the case may be) and should not exceed the maximum hourly quantity.[40]

---

38 In these circumstances, the GSA may provide that the buyer shall be deemed to have made the same nominations as applying for the previous day, or to have nominated the daily contract quantity.

39 From the seller's perspective, part of the reason for prescribing that nominations are to be made in good faith is to afford the seller with some protection from the buyer taking undue advantage of the nominations regime to maximise its own shortfall gas entitlements by increasing the seller's shortfall gas liabilities in circumstances where the buyer is aware of the fact that the seller is constrained in being able to supply the full contractual quantities. In addition to the buyer's nominations being in good faith, the GSA may also provide that where the seller has notified the buyer of gas supply constraints, the buyer shall not be entitled to nominate quantities of gas over and above the nominations then in force. A buyer, however, may argue that such a provision unjustly impedes the buyer's ability to exercise its contractual rights

40 The maximum hourly quantity will normally be the maximum daily contract quantity (or the daily contract quantity, as the case may be) divided by 24.

The GSA may also prescribe a minimum nomination level – for example, if the gas being supplied is associated gas and is dependent on maintaining a minimum level of crude production, or if the operation of the seller's facilities requires a minimum flow of gas.

11.3 Variations

The buyer will want to have the right to vary firm nominations in order to take account of subsequent changes in downstream demand. The seller may be reluctant to afford the buyer such rights on the basis that it will be relying upon the buyer's firm nominations in managing its upstream and midstream operations, and will not wish to incur additional costs and/or increase its risk of defaulting on its supply obligations by having to comply with last minute variations to nominations. Whether the seller is able to afford the buyer a degree of variation flexibility will depend on the operational limitations affecting the seller's facilities. If the seller is able to afford some flexibility, then the buyer's ability to vary a firm nomination will nevertheless be subject to certain time and quantities limitations.

11.4 Forecasts

The buyer will also usually be obliged to give estimates of its forecast gas requirements (eg, for a week or month ahead) and to support these estimates with indicative nominations. These nominations will generally not be binding on the buyer, but will be given in good faith to assist the seller in planning its upstream and midstream operations.

11.5 Undertake and overtake

The GSA may prescribe certain remedies in favour of the seller where the buyer takes a quantity of gas which is more ('overtake gas') or less ('undertake gas') than its properly nominated quantity. Where the buyer undertakes or overtakes gas, the seller may incur loss and therefore the objective of the undertake and overtake gas provisions is to provide for a mechanism which will compensate the seller for its loss. These provisions will also discourage the buyer from undertaking and overtaking gas and therefore bring greater integrity to the nomination provisions.[41]

12. Measurement and testing

The seller will generally be responsible for measuring the quantity and quality of gas delivered under the GSA. Accordingly, the seller will be obliged to install, operate and maintain measuring and metering equipment at the delivery point.

Where the buyer wishes independently to monitor gas quality and quantities (or to monitor the accuracy of the seller's measuring equipment), the GSA will provide

41 The undertake gas provisions may provide for a compensation regime in the form of either an obligation on the buyer to compensate the seller for its actual loss incurred in connection with the undertake quantities, or more commonly liquidated damages in the form or a price premium which is to apply in respect of undertake quantities. Overtake will be an issue in the context of a multi-user pipeline where a buyer's overtake may result in the seller incurring shortfall gas liabilities under other GSAs due to the reduced gas quantities available for delivery to those other buyers.

the buyer with a right to install check meters alongside the seller's equipment.[42] Further, the buyer will also usually have access and audit rights in relation to the seller's measurement equipment in order to monitor the seller's performance.

Where the buyer is concerned about the accuracy of the seller's measurement equipment, the GSA may also provide the buyer with a right to seek independent third-party verification. Disputes arising between the parties in relation to measurement data will usually be referable to an independent expert for determination.

13. Invoicing and payment

13.1 Invoicing and statements

Under most long-term GSAs, invoicing typically occurs on a monthly in arrears basis. The invoice will usually be prepared by the seller and will be accompanied by a monthly statement setting out the information from which the amount due and payable has been derived. A seller will normally prefer robust terms of payment to improve its cash flow, while the buyer will wish to have more favourable payment terms.

The GSA will also provide for an end-of-year reconciliation process pursuant to which the seller will issue to the buyer an annual statement containing information similar to that included in a monthly statement, and indicating whether any adjustment payments need to be made from one party to the other (including any take-or-pay payment owing from the seller to the buyer if the GSA provides for annual take-or-pay).

13.2 Late payment or failure to make payment

To discourage late payment, the GSA will normally entitle the payee to charge default interest on late payments. As the buyer will usually be the payer, the seller will normally seek to negotiate a high rate of default interest to ensure that it is adequately compensated for any payment default and to incentivise timely payment by the buyer.

The seller may also require a right to suspend gas deliveries in circumstances of a continuing payment default by the buyer, or if the buyer has defaulted in making payment on a number of occasions within a specified timeframe.

13.3 Payment disputes

The GSA will normally prescribe a mechanism pursuant to which payment disputes arising between the parties are to be resolved. As most payment disputes will turn on technical matters, the GSA will usually prescribe expert determination as the means of dispute resolution if the parties are unable amicably to resolve the dispute within a specified period of time.

---

42 The GSA will, however, normally stipulate that for the purposes of measuring gas quantities and quality only readings from the seller's measurement are to be taken into account (absent manifest error), although reference may be made to the check meters if there is a problem with the functioning of the seller's equipment.

Whether a party should be entitled to withhold the payment of a disputed amount is sometimes a contentious issue in GSA negotiations. As it is typically the seller who prepares the invoices and accompanying statements and the buyer who is the payer, the buyer will usually insist on the right to withhold disputed amounts pending resolution of the dispute. The seller, on the other hand, will be concerned to protect its cash-flow position and may argue that the buyer should be obliged to pay the full invoiced amount and not withhold disputed amounts, with any adjustment payments (and interest entitlements in respect thereof) being addressed in the dispute resolution procedures.

14. *Force majeure*

A GSA will normally contain *force majeure* provisions. Under most GSAs, a party's ability to claim *force majeure* relief will be further qualified by reference to it having acted in accordance with the standard of a reasonable and prudent operator.

A party affected by a *force majeure* event will not automatically be excused from the performance of all of its obligations under the GSA. For example, under most GSAs a *force majeure* event will not excuse a party from an obligation to pay money or to give notice. Further, a party affected by a *force majeure* event will be obliged to continue to perform its obligations to the extent it can and to take positive steps to bring the *force majeure* event to an end.

In addition to providing for an indicative, non-exhaustive list of events or circumstances which ordinarily constitute *force majeure* (including acts of God and natural disasters), the GSA may also expressly exclude certain events or circumstances from constituting *force majeure* in respect of a party. For example, reservoir failure or a reserve shortfall will usually be expressly excluded from constituting *force majeure* for a seller under a term-supply contract. Similarly, if a party is a government entity, then that party will usually be excluded from claiming as *force majeure* acts of government or changes of law occurring within its jurisdiction.

In negotiating the *force majeure* provisions, the basic objective of each party will be to limit the circumstances in which its counterparty is able to claim *force majeure* relief while seeking to maximise the circumstances when it is able to claim such relief. The seller will wish to be able to claim *force majeure* relief from its gas supply obligations and from its shortfall gas and off-specification gas liabilities in the broadest possible circumstances, including extending *force majeure* events affecting the seller to include events affecting third parties upon whom the seller relies to be able to perform its obligations under the GSA, such as any third-party gas transporters or other contractors.

The buyer, on the other hand, will wish to be able to claim *force majeure* relief from take-or-pay. As the buyer will usually not be under an obligation to take gas, but will be obliged to pay for a minimum quantity of gas over a certain period of time, the buyer's *force majeure* relief from take-or-pay will usually take the form of a downwards adjustment to the take-or-pay quantity corresponding to those quantities of gas which the buyer would have been prevented from taking due to the *force majeure*.

15. Termination

A term-supply GSA will normally be expressed as coming to an end upon the expiry of the gas supply period (discussed in Section 3.5 above). In addition, the GSA will usually also prescribe certain express rights of termination in favour of the seller and/or buyer, including:

- termination by a party pursuant to a material breach by the other party, which breach was not been remedied by the breaching party within a stipulated cure period;
- termination by the buyer for a continued failure by the seller to deliver gas;
- termination by the seller for a continued failure by the buyer to pay monies by the due date;
- termination by a party upon the occurrence of an insolvency event affecting the other party;
- termination by either party pursuant to a prolonged *force majeure* event;
- termination by either party pursuant to a failure to satisfy (or waive) all conditions precedent on and before an agreed backstop date;
- termination by a party as a result of the termination of another project agreement critical to the ability of a party to be able to perform under the GSA;[43]
- termination by a party upon collateral support provided by the other party becoming invalid or ceasing to be in full force or effect; and/or
- termination by a party upon the other party transferring rights or obligations under the GSA in contravention of the transfer restrictions under the GSA.

In addition to any express termination rights contained in the GSA, the parties may also be entitled to terminate the GSA in accordance with applicable law.

Upon the expiry or termination of the GSA, the parties will no longer be obliged to perform their respective obligations under the GSA, although some obligations will be expressed as surviving termination.[44] Further, the GSA may also provide for compensation to be payable from the breaching party to the non-breaching party following termination.[45]

16. Tax

The GSA will usually provide for the apportionment of tax liabilities arising in

---

43 Examples would include termination of the upstream concession, licence or production sharing agreement pursuant to which the seller receives its entitlement to the gas, termination of any intergovernmental or host government agreements relating to the gas project or termination of the gas transportation agreement in the context of a third-party gas transporter.

44 As with any commercial contract, the GSA will also normally provide that termination shall be without prejudice to any rights or liabilities of the parties that accrued prior to termination.

45 For example, if the GSA was terminated pursuant to a breach by the buyer, the GSA may provide that the seller shall be entitled to receive take-or-pay payments for a period of time following the termination as compensation for the buyer's breach. Similarly, if the GSA was terminated pursuant to a breach by the seller, the GSA may provide that the buyer shall be entitled to monetised shortfall gas entitlements for a period of time following termination of the GSA as compensation for the seller's breach. Alternatively, the parties may consider including an alternative formulation providing for the payment of a different measure of damages from the breaching party to the non-breaching party, or acknowledging the right of the non-breaching party to bring a claim for damages against the breaching party as a result of the breach.

connection with the sale and purchase of gas and other activities carried out pursuant to the GSA. Typically, the GSA will provide that the seller is to be liable for all taxes arising upstream of the delivery point, and that the buyer is to be liable for all taxes arising downstream of the delivery point, with each party indemnifying the other party in respect of those tax liabilities.[46]

17. Facilities and maintenance

Where the parties need to construct new facilities and/or modify existing facilities in order to be able to perform their respective obligations under the GSA, the GSA may provide for certain obligations in relation to the construction and/or modification of those facilities. Similarly, the GSA may also impose upon the parties certain obligations relating to the operation and maintenance of those facilities.

During the term of the GSA, the parties will need to carry out periodic maintenance on facilities used in connection with the sale and purchase of gas. As gas is typically supplied in a constant flow, the parties will be concerned to ensure that any downtime attributable to facilities maintenance is minimised. Accordingly, the GSA will usually prescribe a mechanism pursuant to which the parties are to agree procedures for the coordination and synchronisation of their respective facilities maintenance. The parties will usually be entitled to a specified number of days each year during which to conduct facilities maintenance. During periods of maintenance, the parties will be excused from their respective supply and offtake obligations (which will be reflected in the shortfall gas and take-or-pay provisions).

18. Other provisions

Although there is not adequate scope in this chapter to consider all of the provisions commonly seen in a GSA in detail, a GSA would also usually contain the following provisions:

- *Definitions and interpretation provisions:* GSAs typically contain a number of technical terms and it is important that these be accurately defined. As with any commercial contract, the GSA will also normally stipulate rules of interpretation.
- *Assignment and transfers:* a GSA will normally provide that a party cannot assign, novate, transfer or otherwise dispose of any interest under the GSA without the prior written consent of the other party.[47]
- *Liabilities:* in addition to the liabilities provisions discussed above, the GSA will also normally contain generic liabilities provisions addressing (i) the

---

46 In some GSAs, the seller may seek to attempt to pass through to the buyer new taxes or tax increases which come into effect after the date of entry into the GSA on the basis that the seller's project economics were predicated on the basis of tax position as at the date of signing. However, such an approach is unlikely to be acceptable to the buyer as its downstream economics would similarly have been predicated on the tax position existing as at the date of entering into the GSA, and therefore the seller and the buyer should simply bear all tax risk upstream or downstream of the delivery point respectively.

47 As discussed in Section 2, because the identity of a counterparty may have been a significant factor in a party's decision to embark on the gas commercialisation project, the party may wish to ensure that the restrictions on transfer and assignment extend to capture changes of control and privatisation if the counterparty is a state enterprise.

exclusions of liability for consequential or indirect loss, (ii) liability and indemnities for third-party claims, (ii) liability and indemnities for loss or damage to property and injury or death to employees, (iii) monetary caps on the liability of one party to the other, (iv) conduct of claims, (v) duty to mitigate losses and/or (vi) any express remedy for breach contained in the GSA constituting the non-breaching party's sole and exclusive remedy.

- *Insurance:* each party will normally be under an obligation to effect and maintain certain insurances for the duration of the GSA, including insurance in respect of its facilities and third-party liability insurance.
- *Confidentiality:* each party will normally be subject to obligations of confidentiality regarding the GSA.
- *Governing law:* as with any commercial contract, the GSA will stipulate a governing law. In GSAs involving the cross-border sale of gas, the parties will usually stipulate a neutral governing law that is internationally recognised in the petroleum industry as possessing a well-developed body of law that will afford the parties with a degree of certainty and predictability in contractual interpretation and the outcome of claims.
- *Dispute resolution and arbitration:* putting aside disputes which are referable to an expert for determination and informal dispute-resolution procedures (such as alternative dispute resolution), most GSAs will provide that disputes arising between the parties shall either be referred to the applicable courts for litigation or to arbitration. International arbitration, either institutional (such as the International Chamber of Commerce International Court of Arbitration (ICC), or the London Court of International Arbitration (LCIA)), or ad hoc in accordance with the United Nations Commission on International Trade Law (UNCITRAL) rules, tends to be common in GSAs involving the cross-border sale of gas or international parties.
- *Expert determination:* under the GSA certain disputes may be referred to an independent third-party expert for determination. These matters will usually be limited to technical matters such as disputes relating to measurements, calculations, invoicing and/or *force majeure*. The provisions relating to the expert will normally address matters such as appointment, conduct of the expert determination, nature and status of the expert's determination (eg, non-appealable and binding) and the apportionment between the parties of costs relating to the expert determination.
- *Representation and warranties:* each party will normally give standard representations and warranties in favour of the other party.[48] The buyer will also normally insist on the seller warranting that it has title to all gas to be delivered under the GSA and that such gas is free from all encumbrances and adverse claims. In addition, the seller and/or the buyer may insist on the

48 Standard warranties may include (i) that the party has been validly incorporated, (ii) that the party has the requisite authority to enter into the GSA and perform its obligations under the agreement, (iii) that the GSA is binding upon, and enforceable against, the party in accordance with its terms, and (iv) that the party is not subject to any proceedings or litigation which may adversely affect its ability to perform its obligation sunder the GSA.

inclusion of representations and warranties specific to the particular circumstances of the project.

- *Sovereign immunity:* if a party to the GSA is a government entity, then that party may be entitled to claim sovereign immunity or immunity from the execution of enforcement of judgments under applicable law. In such circumstances, the other party will normally insist that such party waives its right to assert such immunity.
- *Application of terms implied by domestic legislation or international conventions:* depending on the jurisdiction, domestic legislation may imply certain terms in relation to the sale and purchase of gas contemplated under the GSA (eg, pursuant to gas, competition or sale of goods legislation). If the GSA relates to a cross-border sale of gas, the United Nations Convention on Contracts for the International Sale of Goods or the United Nations Convention on the Limitation Period in the International Sale of Goods may apply (depending on whether the applicable transit states have adopted those conventions). The parties will need to consider whether the terms implied under the conventions should be included in the GSA, or whether they should be expressly excluded (to the extent permitted by law).
- *Boilerplate provisions:* the inclusion of standard boilerplate provisions will be important.[49]

49 Typical boilerplate provisions would include any provisions relating to entire agreements, time of the essence, costs, relationship of the parties and exclusion of partnership, further assurance, third-party rights (or exclusion thereof), public announcements, waivers, invalidity and severability, variations, notices and/or execution by counterparties.

Crude oil sale and purchase agreements

Mark Morrison
Holman Fenwick Willan

1. Introduction

Contracts for the sale and purchase of crude oil are made by a variety of market participants – including producers, refiners, 'physical' traders (who often buy on FOB terms, charter a vessel, and sell on a CIF or CFR basis), and financial traders (who typically buy and sell on back-to-back terms, except for the price, and rarely take physical delivery). However, the contract terms which are generally used between this range of participants are largely standardised as a matter of form, if not detail.

A common element which links virtually all of these contracts is the fact that crude oil is almost always carried by sea, from producers to refiners. Matching the operational requirements of producers and refiners, while taking account of the uncertainties which often surround the movements of seagoing vessels, is one of the key factors to be addressed in a contract for the sale and purchase of crude oil.

A significant amount of crude oil sales, on which this chapter will focus, is on a spot basis; that is, the oil is traded under a contract for the sale and purchase of a single cargo. Term contracts for the lifting of a number of cargoes over a period of time (eg, 12 months) are not uncommon, but their terms are often more heavily negotiated than is the case with spot contracts and are therefore of less general application.

The aim of this chapter is to provide an overview of the most significant commercial and legal issues in sale and purchase agreements in the current market. The following areas are addressed:

- contract formation and structure;
- the Special Provisions;
- the General Terms and Conditions;
- incorporation of general provisions; and
- new developments.

2. Contract formation and structure

Typically, spot contracts are negotiated over the telephone, during which process the main commercial terms are agreed. These would essentially be:

- the description of the crude oil (usually by reference to origin and/or loadport);
- the quantity to be delivered;
- the delivery period; and
- the price (including how it is to be paid).

Agreement on these key terms may be sufficient in itself to create a legally binding contract.

The main commercial terms are then usually put in writing in a form which is generally referred to as the Special Provisions. This will almost invariably incorporate other more detailed terms by reference. These are usually known as the General Terms and Conditions (the GTCs). Currently, among the most commonly used General Terms and Conditions are those produced by BP Oil International Limited, 2007 edition (the BP General Terms and Conditions). They have been drafted with specific reference to the sale and purchase of crude oil, and have separate sections dealing with FOB deliveries, CFR, CIF and ex-ship deliveries, as well as other delivery methods, and are referred to below by way of example.

The Special Provisions will often include terms which overlap with provisions in the General Terms and Conditions and may expressly replace or vary provisions of the General Terms and Conditions. The terms of the Special Provisions will generally override those contained in the General Terms and Conditions; the BP General Terms and Conditions specially provide that that is the case.

Crude oil is generally traded on FOB terms, and although sales are of course made on a CIF/CFR basis, or ex-ship (DES), this chapter will focus on sales on FOB terms.

3. The Special Provisions

The Special Provisions perform a number of functions. First, and most importantly, they set out the key commercial terms which will invariably be agreed for each transaction. Secondly, they contain specific provisions which override or displace provisions of the General Terms and Conditions which the parties do not wish to incorporate into their contract. Thirdly, they may contain provisions which, for practical and operational reasons, the parties may prefer to be able to see stated explicitly in the Special Provisions, as opposed to having to have the General Terms and Conditions to hand. An example of this would be the term dealing with the passing of title and risk.

3.1 Quality/description

The quality and description provisions of a crude oil contract must be seen against the background of the terms implied by English law.

Under the English Sale of Goods Act 1979, a number of terms are implied into contracts for the sale of goods. For example, goods supplied under the contract must correspond with the description given to them in the contract; they must be of satisfactory quality; they must be reasonably fit for the purpose for which they are supplied; and they must comply with any sample on the basis of which the contract was made. If they fail to meet any of these requirements, then the buyer is entitled to reject the goods, unless the breach is so slight that it would be unreasonable to do so.

The implied terms as to fitness for purpose and compliance with the sample are rarely important in practice in relation to crude oil contracts, and are mentioned here only for the sake of completeness. The quality of crude oil is often very simply described, for example, "quality made available at the time of loading the shipment at the loading terminal", or "XYZ blend crude oil, as normally produced from the field with general characteristics approximately ...". If specifications (or general characteristics) are given, then that is often said to be for guidance only, with deliveries to be "as currently produced".

For many specifications there are well-recognised and published test methods, for example those of ASTM (originally known as the American Society for Testing and Materials). Where the contract states that a particular test method is to be used, that eliminates any argument as to whether the right method has been employed. Where the test method is not specified, testing by any well-recognised method is probably sufficient, although there might well be scope for argument where tests actually performed by different methods produce different results. Contracts often provide for inspection and testing at the port or place of shipment to be carried out by or under the supervision of an independent inspector, and for his findings to be final and binding. (This is not the approach taken by the BP General Terms and Conditions, pursuant to which certificates are used for invoicing purposes only, but the Special Provisions frequently vary that.) English law gives effect to such provisions, and the findings will be final and binding unless the inspector has been guilty of fraud or the inspection/testing has not been in accordance with the contractually specified method, or with normal practice. In other words, even if the inspector makes a mistake, the findings nevertheless bind both buyer and seller. There can therefore be no argument later on. In the absence of such a clause, any findings made by the independent inspector constitute evidence of the quality of the product, but that evidence may not be of any greater value than evidence of any other testing (eg, tests performed at discharge, or even later).

Even where the contract contains a loadport inspector final-and-binding provision, the final and binding effect of his report relates only to the specifications which have been tested, and not to the question of contractual quality overall.

In order to avoid an argument by the buyer that, even though the goods have met the contractual specifications, the seller is in breach because the goods are not of satisfactory quality, sellers frequently include in the contract a term which disclaims any obligation other than that the goods will meet the contract description and specifications. The BP General Terms and Conditions contain a provision to that effect.

3.2 Volume/quantity

Quantity in crude oil contracts can be expressed in volume or in weight. There are two aspects to be considered. The first is the quantity to be delivered and accepted; and the second is the measurement or determination of the quantity actually supplied.

In practice, the contract quantity is expressed in many different ways. Sometimes it is a specified tonnage, which may or may not be subject to a tolerance (eg, 500,000 barrels; or 500,000 barrels ± 5%). Expressions such as 'about' or 'approximately' should be avoided, as they introduce uncertainty, as does the use of the expression 'operational tolerance', at least where a ship is involved. Furthermore, if there is to be a tolerance, or a range, the contract ought to identify the party which is to have the right to determine the quantity (eg, 500,000 barrels ± 5% buyer's option). The exercise of the option is also generally subject to the agreement of the terminal. If the contract does not state which party is to have the option, then the general rule is that in an FOB contract the option is the buyer's, and in a CIF or C&F contract it is the seller's.

Measurement of liquid cargoes and their conversion from volume into weight is a notoriously imprecise science, at any rate where they are loaded into ships. The contract should leave no doubt as to the basis upon which the quantity supplied is to be determined, which is usually the bill-of-lading quantity or the determination made by an independent inspector.

3.3 Price

Currently, it is rare for a price to be agreed on a 'fixed and flat' basis (ie, at a specific monetary amount per barrel). A typical clause in a spot contract will provide that the price in US$ per barrel is to be the average of the daily highs and lows of, for example, Platts Crude Oil Marketwire quotations for Dated Brent, for the five days after the bill-of-lading date, plus or minus a fixed premium or discount. The price per barrel will usually be rounded to three decimal places.

Occasionally in CIF or CFR contracts the date of the vessel tendering notice of readiness at the first discharge port will be taken as the reference point for fixing the price. In the case of CIF and CFR contracts particularly, this kind of pricing mechanism gives a degree of flexibility to the seller, and the seller may be able to perform the contract in such a way as to maximise the price which it receives.

Contracts will sometimes contain provisions for the adjustment of the contract prices. It is common in CIF or CFR contracts for the buyer to have the option to discharge at any suitable port within a specified geographical range (eg, West Europe, Hamburg to Bilbao range). The buyer's choice ought to have an impact on the price, because the cost to the seller includes a freight element. The amount of the freight payable to the shipowner will depend on the length of the voyage. This is dealt with in the sale contract by means of a freight differential provision. In such a case the contract contains a base CIF price, for example, US$140 per barrel CIF basis Rotterdam, and then provides for an adjustment corresponding to the increased or decreased freight payable under the charterparty if the vessel discharges at a port other than Rotterdam.

With long or medium-term contracts, it has historically not been usual (even in times of relative price stability) to fix prices ahead for more than a few months, or perhaps a year. Where the market is in a phase of significant price volatility, then the contract may provide for a formula under which the premium or discount is varied according to the level of the reference grade of crude oil which is used to calculate the price of a particular shipment (eg, the higher the average price of the reference grade of crude oil, then the greater the premium). As a further measure to deal with price volatility, a term contract may also contain a provision for the pricing formula to be reviewed if the price of the reference grade exceeds a certain amount.

3.4 Payment

It is usual for the contract to provide for the price to be paid at a specified time after the date of the bill of lading, or (in the case of CIF/CFR sales) perhaps tied to completion of discharge or to the tendering of notice of readiness at the discharge port. When the seller is content to rely upon the buyer's creditworthiness, no security for payment will be required. Payment will then become due at the agreed time, either upon presentation of a simple invoice from the seller or (more commonly) an invoice plus shipping documents. If payment is to be made against documents (as is usual), then it is desirable to specify in the Special Provisions precisely the documents which will be required. Expressions such as 'usual shipping documents' should be avoided, if possible, as they create uncertainty. The BP General Terms and Conditions specify the documents which are to be tendered in return for payment. These are:

- an invoice;
- 3/3 original bills of lading;
- original certificates of quantity, quality and origin; and
- (in the case of a CIF contract) an original certificate of insurance or a cover note.

It is very common in crude oil transactions for the contract to permit the seller to obtain payment not against the shipping documents but against presentation of the seller's letter of indemnity, sometimes countersigned by a bank, if the shipping documents are not all available when the due date for payment arrives. It is often the case, particularly where the carrying voyage is short and there is a chain of contracts, that the vessel will arrive at its discharge port and/or the time for payment will arise, while the bills of lading are still in the hands of a seller in the early part of the chain and can take months to reach some subsequent sellers. The letter of indemnity is designed to enable the seller to obtain payment even though he is unable to tender all of the required documents. A letter of indemnity constitutes a contract under which the seller (and sometimes also its bank): warrants that title and the free right to use the goods has passed from the seller to the buyer in accordance with the contract; undertakes to supply the shipping documents when available; and agrees to indemnify the buyer against any claims which may be made by third parties claiming to have interests in or rights over the goods.

Where the seller wishes to be sure of payment, he will provide for a letter of credit to be put up by a bank acceptable to the seller and in terms acceptable to him. It is preferable for the contract to provide explicitly for the time by which the letter of credit must be in place, and this is often done. If not, then it must be in place by the beginning of the contract shipment period, and probably in the case of C&F and CIF contracts a reasonable time prior to that. If there is no shipment period specified in the contract (eg, in a CIF contract which provides for a delivery period), it must be in place within a reasonable time after the making of the contract. It is important to note that the time for provision of a letter of credit by the buyer is of the essence of the contract. If it is late, even by a day, the seller is entitled to terminate the contract, and to sue for damages if he has suffered any loss.

It is not uncommon to find a buyer reluctant to pay the full price because he believes that he has a claim against the seller – for example, delivery may have been made late, or there may allegedly be a defect in quality, or the quantity received at discharge may be less than the bill of lading or certified quantity. The buyer therefore wishes to make a deduction from the price to take account of his claim. If payment is by means of a letter of credit and the seller is able to present documents which accord with the terms of the letter of credit, there is in fact no problem for the seller, as there is no means by which the buyer can deduct. Its bank is bound to pay the price in full. But the position is not so clear-cut where there is no letter of credit. Then, if the buyer does in fact deduct, it will be necessary for the seller to take legal proceedings to recover the balance of the price. It is therefore quite common to find a provision in the payment clause which specifically obliges the seller to pay the price in full, without any deduction on account of any set-off or counterclaim.

3.5 Delivery

An FOB contract will always provide for a delivery period (ie, a period during which the goods are to be shipped at the loadport). In principle, and subject to the specific terms of the contract, the buyer must present a vessel at the delivery port in sufficient time to enable the seller to complete loading by the end of the shipment period. Conversely, the seller must make the goods available in sufficient time to enable shipment to be completed by the end of the period. If either party defaults on its obligation as described above, the other is entitled to terminate the contract and claim damages for loss suffered.

In the absence of any indication to the contrary in the contract, in a classic FOB contract the buyer in effect has the right to determine the time within which the delivery period at which the goods are to be shipped, because, subject to giving reasonable notice of arrival of his vessel, the buyer is entitled to present the vessel at any time during the shipment period. What is the position if the delivery period is, say, the whole of the month of March and the buyer, having given reasonable notice, presents his vessel on March 1, but the seller does not make the goods available until, say March 25 and loading is not completed until March 31? Is the buyer obliged to keep his ship waiting until March 25? The answer is that he is so obliged, and that even a lengthy delay such as this does not entitle him to terminate the contract, provided always that delivery is made by the end of the month. His remedy is demurrage (ie, damages at the rate agreed in the contract for delay to the ship).

Under a CIF or CFR contract, it is the seller rather than the buyer who is responsible for provision of the ship. Classic CIF and CFR contracts also contain a shipment period; and if the goods are not shipped within the shipment period, the buyer is entitled to reject the goods and recover damages for loss suffered because of non-delivery. However, crude oil contracts are often not typical, and will very frequently stray from the classic CIF/CFR model. It is common for such contracts to contain a delivery period rather than a shipment period (ie, a period during which it is intended that the goods be discharged at the contractual destination). Sometimes the Special Provisions will contain a combination of both, for example delivery June 26 to 28 "always consistent with scheduled loading at [named terminal] during June 15 to 17". It is likely that clauses of this kind will be interpreted by the courts as imposing upon the seller an obligation to ship on a vessel which is scheduled to arrive, in the ordinary course of events, at any time within the delivery period;

however, a slight variation in wording may be treated as imposing an absolute duty on the seller to ensure that the goods actually arrive at the discharge port on time, which means that the seller bears the risk of transportation delays. Much will depend on the precise wording of the clause. If the seller fails to comply with the relevant obligation described above, the buyer is entitled to terminate the contract and to recover damages for non-delivery if loss has been suffered. Assuming that the goods are made available for discharge in accordance with the contract, must the buyer discharge them in an expeditious manner? The contract will almost certainly contain a demurrage clause, so that if there are delays in discharge which are not attributable to the ship, the buyer will have to pay demurrage. Apart from that, it seems that the buyer is not at risk unless he delays commencing discharge for an inordinate time, probably at least several weeks beyond the end of the delivery period, or unless it becomes clear either that he cannot or will not discharge within such a time. It is only when inordinate delay has occurred, or it has become clear that inordinate delay will occur, that the seller is entitled to take his ship away, sell the goods elsewhere and claim damages for non-acceptance of the goods by the buyer.

Where crude oil contracts contain shipment or delivery periods which are any longer than a few days, it is common for them to contain further provisions intended to narrow the shipment or delivery timeframe. For example:

- an FOB contract with a March shipment period might contain a provision such as "seller to specify three days' loading range at least seven clear days prior to the commencement of such range"; or
- a CFR or CIF contract with a delivery range of July 5 to 15 might contain a provision such as "seller to give at least five working days' notice of a three-day layday range".

The first point to note is that if the party obliged to give such notice does so late, the notice will be invalid. The other party may well accept the notice. If so, all is well. But if it does not accept it, what then? There is a very strong tendency for the courts to treat notice provisions in commercial contracts as being of the essence of the contract, requiring strict adherence. On this basis, the party obliged to give the notice is entitled to give a new notice, nominating a new three-day range, provided there is still sufficient time remaining for a valid notice to be given.

FOB contracts in particular sometimes provide for the delivery period to be narrowed to a laycan. The time of delivery is usually "of the essence" (ie, the goods must have been loaded on board the vessel by the end of the delivery period, and if they are not, then the buyer may terminate the contract). The English courts have recently decided that, in such a case, the buyer is not entitled to terminate the contract if loading has not commenced or contemplated by the end of the laycan period. Thus, the time for delivery is no longer of the essence of the contract, and the buyer is entitled to present the vessel at any time up to the end of the laycan period.

What has been said so far applies to one-off or spot contracts, and in principle the same considerations apply to term contracts. However, in relation to term contracts there is in practice another dimension to be considered. Often the parties will not wish to be tied down to a rigid delivery timetable at the time when they are making the contract. Some contracts provide for, say, one delivery per calendar month for one year, but more often the contract will be more flexible than that (eg, it might provide for quarterly tonnages, or perhaps even just for delivery to be "at a reasonably even rate"). The more vague the delivery provisions are, the more difficult it is to determine their meaning and legal effect, and hence the likely outcome of any dispute.

Any contract should contain as precise details as possible concerning delivery and scheduling as the dictates of commercial flexibility permit. If possible it should:

- specify the intervals at which shipments are to be made;
- specify the quantities (with a tolerance) for each shipment; and
- provide machinery to enable the date for any shipment to be narrowed to a small date range.

3.6 Risk and title

In both FOB and CIF or CFR contracts, as a general rule the risk (in the sense of the risk of accidental loss of or damage to the goods, for example the risk of loss or damage whilst in the course of carriage) will pass from seller to buyer upon the goods being shipped. Theoretically, it might be possible to find specific contract clauses which expressly defer the passing of the risk, but that is very uncommon. The rule that the risk passes on shipment makes good sense. Ideally, the risk should be with the party who is covered by insurance. In an FOB contract the seller will insure the goods up to shipment; thereafter the buyer will have its own insurance. Exactly the same situation pertains with CFR contracts. With CIF contracts the seller insures the transportation risks, but it does so for the benefit of the buyer, and the price to the buyer includes the cost of the insurance. The intention, therefore, in a CIF contract is that the buyer rather than the seller is to be the insured party, and it is logical that the buyer should bear the risk of transportation loss.

In relation to title, it is a basic obligation of any seller to transfer good title to the buyer and to do so at the time at which it has contracted to transfer title. If the seller fails in performance of this obligation, then the buyer is entitled to damages; indeed, the buyer may in suitable cases be entitled to the return of the price if already paid. Speaking generally, a seller cannot transfer good title unless the seller itself has good title.

The prima facie rule that title passes on shipment does not apply if the seller retains control of the bill of lading (eg, by having it issued "to seller's order"). This brings into play the basic rule referred to above that title passes when it is intended to pass. The bill of lading is a document of title. By keeping it under its own control, the seller intends that title to the goods shall not pass immediately.

Crude oil contracts almost invariably contain clauses which specifically deal with the transfer of title. Usually the clause will provide that title, and risk, are to pass upon shipment. Indeed, they can be useful where there are chains of contracts relating to one cargo, where a coherent scheme is created under which title passes simultaneously under all contracts. Sometimes, but fairly unusually, the clause will state that title is not to pass until discharge, or perhaps until payment is made. The principal purpose of a clause such as that is to try to preserve rights against the goods in case the buyer does not pay. But that is a very imperfect way of dealing with a creditworthiness problem. Much the better way, and that usually adopted, is to obtain a letter of credit or a parent company guarantee.

4. The General Terms and Conditions

Almost invariably, spot contracts for the sale and purchase of crude oil will incorporate by reference to a set of general terms and conditions, which in other instances might be referred to as 'boilerplate'. For example, sales of crude oil from Nigeria are almost always subject to the terms of the Nigerian National Petroleum Corporation. General Terms and Conditions are, however, much more than boilerplate, in the sense of terms which may have little significance in practice. In fact, they will generally contain many of the key terms of the contract, and they ought to be reviewed carefully in each case to ensure that they are appropriate to the transaction in question. Taking the BP General Terms and Conditions in relation to FOB contracts as an example, they contain detailed provisions dealing with independent inspection and certification, as well as laydays, nomination of vessels, loading and berthing, the consequences of delays.

In addition, in the BP General Terms and Conditions there are a number of specific provisions which are of general application, irrespective of whether the contract is on an FOB, CFR or other basis. These include:

- responsibility for taxes and duties;
- payment provisions;
- the effect of new and changed regulations;
- *force majeure*;
- limitation of liabilities;
- termination or suspension in the event of liquidation and other causes;
- limitation of assignment;
- facilitation payments and anti-corruption; and
- law and jurisdiction.

The General Terms and Conditions may also contain schedules giving the formats for, say, letters of credit or standby letters of credit, and letters of indemnity.

One area which requires particular comment is that of *force majeure*. There are many different approaches to this issue, and parties will often include a *force majeure* provision within the Special Provisions, rather than rely on what is in the General Terms and Conditions which they have chosen to incorporate.

The approach taken in the BP General Terms and Conditions is that neither party is liable for a failure to perform any of its obligations under the Agreement, in so far as that party proves that the failure was due to an impediment beyond its control. 'An impediment' for these purposes is not narrowly defined but is said to include a number of potential matters such as war, natural disasters, boycotts or problems with supplies of crude oil from the seller's suppliers.

There are a range of consequences, depending on the effect of the impediment: if it makes performance of the contract impossible, then the contract terminates immediately; if the effect of the impediment is to delay performance, then obligations are postponed until, at latest, the last day of the laydays.

There is a specific provision to the effect that the seller is not obliged to purchase alternative crude oil afloat or from other suppliers in order to make good shortages.

There are, however, a variety of other approaches. It is, for example, not unusual to see a more precise definition of what is to amount to an event of *force majeure* (or an impediment), or to suspend performance for a period which goes beyond the end of the laydays. Many traders and other market participants will have their own preferred form of *force majeure* clause, which they will use in place of that in the General Terms and Conditions.

5. Incorporation of general provisions

A particular area of difficulty in crude oil contracts relates to potential uncertainty as to the relationship between the Special Provisions and the General Terms and Conditions. The general principle, which is usually stated explicitly in one or other of those documents, is that where there is a conflict or inconsistency between the General Terms and Conditions and the Special Provisions, then it is the Special Provisions which prevail. It is, however, often possible to read the Special Provisions and the General Terms and Conditions together, without there being any inconsistency between them, although the parties may have intended that the Special Provisions would replace the General Terms and Conditions in certain respects. It is therefore extremely important that the parties should make it clear in the Special Provisions whether they intend to exclude any specific parts of the General Terms and Conditions. This has led to a practice of some market participants having their own standard amendments to the chosen General Terms and Conditions.

6. New developments

Two particular areas have been the subject of recent notable developments. The first is an increasing practice for CIF/CFR sales to move further and further away from the classic CIF/CFR type of contract, pursuant to which the buyer was simply obliged to ship the oil within a defined shipment period and then tender documents for payment. Out of this there have developed CIF 'outturn' contracts, under which title and risk pass on shipment but the buyer only pays for the quantities which are delivered at the discharge port (ie, payment is not made on shipped quantities, and the seller in effect takes the risk of losses in transit). Further, CIF/CFR contracts are increasingly moving towards becoming arrival contracts, rather than shipment contracts, in the sense that the seller undertakes that the vessel will arrive within a specific time window, during which notice of readiness will be presented. Thus, the seller takes the risk of delays during the delivery voyage.

The second area of development is the addition of provisions of a financial nature into what were formerly purely physical trading contracts. For example, there is now a netting clause in the BP General Terms and Conditions. It is also becoming increasingly common, particularly among financial institutions, for provisions to be added into sale and purchase contracts to permit a seller to require that the buyer provides security for the payment price by, for example, a letter of credit, a bank guarantee, or the pre-payment of the purchase price. This is an indication of a trend towards sellers seeking to minimise the financial risks of their transaction.

Shipping arrangements

Denys Hickey
Ince & Co

1. Introduction

This chapter aims to provide an overview of the way in which shipping allows the oil and gas industry to function efficiently in terms of transporting crude oil and refined products, together with liquefied petroleum gas (LPG) and liquefied natural gas (LNG). The shipping industry is a very diverse one, and it operates on the basis of charter forms which may appear fairly arcane to anyone who has not previously been involved with the shipping industry. Ship charters, however, predate the modern petroleum industry by many years, since references to charters can be traced back to Phoenician times, and in England to the fourteenth century.

As a ship type, tankers are relatively new. As late as the middle of the nineteenth century the only oil transported by sea was mainly fish oil, whale oil and vegetable oil. The world's first truly dedicated oil tanker is generally accepted to have been the *Gluckauf*, built in 1886 to carry oil in bulk to Europe. The idea of transporting mineral oil in bulk caught on, and by 1906 99% of it was carried in bulk.

The shipping industry has changed very considerably since the first oil crisis in 1973, at which time the oil majors controlled a significant portion of the world's tanker fleet. Ownership of the worldwide tanker fleet is now much more diverse, as can be seen from the statistics produced by Intertanko reproduced on the next page. There are only a small number of owners controlling more than 10 vessels, and a large number of small independent tanker owners.

Significant changes in recent years include the introduction of double-hull tankers, which aim to reduce pollution in the event of a collision or stranding. In addition, there has been an increasing burden of international regulation, including in particular environmental regulation. Finally, changes to competition law in Europe affect the way in which vessels are operated, particularly affecting shipping pools which market similar types of vessels jointly owned by different owners.

The reason for the importance of shipping to the oil and gas sector is that many of the world's major producing fields are situated in areas such as the Arabian Gulf which are not geographically close to the major consuming markets and are not well served by pipelines. Accordingly, in many cases the only way of transporting crude oil and natural gas is by tankers. In addition, a large proportion of the international transportation of refined products is carried out by product tankers or gas carriers.

Tanker facts – Published by Intertanko

Tanker and combined fleet details as per January 2008 (above 10,000 dwt)
('Chemical' includes chemical/oil tankers)

Size '000 dwt	Fleet No	Order-b No	Fleet m. dwt	Order-b m. dwt	DH No	DH m. dwt	DH share %	Average age	10 yrs+ %	15 yrs+ %	20 yrs+ %	25 yrs+ %
10–60	2,629	1,225	82.2	40	1,602	59.2	72	11.7	43	30	22	9
60–80	342	129	24.0	9.5	271	19.3	80	8.6	32	26	20	5
80–120	742	292	76.2	32.1	614	64.1	84	8.9	36	23	9	2
120–200	361	141	54.7	22.3	306	46.7	85	9.0	37	23	7	3
200+	505	177	148.3	54.3	348	105.7	71	8.4	37	15	2	0
Totals	4,579	1,964	385.4	157.7	2,963	295.0	77	11.5	38	23	10	4
Of which:												
Chemical	1,678	1,189	49.0	37.8	1,425	42.0	86	9.1	50	37	27	7
Comb.	71	–	6.4	–	50	4.4	69	17.2	83	53	26	5

Tanker fleet ownership/control

Ownership	Numbers	m dwt	Share of total	Average age
Independent	3,727	315.3	83%	9.7
Oil company	123	14.2	3%	10.9
State owned	385	24.5	6%	15.7
State oil company	253	31.0	9%	12.8
Totals	4,355	370.8	100%	11.5

As at August 20 2008

2. Types of shipping arrangements

The first and simplest way of meeting shipping requirements is to own and operate the tankers required. This was for many years the model followed by the oil majors who built up very significant tanker fleets. There are, however, several disadvantages associated with this model. The first and most obvious is the lack of flexibility because, unless you are planning to transport oil on a route which never varies, once your ship has discharged in one particular destination it will not necessarily be in the most convenient position to pick up another cargo for owners. This in turn means that it will be necessary to charter out vessels when you do not have cargo of your own to move, or to undertake an empty ballast voyage. In addition, it means that it is less easy to take advantage of the spot charter market if rates are favourable.

A closely related way of meeting shipping requirements is to enter into a 'bareboat' or 'demise' charter, under which the legal owner of the vessel charters the vessel out on a long-term basis on terms that the charterers will take care of all of insurance, maintenance and crewing requirements. A consequence of this is that the charterer will also be regarded for legal purposes as being in control of the vessel and will be legally liable for the operation of the vessel and any resulting liability. Such bareboat charters can have tax advantages in some jurisdictions and can be useful if a company wishes to keep the ships off its balance sheet, or as part of a financing package.

However, the most common forms of shipping arrangements encountered in the oil and gas sector are 'time' or 'voyage' charters. In summary, the difference between the two forms of charter is that under a time charter the vessel is hired out for a period which could be as short as one or two months, but more commonly will be one or more years. With a voyage charter, in contrast, the vessel is only chartered for a single voyage, or sometimes a series of consecutive voyages.

In the case of both time and voyage charters it is normal for chartering to be carried out on the basis of standard forms of charter, the detailed terms of which are subject to amendment during negotiation of the individual charter concerned. The most commonly used time charter forms are BPTime and Shelltime. In the case of voyage charters the most commonly used forms are Asbatankvoy, BPvoy and Shellvoy. It is, however, important to point out that there are many other different company forms in use; and although there are common features, many of the detailed terms vary quite considerably.

In the case of both time and voyage charters, the large charterers tend to have their own preferred additional clauses which are themselves subject to further negotiation during the chartering negotiations. It is therefore very common to see charters where the printed standard form has been amended and charterers' standard additional clauses have also been amended.

The main features of time charters and voyage charters are discussed next.

2.1 Time charters

The main feature of a time charter is that in return for a daily rate of hire the owner agrees to allow the charterer full access to the vessel, and agrees for the vessel to be used within certain geographical limits for the carriage of specified cargoes. Normally, the limits are set fairly widely, but there will always be some limitations, in particular based on the fact that an owner will not want the vessel employed in areas which are subject to hostilities. Equally, he will not want the vessel to be employed in areas such as Canadian waters in wintertime unless the vessel is specifically adapted for ice. There may be other limitations on the use of the vessel depending on her construction, and on whether or not she has permits and approvals to trade freely within the relevant area. In general terms, this means that the standards required for a vessel to trade within Europe or to the United States will be higher than, for example, a vessel which is only required to trade within the Arabian Gulf, or between the Arabian Gulf and the Indian subcontinent. The general trend worldwide is, however, for stricter standards to be imposed, which means that safety standards are continuing to improve.

Under a standard form of time charter the owners are required to pay for the crew, for the maintenance and upkeep of the vessel, and for standard hull and machinery insurance. The charterer will, however, be responsible for providing bunkers (which is a marine term for the fuel used by a vessel) and will normally be responsible for any additional insurances which are required because of the locations at which the vessel is ordered to load or discharge. In conflicts such as the Iran/Iraq war this requirement led to a significant number of disputes because the additional premiums payable can be very significant. A good example of issues that are currently arising concerns additional insurance premiums for vessels trading through the Red Sea which are being targeted by pirates.

Time charters normally contain undertakings by the owners that the vessel has oil major approvals, but there can be difficulties where a vessel loses such approvals, and it is not always made clear whether the owner is obliged to maintain a full set of approvals from the oil majors and major charterers. This is an increasingly important issue because, without oil major approval and approvals from the most important charterers, a vessel can become difficult to employ. This is because not only do the charterers have to be satisfied with the condition of the vessel and her equipment, but the major loading and discharge terminals, which also run their own approval and inspection systems, also have to be satisfied.

In the event that the vessel is unable to perform the operations which are immediately required, because for example of a mechanical breakdown, then the charterers may be entitled to cease paying hire during the time lost. This is on the basis that the vessel will go 'off hire'. Whether a vessel will go off hire will depend on the wording of the off-hire clause and the exact circumstances in which the vessel is prevented from working, and this can give rise to complex issues.

It is, however, important to note that even if the vessel is off hire, it does not follow that the charterers will necessarily be entitled to claim damages. Charterers will only be entitled to claim damages for delays in the event that the owners are in breach of a specific provision of the charter concerning the condition of the vessel or her description or in breach of a warranty as to her performance. The simple fact that the vessel may have suffered a mechanical breakdown will not normally be sufficient to give rise to a damages claim, because time charters usually contain a provision that in the event of a mechanical breakdown the owners are obliged to carry out repairs as soon as they are reasonably able to do so. They are not, however, obliged to carry out such repairs immediately, and the charterers may therefore only be able to treat the vessel as off hire, but not be entitled also to claim damages.

The charterers are entitled to give lawful orders concerning the employment of the vessel under a time charter, but will normally be liable in the event that the orders they give lead to the vessel suffering damage. The basis for this is that owners are entitled to an indemnity for following orders, because the charterers are entitled to employ the vessel on whatever routes they wish. It follows that owners do not have an opportunity in advance to vet the destinations to which the vessel may be sent, and there is a quid pro quo in the sense that in return charterers indemnify owners for any damage or loss which may result.

Time charters normally set out details of the vessel's speed and fuel consumption, and they often provide that if the vessel does not meet the warranted speed and consumption, then compensation will be payable depending on the extent of the underperformance.

Most time charters also have detailed provisions setting out the respective obligations of owners and charterers under the International Ship and Port Facility Security Code (ISPS Code) regime, which is the international code for the security of ships and port facilities.

2.2 Voyage charters

A voyage charter is exactly what its title suggests, which is a charter under which a vessel is employed to carry out a voyage from A to B. It is also possible to have a consecutive voyage charter under which a vessel carries out a series of voyage charters in direct continuation.

The major difference between a voyage and time charter is that with a voyage charter the freight which is payable covers the fuel as well as crew and insurance.

The freight payable under the charter is based on the quantity of cargo loaded, or sometimes on a minimum quantity, and is often calculated by reference to Worldscale. Worldscale is unique to tanker voyage chartering, and is designed to allow a tanker to obtain the same net return per day at the same Worldscale percentage rate regardless of the voyage actually undertaken. Thus, the profitability or loss of different voyages can be easily compared. The freight payable under a tanker voyage charter is therefore very often expressed as "WS XXX". This allows freight to be calculated for the load and discharge ports at which the vessel calls by reference to the published Worldscale rates current at the date of the charter.

A further important difference between a time charter and a voyage charter is that the freight under a voyage charter is calculated on the basis of loading and discharge taking place within a defined period. In most tanker charters, the period of laytime within which loading and discharge should be completed is 72 hours, although it can be longer or shorter for specialised cargoes or ports which may require longer for loading or discharging operations. If laytime is exceeded, then charterers will be liable to pay demurrage at a daily rate for all time by which laytime is exceeded. Laytime and demurrage are highly technical subjects because there are detailed rules concerning what the vessel has to do in order to trigger the commencement of laytime, and there are usually detailed amendments to the standard voyage-charter terms to deal with who is responsible, and what is the effect on laytime and demurrage if delays occur due to bad weather, breakdown of equipment or strikes.

Responsibility for the safety of the ports to which the vessel is ordered is another area in which there is a substantial difference between time and voyage charters. This is because under English law it is assumed that under a voyage charter the owners accept the risks inherent in the vessel going to ports which are named in the charter. However, if the voyage charter provides for loading discharge at any port within a geographical range, then the charterer will be responsible for the safety of the port and berth which is nominated. There can also be great differences between different specific wordings which may be inserted into specific voyage charters.

Voyage charters normally require the vessel to have all of the required approvals and certifications to carry out the intended voyage. It is therefore very common for owners to warrant in the charter that the vessel is in possession of approval from specified oil majors or from other organisations such as Rightship, which is a ship-vetting organisation. It is also fairly common for disputes to arise because vessels can lose such approvals on the basis of an inspection when they go into load or discharge, or because their status changes as a result of some earlier problem which is picked up by a charterer or vetting organisation.

Generally, owners are responsible for all insurance arrangements for the vessel. However, this will not be the case if they intend to send the vessel into a war zone, or into another area where additional premiums may be payable because of the threat of terrorist activity or piracy. In such cases where the danger is evident at the time the charter is entered into, there will normally be specific provision for charterers to pick up the cost of such additional insurance premiums. The position can be different when the danger only arises after the charter has been entered into because of a sudden flare-up. This latter situation gives rise to complex issues which are beyond the scope of this chapter.

2.3 Contracts of affreightment and bespoke charters

There are a number of situations in which a traditional time or voyage charter is not appropriate. An example of a situation which is commonly encountered is with floating production storage and offtake (FPSO) and similar multi-purpose production and storage units. The challenge with these production units is that they only have a finite storage capacity and therefore depend on shuttle vessels to offload crude oil on a regular basis.

There are a number of challenges posed by this kind of arrangement. The first is that the offtaking vessels needs to be compatible with the loading facilities at the floating production storage and offtake. The second is that the operator has to be sure that vessels will turn up on a regular basis to avoid the floating production storage and offtake storage filling up, which could lead to the production unit having to be shut down.

A further challenge is posed by the degree of flexibility which the operator of the floating production storage and offtake wants. It is possible to have a very inflexible contract of affreightment under which the lifting vessel can only be ordered to discharge at a limited range of nearby ports, and the operator of the floating production storage and offtake is not entitled to send the vessel to a discharge port which is further away. The normal solution is to enter into a contract of affreightment under which the parties agree on a minimum and maximum volume of crude oil to be lifted over a period, and agree to a regular schedule of liftings. This is on the basis that the owner guarantees that whichever vessel is used for a particular lifting will be technically capable of loading safely from the production unit.

Very often this kind of arrangement is a bespoke contract drafted on the basis that, in respect of each vessel which loads from the offshore unit, a separate voyage charter will be deemed to arise based on a standard Asbatankvoy or BPvoy charter with modifications. The challenge with this kind of bespoke arrangement, as with any bespoke charter, is to ensure that the terms tie in with the standard voyage charter forms and that in designing something bespoke those who are doing the drafting do not lose sight of any of the important elements normally found in a standard form of voyage charter.

2.4 Refined products

It is worth briefly mentioning particular issues which arise in connection with the carriage of petroleum products which are the product of a refining process. These range from LPG at the top end of the barrel through gasoline, kerosene, gasoil, lubeoil and then down to fuel oil. At the top end of the range, specialised vessels are used, with LPG for example being carried in purpose-built gas tankers.

The main issue which comes up repeatedly with the products at the higher end of the slate, such as gasoil and jet fuel, is the cleanliness of the tanker nominated to carry the cargo. If you are dealing with a time charter, then the master and crew will be obliged to clean the vessel to an appropriate standard to ensure that there is no cross-contamination between previous cargoes which have been carried and the cargo which the vessel loads. Normally, it is fair to say that there are fewer problems with time charters because of the fact that the charterer will have control of the cargoes carried by the vessel and should be very well aware of the steps needed to clean the vessel in between cargoes. In contrast, with voyage charters there are often problems when a vessel has carried a relatively dirty cargo such as gasoil, and then loads a clean product such as gasoline or jet fuel (kerosene). Such charters often refer to the vessel being cleaned to the "charterers' inspectors' satisfaction", but the wording of such clauses can often give rise to disputes, and it is very important to use clear language which leaves no room for disagreement as to the duties which must be undertaken prior to loading the next intended cargo. It is also very important to specify how the cleanliness of the vessel is to be checked, and who gets the final say.

2.5 Liquefied natural gas

Finally, it is worth briefly mentioning the shipping requirements for LNG. Those who have experience of LNG will know that it is natural gas cooled to -160C prior to loading into specially constructed tankers, which are designed to maintain the extremely low temperature of the cargo during carriage.

There are several different designs of LNG tankers, with the newest designs including onboard regasification capabilities, so that any cargo which would otherwise boil off can be re-liquefied and pumped back into the cargo tanks.

Drafting LNG charters is a very specialised area, with a number of different forms of charter currently in use. Charters entered into back in the 1970s, when LNG carriers were first developed, tended to be bespoke documents which were very often written under US law. More recent charters are now often based on either Shelltime or BPTime with specific modifications being included to cater for the peculiar features involved in the carriage of LNG. Most recently, a new charter form, the Shell LNG Voy 1 form, has been introduced, which aims to cater specifically for the features of LNG which require slightly different chartering arrangements. The reader may not be surprised that this does not prevent the need for extensive modifications and additional clauses and, given the normally lengthy period of such charters, they are the subject of detailed and lengthy negotiation.

3. General issues arising under both time and voyage charters

3.1 Pollution

Pollution is an area which all responsible owners and charterers are concerned about.

With voyage charters, the position depends on the jurisdiction in which the pollution occurs. In some 102 jurisdictions it will be governed by various international conventions covering oil pollution which apply to 'persistent' oils, which include crude oil and fuel oil. These international conventions do not cover lighter refined products such as aviation kerosene or gas oil, which can cause significant environmental issues but which are not classified as oil pollution in the normal sense.

However, there are a number of countries which have not signed up to the international conventions, including in particular the United States.

Where the international conventions apply, liability is directed at the owner up to liability limits which are currently the equivalent of approximately US$320 million, although some 21 countries have agreed higher limits of around US$1.1 billion.

In recent years, there have been developments in some jurisdictions which indicate that in certain circumstances charterers as well as owners may face liability for oil pollution. One example is the United States, where there may in certain states be the possibility of a charterer being held liable for pollution. More recently, the French courts have held that Total were responsible for pollution resulting from the *Erika* accident, because of the way in which they approved the vessel prior to chartering. It is also possible that cargo owners could be exposed to liability in Europe under the EU Waste Management Directive.

The position is the same with time charters, although it could be argued that charterers may have more control over the maintenance of a vessel and could therefore face a higher risk of being blamed if a pollution incident occurs as a result of a lack of maintenance (if for example they refuse to agree to the vessel carrying out repairs between voyages).

There is a new convention, namely the HNS convention, which has not yet come into force, which will introduce a liability regime for hazardous and noxious substances, including the refined products which are not covered by the existing oil pollution regimes, and will also cover the carriage of chemicals, LNG and LPG.

Finally, a new convention covering pollution from bunkers has recently come into force.

3.2 Responsibility for cargo

Both time and voyage charters will involve bills of lading being issued for cargo loaded. Where bills of lading are issued, they will normally be subject to a liability regime based on international conventions, the earliest of which is the Hague Convention referred to as the Hague Rules, which came into force in the United Kingdom in 1924.

The Hague Rules lay down a liability regime for the loading, carriage and discharge of cargo and provide that, so long as owners excise due diligence to ensure that the vessel is seaworthy at the commencement of the voyage, they will be entitled to exceptions and limitations of liability. The Hague Rules are directly incorporated into domestic law in many countries, with some countries such as the United Kingdom having incorporated the convention into domestic law. A notable exception is the United States which has, however, enacted similar legislation in the Carriage of Goods by Sea Act 1936.

More recently, the rules have been amended to raise the compensation limits and impose a more onerous regime on owners under the so-called Hague Visby Rules of 1978. The Hamburg Convention of 1978 gave even greater rights to cargo owners. However, although a number of countries have acceded to the Hamburg Rules Convention, they are not yet in force.

It is necessary to understand the existence and the workings of the Hague/Hague Visby/US COGSA liability regime, because it has an impact on risk allocation and insurance arrangements. In addition, it can come as an unwelcome surprise to some people to find that the US COGSA, Hague or Hague Visby Rules may be incorporated into a charter. This is because charters very often incorporate the Hague or Hague Visby Rules or US COGSA, which can for example mean that a charterer can be faced with a time-bar defence when a claim is presented, because under the Hague, Hague Visby or US COGSA regime any claims have to be filed within 12 months or they will be barred.

3.3 Floating production and storage

There has been a vast increase in the number of projects being developed offshore using floating production systems of various types and designs. The early developments utilised converted tankers with process equipment installed on deck, and many units of this type are still in service in regions (such as West Africa) which have relatively benign weather conditions. Increasingly, however, such units are being purpose-built to act as floating production storage and offtake tankers, or just floating storage and offtake.

The challenges associated with charters for such units include the fact that many of the rights and obligations set out in a standard form of time charter will not necessarily apply without modification. Just to take one example, there is a potential tension on a floating production storage and offtake between the role and duties of the marine master and the role of the offshore installation manager (OIM) who has overall charge of the operation of the unit whilst offshore. Another area which requires consideration is the limitation regime, because there can be questions as to whether or not the unit qualifies as a ship, which in turn can have very significant ramifications on liability issues connected, for example, to wreck removal and limitation issues if there is a collision.

There are a number of other issues which have to be addressed, including the maintenance regime, which for floating production storage and offtakes will be different from what it would be with a normal time charter for worldwide trading, where a vessel can schedule dry docking and general repairs at the end of any particular voyage. Clearly, the intention with a floating production storage and offtake is that the unit should stay offshore and should operate for as long as possible without the need for maintenance. This can give rise to tensions between the owners' requirements to carry out maintenance, and the charterers' desire to maintain production from the field on which the floating production storage and offtake is stationed.

3.4 Limitation

Limitation is a concept which is unique to shipping, because ship owners have a right to limit liability to a figure based on their tonnage.

A shipowner's right to limit is based on the size of the vessel, with complex rules about the measurement of vessels governing precisely how the relevant tonnage should be calculated for limitation purposes. This is a very important aspect for charterers to appreciate, because it may have an effect on their liability. Certainly in larger projects, such as projects involving the shipment of LNG, limitation will have a significant effect on the types of insurance arrangements which will need to be put in place.

Gas allocation agreements

Peter Taff
Independent Consultant
Richard Tyler
Lovells LLP

1. Introduction

In this chapter we attempt to explain the concepts of allocation, attribution and substitution and the purpose of allocation agreements by reference to real examples. We also show how allocation agreements are needed and used at different places along the gas chain: upstream, midstream and downstream.

In the second half of the chapter we focus on the example of a typical North Sea upstream allocation system and discuss the issues which are likely to be addressed in the allocation agreement.

2 Principles of allocation

2.1 General

'Allocation' is a concept/process used in both the oil and gas industries to divide a commingled quantity of gas or oil to establish the proportion or part of that commingled quantity that was contributed by each relevant source or company.

The 'relevant sources' might be, for example, each separate gas field connected to an offshore pipeline network where the gas production from all the gas fields commingles into a single pipeline prior to final delivery.

Alternatively, the allocation process might apportion the commingled quantity of gas or oil back to each owner of the produced commodity. So in the example above, if each gas field had several different owners or partners, the allocation process might assess the proportion or part that was contributed by each owner.

Allocation needs to be done at many different places along the gas chain. Allocation could be required at:

- an offshore meter on a gathering platform where production from several different fields or sources first commingles;
- an onshore gas reception terminal where gas from several different offshore pipelines is commingled and processed prior to delivery to buyers; or
- a pipeline flange at a point in an onshore gas network where the commingled gas is owned by several different shippers and is being sold to one or more buyers at that flange (eg, at a cross-border interconnection between two national gas networks, or at the network offtake point to an industrial end-user, such as a gas-fired power station, where the end-user is buying gas in a commingled stream from several different suppliers).

2.2 Methods: volume, weight, energy and/or components?

We referred above to a commingled quantity that needs to be allocated. In theory, the quantity could be stated in many different ways (eg, as volume, weight, or more commonly as energy). The driver for the choice of unit is likely to be whatever is the basis for the commercial contract or agreement between the relevant parties at that location. If various producers are selling gas from a commingled pipeline to various buyers, and the sales contracts are all expressed in terms of energy units, then the allocation of the commingled quantity will be made in terms of energy.

The relative complexity of the allocation process, or allocation rules, will depend on the accuracy being sought, and on how similar or different the various sources of gas are prior to commingling. A few examples are set out below:

- *Simple volume-based allocation.* Gas is produced from two different dry-gas fields which have very similar chemical composition (and hence similar gross calorific value), undergoes minimal processing prior to delivery and is being sold (in energy units) in a commingled stream to a single buyer under two separate gas sales contracts with different prices. In this case it may be sufficiently accurate to divide (or prorate) the measured commingled quantity of energy purely on the basis of the gas production volume measured at each field.
- *Complex component-based allocation.* Gas is produced from two different associated gas fields (A and B) with significantly differing chemical composition (field A has a higher methane content, whilst the gas from field B contains more heavier hydrocarbons and inert gases), is processed in a complex reception plant to remove heavier hydrocarbons and inerts and is being sold (in energy units) in a commingled stream to multiple buyers, under separate gas sales contracts with different prices. In this case, it is likely that the parties involved will want to ensure that the measured redelivered energy is allocated on a basis that reflects the different gas compositions of the source gases, as field A contributes a greater proportion of the methane in the incoming commingled gas stream. Also, as the reception terminal is extracting and redelivering natural gas liquids (NGLs) separated from the gas, the parties will need to allocate the ownership of these valuable liquids (and field B will be the source of the greatest proportion of the liquids produced). In this case, the parties involved will probably opt for a process based on allocation of each separate chemical component in the gas (and liquids). As a simplified example, suppose field A produces 100 units of methane on the day, and field B produces 80 units, and 170 units of methane are redelivered in the gas stream from the processing plant (the remaining 10 units of methane having been used as fuel or dissolved in the separated liquids). Then field A is allocated $100/180 \times 170$ (= 94.4) units of methane in the redelivered gas stream, and field B is allocated $80/180 \times 170$ (= 75.6) units of methane of the 170 units redelivered. The same process is carried out for each of the other components (ethane, propane, inerts etc), so that the redelivered energy in the gas and natural gas liquid streams can then be allocated according to the allocated component contribution in the commingled input stream.

- *Downstream allocation – pro rata to nominations.* Gas is being traded (in energy units) at a cross-border interconnection point of two gas transmission networks between multiple upstream and downstream shippers. As the gas (upstream and downstream) is all commingled, there is no differentiation to be made on gas quality, and hence the allocation process will be primarily one of prorating and matching the measured energy according to the nominations made by the various shippers on either side of the interconnection point.

These three examples illustrate some of the wide range of applications and differences in the complexity of allocation arrangements. There is no easy guideline or rule of thumb to indicate which method is needed in any particular situation. It will be a matter of negotiation between the parties, depending on the stage of the gas chain at which allocation is being made, the differences in the composition of the gas and liquid sources, the differences in the current and future prices of gas (or NGL) sold within the commingled export stream(s), and the cost of implementing the process (which will be significantly greater for a component-based allocation process, where many of the gas and liquid streams will need accurate component measurement equipment).

The three examples also track, to some extent, the changes and developments within the European gas industry (Great Britain in particular).

- In the 1970s, the British gas industry was characterised by having a national monopoly gas buyer (British Gas) and plentiful supplies of gas from dry-gas fields in the UK Continental Shelf Southern Basin bought on the basis of whole-field depletion contracts. A relatively few gas-reception terminals were built on the coast, and offshore pipeline networks developed, bringing gas from a number of different offshore fields/platforms to a commingled delivery point at each reception terminal. Relatively simple volume-based allocation processes were used.
- In the 1980s, the Northern Basin began to be developed and associated gas was produced from oil fields, brought to St Fergus in Scotland, processed to remove the liquids, and then was sold to British Gas (the first such development being the Brent Field). This required much more complex component-based allocation.
- In the 1990s, having established the component-based method in the North, the process migrated south, driven by a number of factors:
  - Newer gas fields had significantly different gas composition (eg, Caister Murdoch), from the earlier developments – higher inerts, for example.
  - Price differences were greater between gas fields delivering into the same commingled stream (as the various contracts had been negotiated and started at different times over a period of 25 to 30 years).
  - New gas sales contract structures were introduced. A commingled stream could now have some gas from a 'whole field depletion' contract and other gas from a supply contract. The seller (and buyer) of gas under the depletion contract would probably want to ensure that the allocation

    process prevented any of its gas being inadvertently delivered under the supply contract.
    - The liberalisation of the market had started and British Gas was no longer a monopoly buyer. The commingled stream could contain gas from one field being sold to British Gas under a whole field depletion contract, together with gas from another field being sold, at the same delivery point, to a different buyer. This often required the re-negotiation of the allocation agreement, and the opportunity was taken to improve the allocation process to give increased accuracy in response to all the attendant changes.
- In the late 1990s, the British gas network was connected to the Continental European system for the first time (via the Bacton–Zeebrugge Interconnector) and multiple gas shippers were selling gas to buyers from the commingled stream at various interface points – at Bacton, at Zeebrugge, at the Belgian/Dutch and Belgian/German borders and at the interconnection point between British and Irish gas transmission systems (Moffat in Scotland). This led to the need for allocation processes at each of these locations to enable the numerous sellers and buyers to administer their respective gas contracts. These have normally been nomination-proration processes as discussed earlier.
- The 2000s have been characterised by further liberalisation of the downstream European gas markets, with more interconnection of traded markets with multiple shippers, sellers and buyers. Through the work of various gas industry associations (eg, EASEE-gas, GIE, EFET), downstream allocation processes have become more harmonised, all largely following the nomination-proration principle, but with added features to handle such things as bi-directional flow and the use of operational balancing accounts (OBAs) between connected transmission system operators (TSOs) (see below).

3. Principles of attribution

The allocation process is primarily about identifying the correct portion of a commingled gas stream that derives from a particular physical source. 'Attribution' is a second stage that considers the quantity actually measured in the redelivery stream against the nominations made during the relevant allocation period, and any other contractual provisions used to arrive at the quantity that is contractually deemed (or attributed) to have been delivered by or to each shipper in the commingled stream at that point.

In a simple allocation system, if there are no such other contractual provisions then the attributed quantity will equal the allocated quantity. The type of contractual provisions that allow the attributed quantity to differ from the allocated quantity could include the following:

- The upstream sellers (or producers) may have made arrangements to help each other with delivery problems, so that gas from one physical source (A) may be allowed to substitute for another source (B) if source B (for example) is suffering some temporary mechanical failure. The allocation process would show the additional production coming from source A, but the necessary quantity would then be attributed to the owners of source B to overcome their delivery problems.

- One contract (A) may have significantly larger flows than the others (B and C), to the extent that it has been agreed that the larger stream will be the 'balancing' flow. This could be at a downstream cross-border interconnection where a large-flow (legacy) gas contract is delivered commingled with gas for much smaller third-party trades. The physical flow control will unavoidably have small deviations from the net nominations made (normally referred to as 'steering differences'). However, the balancing contract or flow takes all of such deviation (up to a specified limit), allowing the other sellers to be attributed gas exactly equal to their nominations. If the flow control deviation exceeds the specified limit (if for example there is an upstream compressor failure), then the process defaults to pro rata allocation of the physical flow for the duration of the incident.
- The upstream and downstream system operators may have an interconnection agreement that incorporates some form of operating balance provision (an operational balancing account or OBA). In this case, any steering difference is attributed to the balancing account of the two transmission system operators and the quantities attributed to each shipper exactly equals its (confirmed) nomination. Thus, the shippers have one level of uncertainty removed in terms of balancing their energy positions within the relevant network (which is useful in reducing their exposure to the risk of balancing charges imposed by the network operator). The operational balancing accounts will have agreed cumulative quantity limits and if at any time the limit is exceeded (eg, due to a large physical failure in the upstream or downstream system), then the process would typically default to one of pro-rata allocation until the failing system becomes operational again and is in a position to bring the operational balance back within the limit.
- At an interconnection point where bi-directional flow is possible, there may be shippers nominating in different directions at any time. The physical flow will be set to be the net of the aggregate commercial flows (ie, the sum of all the nominations in one direction minus the sum of all the nominations in the opposite direction). The allocation process (in the absence of an operational balancing account) will allocate any steering differences between the nominations made in the direction of physical flow and the quantities attributed to the contraflow shippers will be exactly equal to their (confirmed) contraflow nominations.
- Other rules of attribution affecting how steering differences (in the absence of an operational balancing account) or other larger differences between actual measured physical flow and net aggregate nominations are dealt with (otherwise than pro rata) could reflect different orders of priority between shippers according to:
    - whether they have booked (and paid for) firm transportation capacity in the relevant pipeline or network, or are relying on reasonable endeavours

or interruptible transportation capacity; or

- the timeliness of their nominations – whether they have submitted their nomination or changed their nomination after an agreed deadline or gate closure.

4. Principles of substitution

The example above, where there is allowed substitution from one source to assist another, is often used in the upstream, offshore UK gas industry.

The terms, 'allocation', 'attribution' and 'substitution' are closely linked. As explained above, 'allocation' refers to the assessment of the physical contribution of each source to the commingled delivered streams, whereas 'attribution' refers to the contractual confirmation or readjustment of the allocated quantities to reflect quantities actually delivered (in the absence of an operational balancing account), either within the agreed system-wide rules or within rules applicable as between buyer and seller or shipper and transporter. 'Substitution' represents the process in which volumes or energies are lent and borrowed between the several sources which deliver gas into the system. There would normally be an agreed limit to the cumulative amount of substitution that can occur at any time, with rules governing when and how the imbalance must be repaid. The ability of any source to substitute quantities with any other source will be constrained by the contractual provisions which provide for the existence of those rights, whether set out in allocation arrangements, transportation arrangements or gas sales agreements. These provisions will set out not only the allowable limits and repayment conditions, but also the allowable reasons or circumstances (eg maintenance or operational issues restricting the production of the borrowing source) permitting substitution.

Traditionally, there is normally no specific charge made for lending the quantities of gas substituted (the consideration being the subsequent repayment of such quantities), which is perhaps surprising given the volatile nature of the short-term markets that have developed and hence variations in the potential value of the substituted gas. However, one can only assume that the producers, who continue to agree to such terms, see mutual and balancing benefit in the long term to all parties to the free substitution and that they do not favour the alternative of an upstream spot gas market.

5. Upstream vs downstream allocation and title transfer

Up to this point, we have discussed the allocation and attribution of a commingled stream between its sources. By inference this is an allocation upstream of the delivery point (ie, providing the sellers with their entitlements at that point, and confirmation of contractual quantities delivered). However, the downstream TSO (transmission system operator) will have its own default allocation rules, and to ensure a smooth passage of gas entitlement between multiple upstream sellers which are shippers in the upstream system and multiple downstream buyers which are themselves shippers in the downstream system, the process of title transfer between one party and another at the delivery point needs to be examined.

In Great Britain, prior to liberalisation, title transfer was not an issue. There was only one buyer (British Gas) and the buyer was normally party to the upstream allocation agreements.

However, with the advent of multiple downstream national transmission system shippers (in the 1990s), the transmission system operator (Transco[1]) implemented default entry-point allocation rules largely based on prorating the measured entry quantities against the nominations made to it by its shippers. However, there were many pre-existing upstream allocation agreements that had more complex arrangements than simple prorating, and hence Transco allowed different allocations to be input for an entry point if all the parties had an agreed alternative process to provide an Entry Allocation Statement (provided that the aggregate of the quantities in the Entry Allocation Statement exactly matched the Entry Point Daily Quantity Delivered (ie, measured), as such terms were defined in the Network Code.[2] Initially there was no such agreed process and hence there was significant opportunity for a shipper to 'game' the system. Over time a claims-validation process was developed (by the shippers) which essentially created an independent agency to act on behalf of the downstream shippers to validate their respective claims to gas input. The claims-validation process reconciles (after the day) shipper claims and producer statements of gas disposals to the quantity of gas determined by National Grid Gas as entering the national transmission system at the relevant entry point for each gas flow day. It also serves to match individual trades where the transfer of quantities occurs at the entry point. There are rules to adjust claims in the event of 'unders' or 'overs' and/or trade mismatches.

The claims-validation process was necessarily an after-the-day process, because of all the pre-existing upstream allocation rules that could not be changed to suit the implementation of the Network Code.

Other solutions were found at different locations that overcame this aspect. Prior to the commissioning of Bacton–Zeebrugge Interconnector, both of the connected transmission system operators at Bacton (Transco and IUK[3]) were of the view that validation of title-transfer between upstream and downstream shippers was a matter for the shippers to resolve, not the transmission system operators. This presented a considerable commercial risk to the shippers (albeit also a gaming opportunity for any unscrupulous shipper). An informal group of (upstream and downstream) shippers formed a working group and developed the Bacton Agency Arrangements in the months prior to start up (www.bactonagent.co.uk). The process differs from the claims-validation process in that it manages the matching of nominations before and during the day, and calculates shipper entitlements during periods of interruption and curtailment and allocation rules/processes for an agent to carry out in both flow directions at Bacton. By matching all trades before and during the day before the gas flows, there is no misclaimed gas, as gas only flows to satisfy pre-matched trades and nominations. This gives security to all parties in terms of allocation of gas and transfer of gas title, minimising commercial disputes (and removing gaming opportunities).

Since that time, the concept of pre-matching trades and nominations at a

1 Now National Grid Gas plc.
2 Replaced in 2005 by the Uniform Network Code.
3 Interconnector (UK) Limited.

commingled interconnection point has become established in many locations as a common business practice. The transmission system operators have largely recognised that facilitating title transfer and allocation processes is part of their service to their respective shippers.

This has been helped by the work of the transmission system operators, producers and shippers within the EASEE-gas organisation (www.easee-gas.org), which seeks to establish common business practices (CBPs) for the European gas industry by voluntary agreement of all relevant stakeholders.

Of relevance to this examination of allocation processes, common business practices have already been agreed for:

- harmonisation of nomination and matching processes;
- harmonisation of allocation information exchange;
- interconnection agreements; and
- constraints.

Helpfully, the progress of implementation of these common business practices at any and each interconnection point can be readily seen on an Interactive Map developed by GIE (Gas Infrastructure Europe – the association representing gas transmission companies, storage system operators and liquefied natural gas (LNG) terminal operators in Europe) – www.gie.1click.be.

6. Allocation agreements

As indicated above, allocation agreements are used at a variety of different points in the gas chain: upstream, midstream and downstream. There will be different commercial and technical drivers according to the type of gas system involved and the point in the gas chain. These will obviously impact what is covered in the allocation agreement and the nature and content of the allocation, attribution and/or substitution rules that it contains. The allocation agreement will also have to fit appropriately into the framework of commercial contracts between the relevant parties.

To illustrate our comments on various aspects of allocation agreements, we are going to use an example of a fairly typical upstream gas-gathering system in the UK North Sea currently servicing four offshore gas condensate fields (see diagram on next page). The offshore pipeline system and onshore gas processing plant were originally developed by the owners of fields 1 and 2. Fields 3 and 4 are newer fields which have been tied into the pipeline system subsequently. As gas production from the current fields 1 to 4 depletes, there will be ullage in both the pipeline system and the gas processing plant which could provide throughput capacity allowing other (third party) fields or new discoveries to be tied into the pipeline system. Fields 1 to 4 each produce a mixture of oil and gas; most of the oil is extracted offshore and exported via a neighbouring oil pipeline export system. However, the gas gathering system has been designed as a wet gas system and so a proportion of the liquids remains commingled within the gas stream and is delivered together with the gas to the onshore gas processing terminal. At the onshore gas terminal, natural gas liquids are extracted from the commingled gas stream and then fractionated into three separate natural gas liquid streams (propane C3, butane C4 and condensate C5+) to maximise sales value. The remaining dry gas stream is processed to meet NTS (national transmission system) entry specification and can be redelivered either to the national transmission system or piped direct to a gas-fired power station.

North Sea wet gas pipeline system

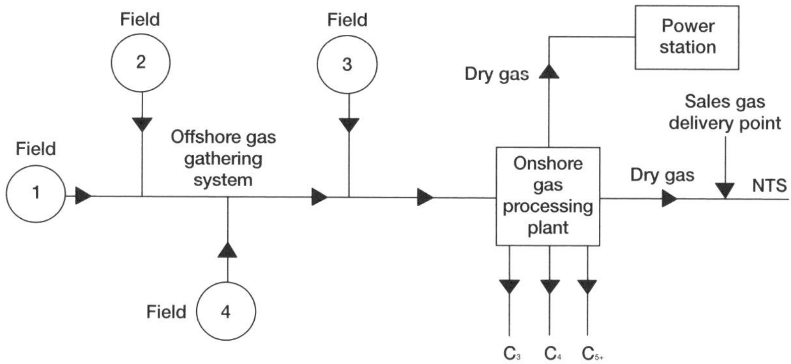

Field 1 ownership:	A 40%, B 30%, C 30%
Field 2 ownership:	A 50%, B 20%, D 30%
Field 3 ownership:	B 50%, C 50%
Field 4 ownership:	A 10%, D 20%, E 70%
Ownership of pipeline and gas processing plant	A 35%, B 27%, C 27%, D 11%

The composition of the gas streams delivered into the offshore pipeline system by fields 1 to 4 differs significantly across the four fields. The composition of gas from fields 1 and 4 is relatively lean, whilst the gas streams from field 2 and 3 are much richer and contain significantly more natural gas liquids. A component-based allocation system has been chosen to take account of these differences in composition, with a view to ensuring that the owners of the fields receive a fair and equitable proportion (of the components and resulting energy content) of each redelivery stream, to take account of their respective input contributions. The allocation agreement will need to include rules and mechanisms to enable the operator of the pipeline system and processing plant to allocate and attribute metered quantities in each redelivery stream to the users of the system (being the owners of fields 1 to 4) on a daily or hourly basis. The precise length of allocation periods will be a matter for negotiation between the parties and may be driven by their need for near-real-time data to facilitate balancing of their positions in the downstream network (in this case the national transmission system).[4]

4 History plays a part here. As an example, the original North Sea allocation agreements were primarily an after-the-day accounting process used to divide up the energy stream delivered to the monopoly buyer, British Gas, between the various gas fields and hence gas contracts. Today a downstream shipper has a need to know its allocated portion of the delivered energy in a much more timely manner, as it has to balance its downstream energy position in accordance with downstream Network Code (or equivalent) rules, which will be based on either hourly or daily balancing. Within-day (hourly or continuous) data on allocation clearly has a benefit in these situations.

Before considering the contents of the allocation agreement in more detail, it is important to consider which other commercial agreements are likely to be in place between the various parties, as the allocation agreement will have to fit into this contractual framework. The likely commercial contracts are listed below:

- There will be a joint operating agreement between the owners of each field and probably a separate lifting agreement governing the rights and obligations of each owner to lift gas from the field.
- For reasons of competition law compliance[5] (and possibly commercial reasons as well), the owners of each field will each sell their respective gas entitlements separately through individual gas sales agreements (GSAs). They have a number of choices. Typically, they could sell their gas to a third party at the entry point to the national transmission system downstream of the onshore gas processing plant or transfer it to their gas marketing affiliate at the same point. In this example, they may have a third option of negotiating a direct sale to the power station.[6]
- There will probably be a joint operating agreement between parties A, B, C and D concerning the ownership and operation of the offshore gas gathering system and the onshore gas processing plant (the system).
- Parties A, B C and D, as owners of the system, will also be parties to a transportation and processing agreement (the TPA[7]) with each set of field owners for fields 1 to 4. The transportation and processing agreement will set out the details of the service to be provided by the owners of the system to owners of the field (essentially gas export via the offshore pipeline system, processing at the onshore plant and redelivery of gas and natural gas liquids) and the tariff to be paid by the field owners for this service. There will usually be one transportation and processing agreement for each field connected to the system.
- Each of the field owners will then probably have agreements for storage, offloading and/or sale of the natural gas liquids redelivered to it.

The allocation agreement is critical to the gas sales agreements and natural gas liquid sales agreements as it will define the quantities available for sale in any time period. The administration and provision of allocation services is usually carried out by the operator of the system and would normally be included as part of the service, as defined under the transportation and processing agreement. In fact in many cases upstream allocation provisions start off as a schedule of allocation principles or an agreed allocation procedure which is included as part of the transportation and processing agreement. However, where a pipeline system and/or processing plant is being used by more than one set of users and there is more than one relevant transportation and processing agreement, the allocation rules applicable to each set

5 Joint gas sales normally involve the sellers fixing their gas sales price and therefore risk infringing Article 81 of the EC Treaty and the Chapter 1 prohibition in the UK Competition Act.

6 A direct delivery to the power station from the processing plant would have the advantage of avoiding any NTS capacity or commodity charges.

7 Not to be confused with third-party access!

of users need to be the same. The rules and mechanisms often become quite complicated with multiple fields and need to be set out in more detail in a separate allocation agreement to avoid uncertainty and to ensure all system users will be dealt with fairly under a single set of consistent rules.

Some gas buyers have historical rights to be party to the allocation agreement and would argue that they have a demonstrable need to be a party, especially where they are buying gas from more than one gas field in the commingled system under more than one gas sales agreement (and hence at differing gas prices). This was particularly the case where buyers bought gas under dedicated field-depletion contracts. Today, with most gas bought under supply contracts (ie, not depletion based), there is less argument for a buyer to want assurance and an audit trail to ensure that a particular hydrocarbon molecule originated from a particular gas field. Producers and upstream gas sellers will tend to resist gas buyers being party to the allocation agreement. There will also be a concern that gas buyers may be able to use information disclosed under allocation agreements for gas trading purposes, rather than for verifying compliance with the relevant gas sales agreement.

6.1 Allocation principles

Allocation agreements will often set out a series of allocation principles, with the intent that the detailed allocation and attribution rules should be consistent with such principles. The principles will establish the essential basis of allocation – whether based on a pro rata allocation of volumes, or on balance of energy, or on a mass component basis, or on a combination of these methods. The allocation principles may define input and output streams to be metered and may set certain metering standards.[8]

The allocation agreement is likely to set out certain other allocation principles such as:

- the allocation and attribution rules shall be fair and equitable and shall be applied by the operator to all users of the system in a non-discriminatory fashion;
- the allocation and attribution rules may be modified in accordance with the modification procedure (to improve fairness or accuracy), but no modification may be made which introduces material and/or systematic bias into the allocation process; and/or
- the basis for priority rules as between users.

6.2 Allocation/attribution priorities

It is usual for upstream gas allocation systems to be driven by the gas redelivery nominations of the system users as, particularly where gas production is the main value driver for a field, gas sales agreements are likely to be buyer nominated and gas buyers are likely to have flexible nomination rights. The system user will want to be

8 The metering standards are likely to be amplified by a substantial set of measurement provisions. Measurement and metering is a very technical area and is, of course, crucial to the accuracy and fairness of any allocation system. Measurement provisions are often contained in a schedule to the allocation agreement or sometimes in a separate measurement manual.

able to reflect his gas buyer's nomination rights under the allocation agreement and, as part of the service under the transportation and processing agreements, the system operator will be expected (by the system users) to operate the system so as to deliver in each allocation period the aggregate of users' nominations at each gas redelivery point (in this case, the power station and the national transmission system) with a high degree of accuracy. System users will not normally nominate redeliveries of specific quantities of natural gas liquids, but will be obligated to take delivery of and export from the gas processing plant (usually by pipeline) whatever quantities of natural gas liquids are allocated and attributed to them, as a result of processing the required quantity of gas to ensure that the gas nominations are met.

In determining amounts to be attributed to system users in each output stream in each allocation period, upstream allocation agreements often take into account additional criteria over and above the system users' respective inputs into the system and their nominations for gas redeliveries from it, for example:

- whether the user had booked firm transportation and processing capacity in respect of such nomination, or whether the user is relying on a reasonable endeavours (ie operationally interruptible) transportation and/or processing right; and
- whether the user's nominations were timely or were given or changed after an applicable nomination gate closure (typically this would give higher priority to nominations made on Day D-1).

The attribution rules may incorporate the above concepts into an attribution hierarchy, which is used to allocate (between the users) any shortfall or excess amounts of aggregate metered gas redelivery quantity (eg, to the national transmission system) in an allocation period as compared with users' aggregate nominations. The *raison d'être* for incorporating concepts such as firmness of transportation/processing capacity and timeliness of nominations into the attribution hierarchy is to give value to the higher cost of booking firm capacity and to incentivise users to nominate (or re-nominate) in a timely fashion.

6.3 Pipeline stock

Gas pipelines of a significant length are able to store a substantial amount of gas and can operate safely within a range of pressures and operating conditions. The ability to store gas in the offshore pipeline system as 'linepack' without immediately delivering it to the onshore gas processing plant potentially gives the users of such facilities increased flexibility and gas deliverability.

One question for the transportation and processing agreement and for the allocation agreement is whether the users of the system should be allowed to use the pipeline storage capability as part of the service they have paid for, whether they should pay extra for it, or whether the benefit of such storage capability should be reserved for the owners and the operator of the pipeline system.

Where the users are not entitled to access the pipeline's storage capability, in each allocation period their inputs into the system need to balance (on an energy basis) their offtakes from the system in gas and natural gas liquids, except where the system operator agrees otherwise. In circumstances where the users are entitled to share in the pipeline's storage capability, this is usually given effect in the allocation agreement through the concept of pipeline stock accounts.

The idea of pipeline stock accounts is to give each system user or field group the right (and obligation) to manage its own stock of gas in the pipeline within certain operational limitations. This gives each of the system user's a right to share the storage and linepack capability of the offshore pipeline system, but the responsibility to manage its stock in such a way that the system operator is able to operate it within safe operating parameters. Usually, each system user or field group will be required to establish and maintain a minimum pipeline stock and will not be entitled to allow its pipeline stock to exceed a maximum level. The allocation agreement will prescribe sanctions (probably rights for the system operator either to buy or sell gas on the system user's/field group's behalf in order to bring the relevant pipeline stock account within the permitted range), if a system user/field group breaches either its minimum or maximum limit. Provided that they remain within the permitted range, pipeline stock accounts give system users/field groups access to a share of the flexibility/linepack capability of the pipeline system. This assists system users in supporting their gas delivery obligations (eg, if their field experiences operational difficulties) and may allow users to maximise deliveries to the downstream network to meet price and demand peaks.

A similar concept has been incorporated downstream, in the contractual arrangements for users of the Bacton–Zeebrugge Interconnector. Here the shippers each 'own' and operate a share of the pipeline inventory on a pipe-within-a-pipe basis.

6.4 Substitution

The concept and purpose of substitution has been considered above (see Sections 3 and 4 of this chapter) and this fulfils a similar function to pipeline stock and may provide additional delivery support. Substitution provisions for fields connected to an offshore pipeline system are often included in the allocation agreement.

6.5 Fuel gas

The operation of the offshore pipeline system and the gas processing plant will consume fuel (eg, in gas compression, extraction and fractionation of natural gas liquids and in removal of contaminants). The allocation agreement and probably also the transportation and processing agreements will entitle the system operator to use gas from the commingled stream as fuel gas. There may also be an element of shrinkage across the system.

The allocation agreement will contain provisions for the allocation of fuel gas and shrinkage amongst the system users. Generally, this will be done pro rata to throughput during the relevant period. Where fuel gas has been consumed to remove certain contaminants from the gas stream and measurements (eg, by gas chromatograph or sampling) indicate that such contaminants have been introduced by a particular field, the allocation agreement may include provisions to enable the relevant fuel gas usage to be allocated to the owners of that field. Fuel gas and shrinkage allocation can be implemented by the system operator making an appropriate deduction from the stock accounts of all system users/field groups on a periodic basis.

6.6 Change/modification mechanisms

An allocation agreement needs to be a living document which is capable of adjustment to new circumstances, for example:

- extensions or modifications to the pipeline system or gas processing plant;
- the admission of new fields to the system; or
- the need to correct or improve metering or allocation or attribution processes.

By their very nature, allocation agreements are multi-partite agreements and some North Sea allocation agreements have up to 50 parties. This means that the modification process would be unworkable if unanimity were required for all changes. For this reason the modification provisions in an allocation agreement are very important. They will usually allow the operator to make certain (necessary) changes provided that they meet certain strict criteria. They will also allow the operator or users to propose other modifications which, subject to possible operator veto on cost/practicability grounds, will be adopted if endorsed by a specified majority of the users.

The allocation agreement may limit the type of modifications (or parts of the allocation agreement) or the grounds on which modifications may be proposed (particularly if they are not subject to a majority voting procedure). There may be requirements for all modifications that they:

- are in accordance with good oil and gas field practice relating to allocation, attribution and measurement of gas and natural gas liquid streams;
- do not introduce any material or systematic bias between the users; and
- are in accordance with the allocation principles set out elsewhere in the allocation agreement.

Whether or not modifications meet relevant criteria (which affect the basis on which they can be adopted) may, in the event of a dispute, be subject to expert determination.

6.7 Admission of new users

An allocation agreement can only work where all the users of the relevant system are bound by its terms. Accordingly, there needs to be a failsafe mechanism for the admission of new users, in the event of the admission of a new field to the system or the acquisition of an interest in an existing field by a company which is not currently a party to the allocation agreement. This can be achieved relatively easily from a drafting perspective and the operator will usually have the right to sign (on behalf of all existing users) an accession agreement with any new user. There is also likely to be a mechanism for users to retire from the allocation agreement once they have ceased using the system.

6.8 Cutback rules

One important issue in transportation and processing agreements and in allocation agreements is what happens if there is an operational event which reduces capacity in all or a part of the pipeline system or the processing plant. How will the remaining capacity be allocated and used? It is important that the 'cutback rules' are applied in a non-discriminatory fashion to all users of the relevant system. For this reason such cutback rules will often be set out in the allocation agreement, rather than in individual transportation and processing agreements.

There is a limited range of typical options for cutback rules. Where a particular incident or capacity constraint can be shown (at the time) to have been caused by a particular field, the operator may be permitted/required to target the cutback at the owners of that field. Where blame cannot be attributed to particular users, in most cases the remaining capacity will be allocated to users pro rata to the amount of firm capacity they hold (ie interruptible or reasonable-endeavours capacity will be cut back first). Among firm capacity holders, an allocation agreement may provide for remaining capacity to be allocated to users pro rata to their firm nominations on the first day of the cutback and only to default to pro rata to firm capacity if the capacity constraint continues into a second day.

6.9 Allocation and attributions algorithms

Gas and oil allocation and attribution systems will be computerised. Often computer programmers will be busy writing the computer program at the same time as the parties and their lawyers are negotiating and drafting the allocation agreement. It is obviously important that the two match up accurately or else the operator will not be able to apply the allocation rules in the allocation agreement. This means that the person who is directing the IT part of the project needs to have substantial input into the allocation agreement. It helps if the main negotiator of the allocation agreement is in control of both processes and has considerable technical expertise. Some or all of the detailed allocation and attribution algorithms used in the computer process are often set out in a schedule to the allocation agreement. In the authors' experience, it is also helpful on occasion to attach as a schedule a description of the mathematical model on which the allocation and attribution processes are based.

6.10 Contamination liabilities/cross-user liability agreements

One characteristic of a multi-field pipeline and/or processing system which needs to be considered, is the possibility of off-specification gas being injected into the system. In many cases, this may not be too problematic, as by its nature a multi-field system has significant blending capability (assuming all or most fields are producing). However special processing equipment may be required to deal with particular contaminants (eg, H_2S, Mercury, CO_2, mercaptons) and the costs of installing and operating this equipment ought to be targeted at the right users/fields. This can be dealt with to a minor extent by rules on fuel gas in the allocation agreement (see Section 6.5 above), but it is really an issue for negotiation and debate in the transportation and processing agreements and possibly specific agreements dealing with removal of known contaminants.

Real problems may occur where unexpected quantities of a known contaminant or an unexpected contaminant are injected into a pipeline or processing system. This can lead to the whole commingled stream becoming contaminated and failing to meet downstream specifications. In turn, the system may need to be purged, resulting in loss of the pipeline stock and also in considerable downtime for the system.

The liabilities as between field groups and the system owners for off-specification gas will usually be dealt with by cross-indemnities in each relevant transportation and processing agreement. The field owners will indemnify the system owners in respect of losses under specified heads of damage caused by the field owners injecting off-specification gas. The system owners will in turn indemnify the field owners in respect of off-specification redeliveries of sales gas, but such indemnity will usually be disapplied where the relevant field or another field has injected off-specification gas into the system in breach of its transportation and processing agreement.

The transportation and processing agreements do not regulate liabilities for off-specification gas as between users in different fields and therefore there is a possibility that, given sufficient evidence, one user group could sue another user group in tort (presumably negligence) in respect of an off-specification incident. Some pipeline systems require all users to enter into a cross-user liability agreement (CULA) to address this issue. Often cross-user liability agreements will set up a 'hold harmless' framework between users to prevent such tort claims, save where the incident has been caused by wilful misconduct or sometimes gross negligence (such terms to be defined in the cross-user liability agreement).

In the event of an off-specification incident caused by wilful misconduct or gross negligence, the cross-user liability agreement will usually require the recalcitrant user(s) to indemnify the innocent users up to a specified aggregate limit. This effectively substitutes a direct contractual remedy for any possible tort claims and imposes a higher requirement as to culpability than normal negligence. The cross-user liability agreement will also have to deal with the claims process and what happens if the aggregate limit is exceeded.

Gas balancing agreements

Maine Stephan Goodfellow
George F Goolsby
Baker Botts LLP

1. Introduction

Gas balancing agreements represent the oil and gas industry's response to the gap between expectation and reality arising from the model form of joint operating agreement's expectation that each owner in the well will make a reasonable, good- faith effort to take and dispose of its full share of natural gas production as produced and the reality that, so long as each owner markets his own gas, short-term, periodic, long-term and even permanent imbalances will arise. Given the evolution of natural gas markets in the United States and the complexities involved in individually marketing gas production, it should come as little surprise that gas imbalances frequently arise. And, given the substantial perceived value a producer places on the right to market its own share of gas production, there is little prospect that the imbalance issue will soon fade away.[1]

1 While it is beyond the scope of this chapter to discuss the evolution of natural gas marketing in the United States over the last 50 years, suffice it to say that until federal deregulation of interstate sales for resale by producers of natural gas and the related unbundling of interstate pipeline services, which occurred primarily during the period 1978 through 1985, gas imbalances occurred less frequently. Greatly simplifying, until these regulatory changes occurred, producers who sold gas destined to cross state boundary lines were required to make those sales for the life of the production to whichever interstate pipeline served that production area. The interstate pipelines were merchants, serving as wholesalers which purchased and resold huge quantities of gas. Interstate pipelines were often the sole market for the gas, and all of the producers in the well, unit or field typically sold to that interstate pipeline. While the producers might have separate contracts, typically the interstate pipeline purchaser took in proportion to ownership, so imbalances among those selling to the same interstate pipeline were relatively rare. It was possible, from time to time, for a producer to make so-called 'direct sales' to an industrial end user, but as a general matter the interstate pipelines were merchants only and were not in the business of transporting gas to be sold by producers to end users or local distribution companies. Instead, the interstate pipelines themselves served those markets by reselling gas they purchased from more-or-less captive producers to more-or-less captive end-users and local distribution companies served by that interstate pipeline. Imbalances occurred when the source of supply (eg, well, unit or field) had a separate pipeline connection to intrastate markets – that is, markets within the state where the natural gas was produced or, more rarely, when there was but one pipeline purchasing under differing terms. Assuming that steps were taken from the outset of production to keep the production stream going in *intrastate* commerce contractually and physically separate from that going in *interstate* commerce, producers in states such as Texas and Louisiana, in particular, could sell gas within those states at unregulated prices, sometimes to intrastate pipelines and, less often, to other intrastate customers. Thus, imbalances could arise in a true 'split stream' context where both an interstate pipeline and an intrastate pipeline served the same source of supply and the several producers chose to market to each of them. After wellhead deregulation and the unbundling of interstate pipeline services, the interstate pipelines (as, in time, the intrastate pipelines) were no longer the mega-wholesalers of gas, but abandoned the merchant function in favour of being solely transportation service providers. Over time, marketing companies of various types and affiliations entered the void created in the market, with the result that producers could sell directly to markets of their choice or they could sell to a number of marketing companies who, in turn, developed a sales market with various end-users and local distribution companies along the route of one or more pipelines who connect the source of supply with that sales market. Some producers and interstate pipelines have set up marketing affiliates by which to aggregate and market gas; independent marketing companies are also common. The upshot is that in today's marketplace there are numerous ways to market gas and numerous counterparties, so that individual producer marketing means, almost by definition, that imbalances will occur.

The issue of gas imbalances involves laws dealing with rights in real property, personal property rights and contract law. Under the laws of many states in the United States, if there are multiple lessees under a lease, each of the lessees is typically classified as a co-tenant, with each co-tenant owning and having the right to take and dispose of its percentage share of the natural gas as it is produced from the lease. But co-tenancy law alone provides an unsatisfactory basis upon which to proceed without taking into account oil and gas industry requirements. As a result, the industry developed forms of joint operating agreements which, together with industry experience, have further defined how each producer shares in the common production stream and, if necessary, accounts to its co-producers for any takes it may make in excess of its share.[2]

While the producers of a lease, unit or well share in a 'cost project' when they agree to operate under a joint operating agreement, at least in the United States they do not often elect to share in a revenue project through, for example, the joint marketing of the full natural gas stream as a group. Instead, each producer is entitled to receive in kind its share of production when produced, as its percentage share is recorded on Exhibit A to the typical joint operating agreement. As explained later in this chapter, in addition to the benefits each producer receives from being able to market its share of gas for its own account, under United States law joint marketing has historically triggered undesirable federal tax impacts which further encouraged individual, rather than joint, marketing of production. It also implicates antitrust concerns if not properly structured. The result is that, with exceptions, industry practice has been for each producer to own its share of gas production as and when produced and exercise the individual right to market as it sees fit. Rather than jointly market at the producer level, a more common practice has been for a larger producer, through its marketing affiliate, to purchase production from other co-producers. Such an arrangement may or may not mitigate wellhead imbalances, depending upon the terms and provisions of the gas purchase arrangement, how long that arrangement remains in place, and how many co-producers from the common source are selling to the marketer under the same or similar terms.

Professor Pat Martin has observed that the production imbalance problem arises from the fact that most state laws (and especially those for pooling or unitising multiple leases into one tract for drilling purposes), coupled with the provisions of the joint operating agreements developed over time by the industry, do not follow either a 'true co-tenancy' or 'capture' philosophy.[3] In fact, they establish a hybrid approach. In a true co-tenancy, each co-tenant has an undivided ownership right in

---

2 The producer's share of production depends upon the facts, but ultimately is expressed as a fractional or percentage share as shown on an exhibit to the joint operating agreement. For example, the 1989 AAPL Form 610 Model Form Operating Agreement records that information for all parties on Exhibit "A" and Article III.B declares that:
"B. Interests of Parties in Costs and Production:
Unless changed by other provisions, all costs and liabilities incurred in operations under this agreement shall be borne and paid, and all equipment and materials acquired in operations on the Contract Area shall be owned, by the parties as their interests are set forth in Exhibit 'A.' In the same manner, the parties shall also own all production of Oil and Gas from the Contract Area subject, however, to the payment of royalties and other burdens on production as described hereafter."

3 Patrick H Martin, *The Gas Balancing Agreement: What, When, Why, and How*, 36 Rocky Mtn. Min. L. Inst. 13-7 to 13-10 (1990).

each molecule, such that any sale of the natural gas is, by definition, a sale for the benefit of all of the owners of the natural gas stream, regardless of who makes the sale. While each co-tenant may have individual discretion to enter into a sales agreement, if it does so the co-tenant acts for all and must account to all when it makes the sale. Under such an ownership approach, there cannot be a production imbalance, simply because each co-tenant owns each and every molecule. At most, there can be a failure of the selling co-tenant to account properly to the other co-tenants for the proceeds of the sale.[4] At the other end of the spectrum, a true 'capture' approach presupposes that each producer has the right to produce and take its allocable share, but when another co-producer fails to take its own share, that share is forfeited, abandoned or otherwise lost to the first producer – which, in fact, takes and markets the natural gas for its own account. Again, no *production* imbalance arises, simply because all production is accounted for as produced – all of it becomes the property of the one that actually takes and markets the gas stream for its own account. And no accounting to the other co-producers is required because 'capture' presupposes that only by actually taking one's share of the gas stream does one acquire personal property rights in the resultant production.[5]

Given an underlying legal, contractual and natural gas marketing regime where production imbalances very likely will arise whenever there are multiple owners of a common source of supply, what happens when one of the co-owners, for whatever reason, either chooses, or fails in its efforts, to take and market its allocated share? This chapter will briefly discuss that issue by focusing attention on three questions. First, what must parties to a joint operating agreement consider when planning for the contingency that their respective shares of natural gas production may go out of balance during the life of the common source of production. Secondly, how do gas balancing agreements address the problem and what limits, if any, exist on the co-producers' ability to agree contractually on the terms of a gas balancing agreements? And, finally, what are the implications of the answers to the first two questions on the use of natural gas balancing agreements in jurisdictions other than the United States?

2. Anticipating and addressing gas imbalances

Given multiple owners and the vagaries of individual marketing, gas production imbalances often arise during the productive life of a well.[6] As previously described, an imbalance arises when parties to a joint operating agreement or similar arrangement take and sell natural gas disproportionately to their ownership in the well, unit or field. In industry parlance, the party which sells more natural gas than its ownership share is 'overproduced', and the party which sells less than its ownership share is 'underproduced'. Imbalances arise in different ways and in different contexts, sometimes by design but often by happenstance.[8] As Professor

---

4 *Ibid* at 13-9.
5 *Ibid.*
6 Ernest E Smith and Jacqueline L Weaver, *Texas Law of Oil and Gas* §17.6, at 17-51 (Bender 2007).
7 *Ibid.*
8 Patrick H Martin, *The Gas Balancing Agreement: What, When, Why, and How*, 36 Rocky Mtn Min L Inst 13-7–13-10 (1990).

Martin has observed, how imbalances arise certainly affects people's attitudes about whether to enter into a gas balancing agreement and what terms should be included.[9] For example, there may be two pipelines connected to the same source of supply, each of which is taking gas at different rates. This is a true 'split stream' scenario where there is little or no sense that the overproduced or underproduced party is at fault. Similarly, even where there is only one connecting pipeline, the pipeline may refuse to take natural gas from all the parties in the field or unit, or from one of the co-tenants in a well.[10]

The equities in these situations differ from others, however. Contrast the above situations with the situation when a party simply decides that in its opinion current natural gas prices are too low and, as a result, it elects not to sell its share on a current basis. By delaying its takes, it hopes to sell in a better market. But its action has implications for all of the co-lessees with respect to the duty to market under the lease. Given this duty, the other co-owners may not be willing forgo their own takes, choke back production or shut the well and risk liability to the lessor for failing to market and risk harm to the well if production is shut in. In the meantime the non-taking co-owner does not mind that the other producers are selling the gas, especially if that co-owner has the benefit of a gas balancing agreement, because the balancing agreement allows the co-owner to 'store' its gas, and the ongoing sale by the other co-owners satisfies the lease requirements and avoids choking back production and risking harm to ultimate recovery from the well.[11]

A variation of this scenario is the owner who wishes to make seasonal sales in a market where winter prices (for heating loads) or summer prices (for cooling loads) are historically higher than off-season prices in the marketplace. The perceived inequity in these arrangements is that only some, but not all, of the co-owners can use that strategy, and will resent this manipulation all the more if, indeed, the market is better and by manipulation the delayed taker gets a better price. If, however, the market does not turn out to be so favourable, the non-taker may further delay or forgo its takes, especially if the gas balancing agreement provides for cash balancing, with the result that the non-taker may demand monetary compensation from the other owners out of their proceeds. This 'heads I win, tails you lose' approach can often lead to significant discussion among co-owners seeking to negotiate gas balancing terms that are fair and evenhanded to all parties. As will be seen, many agreements specifically bar this kind of manipulation.

Still other reasons that production imbalances may arise do not have the same

---

9 *Ibid.*

10 See *Transcontinental Gas Pipeline Corp. v State Oil & Gas Board*, 457 So.2d 1298 (Miss. 1984), rev'd, 474 U.S. 409, 550 (1986), and *Transcontinental Gas Pipe Line Corp. v American National Petroleum Co.*, 763 S.W.2nd 809 (Tex. App. 1988).

11 To elaborate, many leases do not contain so-called shut-in royalty provisions by which all of the lessees could decide to shut in all production and simply pay an 'in lieu of' payment to the lessor. Even if the lease has such a provision, shutting in wells during periods when prices are low could have deleterious effects for the well and, therefore, lead to a claim of failure by the lessees to act as prudent operators. Finally, when the well is an oil well producing associated gas, the oil has paramount value and it is not possible to shut in gas production. As a result, only some, but not all, of the producers can typically make the election to go underproduced, thus exacerbating the negative reaction of the taking producers to one of their number electing to play the market at their expense.

danger of inequity: through no fault of the producer, the pipeline could be delayed in connecting to the source of supply, the pipeline could experience a *force majeure* event, or the pipeline could be otherwise unavailable.[12] Finally, the relative size of the producers could be a factor, as when one owner is dominant in a field and smaller co-owners have difficulty in marketing their shares of the gas stream.[13] As with any decision to contract, the parties should carefully consider the circumstances to determine how best to address the imbalance contingency without creating opportunities for undue gamesmanship.

Imbalances can be resolved in two ways: balancing in kind and cash balancing.[14] Balancing in kind allows for the underproduced party to make up his share by temporarily increasing production at the expense of current takes by the overproduced party.[15] On the other hand, cash balancing requires the overproduced party to pay the underproduced party (either periodically or at well depletion) for the underproduced party's share of the gas the overproduced party produced and sold.[16]

3. Gas balancing in relation to the joint operating agreement

Before examining the terms which might be included in a gas balancing agreement, we should first be clear about what the main articles in a typical joint operating agreement provide regarding the working interest owners' rights and the ability of the operator to avoid or mitigate the imbalance problem. In the United States the most commonly encountered form of joint operating agreement is one of the four forms promulgated over the years by the American Association of Petroleum Landmen, or AAPL. Commonly known as AAPL Form 610, this document exists in 1956, 1977, 1982 and 1989 versions. Among other provisions that differ among these four forms is that pertaining to 'Taking Production in Kind', which appears in Article VI of these forms. For illustrative purposes reference is made to Article VI.H of the APPL Form 610 Model Form Operating Agreement (1989) entitled "Taking Production in Kind: No Gas Balancing Agreement". To be clear, subarticle H (no gas balancing agreement) is an alternative to subarticle G of that form, which is used

12 The emphasis on 'through no fault of the producer' is important because producers sometimes hope to move their gas on the pipeline using cheaper 'interruptible' service rather than paying for more expensive 'firm' service. If, as a practical matter, only firm service gas actually moves on the pipeline, the result is that the producer who contracted for interruptible service will not be taking its share. One would then assume that the other producers are taking the imbalance under the gas balancing agreement, but whether that is true depends upon what maximum firm service volume they contracted for with the pipeline. If they contracted for only their percentage share of production, the pipeline may not take the extra imbalance gas, with the result that the producers may be required to limit that production for the month. Not surprisingly, none of the producers will be pleased with this situation, and those which contracted for firm transportation service will be particularly displeased with the one which did not.

13 Some states regulate pipelines subject to their jurisdiction by requiring the pipeline to take in proportion, or to be a so-called 'common purchaser' of gas. The statutes can be of assistance to a smaller-interest owner or owner of a single well which is having difficulty finding a market or pipeline connection. Texas has both such regulatory provisions, albeit that there have been only a handful of contested proceedings under the common-purchaser statute. Given high demand for natural gas, this problem is now less significant.

14 See Smith and Weaver § 17.6 at 17-53.

15 *Ibid* at 17-52.

16 *Ibid* at 17-53.

when the parties have agreed upon and attached a form of gas balancing agreement as Exhibit E.[17] In the 1989 version, when the parties have elected to use a gas balancing agreement pursuant to subarticle G, the gas balancing agreement contains all of the terms for gas and the text of subarticle G itself relates solely to imbalances of oil. In contrast, if the parties elect not to have a gas balancing agreement, subarticle H addresses both oil and gas and provides as follows:

"H. Taking Production in Kind (No Gas Balancing Agreement):

Each party shall take in kind or separately dispose of its proportionate share of all Oil and Gas produced from the Contract Area, exclusive of production which may be used in development and producing operations and in preparing and treating Oil and Gas for marketing purposes and production unavoidably lost. Any extra expenditure incurred in the taking in kind or separate disposition by any party of its proportionate share of the production shall be borne by such party. Any party taking its share of production in kind shall be required to pay for only its proportionate share of such part of Operator's surface facilities which it uses.

Each party shall execute such division orders and contracts as may be necessary for the sale of its interest in production from the Contract Area, and, except as provided in Article VII.B., shall be entitled to receive payment directly from the purchaser thereof for its share of all production.

If any party fails to make the arrangements necessary to take in kind or separately dispose of its proportionate share of the Oil and/or Gas produced from the Contract Area, Operator shall have the right, subject to the revocation at will by the party owning it, but not the obligation, to purchase such Oil and/or Gas or sell it to others at any time and from time to time, for the account of the non-taking party. Any such purchase or sale by Operator may be terminated by Operator upon at least ten (10) days written notice to the owner of said production and shall be subject always to the right of the owner of the production upon at least ten (10) days written notice to Operator to exercise its right to take in kind, or separately dispose of, its share of all Oil and/or Gas not previously delivered to a purchaser; provided, however, that the effective date of any such revocation may be deferred at Operator's election for a period not to exceed ninety (90) days if Operator has committed such production to a purchase contract having a term extending beyond such ten (10)-day period. Any purchase or sale by Operator of any other party's share of Oil and/or Gas shall be only for such reasonable periods of time as are consistent with the minimum needs of the industry under the particular circumstances, but in no event for a period in excess of one (1) year.

Any such sale by Operator shall be in a manner commercially reasonable under the circumstances, but Operator shall have no duty to share any existing market or transportation arrangement or to obtain a price of transportation fee equal to that received under any existing market or transportation arrangement. The sale or delivery by Operator of a non-taking party's share of production under the terms of any existing contract of Operator shall not give the non-taking party any interest in or make the non-taking party a party to said contract. No purchase of Oil and Gas and no sale of Gas

---

17 It is not mandatory that the gas balancing agreement be made an exhibit. A separately signed gas balancing agreement will also suffice for purposes of the 1989 version.

shall be made by Operator without first giving the non-taking party ten days written notice of such intended purchase or sale and the price to be paid or the pricing basis to be used. Operator shall give notice to all parties of the first sale of Gas from any well under this Agreement.

All parties shall give timely written notice to Operator of their Gas marketing arrangements for the following month, excluding price, and shall notify Operator immediately in the event of a change in such arrangements. Operator shall maintain records of all marketing arrangements, and of volumes actually sold or transported, which records shall be made available to Non-Operators under reasonable request."

Note that while a fair amount of detail is included in this provision, it still leaves many questions unanswered and engenders uncertainty respecting potential imbalances. Indeed, the only remedy is the invitation to the operator either to purchase the imbalance volumes or to market those volumes on behalf of the non-taker. But the operator has the option, and not the duty, to step in and take the excess gas in his role as operator. Specifically, the operator is granted limited authority (but does not have the obligation) to take possession of the oil and natural gas production of any party who does not plan to take its share of current production and either (i) purchase that share of production or (ii) market the hydrocarbons on behalf of the non-taking party.[18] By so doing, an imbalance is avoided because the operator's actions provide an alternative way for the party who has not made plans to take its share to rely on the operator to take and dispose of its share of the hydrocarbons on a current basis. Significantly, however, the operator's authority to market for the non-operator is limited by the terms of the joint operating agreement. These limitations derive from industry practice and are shaped by two federal tax rulings.[19]

To comply with the tax requirements, the joint operating agreement states that the operator's authority to purchase or sell is revocable and is limited to a reasonable period, not to exceed one year.[20] More fundamentally, however, many operators will not opt to take any excess production under this provision because of two very significant risks: first, under the 'on behalf of' provision, the operator acts as agent for the owner and may be subject to fiduciary duties that make acting as the non-taker's agent legally unacceptable; and secondly, controversies about whether the price the operator paid (if it purchases the gas) or received (if it markets the gas on behalf of the non-operator) are quite common. For these reasons, a careful operator will refuse to exercise its rights as operator under this provision unless it enters into

---

18 Eugene Kuntz, *Gas Balancing Rights and Remedies in the Absence of a Balancing Agreement*, 35 Rocky Mtn Min L Inst. 13-16 (1989); see also AAPL, Form 610 art VI(G)).

19 If the operator does not limit its marketing to the terms specified in the joint operating agreement by, for example, violating the rule against marketing beyond the one-year period stated in the agreement, the parties who are involved in the sale risk being taxed as an association taxable as a corporation (I.T. 3930, 1948–2 C.B. 126; I.T. 3948, 1949–1 C.B. 161). Simply stated, the parties involved in the sale could be treated as if they have formed a type of business association which is taxed as if a separate corporation owned by them is making the sale. The result is to create an extra layer or level of federal taxation: their 'corporation' pays taxes and, once they receive their individual proceeds from their 'corporation', they are taxed again on what they receive. There have been changes to the tax code which, if used, avoid this result, but the failure to realise that these kinds of tax structuring decisions must be made can prove costly.

20 Kuntz, at 13-17.

a separate written agreement with the non-taking party which addresses these and other issues in detail. Still, if such arrangements are in place, the purchase or sale by operator provisions can avoid short-term or episodic imbalances.[21]

Because an operator typically owns an interest in the well, it may elect not to take and market the gas *in its role as operator* under the above-described provision and may instead, *in its role as a co-producer and for its own account*, take some or all of the excess gas. In that case, an imbalance arises and the operator is simply an overproduced party. But this true imbalance arises only when the operator purports to take and sell the available share of gas as its own.[22] As previously mentioned, when the operator does elect to purchase from or sell on the non-operator's behalf, there is no production imbalance but the operator risks becoming embroiled in disputes, most typically about the price to be paid to or settled with the non-operator.[23]

Again, when subarticle H of the 1989 AAPL Model Form 610 is chosen and the parties have not entered into a gas balancing agreement, their rights are determined primarily by the terms of the joint operating agreement and underlying state law principles of co-tenancy.[24] Certainly, this subarticle of the 1989 AAPL Model Form 610 does not provide for the many contingencies that could arise when oil or gas production gets out of balance.[25] Among other obvious deficiencies is that the joint operating agreement does not specify whether an imbalance will be corrected by balancing in kind, periodic cash balancing, or cash balancing at well depletion. Indeed, it is absolutely silent on the matter.

4. Balancing in kind versus cash balancing

Although there is a paucity of case law on the subject, when there is a joint operating agreement but no gas balancing agreement specifying a remedy, some courts have held that balancing in kind is the preferred method of resolving an imbalance: *Pogo Producing Co. v Shell*, 898 F.2d 1064, 1067 (5th Cir. 1990) (holding that Pogo was not entitled as an underproduced party to demand cash balancing simply because it was unable to market its share of gas, at least as long as the well was not near depletion); and *Doheny v Wexpro Co.*, 974 F.2d 130, 133 (6th Cir. 1992). The court in *Pogo* recognised, however, that there may be situations when balancing in kind may be inequitable, such as when insufficient reserves remain for the underproduced party to make up its share of production before depletion, or when well allowables or other regulatory constraints restrict total production such that achieving a zero balance

---

21 Note that Louisiana law provides that its state agency has the authority to require one party to take and dispose of gas for another party to protect correlative rights (*Amoco Production Company v Thompson*, 615 So.2d 376 La. Ct. App. 1987).

22 Smith and Weaver §17.6 at 17-52.

23 *Ibid.* See also *Holloway v Atlantic Richfield Co.*, 970 S.W.2d 641 (Tex. App.–Tyler 1998, no pet.) (dispute over the 'best price obtainable in the area', which was the standard contained in the 1977 and 1982 versions of the AAPL Model Form 610). Note that typical industry practice is when parties are overproducing, they do so in proportion to their ownership interests. Similarly, when there is more than one underproduced party and both wish to make up, they do so in proportion to their ownership interests.

24 Smith and Weaver §17.6 at 17-51.

25 *Ibid.*

through balancing in kind would be impossible. Again, these are situations when no gas balancing agreement is in place and underproduced parties were seeking relief based solely on the terms of the joint operating agreement and state-law co-tenancy principles. The principal benefit of balancing in kind is that it best preserves the underproduced parties' ability to perform in the manner originally intended, namely taking and selling their share of the natural gas for their own account. As will be seen, numerous difficulties attend cash balancing, so it is not surprising that finding a way for the underproduced party to receive gas in kind is the preferred method.[26]

Cash balancing is the second means to resolve imbalances, but cash balancing also presents problems in achieving an equitable result.[27] Certainly, when there is no gas balancing agreement, neither the overproduced parties nor a court will be keen to allow the underproduced party to play the market for gas by, for example, delaying its takes of production in a rising market to obtain higher profits later.[28] Quite aside from the equities involved in how the imbalance was created, the most fundamental issues in cash balancing are the price to be paid to the underproduced party to compensate for its loss of production and when that payment is made. In putting together a gas balancing agreement that calls for cash balancing, numerous price bases can be argued. The settlement price could be (i) the price actually received by the overproduced party at the time the imbalance volumes were sold; (ii) the price received most recently by the overproduced party; (iii) the market value at the time of sale or current market value; or (iv) the best price obtainable in the area at the time of sale or currently.[29]

One problem with requiring a settlement using the price actually received by the overproduced party is that it gives the underproduced party the benefit of the overproduced party's market, which may be superior to that of the non-taker and may indeed have motivated the non-taker's decision not to take. Additionally, using actual sales proceeds is intrusive, requiring the overproduced party to reveal much about his internal business and marketing affairs, some of which may be confidential. So long as the sales data is historic, no antitrust issues are likely; but using current data in a real-time situation could also raise antitrust concerns. Lastly, if the overproduced party is selling to its own marketing affiliate or if there are other post-production costs paid to affiliates for treating and gathering, determining the price actually received by the overproduced party in order to make the calculation can become a point of controversy, much as it is with royalty owners under 'proceeds' type leases. Using an objective market-value approach in the absence of direct reference to index prices or other specific market data runs great risk of disagreement.

Comparability has long been an issue with any market-value type of

---

26 While it is rare, there are gas balancing agreements which provide that underproduction can be made up from sources of supply owned by the overproduced party other than the well or unit from which the imbalance was created. Quite aside from the practicalities of using gas from other leases for this purpose, such an approach raises concerns about how the royalty obligations are to be met on the second lease when gas is used to settle imbalances on the first lease.

27 See Smith and Weaver §17.6 at 17-53 to 17-54.

28 *Ibid* at 17-54. See also *United Petroleum Exploration, Inc. v Premier Resources, Ltd.*, 511 F. Supp. 127 (W.D. Okla. 1980) (ordering immediate cash balancing based on the price received by the operator).

29 *Ibid.*

determination. In addition, while using index prices or other similar posted prices is recommended, some producers may be reluctant to agree on an objective standard for fear that the settlement value may be higher than the amount per unit they actually received. Of course, if the gas was sold using the same index pricing, this concern is avoided. But regardless of the pricing basis chosen, in the senior writer's experience no producer will intend to agree to pay out more than it actually received for the imbalance volumes absent extraordinary circumstances. That is also why a producer might object to using current values instead of tying the value to the time when the imbalance occurred. While it is true that the overproduced party will have received the time value of the proceeds since the sale, most producers will not perceive that time value benefit as justifying a risk of settling on a price basis higher than what they received. Mention has previously been made of using a standard such as 'the best price obtainable in the area' in the context of operator purchases of excess gas under Article VI.H of the 1989 AAPL Model Form. Certainly, that standard may give rise to disagreement about access to and the quality of the database, and whether the sale is comparable to the subject situation. If that is tied to publicly available index prices however, those issues are mitigated.

The timing of cash balancing payments (either immediate, periodic, or at depletion) can also be disputed.[30] Immediate cash payments run the risk of appearing as a backdoor means of joint marketing, depending on the circumstances. They also beg the question of whether any form of resumed takes or in-kind balancing will be available to resolve the imbalance in preference to cash balancing. Periodic payments do have the benefit of keeping the absolute magnitude of imbalances in check. In addition, some producers prefer to settle the matter all at once rather than piecemeal, especially if price is a contentious issue. Cash balancing after the reservoir has been reduced to the point that balancing in kind can no longer resolve the problem appeals to many, but some argue that by that relatively late point in the life of the well it makes more sense to wait until depletion has occurred and simply settle up in one transaction. As practical as that sounds, however, one should keep in mind the risk that the dollar amount owed could be significant, that time value concepts may not be fully compensated for, and that often the debt is an unsecured debt of the overproduced party. Thus, credit risk issues are magnified if the imbalance volumes are significant and depletion is years away. At bottom, waiting until depletion to settle accounts runs the risk that the overproduced party may be unable to satisfy a large cash liability.[31] If that risk is substantial, an immediate or periodic cash balancing may be preferable. In addition or in the alternative, the producers could grant each other security interests in their respective interests in the well or the proceeds of sale, but if it is a one-well property that is depleted, such security may be of limited value.

5. Addressing risks through a gas balancing agreement

Despite issues attending in-kind and cash balancing, doing without a balancing

30 Smith and Weaver §17.6 at 17-53 to 17-54.
31 *Ibid* at 17-55.

agreement is unwise. The failure to agree on gas balancing terms when the parties enter into a joint operating agreement or before production begins means that no-one is sure what will happen if accounts go out of balance and an underproduced party is left to scramble for a remedy under a number of legal theories. While most of the cases deal with various contractual and co-tenancy theories, it should be borne in mind that tort theories could also be asserted, such as conversion or intentional interference with contracts, in an attempt to recover the value of underproduction. Thus, as a practical matter, it is seldom wise to proceed without a gas balancing agreement that makes clear in advance the parties' rights in the event of an imbalance.

By entering into gas balancing agreements the parties to a joint operating agreement can displace whatever result might otherwise occur in the absence of agreement by specifying in advance the method by which imbalances will be resolved.[32] In doing so, the parties avoid leaving the determination of their rights to statutory, common law or equitable principles, or to a silent, vague or inadequate joint operating agreement.[33] A gas balancing agreement is like other contracts typically used in the oil and gas industry, in that it requires the parties to anticipate problems and allocate the risk and responsibility for those problems to the appropriate party.[34]

6. Model form agreements

The American Association of Professional Landmen (AAPL), the Rocky Mountain Mineral Law Foundation (RMMLF), and the Association of International Petroleum Negotiators (AIPN) all publish forms of gas balancing agreements.[35]

As previously discussed, the AAPL Form 610 Model Form Operating Agreement (1989) includes two options for the parties to consider respecting imbalances. As the first choice, under Article VI.G the main articles address only oil imbalances because under that election the parties agree to enter into a gas balancing agreement, either as Exhibit E or by separate agreement. Note that the Article VI.G option is nothing more than an agreement to agree to a gas balancing agreement unless and until the parties actually attach or enter into a gas balancing agreement (*Pogo*, 898 F.2d at 1065–66). The district judge in *Pogo* found that even though the parties may well have intended to use the AAPL form of gas balancing agreement by including Article

32 Smith and Weaver § 17.6 at 17-57.

33 *Ibid.*

34 36 Rocky Mtn Min L Inst 13-1, 13-50 (1990).

35 The AAPL publishes AAPL Form 10-E, the Rocky Mountain Mineral Law Foundation publishes Form 6, and the AIPN includes a gas balancing option in its Joint Operating Agreement. See Mark D Christiansen, "A Comparison of the Model Form Gas Balancing Agreements - Catching up with a Changing Market Environment" (40 Rocky Mtn. Min. L. Inst. 16-1 (1994)) (discussing differences between the AAPL and Rocky Mountain forms). The senior author of this chapter well remembers how, in 1975, as a new lawyer, he was given as one of his first assignments the task of drafting from scratch a gas balancing agreement that would be used by several small producer clients. While more senior lawyers could describe the purpose of such an agreement and some of its possible mechanics, there simply were no published forms at the time and what versions existed tended to be company proprietary versions. Certainly, there were no expert committees who had carefully thought through the issues to produce an industry form, and experience with gas imbalances was much more limited. A debt of gratitude is owed to AAPL, RMMLF and AIPN for their contributions in developing the modern forms.

VI.G, in the absence of an actual gas balancing agreement, the general preference for balancing in kind applied because the parties had not effectively contracted for cash balancing. The second choice under the 1989 AAPL Form 610 is to elect to use Article VI.H which, as previously discussed, pertains to both oil and gas and does not include a gas balancing agreement. That election basically addresses imbalances solely by reference to the authority of the operator to mitigate the problem, if it so elects, by either purchasing the imbalance volume or marketing it on behalf of the non-taking producer.

Perhaps the most complete form of gas balancing agreement is the AAPL Model Form Gas Balancing Agreement (Form 610-E) (1992). That agreement requires that each party to the joint operating agreement make a reasonable, good-faith effort to take its full share of production to the extent necessary to maintain the subject leases in effect, to protect the producing capacity of the well or reservoir, to preserve correlative rights, and to maintain oil production when gas is produced in association with oil.[36] Note that compliance with each of these duties serves as the predicate for a party's right to seek the agreed remedies for an imbalance. We have previously discussed, for example, that it is essential to produce the well to maintain the lease and in a manner which protects its productivity capacity. Similarly, the reference to preserving correlative rights (ie, each party's right to take from the common source) underscores the intent to provide a fair opportunity for all owners to enjoy the benefits of ownership to the extent of their interest in the common source. And, finally, the reference to maintaining oil production when gas is produced in association with oil emphasises the economics of the situation and countenances production by some, even if other producers cannot currently take their shares of oil and gas as produced.

As with Article VI.H, the form of gas balancing agreement authorises the operator, *at the operator's option*, to take a non-taking party's share of production and either purchase it or market it on behalf of the non-taker.[37] By so doing, an imbalance is avoided but, as noted above, the operator's ability to purchase or to market for non-operators is limited to a maximum one-year period. When the operator does not or cannot act to avoid an imbalance, the form then further provides several options by which an underproduced party may make up its underproduction. For example, the form provides for balancing in kind, but gives the parties the right to agree to limit that remedy in several ways.[38] These limitations include seasonal restrictions (to avoid intentional underproduction in order to play the seasonal market) and a provision restricting a party's further overproduction once that producer has produced 100% of its expected share of production from a well or supply source.[39] This last constraint recognises that, if in-kind balancing is to be an effective remedy, there must be an effort to limit ultimate takes by overproducers so that enough gas

36 AAPN Form 610-E § 3.20. See also Edward B Poitevent, "The American Association of Petroleum Landmen's Model Form Gas Balancing Agreement and Instructions", *Landman*, May to June 1992, at pp 18–21 for a discussion of the AAPL Model Form Gas Balancing Agreement.

37 AAPL Form 610-E § 3.6.

38 *Ibid* at §4.

39 *Ibid* at §§4.2 to 4.3.

remains in the reservoir to allow the underproduced party to make up its underproduction. While this is a logical constraint, it may be difficult to determine what amount of hydrocarbons will actually be produced from the reservoir and, therefore, whether the limit has been met by an overproduced party. At best, the parties must content themselves with reasonable estimates. Moreover, once the overproduced parties cease further takes, if the underproduced party still fails to take the full well stream, lease maintenance issues and maximum efficient operations concerns arise. In such circumstances the overproduced parties may have no choice but resume takes.

Cash balancing is also provided for in the AAPL form, either at well depletion or at any time before, as the parties elect.[40] Additionally, there are several options available to the parties concerning the method of payment (eg, directly between parties or through the operator) and methods of valuing the underproduced party's share.

The RMMLF Form 6 gas balancing agreement (1990 version) contains a number of elective provisions that are intended to avoid some of the hardships or inequities that can arise when an underproduced party makes up its underproduction. For example, Section 2(b)(ii) provides that an underproduced party may never make up production during the months of December, January, February, and March. Note that if the relevant gas sales market is Florida, these months would be the summer months when the cooling loads provide the best market. Similar to a provision found in the AAPL form, Section (2)(e) of the RMMLF form authorises the operator to cut off further takes by an overproduced party once that party has taken all expected production attributable to its interest from the area. This both limits imbalances at well depletion and gives the underproduced party some opportunity to get in balance. The RMMLF form provides for cash balancing at well depletion, but, unlike the AAPL form, does not include the option of periodic cash balancing. Particularly noteworthy is that the RMMLF form does not provide an option for the operator to either purchase or sell a non-operator's gas on its behalf. If that is desired, the RMMLF form would need to be modified to include AAPL provisions or carefully married to the AAPL Form 610 joint operating agreement.

The AIPN Joint Operating Agreement takes a different approach to gas balancing from the AAPL Form 610. The AIPN form contains two options, the first of which lays out basic principles for gas balancing but invites the parties to negotiate a separate gas balancing agreement in accord with the principles.[41] If the parties do not enter into a separate gas balancing agreement, the parties are then bound by the principles set forth as the default gas balancing agreement in § 9.3(A). Clearly, the most significant characteristic of the AIPN approach is that it does not provide for cash balancing. Instead, an underproduced party is warned in no uncertain terms that its share of current production is subject to forfeiture if it does not take its share. In this regard, the first term of the optional gas balancing language provides: "further provided that such under-taking Party shall lose its right to such make-up Natural

40 *Ibid* at § 7.
41 Association of International Petroleum Negotiators, Joint Operating Agreement §9.3 (2002).

Gas if it has not taken delivery of the make-up Natural Gas within _________ [months/years] after the excess Natural Gas was originally taken"[42] The AIPN form also gives the parties the option not to use the default gas balancing agreement set forth as principles. That option might be chosen, for example, if they agree to enter into their own gas balancing agreement providing different terms but otherwise subject to the contract. Finally, and consistent with the RMMLF form, the AIPN form does not provide an option for the operator either to purchase or sell the non-operator's gas on its behalf. If that options is desired, some custom drafting will be necessary.

This very brief review of available forms of gas balancing agreements serves to emphasise the importance of the issues which typically arise in maintaining balanced production accounts and the significantly divergent views expressed by the several panels of experts who have been instrumental in developing the forms. Clearly, many experts favour forcing balancing in kind and disfavour cash balancing. Others are more even-handed, at least in the sense that the menu of options includes both in-kind and cash balancing options. So, too, does the role of operator vary in these formulations. Only the AAPL form continues to define a role for the operator to resolve or mitigate imbalances through either purchasing the imbalance production or marketing it on behalf of the non-taker.

7. Enforceability

With respect to the enforceability of gas balancing agreements, courts have held that the parties may specify by contract the means by which they may restore a gas imbalance. But, as Professors Smith and Weaver note, "Reliance upon a single method of balancing may also result in grave inequities if the assumption underlying its adoption proves incorrect".[43] That admonition has been the subject of several cases. For example, *Chevron USA, Inc. v Belco Petrol. Corp.*, the Fifth Circuit, interpreting Louisiana law, held that where the parties had mentioned only balancing in kind in their gas balancing agreement, and had left cash balancing completely out of the agreement, cash balancing was not available to the underproduced party even though there was not enough gas remaining in the reservoir for the underproduced party to produce its percentage share.[44] Specifically, the court stated[45]:

"Given this specific designation of a particular method of in-kind balancing as the proper way of reconciling the account, there is no room for the contention that the parties left open the possibility that cash balancing or some other form of balancing might nonetheless be used. Because the contract, on its face, only provided for in-kind balancing, Belco breached no contractual duty to Chevron when it refused to pay Chevron in cash."

The agreement specifying balancing in kind as the remedy thus placed the risk of lost production squarely on Chevron as the underproduced party. The court held that Chevron's claim that its gas was sold by Belco, the overproduced party, and that Belco

42 *Ibid* at § 9.3(A)(1).
43 Smith and Weaver § 17.6 at 17-59.
44 755 F.2d 1151, 1154 (5th Cir. 1985).
45 *Ibid.*

therefore had a duty to account was an equitable claim of unjust enrichment, which claim did not supersede the contrary terms of the contract between the parties.[46]

Chevron has been followed by the Louisiana state courts – see *Amoco Prod Co. v Fina Oil & Chem. Co.*, 95 1185 (La.App. 1 Cir. 2/23/96); 670 So.2d 502. The facts in Amoco are similar to those in *Chevron*. Amoco claimed that it was entitled to cash balancing to restore an imbalance after well depletion despite having omitted a cash balancing provision from the gas balancing agreement. The court noted that the balancing in kind clause in the agreement did not limit itself solely to the period when the wells were producing, or if enough gas remained for an underproduced party to recover its underproduction. The court held that, at a minimum, "*Pogo* and *Chevron* establish that, where the parties have agreed to the method of balancing and failed to provide for cash balancing, that agreement will be given effect, even if it deprives a party of its pro rata share of the gas".[47] The court added, "a fair interpretation of *Chevron* is that a *failure to mention cash balancing in a balancing agreement will preclude that remedy, even if the well depletes*" (emphasis added).[48] As a result, parties who are evaluating which form to use should carefully consider whether to use a form providing only for balancing in kind, even if it has provisions that attempt to assure the reservoir will have sufficient gas to allow make up. Those protections may not work, and if they do not, no cash balancing will be available.

The 14th Court of Appeals of Texas has also added the issue of the limitations imposed on the parties in seeking relief under a gas balancing agreement.[49] The gas balancing agreement in *Lowmar* stated that it was the parties' intent to use the gas balancing agreement to bring the parties' accounts into balance as soon as possible and not to use gas balancing rights as a means to store gas, delay marketing or otherwise withhold the gas from the market.[50] Energy Development, as the underproduced party, contended that the imbalance arose because it was unable to sell its share of the gas to its parent company, to which it argued it was contractually bound to sell.[51] Because the imbalance allegedly arose from a situation beyond its control, and Energy Development asserted that it was entitled to exercise its rights as an underproduced party. The court held that because Energy Development's gas purchase contract with its parent permitted Energy Development to sell gas to another pipeline company, and Energy Development had not taken steps to receive and market its full share of gas, it breached the gas balancing agreement and was not entitled to exercise its rights as an underproduced party.[52] The court further found that Energy Development was using the gas balancing agreement as a storage mechanism, which violated its duty to the other working interest owners under the agreement. The breach by Energy Development excused Lowmar from liability under the gas balancing agreement.

---

46 *Ibid.*

47 670 So. 2d 502, at 514.

48 *Ibid.*

49 See *Energy Dev. Corp. v Lowmar Exploration Co.*, No. 14-98-00619-CV, 2000 WL 795893 (Tex. App.—Houston June 22, 2000, no pet.) (not designated for publication).

50 *Ibid* at *6.

51 *Ibid* at *2.

52 *Ibid* at *8.

Although not designated for publication, the 14th Court's opinion in *Lowmar* clearly indicates that the parties are free to contract with respect to gas imbalances and that such agreements will be enforced in accordance with their terms. It also suggests the wisdom of including provisions clearly stating when a party cannot demand a remedy because it went underbalanced in breach of the agreement. Parties who violate such agreements will not later be allowed to exercise rights thereunder. Because Energy Development physically and contractually could have taken its share of the gas and simply chose not to, the court concluded that Energy Development was using the gas balancing agreement as a storage mechanism. That use put Energy Development in breach. The court in *Lowmar* noted that a party who is in default cannot itself maintain a suit for breach of contract.[53] Finally, the court noted that a breach by one party of reciprocal promises in a contract excuses performance by the other parties.

8. Gas balancing in a global context

Gas balancing issues are not confined to gas markets in the United States. While this chapter briefly describes how gas balancing agreements evolved in the United States context, gas balancing agreements are becoming more relevant in worldwide operations. Historically, much of the direct investment in hydrocarbon exploration has been devoted to finding oil, not gas. Not only is oil relatively more valuable, but it is more easily transported than gas and can be more easily delivered into international markets. Indeed, until the advent of liquefied natural gas (LNG) technologies and the development of worldwide gas markets based on the liquefied natural gas trade, natural gas, while used in many developed areas having sophisticated gas pipeline grids, was often treated as a waste production in oil production. In emerging economies having no local natural gas markets, producers often flared the gas and were disappointed when their drilling efforts found gas reservoirs rather than oil. Given increased worldwide demand for all forms of relatively clean-burning fuels, natural gas is enjoying much greater demand.

Under these circumstances, it is fair to assume that natural gas resources will continue to be developed, and as they are developed multiple markets will emerge. At present, much of the development is focused on liquefied natural gas and other high-value projects, but even in Western Africa, Trinidad and Tobago, the Far East and South America, where liquefied natural gas projects are being developed, not all of the gas can or will go to those projects. It is common, for example, for the host country to allocate gas production to different markets and to require that some percentage be used, or reserved for use, in local markets. Many projects include the national oil company as the government's representative and/or as a project participant, with a related requirement that the NOC assure that local requirements are met. Thus, even though there is tremendous pressure to aggregate gas supplies to serve major liquefied natural gas and similar projects, there will also be pressure to serve other markets. Moreover, many production sharing agreements and concessions allow the contractors or holders separately to take and market their

53 2000 WL 795893, at *5.

shares of gas production. As a result, while it is unlikely that gas imbalance issues will rise to the level experienced in the United States gas industry, there will be occasions when a gas balancing agreement will be relevant. In those instances, the familiarity with the industry forms, coupled with a thorough knowledge of the local situation to inform necessary modifications to fit the facts, will prove useful in addressing potential imbalances. Fundamental issues such as how imbalances may arise and whether in-kind balancing versus cash balancing are practical solutions should be considered. If cash balancing is viable, what price to use and when to settle accounts must be considered. On the other hand, if in-kind balancing is the sole remedy, how production will be monitored to enforce production limits whether forfeiture concepts can operate in the local environment must be considered. And, as with the United States experience, the parties must consult with local law experts to determine whether their right to contract a result is consistent with their rights to explore and develop the resource and will conform to national oil company and local market service requirements.

9. Conclusions

In summary, the case law suggests that parties entering into joint operating agreements should also agree on a gas balancing arrangement to more fully and completely protect their rights in the event of an imbalance. Not doing so results in an unacceptable level of uncertainty and the potential loss by an underproduced party of substantial value. The agreement lays out a plan to bring the parties' production accounts back into balance if, for whatever reason or for specified reasons, the accounts go out of balance. While many agreements rely solely on balancing in kind, other agreements add cash balancing as a backstop mechanism when in-kind means are unavailable. In the absence of a gas balancing agreement, balancing in kind is the preferred method of bringing production accounts back into balance, unless balancing in kind would be inequitable to the underproduced party. An inequity arises, for example, when the reservoir is substantially depleted before accounts can be brought into balance. At least under US law, enforcing co-tenant rights or pursuing other property, contract or tort theories to recover underproduced gas, or the value of that gas, when there is no express gas-balancing agreement is a risky strategy. Agreeing in advance to a form of gas balancing agreement removes uncertainty and best defines the parties' rights. When the parties enter into a gas balancing agreement, they have broad latitude to fashion the procedures and remedy. What they agree is then treated by the courts as the exclusive means of resolving any imbalance, even if the means they choose ultimately produces an incomplete or arguably inequitable result. If a party enters into an ill-considered gas balancing agreement, the courts are unlikely to come to the party's rescue. Gas balancing agreements may be useful in any international setting when there are multiple participants under a production sharing agreement, concession, joint operating agreement or similar arrangement and the production is to be separately owned and marketed. Care should be taken, however, to assure that local law principles do not limit, negate or condition the effectiveness or operation of this contractual arrangement.

No agreement can provide for every possible contingency, but the parties are in the best position to assess the situation and negotiate an agreement that takes into account their mutual interests and expectations. Some major issues that should be addressed are:

- what type of balancing, in kind and/or cash balancing, to include, and how the two relate if both are included;
- what timing for balancing is desired, including how much of the future production the underproduced party may take to make up his underage and, for cash balancing, whether to have periodic cash payments versus settling accounts only at depletion;
- whether to include limitations on when in-kind balancing can occur, such as disallowing 'storage' uses or providing that make-up cannot occur during peak months;
- whether to include any time limitation on how long an underproduced party has to make up his underproduction before forfeiting the right to do so or on an overproduced party to provide an opportunity for the underproduced party to make up in kind;
- whether and how to address the issue of lease maintenance, maximum efficient well operations and/or gas productions in association with oil in fashioning in kind make up procedures;
- whether to authorise the operator temporarily to market for other parties; and
- what price to use for cash balancing and whether and how to address credit risk issues.

This list is not exhaustive. It should, however, assist anyone who is preparing or evaluating a gas balancing agreement in considering many of the attendant issues and risks. The good news is that, with several industry forms now available, parties are in a better position to reach an informed agreement addressing the major issues than was previously the case. Still, there is no 'one size fits all' solution, and a producer should approach these agreements on a case-by-case basis to assure it responds to particular facts.

Buying and selling upstream assets

Erin Dyer
Ashurst LLP
Sharon Wilson
Freehills

1. Introduction

As developing nations seek to secure energy supply there has been a significant increase in the global demand for energy, particularly oil and gas resources. As a result the competition for upstream assets has become intense. In order to maximise the value of an asset and the likelihood of concluding a successful deal, it is important for the buyer and the seller to consider the most appropriate transaction structure and to identify the key issues early in order to streamline the process to the benefit of both parties. This chapter examines some of the key legal and commercial issues involved in buying and selling upstream oil and gas assets.

The first part of the chapter considers the important and necessary preparatory work involved in an acquisition and includes a brief examination of the various transaction structures used to buy and sell upstream assets. The second part focuses on the sale and purchase agreement (SPA) itself, in particular those issues which are unique to the purchase of upstream oil and gas assets.

2. Preliminary considerations

2.1 Upstream assets

One of the seller's first steps in conducting an upstream transaction is to identify precisely the asset that is for sale.

The host country will have granted petroleum exploration, development and/or exploitation rights for a specific geographic area, known as the contract area or licence area. These rights are contained in a production sharing contract, concession or licence (host government agreement). Where more than one company is involved in the exploration, development and/or exploitation of the area, the relationship between each of the companies is governed by a joint operating agreement (JOA). Other chapters have expanded on these topics.

The asset which is the subject of an upstream transaction usually comprises the following elements:

- an undivided interest in the host government agreement;
- an undivided interest in and under the joint operating agreement;
- an interest in the other agreements relating to the exploration, development or production of petroleum, including unitisation, sales, transportation agreements and technical data agreements; and

- physical assets in connection with the exploration, development or production of petroleum.

(In this chapter, such an asset will be referred to as the 'upstream asset'.)

2.2 Decision to sell

The commercial decision to buy or sell upstream assets is often underpinned by strategic considerations and, importantly, the phase of the asset – whether exploration, development or production.

Upstream assets may be sold for many reasons, including where:

- the seller is seeking to share or reduce its risk exposure to an asset, or to rationalise its portfolio of assets with the aim of striking an appropriate balance between exploration phase and production and development phase assets;
- the asset is approaching abandonment and significant expenditure is required in relation to plugging wells and other abandonment activities;
- the asset does not meet the seller's benchmark rate of return;
- no reserves upside exists, or expensive enhanced oil recovery techniques are required for further production;
- the political risk associated with the host country is no longer acceptable to the seller (or the seller's country limit is breached); or
- the seller seeks to use proceeds from the sale to finance other activities.

The drivers for the transaction are likely to influence the manner in which the seller structures the transaction from a commercial and legal perspective.

2.3 Planning

In addition to the matters described above, there are a number of other key issues that the parties will need to consider at a preliminary stage that may impact on the timetable and structure of the transaction, including:

- timing constraints for either party (eg, where transaction proceeds are used to fund the purchase or development of other assets);
- commercial priorities of both the buyer and the seller (eg, the seller may wish to divest a package of assets, or the buyer may wish to secure operatorship of an asset as part of the sale process);
- the nature of consents and conditions necessary for an effective sale;
- whether there are any associated transactions (eg, the buyer may be selling part of the upstream asset to a third party on a back-to-back basis); and
- tax implications of the transaction. Tax advice should be sought early in the transaction, as the choice of structure will have a bearing on the tax position of both the buyer and the seller. Tax treatment is a complicated area, which depends on the jurisdiction involved and is beyond the scope of this chapter. While tax considerations are important, they should not prevent either party from achieving their commercial objectives for the transaction.

The seller will also need to decide on the most appropriate sale process for the particular upstream asset. A formal bid process soliciting competing bids from a number of (sometimes pre-qualified) buyers may be adopted, or the seller may undertake a one-on-one negotiation with a buyer. In addition, the seller may also choose to first agree a heads of agreement before negotiating a fully termed sale and purchase agreement.

3. Transaction structure

The most common transaction structures used in relation to buying and selling an upstream asset are:

- an asset sale;
- a farm-out;
- a share sale; and
- an asset swap.

Each of these structures is considered below.

3.1 Asset sale

An asset sale is the direct acquisition of the upstream asset from the entity which owns the upstream asset. An asset sale is often preferred where the transaction involves a small number of assets or where the assets are held by an entity holding a number of other assets which it intends to retain.

One of the principal advantages of an asset sale from the buyer's perspective is that the buyer can obtain a clear understanding of the liabilities which it will assume on completion of the sale. The buyer need not be concerned about liabilities which attach to the corporate entity of the seller and that are not expressly described in the sale and purchase agreement as being assumed by the buyer. Accordingly, the buyer's due diligence is usually simpler than a due diligence for a share sale, as it will need to conduct due diligence only on the upstream asset being purchased. In an asset sale, any liabilities incurred by the seller in respect of its activities unrelated to the upstream asset will remain with the seller and will not be transferred to the buyer unless the buyer specifically agrees to assume those liabilities. Compare this situation with a share sale, where liabilities of the target company will be transferred to the buyer unless specifically retained by the seller through the provision of indemnities or otherwise.

One of the principal disadvantages of an asset sale is that the transaction is likely to be subject to any third-party consents or conditions. These matters are considered in Section 5 below.

3.2 Farm-out

A farm-out (or farm-in) is unique to the oil and gas and mining sectors and is a variation on an asset sale transaction. While there are many similarities between an asset sale and a farm-out, a farm-out can be distinguished in several key respects.

In a farm-out, the seller (called a 'farminor' or 'farmor') agrees to assign an interest in the whole or a part of an upstream asset in return for the buyer (called a 'farminee' or 'farmee') paying an agreed share of defined actual work programme costs (eg, 15% share of costs in return for a 15% interest in the upstream asset). In addition to paying an agreed share of actual work programme costs, the farminee will usually pay what is known as a 'promote' or a 'carry'. A 'promote' or 'carry' is a contribution by the farminee to the farminor's share of work programme costs, which may include both reimbursement for historical expenditure and prepayment of future budgeted expenditure. For example, a farminee may farm-in to a working interest on a '2 for 1 promote' meaning that for every $1 spent by the farminor on work programme costs, the farminee is required to spend $2. Usually, under the relevant host government agreement, expenditure payable under a promote or a carry is cost recoverable by the buyer and is capped, often at the budgeted cost of the minimum work obligation under the applicable host government agreement.

A farm-out is traditionally used for assets which are in the exploration or pre-development phases (with pending minimum work commitments), and often the seller will retain some interest in the upstream asset along with operatorship. A farm-out enables the farminor to reduce its interest in an upstream asset by sharing risk and bringing in new expertise or capital to fund work obligations. In a high-asset-value investment environment, farm-out transactions are attractive to buyers as a result of their relatively lower upfront capital investment (as there are unlikely to be existing reserves in place prior to the farm-out) and larger upside potential, where the farm-out activities result in a discovery.

The key issues which arise during a farm-out transaction include:

- determining the description of the farm-out obligation, including the nature of the work to be conducted, timing for completion and location of work (eg, identifying where wells will be drilled or providing for a mechanism to agree the location of such wells). This will require close liaison between the parties' technical, legal and commercial disciplines so as clearly to define the works to be performed;
- whether the assignment of the upstream asset will take place concurrently with the execution of the farm-out agreement (subject only to a condition precedent in respect of necessary approvals), or once the farminee has 'earned' its interest, by contributing to expenditure or completing the farm-out activities. In many jurisdictions an assignment must take place up front to ensure cost recovery or tax deductibility of earn-in spend, with the actual earn-in being a condition subsequent to the transaction;
- whether to include a substitute well provision (either a firm commitment or an option) if the original commitment encounters difficulty, providing the farminee with another chance to earn its interest and allocating the rights to any cost recovery in respect thereof; and
- the farminee's entitlement to past data once the farm-out has been completed. In this regard the parties should consider the liability for costs ancillary to the farm-in – for example, the underlying seismic licence may contain an uplift payment in respect of any new joint venture participants obtaining access to seismic data acquired under the existing host government agreement and the joint operating agreement. If the costs of this uplift are not expressly provided for in the farm-out agreement, the farminor may be required to pay this uplift.

3.3 Share sale

In a share sale transaction, the buyer buys shares in the entity which (directly or indirectly) owns the upstream asset. A share sale transaction may take the form of a non-contested or contested acquisition (if the target company is a public company), or a privately negotiated takeover (if the target company is a private company). The focus of this chapter is limited to privately negotiated acquisitions.

A share sale is often preferred for larger transactions involving a significant number of upstream assets, where there is a dedicated special-purpose entity holding the upstream assets, or where joint-venture or government consents may prevent the completion of the transaction if it is conducted as an asset sale.

The major advantage of a share sale for both parties is that pre-emption is unlikely to be a barrier to the sale, as many upstream joint operating agreements do not include conditions which restrict a transfer of shares in the company holding the upstream asset.

Another major advantage of a share sale for the buyer is that the buyer may have access to the target company's tax losses, which may be used to offset taxable income within the buyer's group. For the same reason, the seller may prefer an asset sale in these circumstances to use the tax losses within the seller's group after the sale of the upstream asset.

In a share sale the parties will have to address what will be done with any assets or liabilities held within the target entity that the seller does not wish to sell or the buyer does not wish to purchase or assume. During the initial structuring of the transaction, the parties will need to consider whether it is possible, both in a practical sense and having regard to applicable laws, to transfer such assets and liabilities out of the target entity before the completion of the sale. Where liabilities cannot be transferred out of the target entity, the buyer may request indemnities from the seller in respect of the specific liabilities which are to be assumed by the buyer. Therefore, the buyer's due diligence for a share sale is likely to be more extensive as it will need to identify any such liabilities prior to the acquisition and seek to remove them from the target entity, obtain appropriate indemnity or warranty protection, seek an adjustment to the purchase price or use a combination of these.

3.4 Asset swap

An asset swap is another variation on an asset sale transaction. It may be a simple exchange of assets, or a more complex transaction involving several parties and several interests. More usually, a swap consists of two transfers, each transfer being the consideration for the other. There may also be cash payments or other adjustments to achieve commercial parity in respect of the consideration paid for each transfer. Asset swaps are relatively uncommon due to the difficulties in finding comparable assets to swap and willing swap counterparties.

Key issues which the parties should consider for an asset swap include the following:

- As with any transaction where a buyer provides non-cash consideration, it may be difficult to attribute a monetary value to each asset, which is often required for tax purposes. This is particularly the case with exploration assets.

- The consequences of a partial failure of consideration (eg, where one swap fails due to pre-emption by a joint venture participant).
- The extent of conditions precedent required, including consents, conditions and approvals.
- The bona fides of each party. In some cases an asset swap proposal may amount to a 'fishing expedition' for information.

4. Due diligence

In the due diligence phase of the transaction the buyer will review all relevant financial, legal and technical information in relation to the upstream asset, and in the case of a share sale, the target company.

Due diligence is important not only to identify and quantify the risks associated with the sale, but also to verify the value of the upstream asset and to determine the protections (warranties and indemnities) which will be required by the parties in relation to the sale.

The buyer will often insist that completion is conditional upon satisfactory results of due diligence. Typically, such a request is strongly resisted by the seller on the grounds that it increases the risk that the buyer will not proceed to completion or will seek to reopen the terms of the sale and purchase agreement after signing – in essence it amounts to a one-way option in favour of the buyer not to proceed to completion.

The seller will also need to consider the best method for information disclosure and the level disclosure provided. Increasingly, sellers will provide buyers with a virtual (or electronic) data room to enable multiple buyers to appraise the assets concurrently. Whether the seller provides concurrent access to information relating to an asset will depend on any exclusivity or 'no-shop' arrangements which the seller may have agreed with potential buyers. It will also depend on the confidentiality restrictions in the underlying documentation. Often, agreements will provide that information may only be disclosed to bona fide buyers. There may also be host government restrictions on disclosure of information outside the relevant country.

Legal due diligence should focus on a number of areas, including principally those set out next.

4.1 Title

This should cover:

- verifying the seller's good title to the upstream asset, including the seller's working interest in respect of the asset;
- identifying issues or irregularities with the chain of title; and
- how secure the seller's title is. For example, is the asset in a joint development zone? Are there any applicable treaties? Is unitisation of the asset possible or likely?

4.2 Encumbrances

Identifying encumbrances which may affect the upstream asset, including any local participation rights, bonus payments, overriding or net profits royalties or charges, is important.

4.3 Key contracts

This covers:

- identifying and understanding the effect of the terms of key documents (on the sale process and the ownership/operation of the upstream asset post completion) under which the seller derives its rights, such as joint operating agreements, bidding agreements, unitisation agreements, gas sales and gas transportation agreements and marketing agreements;
- identifying any onerous obligations which may adversely affect the value of the upstream asset; and
- determining joint operating agreement voting percentage rights and whether they are commensurate with the interest acquired.

4.4 Conditions and consents

These matters, including pre-emptive rights, are considered in detail below.

4.5 Liabilities

This involves identifying expenditure commitments and any other liabilities (actual or contingent) which exist in relation to the upstream asset.

4.6 Abandonment

This refers to:

- identifying the applicable decommissioning and abandonment regime, whether in the upstream asset agreements or the legislation of the host government;
- determining whether the abandonment security provided by the joint venture participants, in particular by the seller, is sufficient; and
- determining the buyer's abandonment obligations (financial or otherwise) after completion.

5. Conditions and consents

The buyer and the seller will need to consider whether there are any restrictions on transferring the upstream asset in the joint operating agreement, host government agreements or other key contracts (eg, offtake agreements, service contracts, pipeline arrangements or financing agreements).

Possible restrictions on transfer take the form of:

- third-party consents, including joint venture consents;
- government consents and approvals; and
- conditions on transfer or on a change of control.

5.1 Third-party consents

The buyer and the seller will need to identify the required third-party consents on the transfer of the upstream asset (in an asset sale) or a change of control of an entity holding the upstream asset (in a share sale) and the circumstances where consent may be withheld. Third parties include joint-venture participants, parties to other contracts related to the upstream asset, and lenders where finance is in place.

The third-party consent requirement may allow the third party to withhold consent to the transfer absolutely (at its sole discretion), on reasonable grounds or on grounds that the prospective buyer does not have the financial or technical capability to perform the obligations under the relevant contract. In most agreements in the upstream oil and gas sector, however, apart from study-and-bid agreements, an absolute right to withhold consent is rare.

If the sale involves the transfer of operatorship of an upstream asset, it is usual for the joint operating agreement to provide that the transfer of operatorship requires the approval of the operating committee in accordance with the voting thresholds described in the joint operating agreement.

5.2 Governmental consents and approvals

In addition to any third-party consents, a change in ownership or a transfer of operatorship of an upstream asset is also likely to require consent of the host government under the applicable regulatory regime and/or the relevant host government agreement. The seller may also require the consent of the relevant national oil company. These consents may or may not extend to a change in control. In addition, approvals and/or registrations of regulatory authorities (ie, the oil and gas administrator) and foreign investment boards may also be required.

Notwithstanding the formal requirements of a host government, in the interests of a good working relationship most international oil companies voluntarily decide to keep the host government informed of transfers of interests in the upstream asset by indirect or direct means.

5.3 Conditions on transfer or on change of control

In addition to consents, there may also be conditions which must be satisfied prior to the sale in order to ensure that the transaction is effective. The buyer and the seller will need to identify the effect of any conditions applying to the transfer, the procedure and the timing associated with such conditions and the likely impact on the sale process.

Many of the conditions on transfer are found in the joint operating agreement. The conditions on transfer of a participating interest under a joint operating agreement include pre-emption rights, first rights of refusal and first rights to negotiate. These conditions are discussed below. While this chapter describes these conditions in the context of the joint operating agreement, similar conditions may also be contained in host government agreements.

By identifying the applicable conditions, the buyer and seller will be able to implement a strategy that best ensures that the contemplated sale is completed on schedule, is legally binding on completion and does not result in the imposition of additional onerous conditions on the buyer.

(a) Pre-emption rights and first rights of refusal

There is no commonly accepted legal definition of a pre-emption right (sometimes referred to as a first right of refusal) and each joint operating agreement must be taken on a case-by-case basis and carefully reviewed to determine its effect.

The underlying principle of a pre-emption right is that a joint-venture participant should have the right to buy the upstream asset from the seller on the same terms and conditions agreed with a prospective buyer. While pre-emption right provisions vary from case to case, a common form is contained in the AIPN standard form of joint operating agreement, which provides that once the final terms and conditions of an upstream asset transfer have been fully negotiated, the seller must offer those terms and conditions to the other joint-venture participants. Each of the other participants has the right to accept the offer to buy the upstream asset on the terms and conditions presented by the seller and in proportion to its existing interest in the upstream asset. If none of the other participants exercises its right to the offer, then the seller may transfer the upstream asset to the proposed buyer on terms no more favourable than those presented to the other participants. In practice, where a pre-emption right exists, it will mean a delay to the sale process of usually 30 to 60 days (or the duration of the pre-emption period) while the joint-venture participants decide whether or not to exercise their pre-emption right.

The buyer should also note that the joint-venture participants may also have the right for their participating interest to 'tag along' with the seller's transaction – that is, to require the buyer, as a condition of buying the seller's interest, also to buy their participating interest on the same terms.

There may be ways in which a transaction can be legitimately structured so as to avoid triggering a pre-emption right. Where the pre-emption right entitles the joint-venture participants to match the deal done with the buyer, one argument commonly advanced is that if the transaction can be structured in such a way that the joint-venture participants cannot physically match it, then the pre-emption right may be defeated. The buyer may seek to achieve this position by offering non-cash consideration which the other joint-venture participants do not have (ie, an interest in another field, equity, or loan notes) and therefore cannot match, or by structuring the transaction as an indivisible package deal involving a package of interests which, under the terms of the sale and purchase agreement, cannot be split.

Another method to avoid triggering a pre-emption right is for the buyer to acquire the shares of the seller (provided that the joint operating agreement does not contain change-of-control provisions). Alternatively, where the sale of the particular company holding the upstream asset is not attractive to the parties, the seller may transfer the upstream asset to an affiliated company of the seller (usually newly formed), as this can normally be done without the consent of the other joint venture participants. The buyer will then purchase the share capital of the newly formed affiliated company (the process being known as the 'hive-up' or 'affiliate' route). For a hive-up route to be effective, the seller must transfer the upstream asset to its affiliated company while it remains an affiliate of the seller and before any steps are taken which may result in beneficial ownership vesting in the buyer. Caution should be exercised in employing this disposal method, as joint operating agreements often have provisions designed to prevent such a transaction by restricting the affiliated company from transferring the upstream asset to a third party within a specific time period.

The effect and implications of pre-emption provisions will be entirely dependent on the precise terms of those provisions and the structure of the particular transaction proposed. The terms should therefore be carefully analysed and understood before any steps are taken.

(b) First right of negotiation

A first right of negotiation provides that if the seller intends to sell an upstream asset, prior to discussing the sale with prospective buyers it must first give notice to the other joint-venture participants and invite them to submit offers for the upstream asset. The other participants will then have a specified period within which to make an offer for the upstream asset, and if more than one of the other participants wishes to buy the upstream asset, then the offer price will typically be the highest price which any of them is willing to pay. If, following a period of negotiation between the parties, the seller does not find the offer acceptable, it may within a further limited period negotiate with prospective buyers to transfer the upstream asset. Some first rights of negotiation require that this subsequent agreement with the prospective buyer must be on terms more favourable to the seller than the offer from the other joint-venture participants. Without this final condition, a first right of negotiation is perhaps the weakest of restrictions on transfer of an upstream asset. In this regard, the first right of negotiation provides more certainty to the prospective buyer that the sale will be completed than a pre-emption right or a first right of refusal.

6. Sale and purchase agreement (SPA)

At the heart of any transaction for the sale of an upstream asset is the sale and purchase agreement. While a sale and purchase agreement for an upstream asset contains many provisions common to sale and purchase agreements for the sale of other types of assets, there are some legal and commercial principles which are unique to the sale of upstream assets which deserve special consideration.

6.1 Documenting the transaction

The format and the content of the sale and purchase agreement will depend upon whether the transaction is a share sale or an asset sale.

A share sale involves the negotiation of a share sale agreement under which a buyer buys shares in the company which (directly or indirectly) owns the upstream asset. In addition to the share sale agreement, a share sale will also involve the preparation of other documents including a tax indemnity and other corporate documents required to effect the sale, such as share transfers, directors' resignations and appointments.

An asset sale involves the negotiation of an asset sale agreement between the owner of the upstream asset and the prospective buyer. The asset sale agreement will describe the upstream asset being purchased. In addition to the asset sale agreement, an asset sale will also involve the preparation of other documents, including an assignment of the seller's interest in the asset, novation of the joint operating agreement and other relevant agreements, third-party consents, waivers of pre-emptive rights and any necessary host government consents and approvals.

6.2 Upstream asset

The sale and purchase agreement should specifically define the upstream asset which will be sold and purchased and will usually provide that the upstream asset (or, in the case of a share sale, the shares in the target company) will be transferred on completion, free of encumbrances (including charges and royalties). If the buyer agrees to buy the upstream asset subject to specified encumbrances such as a royalty, these encumbrances should be individually described in the sale and purchase agreement.

6.3 Parties

Like any sale and purchase agreement for the purchase of assets or shares, the buyer should assure itself that the seller named in the sale and purchase agreement owns the assets or the shares which are the subject of the transaction. It is in this regard that the chain of title investigation conducted during the due diligence phase becomes important. In addition, the buyer will need to assess whether the seller has the financial capacity to meet post-completion obligations, such as satisfying warranty or indemnity claims, and in this regard the buyer may require a guarantee, retention of a portion of the purchase price or other financial support from the seller.

The seller will also need to make a credit assessment of the financial capacity of the buyer to pay the purchase price at completion and, similarly, may require a parent company guarantee or other credit support to secure performance of the buyer's payment obligations, as well as its ongoing undertakings with regard, for example, to abandonment liabilities.

6.4 Key dates

There are three key dates for the purpose of an upstream asset transaction:

- the effective date;
- the signing date of the sale and purchase agreement; and
- completion.

While the signing date is straightforward, the concepts of the effective date and the completion date require further consideration.

An upstream asset transaction is often based on an effective date, being a nominated date on which economic risk and benefit of the upstream asset is deemed to have passed to the buyer, despite physical and legal transfer of the upstream asset occurring at a later date (ie, at completion).

For ease of accounting purposes, the seller will often select an effective date which is consistent with the timing of annual work programmes and budgets (in the case of the sale of a single upstream asset) or a date immediately following the end of a reporting period such as the first day of the seller's fiscal year (in the case of a package of upstream assets).

All revenue and expenses (including the proceeds of pending insurance claims and interest on those amounts) attributable to the period *prior to* the effective date in relation to the target assets will be for the seller's account. Subject to completion occurring, revenue and expenses attributable to the period *on and from* the effective date will be for the buyer's account. As these amounts may not be known at the time of signing, or possibly even at completion, the sale and purchase agreement will need to include a price adjustment mechanism to ensure that the seller and the buyer are put in the same economic position as if the physical and legal transfer of the assets or shares occurred on the effective date. Price adjustment mechanisms are considered in Section 6.7 below.

Completion occurs once all conditions precedent have been satisfied or waived (see below). The sale and purchase agreement should clearly specify the time, place and activities that will occur on completion and which are required to be achieved to allow completion to take place.

On completion, the buyer will pay the purchase price and the seller will deliver the upstream asset. For a share sale, the upstream asset is delivered to the buyer through delivery of executed share transfers and share certificates. For an asset sale, the upstream asset is delivered to the buyer through delivery of the legal assignments and transfers of the relevant host government agreement, and deeds of assignment and/or novation of any operational agreements. The concepts of assignment and novation are considered in Section 7 below.

6.5 Conditions precedent

If the sale and purchase agreement is not subject to any conditions precedent, the buyer and the seller can sign and complete the transaction simultaneously. However, it is common for upstream asset sale-and-purchase agreements to contain conditions which must be fulfilled prior to completion of the transaction. Nevertheless, the parties should attempt to minimise the number of such conditions precedent so as to limit uncertainty and reduce the risk that completion does not occur.

As described above, the conditions required to be waived or satisfied prior to completion should be determined early in the sale process. The timeline for completion will need to accommodate the timeframes for obtaining consents or satisfying conditions identified in the due diligence process.

The typical conditions precedent in an upstream sale and purchase agreement may include:

- notice of waiver or non-exercise of pre-emption rights or first rights of refusal from joint venture participants;
- consents from joint venture participants and other third parties;
- on an asset sale, the novation of the joint operating agreement and assignment of other contracts;
- antitrust and other regulatory approvals;
- releases of mortgages, charges or other encumbrances over the assets or shares;
- financing – particularly in a bid situation, the buyer will be expected to demonstrate funding in support of its purchase of the upstream asset, including for example the provision of a bid deposit; and
- completion of any pre-sale restructuring – for example, in a share sale the seller may need to transfer assets it wishes to retain from the target company to another company within the seller's corporate group.

Parties are often placed under an obligation to use reasonable or occasionally best endeavours to satisfy the conditions precedent. There will be no obligation to complete the transaction until the conditions precedent have been waived or satisfied. However, a party may waive the conditions precedent included for its benefit.

The sale and purchase agreement should provide that the conditions precedent are satisfied or waived within a specific time period (or 'drop dead date') and that failure to satisfy or waive the conditions within that time period gives rise to a right by either party to terminate the sale and purchase agreement, unless the parties are able to agree to an extension. The time period or drop dead date should be realistic and consistent with the time required to satisfy the conditions but not so long that there is a risk that the purchase price may no longer reflect the market value of the upstream asset.

Finally, conditions precedent should be objective and with a clear description of the event to take place. Vague and subjective conditions give rise to the risk of abuse by an opportunistic buyer or seller seeking to terminate the sale and purchase agreement prior to completion.

6.6 Interim period

The 'interim period' is the period between the signing of the sale and purchase agreement and its completion. During this period, subject to completion occurring, the seller is effectively the caretaker of the upstream asset on behalf of the buyer. As a result, the sale and purchase agreement contains buyer protections which ensure that the seller preserves or does not adversely affect the value of the upstream asset or the business of the target company. The buyer must be careful to ensure that any restrictions placed on the seller during this period do not affect the seller's ability to manage the upstream asset. Unreasonable restrictions may be self-defeating and diminish value, and a balance needs to be struck between protecting the buyer's investment and allowing the seller to manage the upstream asset.

A particular concern of the buyer is to ensure that it receives timely and sufficient information regarding the upstream asset. In this regard the buyer may:

- require the seller regularly to communicate and provide information to the buyer regarding the upstream assets or the business of the target company;
- require the right to attend operating committee meetings as an observer (if the joint operating agreement will permit this); and
- require the seller to consult with the buyer, or possibly even vote in accordance with the buyer's directions, when voting on work programmes and budgets or authorisations for expenditure for joint-venture operations. Where the seller must vote in accordance with the buyer's directions, difficulties may arise if completion does not occur.

The confidentiality obligations in the joint operating agreement will determine, to some extent, the type of information that the seller can disclose to the buyer during the interim period. If confidentiality obligations restrict the ability of the seller to disclose information, the buyer may at least require the seller to use reasonable endeavours to procure the necessary disclosure consents from joint-venture participants and/or the host government.

In addition to information provision obligations during the interim period, the seller will generally give a number of specific undertakings, such as:

- to continue to make and receive all payments and operate in the ordinary course of business;
- not to vary or terminate any material agreements, or enter into any new material agreements;
- to take all necessary steps to preserve, maintain and protect the upstream asset (or the business of the target company);
- not to buy or sell assets without the prior consent of the buyer; and
- not to enter into any agreement for capital expenditure or to purchase fixed assets in excess of a specific monetary threshold.

6.7 Purchase price and adjustment mechanisms

The sale and purchase agreement should clearly define all matters relating to the price, including the type and value of the consideration, the allocation of the consideration between the elements of the upstream asset, the timing and method of payment and the applicable price adjustment mechanism.

The consideration may be paid in cash, in shares, by assumption of future expenditure obligations or 'carry', by means of an asset swap, by equity or loan notes, or by a combination of these. The consideration may also include the right for the seller to receive an overriding royalty or net profits royalty (either paid in cash or in kind), based on the value of future production from the upstream asset. Where a royalty forms part of the consideration, the sale and purchase agreement will need clearly to set out the method of calculating and paying the royalty and also contain provisions which ensure that the obligation to pay the royalty can still be enforced by the seller if the upstream asset is later sold by the buyer.

In an asset sale, the value of the upstream asset is apportioned between plant, machinery and other tangible fixed assets, with the balance allocated to intangible assets including the licence or rights under the production sharing agreement or the concession. It is important that the allocation achieves the maximum tax benefits for the buyer and the seller (whose interests may well conflict). Subject to the buyer's tax position, it is generally more tax effective if the buyer can apportion most value to tangible fixed assets to maximise depreciation on capital allowances.

Payment may be structured as a single payment paid entirely at completion, or as a payment at completion followed by fixed deferred payments payable at specific times or contingent upon certain events (eg, completion of an exploration well). The sale and purchase agreement may also require that a deposit is paid on execution of the sale and purchase agreement and in this case the sale and purchase agreement will need to be clear as to the circumstances in which it can be retained by the seller or returned to the buyer.

In a simple transaction, the price will be fixed at execution. The buyer and the seller will agree a price based on a certain level of working capital in the target company. If this level changes before completion, an adjustment will be made to the price. There are several methods of adjusting working capital, but in many cases the sale and purchase agreement will contain a price adjustment mechanism which is designed so that all expenditure and receipts attributable to the period before the effective date are for the account of the seller, and all expenditure or receipts attributable to the period on or after the effective date are for the account of the buyer. An alternative structure is for the base price for the upstream assets to be agreed, with subsequent adjustment up or down to reflect the value of working capital at the effective date, and payments and receipts since the effective date.

A basic price adjustment mechanism will take into account changes in working capital (including hydrocarbon stocks, lifting position, debtors, creditors, cash balance) since the effective date and income and costs between the effective date and completion, including development expenditure in the case of a development phase asset.

It is critical that the purchase price provisions clearly set out the basis on which the adjustment is made (including accounting principles) and that an effective mechanism for resolving disputes is agreed. It is often useful to include a worked example to ensure the provisions operate as intended.

An example of a simple price adjustment procedure is as follows:

- the buyer pays an agreed estimated amount at completion;
- the seller calculates the price adjustment (based on agreed accounting principles) and provides details of its calculation in a draft completion statement, which is provided to the buyer within a specific period after completion;
- the seller and the buyer agree the final form of the completion statement within a specified period after the seller has provided the draft completion statement;
- where the buyer and the seller are unable to agree the price adjustment, the matter is referred to dispute resolution (typically expert determination); and
- once a price adjustment has been agreed or determined, the buyer or the seller (as the case may be) pay any balancing amount (usually with interest).

6.8 Warranties

Warranties are contractual promises by the seller as to factual matters relating to the target asset or company. The warranties outline the basic assumptions which underpin the price and the nature of the upstream asset purchased. While the buyer will also provide some warranties (eg, in relation to its corporate existence), it is the seller's warranties that are of critical importance.

Put simply, damages for a breach of warranty are calculated by reference to what is required to put the claimant into the position he would have been had the warranties been true or, in other words, for loss of bargain. In the sale and purchase agreement, the buyer's right to damages for breach of warranty will usually take the form of an adjustment to the price on the basis that the buyer has paid too much for the upstream asset or target company based upon incorrect information. In this way, provided that the buyer ensures that the seller warrants that the information provided during the due diligence process is accurate and complete, the warranties give weight to the due diligence process.

Warranties may be given at execution of the sale and purchase agreement and may also be repeated at completion. Warranties at completion will be particularly requested by the buyer where there is likely to be a lengthy period between execution of the sale and purchase agreement and completion. The extent to which warranties are repeated at completion goes some way to determining the allocation of risk between the buyer and the seller during the interim period.

Warranties may be drafted in several ways, from an absolute warranty with no qualification (so that all risk in relation to the matters warranted rests with the seller) to a warranty qualified by the knowledge of the seller or with respect to materiality thresholds (so that some risk in relation to the matters warranted is borne by the buyer). The buyer should not agree to 'standard form' warranties and should take special care to ensure the warranties are consistent with the assumptions made by the buyer when deciding to purchase the upstream asset. The agreed warranties should reflect the parties' commercial objectives and will also reflect the respective bargaining strengths of the parties.

In addition to qualifications contained in the warranties themselves, the seller's warranties will generally be qualified by the matters described in a disclosure letter or schedule which is agreed during negotiation of the sale and purchase agreement. The disclosure letter carves out specific details about the upstream asset from the warranties (eg, details about a dispute in relation to the assets where a warranty exists that there are no disputes in relation to the upstream asset). The matters described in the disclosure letter need not relate to specific warranties, but may be expressed to qualify the warranties as a whole. The letter is generally delivered to the buyer in a final form from the seller immediately prior to signing the sale and purchase agreement.

The types of warranties contained in the sale and purchase agreement will depend upon the nature of the upstream asset and the degree of prior knowledge that the buyer has in relation to the upstream asset, but will typically cover areas such as the following:

- *Title to assets* – the seller will warrant that it is the legal and beneficial owner of the assets (including its undivided share in the relevant production sharing agreement, concession or licence) free from encumbrances.
- *Host government agreement* – the seller will warrant matters relating to the host government agreement being in full force and effect, whether any breach exists, and matters relating to the revocation of the licence or termination of the service or host government agreement by the relevant government authority.
- *Surrender, withdrawal* – the seller will warrant in relation to the extent of surrender or withdrawal from the contract or licence area and whether any surrender or withdrawal is pending.
- *Sole risk, non-consent operations* – the seller will warrant the extent to which the seller has participated in sole risk or non-consent operations under the joint operating agreement.
- *Abandonment* – the seller will warrant (to some extent) that all wells in the contract or licence area have been plugged and abandoned in accordance with good and prudent oilfield practice and relevant laws, and will also

warrant in relation to the extent of payments made on account of or by way of provision for future abandonment obligations.

- *Environmental liability* – the seller's warranties on environmental matters will include obtaining and complying with environmental consents, the extent of liabilities arising under environmental laws or pending actions and existence of hazardous substances or waste.
- *Operatorship* – the seller will warrant matters relating to resignations, conduct of operations in accordance with good oilfield practice, breach of joint operating agreement obligations and compliance with applicable laws. Where the seller is not the operator, these warranties will usually be qualified with respect to the seller's knowledge.
- *Work programme and budgets* – the seller will warrant that, other than as contained in documents disclosed in the data room, there are no approved budgets, programmes and commitments for expenditure (pursuant to approved authorisations for expenditure) in relation to the host government agreement.
- *Reserves* – it is usual for the seller to exclude warranties relating to the quantity of reserves, geological, geophysical or technical engineering interpretations or forecasts, the amount of cost-recoverable hydrocarbons and the cost recoverability of any operating expenses under the terms of the host government agreements. These are matters for the buyer's technical advisors to determine.
- *Cost recovery pool* – the seller may also warrant the extent to which recoverable costs under the host government agreement are available to the buyer.

There will generally be many other warranties contained in the sale and purchase agreement. The content of the warranties will depend on the nature of the upstream asset and the relative negotiating strengths of the buyer and the seller.

6.9 Indemnity and limitation of liability

The indemnities included in a sale and purchase agreement will depend on the nature of the upstream asset but will commonly reflect the pre- and post-effective-date risk allocation, such that the seller agrees to indemnify the buyer against liabilities attributable to the period prior to the effective date, and the buyer agrees to indemnify the seller against liabilities attributable to the period on and from the effective date. In addition, based on the results of due diligence, the buyer may seek further indemnities from the seller in respect of specific liabilities. The seller will also commonly seek a full indemnity in respect of future abandonment obligations.

While warranties provide some protection for the buyer, indemnities further strengthen the buyer's position to ensure that the assets acquired reflect the buyer's understanding of the upstream asset. The advantage for the buyer in obtaining indemnity protection over warranty protection is that the buyer can be compensated on a simple dollar-for-dollar basis for the liability in question, without having to prove the buyer's loss of bargain.

In most sale and purchase agreements, the seller of an upstream asset will seek to limit its liability to the buyer. The seller of an upstream asset may limit its liability in the following ways:

- *Time period limits* – the seller will require the buyer to bring claims within a specific time period. It is common to see limits of one to three years from completion for breach of warranty and seven years (or longer – Indonesia has a ten-year statute of limitations for tax) from completion for tax warranties. Clearly, the seller will seek to limit its exposure by keeping this time period as short as possible.
- *Excluding liability for* de minimis *claims* – the seller will seek to exclude liability for any claim less than a specified percentage of the purchase price or a specified monetary amount. Depending on the circumstances, a typical starting position for the seller might be 2% of the purchase price. The buyer will seek to remove or reduce the amount of any *de minimis* limitation.
- *Baskets* – A basket provides that the seller will not be liable for claims unless the aggregate of claims (excluding *de minimis* claims) exceeds a percentage of the purchase price or specific monetary amount (the 'basket amount'). A basket may be structured on an excess liability or an overflow basket. An excess liability basket only allows the buyer to claim for amounts in excess of the agreed basket amount. An overflow basket allows the buyer to claim the basket amount plus all amounts in excess of the basket.
- *Overall and per claim caps* – in almost all cases, the liability of the seller will be capped on a per claim basis and on an overall basis with reference to a percentage of the purchase price or a specific monetary amount. While the seller will customarily propose a low cap (say 10% of the purchase price), the final position agreed between the parties may reflect somewhere between 20% and 100% of the purchase price.
- *Consequential loss* – Liability for consequential loss is usually sought to be excluded by the seller, but the buyer will need to take care with the way in which this is worded, given that it is paying for a future revenue stream.

In a share sale, specific tax liabilities are generally allocated in a tax deed of indemnity. While tax indemnities are beyond the scope of this chapter, it sufficient to note that the objective of the tax indemnities is to protect the buyer against future tax liabilities which may arise and which are attributable to the period prior to the effective date, but are unknown as at signing or completion.

6.10 Decommissioning and abandonment liability

Given the significant expense involved with decommissioning and abandonment of an upstream asset and the fact that parties owning an upstream asset are usually (under the relevant legislation) jointly liable in respect of the same, apportionment of responsibility for decommissioning is an important part of a sale and purchase agreement for upstream assets. Many legislative regimes impose liability for decommissioning costs on the owners of an upstream asset at the time that the abandonment activities take place, and accordingly the buyer may wish to seek an indemnity from the seller to protect itself against any inadequate provision by the seller for decommissioning costs prior to the effective date (in addition to any warranty protections which have been agreed). Alternatively, some legislative regimes provide for decommissioning and abandonment to be separated from the ownership of the upstream asset and to endure even after a transfer of the relevant upstream asset. Therefore, a seller of an upstream asset may find that they are liable for a portion of decommissioning and abandonment liability based on the period of time they held the asset, despite not holding the asset at the time decommissioning and abandonment takes place. If the transaction involves the buyer taking on this liability, the seller should consider requiring (and joint venture participants will likely require) the buyer to provide sufficient security in respect of its liability for decommissioning and abandonment costs for the period on and from the effective date.

6.11 Termination rights

Where there is a gap between the signing of the sale and purchase agreement and completion, in addition to termination rights by either party for failure to satisfy or waive the conditions precedent it is common for the buyer also to require the right to terminate the sale and purchase agreement in circumstances where the seller has committed a material breach of the agreement, and/or where a material adverse event has occurred which affects the upstream asset.

Material breaches by the seller may extend to breach of a seller's warranty or breach of the seller's obligations during the interim period. The seller will strongly resist the buyer terminating the sale and purchase agreement for breach of warranty, and will generally seek to limit the buyer's rights to terminate the agreement between signing and completion.

If the buyer has paid a deposit on signing and the sale and purchase agreement is terminated due to the seller's failure to comply with the terms of the sale and purchase agreement, then the deposit will be returned to the buyer. If the seller is entitled to keep the deposit on termination, it is important that the retention of the deposit is expressed to be a genuine pre-estimate of the seller's loss, otherwise, as a matter of English law, the provision can be construed as a penalty and the clause held to be invalid. In addition, the buyer should provide that retention of the deposit is the seller's sole remedy in respect of the termination of the sale and purchase agreement.

7. Assignment and novation

In an asset sale, the buyer will take an assignment or novation of the seller's interests in the agreements relating to the upstream asset, including the joint operating agreement, offtake and other agreements and host government agreements.

In particular, an assignment of a participating interest in the joint operating agreement will usually require the buyer to covenant with the other joint-venture participants to be bound by and observe the conditions of the joint operating agreement, including operator obligations where the transaction involves a change of the operator.

It is important that the legal formalities for assignment or novation of the relevant agreement are complied with. The nature of these formalities depends upon the relevant jurisdiction. Under English law, it is important to bear in mind that where the parties seek to transfer the burden of a contract from the seller to the buyer, the parties should execute a novation deed.

8. Tips for a successful transaction

For both the buyer and the seller the objective will generally be to maximise value and minimise risk for themselves and complete the sale in as short a time as possible. Practically, there are a number of things that the buyer and seller can do to ensure a successful outcome:

- Both parties should have a clear picture of the commercial objectives for the transaction and ensure that these objectives are not overshadowed by legal and tax requirements.
- Both parties should assemble the right team (both internally and externally). The parties may need specialists in tax, technical, finance, legal and specialist M&A. The team should be able to communicate freely to unlock value across complementary disciplines. The team should understand the 'market' for assets and how that market influences the underlying risk allocation in upstream sale and purchase agreements.
- Both parties should do most of the work before commencement of sale and purchase agreement negotiations, including a thorough due diligence process, structuring and tax advice and assessing the likely impact of consent requirements and conditions. Failure to acquire tax advice at an early stage may materially impact on value (eg, where the most tax efficient acquisition vehicle is not used by the buyer).
- If the buyer is using external financing to fund the transaction, it should ensure that the financing timetable is consistent with the sale process.
- The seller should provide timely, clear and accurate information to government authorities and joint venture participants. Failure to do so is likely to result in a delayed or frustrated sale process, as consent from these parties is usually essential for completion.
- Open communication between the buyer and the seller, the host government and any joint-venture participants will ensure not only a smooth completion process, but also a harmonious working relationship after the completion of the sale.

Gas processing

Nina Howell
Garry Pegg
Hogan & Hartson

1. Scope and introduction

This chapter considers arrangements for the processing of natural gas produced on the UK continental shelf (UKCS) at receiving facilities located onshore in the United Kingdom. The focus of the chapter is primarily on legal and regulatory issues, including third-party access, that will be relevant to both owners of gas processing facilities (facility owners) and gas producers seeking to secure capacity rights in the gas processing facility (gas producers). As part of this exercise we have considered the main terms and conditions that would be expected to be seen in a gas processing agreement between the facility owner and the gas producer. So that these issues can be considered in context, we have provided some background information in Section 2 about the United Kingdom's gas processing facilities and the process for treating gas.

2. Background information

2.1 The United Kingdom's main gas processing facilities

In the United Kingdom there are seven main gas processing facilities (also called beach terminals) at St Fergus (Aberdeenshire, Scotland), Teesside (north-east England), Barrow-in-Furness (Cumbria), Easington (Yorkshire), Point of Ayr (north Wales), Theddlethorpe (Lincolnshire) and Bacton (Norfolk). The UK–Belgium Interconnector feeds into Bacton, which is one of the largest gas terminal complexes in the United Kingdom, and St Fergus is the UK receiving facility for the UK–Norway Vesterled pipeline. These gas processing facilities receive natural gas from gas producers operating more than one hundred fields on the UK continental shelf. These facilities are distinct from the United Kingdom's liquid natural gas import terminals which are outside the scope of this chapter.

2.2 Ownership of gas facilities

Gas processing facilities are a key component of the gas supply chain. Gas field development necessarily involves the construction of a pipeline to transport gas from the reservoir to the beach, and a gas processing plant at the beach to make the produced gas fit for purpose. Often at the beginning of their lives both the pipeline and the associated gas processing facility are dedicated to a single reservoir and both are owned by a consortium made up of all or some of the owners of that reservoir (typically the parties to the relevant joint operating agreement). As with pipelines, economy of scale is a key consideration when contemplating the construction of a gas processing facility and, consequently, gas processing facilities are built with capacity to receive and process gas in excess of production from the founding reservoir in order to accommodate future gas production. This means that as new fields have come on stream, existing gas processing facilities have absorbed production from these new developments. The involvement of new participants and the move away from dedicated pipelines and facilities have resulted in some erosion of ownership by founding consortia. However, today gas processing facilities (like pipelines) are still typically owned by producer consortia (ie, unincorporated joint ventures) and run for the group by a single operator.

2.3 Function of gas processing

The function of gas processing is to treat raw gas so that it is ready for export into onshore pipelines as processed gas for distribution to end users. Processing is necessary because raw natural gas produced at the wellhead is not sufficiently pure for residential, industrial or commercial uses. Furthermore, gas required for residential, industrial and commercial purposes must consist principally of methane. Methane produces less carbon dioxide and is therefore more environmentally friendly than other fuels.

2.4 Processing offshore

Typically, some processing will take place offshore. Where the new development is being tied in to existing infrastructure, offshore processing will be carried out under a transportation and processing agreement (commonly known as a TPOSA) between the gas producer and the owners of the pipeline and associated infrastructure that will bring the gas to the beach. The transportation and processing agreement will set out both (i) the terms under which the gas producer's gas is transported from the reservoir to the beach; and (ii) the processing services that will be provided to the gas producer upstream of the beach terminal. The latter will typically include the removal of free liquid water and natural gas condensates at or near the wellhead and the injection of chemicals required to ensure that the gas producer's gas is compatible with the transporters' infrastructure. The water is disposed of as waste water and the condensate is usually transported by pipeline to an oil refinery. The gas is then transported by pipeline to the gas processing facility. The tariff payable under a transportation and processing agreement is generally higher than the tariff payable under a classic transportation agreement which does not include any processing services. Any liquids and solids not removed in offshore production separators must be separated from the gas and this is done in 'slug catchers' and/or filter-separators, as the submarine pipeline arrives in the onshore gas processing facility.

2.5 Processing onshore

Completion of the processing of natural gas will take place at the onshore gas processing facility. Each gas processing facility will be tailored to process gas of the composition of the reservoirs feeding into the gas processing facility. As no two gas reservoirs are the same, the treatment process will necessarily differ at each gas processing facility and consequently each gas processing facility will have its own bespoke process technology. What follows is a high-level illustration of the process that occurs at most of the United Kingdom's gas processing facilities:

- First, hydrogen sulphide and carbon dioxide are removed as part of the initial purification process.
- Next water vapour, mercury and nitrogen (in that order) are removed.
- Natural gas liquids (NGLs) are then removed. Natural gas liquids include ethane, propane, butane, iso-butane and natural gasoline, and these are sold separately for different commercial uses.
- Finally, the residue from the NGLs, which is composed almost entirely of methane, is ready to be transported to end user markets.

Almost all gas that is processed at the beach terminal in the United Kingdom is delivered into the National Transmission System (NTS) for onward delivery to end users. The NTS is the high-pressure part of the National Grid's transmission system and consists of more than 6,600 kilometres of pipeline crossing the United Kingdom. Some processed gas may remain at the gas processing facility for use as fuel to operate the facility. It is also fairly common for other infrastructure, such as power plants and desalination plants, which use gas as their fuel stock, to be strategically located in the vicinity of a gas processing facility so that processed gas can be delivered directly to the adjacent plant. An example of this is the Teesside power plant that is located close to the Teesside gas processing facility.

3. Third-party access

3.1 Gas Act 1995

Prior to the enactment of the Gas Act 1995, there were no express obligations imposed by law on facility owners in the United Kingdom to grant third parties access to spare capacity (also called ullage). The Pipe-lines Act 1962 did, however, already recognise the concept of third-party access to pipelines. The Gas Act 1995 extended EU Directives on third-party access to the United Kingdom's gas infrastructure, including gas processing facilities, with the objective of creating greater competition and removing any discriminatory behaviour by facility owners.

The Gas Act 1995 introduced transparency to the terms on which facility owners are willing to provide processing capacity to third-party gas producers. This was achieved by Section 12(1) of the Gas Act 1995 (as amended by Schedule 3 of the Gas (Third Party Access and Accounts) Regulations 2000) which requires facility owners to publish at least once a year the 'main commercial conditions' for access to capacity in the facility for gas processing. 'Main commercial conditions' are defined as:

> *"(a) such information as would enable a potential applicant for a right to have gas processed by a gas processing facility or conveyed in a relevant gas pipeline to make a reasonable assessment of the cost of, or the method of calculating the cost of, acquiring that right; (b) the other significant terms on which such a right would be granted; and (c) such other information as the Secretary of State may from time to time specify by notice".*

The main commercial terms published by owners of the different gas processing facilities in the United Kingdom are broadly consistent in both scope and content and must be prepared in accordance with guidelines produced by the Department of Business Enterprise and Regulatory Reform (DBERR). The guidelines require the main commercial terms to be available upon request from a potential user of capacity and require facility owners to publish all "pertinent contractual terms and conditions" on use of the infrastructure and on payment. The guidelines extend 'pertinent contractual terms and conditions' beyond purely commercial matters to include details of the liability and indemnity regime that will apply as between the facility owner and the gas producer. Typically, key terms and conditions are as follows:

- Specified indicative tariffs on a unit-cost basis for the processing of gas based on standard arrangements. Actual tariffs will vary as a function of a number of parameters, including gas quality, water content and modification costs.
- The indicative tariff will be reviewed annually and revised to reflect the cost of inflation.
- Any tariff is indexed-based on a standard published index.
- Where tie-ins or additional onshore equipment are required to process third-party gas at the gas processing facility, the associated capital expenditure is charged directly to the gas producer which requires the additional equipment.
- Where equipment is exclusive to a particular gas producer the operating expenditure for such equipment will also be for the sole account of that gas producer.
- The redelivery point will be into the NTS.
- Gas delivered by the gas producer to the gas processing facility must meet defined specifications for that facility. Generally, gas must be free from objectionable odours and from materials and dust or other solid fluid matter, waxes, gums or gum-forming constituents and any solids.
- Each gas producer must make a capacity booking for each contract period (usually October to March and April to September), and each booking will normally be made three months in advance of the start of the contract period.
- Capacity bookings will have send-or-pay (see Section 5.6) obligations (or minimum bill) attached to them at a level to be specified by the facility owner.
- Gas producers are relieved of their send-or-pay obligation during periods of *force majeure* and scheduled maintenance.
- Gas producers have carry-forward rights.
- Gas producers are required to enter into the allocation and attribution agreement for the facility. This is because gas delivered to and processed at each facility will usually come from a number of fields with differing groups of owners. Therefore, an allocation and attribution system is necessary to ensure that each party receives its correct share of the volume of gas redelivered.
- Certain priority rights will be invoked in the event of a curtailment in the

available capacity at the gas processing facility. As a general rule, available capacity will be made available first to the founding gas producers. Additional users will generally share the remaining available capacity on a pro-rata basis (ie, 'sharing the pain').

- Processing services are suspended during planned shutdown and modification periods. The main commercial terms will specify the allowable maintenance and modifications days.
- No claims are allowed between gas producers and facility owners in respect of property loss or consequential loss relating to performance under the fully termed gas processing agreement unless that loss is caused by the wilful misconduct of a party. Each party is required to indemnify and hold harmless the other party in respect of injury or death of its employees (ie, a mutual hold harmless regime).

The publication of the main commercial terms for each gas processing facility in the United Kingdom has created a framework within which facility owners and gas producers can negotiate the fully termed gas processing agreement. This in turn has significantly simplified and shortened the process for negotiating these agreements. That said, as is so often the case, 'the devil is in the detail' and the process for reaching agreement on the fully termed gas processing agreement can still be complicated and time consuming. Section 5 provides a more detailed description of the terms that are generally included in a fully termed gas processing agreement.

3.2 The Infrastructure Code of Practice

The Offshore Infrastructure Code of Practice (ICOP) sets out principles and procedures to guide both facility owners and gas producers in negotiating third-party access to oil and gas infrastructure. Its name is somewhat misleading, as its application extends beyond offshore infrastructure to onshore gas processing facilities. The Offshore Infrastructure Code of Practice has no statutory force and is not a legally binding agreement. However, the principles enshrined in it are universally observed by UK oil and gas sector. In the context of gas processing, the relevant participants are: (i) UK facility owners, (ii) owners of capacity in a gas processing facility, and (iii) gas producers. The effect of the Offshore Infrastructure Code of Practice has been to enhance the process for securing third-party access already embodied in the Gas Act 1995 by establishing clear parameters within which to negotiate third-party access to UK continental shelf infrastructure. The underlying principle of the Offshore Infrastructure Code of Practice is that access to infrastructure should be transparent and non-discriminatory.

The development of the onshore (or downstream) gas trading market in the United Kingdom has accentuated the need for timely negotiation of third-party access to gas processing facilities. This is recognised by the Offshore Infrastructure Code of Practice, which imposes on facility owners a duty to facilitate timely and efficient operation of the allocation, attribution and substitution processes. To this end, facility owners are required to give gas producers access to information which will enable the gas producer to understand the basis of their allocation and attribution and which, in turn, will enable gas producers to assist their customers to compete on level terms in the UK downstream gas trading market.

The Offshore Infrastructure Code of Practice also acknowledges that in the process of negotiating third-party access, facility owners will receive information from gas producers applying for capacity rights which is of a potentially commercially sensitive nature. To address this, the Offshore Infrastructure Code of Practice requires facility owners to impose clear controls on dissemination of such information, and they are prohibited from using the information in a way that is preferential to the facility owner or its affiliates.

One very important function of the Offshore Infrastructure Code of Practice is to set out a clear process for resolving disputes between facility owners and gas producers in respect of third-party access, so that disputes are resolved in a manner that is fair and reasonable and in line with effective competition. The Offshore Infrastructure Code of Practice provides that if a third-party gas producer is unable to agree satisfactory terms of access to capacity in the gas processing facility with the facility owner, and it appears to the third-party gas producer that there is no reasonable prospect of achieving a satisfactory outcome, the gas producer can make an application to the Secretary of State for Business, Enterprise and Regulatory Reform to require access to be granted and to determine the terms on which it is to be granted. The secretary of state is empowered by the Gas Act 1986 to resolve the dispute and, if applicable, to determine the terms (including the tariff) upon which access will be granted.

The Offshore Infrastructure Code of Practice also establishes a procedure for gaining access to UK continental shelf infrastructure (including gas processing terminals). It requires the gas producer to approach the operator of the gas processing facility in the first instance with details of its requirements for access. The operator will then formally approach the facility owners with a written request containing a statement of the gas producer's requirements and any other relevant information. At an initial meeting between all the parties, a timetable will be agreed for the negotiation process, including timeframes for any technical work that may be required.

3.3 Exemption from third-party access

Exemption from the application of third-party access rights may be granted in special circumstances. The power to grant such exemptions has been devolved to the Office of Gas and Electricity Markets (OFGEM) (which is governed by the Gas and Electricity Markets Authority), but remains subject to EU approval. In deciding whether to allow an exemption, OFGEM will consider, among other things, the participants' market shares and any other concerns related to capacity hoarding.

4. The regulatory authorities

Offshore and onshore infrastructure in the United Kingdom is subject to different legal regimes. It is well known that DBERR (at the time of writing acting through the Department of Energy and Climate Change (DECC)) is responsible for regulation of the upstream oil and gas sector and OFGEM is responsible for regulation of the downstream gas network. The question arises whether onshore gas processing terminals fall within the offshore legal regime or the onshore legal regime, as they appear to sit between the two. Geographically they are onshore at the beach, but at the same time onshore gas processing is considered to be the final part of the upstream supply chain and, until processed gas enters the NTS (or is transported elsewhere), the gas remains within the control of the upstream participants. So is DBERR or OFGEM responsible for regulating the United Kingdom's gas processing terminals? The answer is both, to differing degrees.

DBERR does not have an internal section dedicated to oil and gas operations which take place onshore. It does, however, have responsibility for monitoring the Offshore Infrastructure Code of Practice and ensuring adherence to it and, as discussed in Section 3.2 above, for resolving any disputes in respect of third-party access to gas processing facilities.

OFGEM is responsible for the regulation of the UK onshore gas market and monitors compliance with the onshore regulatory framework. It is immediately apparent from relevant legislation (notably the Gas Act 1995) and publicly available sources of information that OFGEM is responsible for the regulation of gas storage facilities located onshore in the United Kingdom. What is less clear is the scope of authority that OFGEM has in respect of the United Kingdom's onshore gas processing facilities, and to date little has been written about regulation of these facilities. OFGEM's powers and duties in respect of gas processing facilities are largely provided for in statute and include responsibility for granting exemptions to third-party access (as discussed in Section 3.3 above).

5. Gas processing agreements

This section sets out details of the main provisions that would normally be included in a gas processing agreement. These provisions are broadly consistent with the provisions that are generally included in agreements for the processing of oil in the United Kingdom's oil processing terminals.

5.1 Parties

As a general rule, each gas producer with entitlement to production from a field (under the terms of the joint operating agreement for the field) will individually contract with the facility owners under a single gas processing agreement. It is fairly common for the operator of the facility to contract in its own right and to assume responsibility for the performance of specific obligations under the gas processing agreement.

Gas producers and facility owners are required to operate their respective facilities in a diligent and prudent manner, which is often defined by reference to the standard of a 'reasonable and prudent operator'.

5.2 Scope of services

The gas processing agreement will spell out exactly what services the facility owner will provide to the gas producer. There are generally two types of service:

- those which are provided in return for the payment of an agreed tariff (tariff services); and

- 'non-tariff services', for which the facility owner will charge the gas producer separately.

Tariff services will generally include:

- receipt of a volume of raw gas meeting the agreed delivery specification up to the firm capacity nomination of the gas producer;
- performance by the operator of the facility (on behalf of the facility owners) of the processing methodologies and production of processed gas product; and
- redelivery of processed gas product at the delivery point which complies with the agreed redelivery specification. In the United Kingdom, the redelivery point is usually the NTS and the NTS has its own delivery specifications.

Non-tariff services are generally services that are not of a routine nature, but which may be required over the life of the gas processing agreement. One example is where modifications or additional equipment are required at the gas processing facility to accommodate the gas producer's gas. In this scenario, the facility owner will provide the required modifications or equipment on a full-cost reimbursement basis at no (or little) risk to the facility owner. Any modifications or additional equipment will become the property of the facility owner. Another example is the provision of additional chemicals by the facility owner, in the event that it becomes necessary to treat the gas producer's gas with specific additional chemicals to ensure gas redelivered to the redelivery point after processing meets the specifications for the redelivery point.

5.3 Service commencement date

It is usually in the interest of both the facility owner and the gas producer to agree a 'commencement date' when their respective obligations to each other will commence, regardless of whether the facility owner is ready to receive gas for processing or the gas producer is ready to commence deliveries of gas to the gas processing facility. This is achieved by the inclusion of a 'funnelling' or 'window' mechanism.

The gas producer will be keen to ensure that there is a fixed commencement date when the processing services will begin. This is to ensure that the gas producer's scheduled start of first commercial production is not frustrated by the gas processing facility not being ready to receive its gas. It is likely that the gas producer will have entered into one or more gas sales agreements for the sale of its produced gas and the gas producer will need to know that it will have processed gas available to it, so that it can honour its obligations under its gas sales agreements and can start receiving revenue from its gas sales. The readiness of the facility owner will be less of a concern where receipt of the gas producer's production does not require any modifications to, or additional equipment at, the receiving gas processing facility. This is because the risk of delay caused by modifications or adding the new equipment is removed.

If the facility owner is not ready to start receiving gas on the commencement date for any reason (including delays incurred in completing any modifications or in installing any additional equipment or infrastructure that is required at the processing facility), the gas producer is likely to suffer substantial loss from lost or deferred production. It is also likely that the gas producer will incur liability to a gas buyer who is expecting to purchase volumes of gas from the commencement date under a gas sales agreement with the gas producer. The gas producer will seek to offset this liability under the gas processing agreement. Typically, the gas producer will seek monetary compensation to offset any liability it incurs under its gas sales agreements and the facility owner will seek to limit the amount of compensation it is willing to pay to the gas producer (if any). There will usually be discussion about whether the parties can recover consequential loss (see Section 5.10) and the outcome of this discussion may affect the extent to which the gas producer can recover its losses from the facility owner. The usual exclusions from liability will apply for *force majeure* (see Section 5.12).

For the facility owner, the commencement date marks the time when the gas producer's send-or-pay obligation commences, so the gas producer is obliged (with very limited exceptions) to pay the tariff to the facility owner from this date even if the gas producer is not ready to start deliveries to the gas processing facility.

5.4 Capacity reservations

This clause will reserve for the gas producer an agreed level of capacity in the facility. The facility owner will 'sterilise' this capacity so that it can only be utilised by the gas producer. The gas producer will be under an obligation to make a capacity payment (see Section 5.6 below) for a portion of that reserved capacity whether it is used or not and irrespective of the quantity of gas that is actually processed. This send-or-pay (or minimum bill) obligation guarantees a minimum revenue stream for the facility owner and guarantees the gas producer a minimum level of capacity in the gas processing facility.

It is common for the facility owner to accept gas for processing over the nominated firm capacity (excess gas) on a reasonable-endeavours or discretionary basis.

5.5 Tariff

As mentioned at Section 5.2 above, the facility owner will charge the gas producer a tariff in relation to the tariff services. The tariff is normally expressed as a formula assessed on the volume of gas processed at the facility. In charging the tariff, the facility owner is looking to recover both infrastructure and operating costs whilst receiving a return on the business of processing the gas.

There may be regulatory issues to consider in charging a tariff to the gas producer especially in relation to the Gas Act 1995 and third-party access to the facility (see Section 3.1). In summary, the tariff must be fair and reasonable.

The agreement should also stipulate the currency under which the tariff is payable and deal with indexing the tariff to take into account general inflation.

Mention should be made as to whether any form of tax is included in the tariff, such as VAT or environmental taxes. The facility owner will normally request reimbursement of any tax incurred via its processing of the gas on behalf of the gas producer.

5.6 Send-or-pay

The facility owner will usually require the gas producer to enter into a 'send-or-pay' commitment in order to guarantee itself a minimum income. Under such a commitment, the gas producer will pay for the processing of a defined base volume of gas in a year regardless of whether or not those volumes are delivered to the facility.

send-or-pay essentially offsets some of the risk on the facility owner in recovering part of the initial capital outlay on the facility and its operating expenses. Where the capital outlay in the facility has already been recovered, it is usual for the facility owner to argue that a send-or-pay obligation is the quid pro quo for guaranteed processing capacity in the facility for the gas producer. To the extent that capacity is sterilised (ie, dedicated to a particular gas producer), it represents a lost opportunity for the facility owner if it is not used by the gas producer and the facility owner will attach a cost to that lost opportunity (the cost being the send-or-pay obligation).

The send-or-pay commitment level is freely negotiable between the facility owner and the gas producer, but it tends to fall within the 65% to 80% range.

The facility owner will usually want the send-or-pay obligation to start on the commencement date of the gas processing agreement (see Section 5.3). It is normal for the send-or-pay obligation not to apply where volumes of gas from the gas producer are reduced as a result of particular circumstances, such as constraints in either the facility or a *force majeure* event impacting upon either the facility owner or the gas producer.

Minimum send-or-pay obligations are usually settled on a monthly basis, with overall calculations made on an annual basis. It may transpire that a gas producer has made an overall send-or-pay payment in a year, but it has not fully utilised its reserved capacity in the facility. In circumstances such as these, the gas processing agreement may provide for make-up/carry-forward rights or a discount in future years when the gas producer's use of capacity might exceed its reserved capacity. As the objective of send-or-pay is to produce a guaranteed minimum income over the life of the gas processing facility, the facility owner may agree to this offset; however, this will be a matter for negotiation between the parties at the contract stage. Such mechanisms dealing with make-up/carry-forward rights can take the form of fairly complex provisions in a gas processing agreement.

5.7 Throughput restrictions

There will need to be provision in the gas processing agreement permitting the facility owner to reduce the volumes of gas it is required to take delivery of in certain situations and a blanket provision stating when it may stop taking delivery altogether. Examples of where the facility owner will need to invoke the blanket provision include:

- to address environmental or safety issues;
- to conduct maintenance on the facility;
- in the event that the gas producer fails to meet the delivery specification; and
- in the event of a breakdown or a failure in the gas processing facility.

Usually, the facility owner will not incur any liability to the gas producer for suspension of the services in the situations cited above unless the suspension was necessary because of some wrongdoing on the part of the facility owner.

In prolonged periods when the facility owner is unable to provide the processing services, the gas producer will wish to ensure that it is able to switch to an alternative means of gas processing under temporary arrangements with other facility owners if it is physically possible to achieve this. The facility owner will often be required to give reasonable notice as to when it will be ready to resume the services, so as to mitigate any cancellation charges involved in such temporary arrangements. Such interruptions to delivery will only usually be permitted on a defined number of occasions in each year.

A standard remedy for the gas producer in circumstances where the facility owner is unable to receive volumes of gas for processing is for the facility owner to provide the gas producer with compensation in the form of 'tariff-free volumes of gas'. This remedy can be invoked for the facility owner's failure to receive gas from the commencement date and thereafter for a failure to receive and process gas during the life of the gas processing agreement. Tariff-free volumes permit the gas producer to deliver a quantity of gas to the facility owner without having to pay the requisite tariff in relation to that delivery. In addition to providing compensation to the gas producer for any lost or deferred production, this provision will act as an incentive on the facility owner to ensure capacity is available.

5.8 Curtailment

In the event of any constraints on the system restricting the ability of the facility owner to take delivery of gas, the rules for allocation of any available capacity between all users should be clearly defined in the gas processing agreement.

Although the gas producer will want to be given priority or at least equal rights to other users with capacity in the facility, in some scenarios priority rights may already have been awarded elsewhere (ie, to earlier users of the gas processing facility).

5.9 Measurement and testing

The facility owner will normally consent to install and have in place all measurement and testing facilities in the facility and to permit a representative of the gas producer to observe the operation of the measurement and testing facilities.

The facility owner will also provide the representative of the gas producer at their request with any measurement or test data that they may require for their audit. The gas producer should limit the frequency of its requests to circumstances that reasonably require it.

In the gas processing agreement, the facility owner and gas producer should set out the standards to which the quantity of gas will be measured and how it will be analysed. The standards will usually be based on internationally accepted standards in the industry, and the results should be published objectively.

At the beginning of each month, the gas producers should inform the facility owner of the final quantities of gas delivered.

5.10 Liabilities and indemnities

The gas processing agreement will set out liability and remedies for specific events such as delivery of off-specification gas, failure to process or deliver, or throughput restrictions.

Outside of the agreement on liabilities and remedies for specific events, the standard approach towards liability in gas processing agreements is to adopt a mutual 'hold harmless' regime. Under this 'knock for knock' model, the facility owner and gas producer will each accept liability for loss or damage to specified facilities and property and for death or personal injury to employees. This would be the case even if the loss or damage is caused by the other party. At its most basic, the regime holds that each party must bear its own losses and liabilities.

The knock-for-knock regime will often (but not always) extend to each party's consequential loss and therefore this provision will need to take into account the definition of 'consequential loss'. Consequential loss has a well-established meaning in English Law. The standard definition comprises losses that can reasonably have been supposed to have been in the contemplation of the parties at the time they entered into the contract. This can include indirect losses flowing from a breach. Consequential loss is therefore anything that is beyond what is considered normal loss flowing from a breach of contract and can include lost profits or expenses incurred through the breach, subject to the rules on remoteness.

The definition of consequential loss under gas processing agreements is normally much broader in scope than the general legal principle and will encompass losses beyond those which were supposed to have been in the contemplation of the parties at the time the contract was made. It is common for the definition of consequential loss in a gas processing agreement to set out an exhaustive list of the events that will be covered by the definition, including lost profits, loss of use, loss or damage incurred, losses associated with business operation, and loss of bargain, contract, expectation or opportunity.

A further consideration is whether the mutual hold-harmless regime is disapplied where the loss is caused by the wilful misconduct of a party. It is common to hold one party liable for the losses of the other party (ie, to disapply the mutual hold-harmless regime) where the loss is caused by wilful misconduct of the first party. Wilful misconduct will need to be defined in the gas processing agreement, as it does not have a recognised meaning under English Law. Where the facility owner and the gas producer have agreed caps on liability, they will need to consider whether the cap should be disapplied in circumstances of wilful misconduct.

Consideration should also be given as to whether the benefit of the indemnity protection should extend beyond the parties (and typically their respective affiliates) to their contractors and sub-contractors.

5.11 Ownership and risk of loss

The gas processing agreement will usually make it clear that the risk in, and property rights relating to, the gas while it is in the gas processing facility will remain with the gas producer at all times, and the gas producer should insure the volumes of gas against risk of loss or damage throughout.

5.12 *Force majeure*

The *force majeure* clause should clearly define the limitations of relief available to the parties.

This clause should relieve any party from liability for failure to perform any of its obligations under the agreement caused by circumstances which are judged beyond its control. The affected party is normally required to continue to perform its obligations to the extent possible.

A non-exhaustive list of the circumstances that may give rise to *force majeure* is often included in the gas processing agreement, with a catch-all provision that *force majeure* relief will also be available regarding any other event outside a party's control when acting as a reasonable and prudent operator, unless it is specifically excluded in the agreement.

It will also be worth including a provision that deals with the obligations of each party during the period when *force majeure* is being claimed, how the relief afforded by *force majeure* should be managed in the interim period, and where there has been a prolonged event of *force majeure*, whether the parties are able to terminate the entire agreement.

5.13 Dispute resolution

A dispute resolution clause should provide for how disputes are to be resolved and aim to ensure that the agreement remains in operation to the greatest possible extent until the dispute is finally determined. To take account of this, a clause should be included in the gas processing agreement stating that, whenever a dispute arises, the parties must continue to perform their respective obligations and covenants to the greatest extent possible.

There are several dispute resolution mechanisms the parties may choose to include in the agreement and they all have varying levels of cost, formality and speed of resolution. Below are some of the more common dispute-resolution mechanisms adopted in gas processing agreements:

- *Expert determination.* Expert determination may be used for disputes of a technical nature, such as whether gas delivered or redelivered met the agreed specifications. Under this process the parties together will appoint an independent expert who will adjudicate on the matter in dispute. The agreement will normally state that his decision will be final and binding on the parties, or provide the procedure under which his decision can be appealed to the courts. It will be important to make provision regarding which party has responsibility for payment of costs.
- *Arbitration.* This clause will define the type of dispute to be referred to arbitration, the venue and language of the arbitration, the mandate and procedural law applicable and the procedure for the selection and appointment of the arbitrators. It will also make provision for resolving any failure to agree on any aspect of arbitration. The parties will decide on the rules that will regulate the procedure of the arbitration. It is common practice to refer disputes under gas processing agreements to arbitration.
- *Litigation.* The agreement may state that disputes are to be settled in court.

In addition to providing for dispute resolution there should be a governing law clause included in the agreement, stating the law applicable to the gas processing agreements. For gas processing agreements relating to facilities located in the United Kingdom, English law will be the governing law (except in rare cases where Scottish law may be adopted).

5.14 Term and termination

The term of the gas processing agreement will ideally continue until the sources from which the gas producers obtain their gas permanently cease production (ie, at the end of the field life). This is difficult to predict accurately, since prediction of gas reserves and rates of production is often imprecise; but it is common, notwithstanding these difficulties, to identify at least a minimum term.

The agreement may otherwise be terminated because an event entitling a party to terminate has arisen, and the right of termination has been exercised.

The termination clause of the agreement may permit early termination under any one or more of the following circumstances:

- if the relevant approvals and consents are not obtained by the commencement date;
- a failure by the gas producer to deliver any gas within a specified number of days of the commencement date for reasons other than *force majeure*;
- a failure by the facility owner to take delivery of the gas or provide the services for a predetermined period for reasons other than *force majeure*;
- a failure by the gas producer to deliver gas for a predetermined period during the term of the agreement;
- termination of the agreement by one party because of the other party's insolvency. Insolvency should be defined as under statute; and
- a *force majeure* event which has resulted in the suspension of the services and has continued for a predetermined period (specified in the *force majeure* clause), causing the frustration of the entire agreement.

Notice of termination should be provided by either party within the time limits set out prior to the date of termination. The clause should also state that the obligations and rights granted to the parties under the agreement shall survive any termination of the agreement.

There will also need to be provision made for post-termination consequences such as continuing covenants and obligations regarding confidentiality and the limitations of liability between the parties.

A clause dealing with damages and compensation should be inserted, and this should set out the rights of the parties to claim damages or compensation due to losses which they may have suffered as a result of wrongful termination.

5.15 Miscellaneous

This section of the gas processing agreement will set out the standard boilerplate clauses to be included in the agreement. The following provisions may be included:

- a list of the designated representatives of each party to the agreement, the authority of each representative and the procedure under which each party may change their representative;

- how any communications or notices under the agreement are to be transmitted between the parties (ie, the permitted formats in which communications or notices are to be given, the methods of delivery and when such communications shall be deemed to have been given); the addresses for the service of such communications for each party will also be given. There will often also be discussion whether notice by e-mail is permissible;
- the procedure for transferring the rights and obligations under the agreement and defining the extent to which such rights and obligations may be transferred should also be included;
- a clause dealing with 'waiver of rights', which will usually emphasise that such a waiver shall not apply to future defaults;
- a provision obliging the parties to keep all information and documents pertaining to the agreement confidential, together with a limited set of circumstances in which a party can disclose such information without the consent of the other party;
- a clause stating that the implementation of the entire agreement is conditional on the obtaining of all necessary consents and approvals from various agencies and, where applicable, which party is responsible for obtaining such consents and approvals – this may be documented as conditions precedent to the effectiveness of the gas processing agreement;
- a provision stating that the agreement represents the entire agreement between the parties and that it supersedes any prior agreement concerning the provision of services;
- an insurance provision requiring each party to take out and maintain insurance up to a minimum value with reputable insurers in respect of any loss or damage to the gas or the facilities;
- how any liabilities for taxation are to be allocated between the parties; and
- the warranties and representations to be given by the parties.

Decommissioning of upstream oil and gas facilities[1]

Flávia Kaczelnik Altit
Mark Osa Igiehon
Shell International BV

1. Introduction[2]

The decommissioning of disused offshore oil and gas structures has posed a plethora of legal, regulatory and technical challenges for international law, states and the oil and gas industry. This chapter discusses the progressive development of international law on the subject; how the international oil and gas industry as well as international law have struggled to find the right balance in formulating rules and standards for disposal of disused structures; the seminal effect of the Brent Spar episode on the development of international law and policy; and current law and practices across regions and selected jurisdictions. The chapter identifies evolving legal, policy and removal trends and innovations, and discusses regional law and policy developments in the Gulf of Mexico and North Sea (North East Atlantic), which are suggested as pivotal to general international law. The chapter concludes with aspects of the decommissioning challenge that can now be considered as resolved and those aspects that remain unfinished and with discussion of some particularly challenging issues and jurisdictions.

2. Abandonment or decommissioning

'Decommissioning' describes the set of activities to be undertaken to manage and dispose of installations and platforms and eliminate environmental footprint once a producing field is nearing, or reaches, the end of its economic life. In this chapter, the discussion is focused on the decommissioning of those oil and gas installations typically placed on the continental shelf, as these are the subjects of international law. It is estimated that there are more than 6,500 such offshore installations in place around the world.[3]

Decommissioning may involve leaving in place, dismantling, removing or sinking disused facilities. Other technical activities forming part of decommissioning include plugging and abandonment of wells, pipelines, risers and related facilities. The option to be selected will take into consideration the impact on the environment, the safety of personnel and other users of the sea, the reputational impact of any decision and the most cost-effective solution.

Terminologies associated with decommissioning are very interesting and have

1 This chapter is a modified version of a paper originally published by the Rocky Mountain Mineral Law Foundation in the Proceedings of the 53rd Annual Rocky Mountain Mineral Law Institute (2007).
2 The views expressed in this chapter are personal to the authors and do not reflect official Shell position.
3 www.info.ogp.org.uk/decommissioning.

evolved alongside international law on the subject. 'Abandonment', 'removal' and 'disposal' are terms commonly used to describe the process of managing and/or disposing of disused installations. However, the most appropriate term is 'decommissioning', and this is the term which is increasingly gaining currency within the oil and gas industry, as well as among international law commentators. This trend contrasts with the previous tendency to use the term 'abandonment'. It was initially suggested that offshore oil and gas installations should be likened to shipwrecks. It was argued that on disuse, offshore oil and gas installations could be abandoned by the operator, similar to the right of a shipowner to abandon a shipwreck, without any further legal liability or responsibility for the same.[4] It is, however, now commonly accepted as a general principle of international law as well as a requirement of international treaties that the relevant coastal state is responsible for ensuring that disused installations are removed from the continental shelf, or otherwise handled in accordance with the rules of international law.

3. Decommissioning outlook and activities

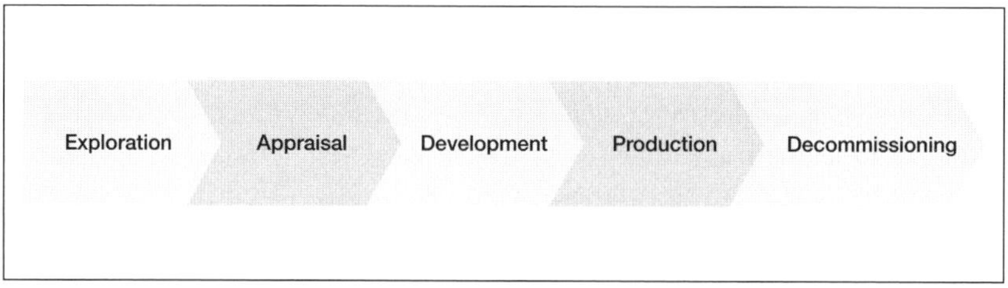

Decommissioning activities form part of the licence to operate. Although decommissioning occurs at the tail end of the upstream oil and gas industry activity cycle, it entails a number of challenges. These include giving consideration to the potential effect on the environment, concerns regarding sustainable development, the level of preparatory work involved, the complexity of the removal activity, high costs and the challenges of a rather complex regulatory structure. It is now obvious to the oil and gas industry, as well as to international law commentators, that the challenges of offshore decommissioning are quite considerable and not to be underestimated – see the diagram on the next page for the scale of the structures involved.[5] Careful planning and preparation (including anticipatory plans during the development phase of an offshore field) are now good practice and a timely plan, properly conceived, is essential to the success of a decommissioning project.[6]

4 See Bruce M Kramer and Gary B Conine, *Joint Development and Operations in International Petroleum Transactions,* Second Edition, Rocky Mt Min L Fdn, 2000, p 651: *"The difficulty with the term 'abandonment' is that it is wrongly believed that the liability of the owner or the operator of the installation continues forever. It should be noted here that the rules on abandonment of a wreck are quite different. Under §531 of the Merchant Shipping Act 1894, as amended, a shipowner is under a duty to remove a wreck if it constitutes an obstruction or hazard to navigation and is liable for any damages suffered by a passing ship if such damage is caused by the lack of marking. (Once the harbour authority or the P&I Club has accepted notice of abandonment, however, the owner normally is relieved of further liability.)"*

5 Diagram used by the kind permission of OGP; © OGP International Association of Oil and Gas Producers: http://info.ogp.org.uk/Decommissioning/Solution.html.

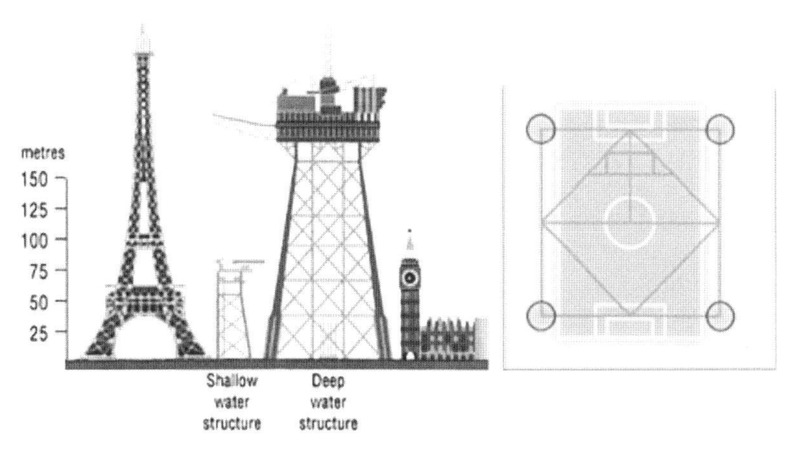

Decommissioning activities are now expected to increase across the global oil and gas industry, with peak decommissioning activity levels likely to be concentrated in the two main regions of the United States' Gulf of Mexico and the North Sea, at least for the foreseeable future. In the United States' Gulf of Mexico, at least 210 installations have been removed to date. However, it is thought that as many as 1,000 other fixed installations have ceased production but are yet to be decommissioned. To address the backlog, the US Minerals Management Service (MMS) directed that by the end of 2006 all inactive offshore platforms should be reactivated or put to some other agreed use, or removed entirely.[7] It remains to be seen, how much progress has been made towards meeting the end-2006 target set by the MMS.

Across the North Sea, some 40 fields have been abandoned[8] to date with a further 66 in the process of, or awaiting, abandonment. Of the 40 fields abandoned, 23 are in the United Kingdom, 11 in Norway and six in the Netherlands.[9] The trend definitely shows an increasing rate of decommissioning and a decreasing rate of new fields or installations. In the United Kingdom, it is expected that some 280 installations (out of some 470 installations altogether) will be decommissioned during the peak removal years from 2012 to 2024 (see graph on next page).

The impending increase in the level of decommissioning activities, particularly in the Gulf of Mexico and the North Sea, is a clear indication that the subject will become even more pressing for the international oil and gas industry, interested non-governmental organisations and other stakeholders as well as international law commentators. The graph below[10] shows the estimated dates for decommissioning of

6 In the UK continental shelf, it is recommended that planning begin not less than three years before cessation of production.

7 Scottish Enterprise, *Gulf of Mexico 2005 Oil and Gas Report*, pp 4 and 38.

8 Considering that fields described here also include fields permanently shut-in but not necessarily decommissioned yet, the choice of the term 'abandonment' seems appropriate.

9 Wood Mackenzie, "Decommissioning in the North Sea", in *Upstream Insights*, November 2006.

10 Graph used by the kind permission of UK Offshore Decommissioning Unit; © UK Department of Energy and Climate Change: https://www.og.berr.gov.uk/upstream/decommissioning/forecast_rem.htm.

offshore oil and gas installations in the United Kingdom continental shelf and demonstrates that the oil and gas industry is moving into full-scale decommissioning at least in the North Sea.

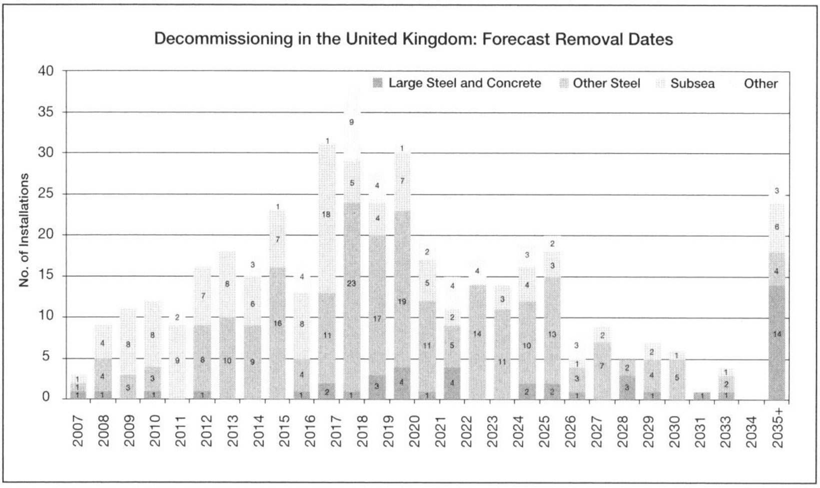

As to costs, Wood Mackenzie estimates that future decommissioning in the North Sea will cost some US$42 billion (2007 prices) with the bulk of that to be spent in Norway (48%) and the United Kingdom (40%).[11] The International Marine Contractors Association estimates that global expenditure on decommissioning will exceed US$75 billion.[12] It is therefore clear that the costs to be expended by the oil industry (in many cases to be contributed to by host governments either directly or indirectly through fiscal means) are sizeable. One question therefore is how the various parties who are to bear the costs of decommissioning can arrange to do so in a thorough manner. The issue of how to ensure that there are companies or corporate entities available and able to meet the cost of eventual decommissioning, at the end of a field's life, remains problematic in many jurisdictions. This is clearly unfinished business.

4. Relevant and topical issues

4.1 Liabilities

Perhaps among the biggest legal challenges relating to decommissioning activities are the issues of liability and responsibility for undertaking decommissioning and removal. The issues and questions include:

- Who is to undertake decommissioning activities?
- Who is to bear the costs of the decommissioning?

11 Wood Mackenzie, as n 9.
12 International Marine Contractors Association's Press Release 09/06: http://www.imca-int.com/core/imca/news/press/0609.html.

- Do past licence holders retain liability after divestment?
- What about perpetual liability? Do the operator and/or non-operator partners retain liability beyond the end of the decommissioning activities? For example, who will be responsible for any deterioration of installations and pipelines if they are left in place?
- In a joint venture environment, do all companies' present financial capabilities? What are the consequences if they are jointly and severally liable?
- Is it possible to provide accurate cost estimates for future decommissioning?

4.2 Cost recovery, accounting and tax

Accounting for decommissioning costs will vary according to the legislation of each country. The tax treatment of the cost of decommissioning is key to the recoverability of such costs, and such recoverability is not always certain. Points helpful to determining the most appropriate way of accounting for such costs are whether there are statutory or contractual obligations in place; whether there are requirements to contribute to abandonment funds; whether such funds are properly secured for future use; and whether they will suffice.

On the tax side, it is desirable that the decommissioning funds set aside for future obligations can be accounted for as expenses. Not all tax regimes allow this, considering that costs have not yet been incurred.

4.3 Decommissioning funds and other forms of security

Decommissioning costs are extremely high and will be incurred when the field is no longer producing at its highest level (if at all). Hence, securing funds early for eventual decommissioning activities, and preferably well ahead of time, is a good preparatory measure. However, in view of questions relating to what type of security is required or accepted, and for what period of time, along with the tax treatment and the costs of such security, the otherwise sound preventive measure of providing early security has proved to be problematic in many jurisdictions.

Ordinarily speaking, the best security is a decommissioning fund, by which certain sums are contributed from time to time during the economic life of the field, in order to build up a cash fund. Such a fund will then be utilised to finance removal or decommissioning activities in the future, when production ceases.

There are various forms of security, including abandonment funds, trust funds, letters of credit, performance bonds and parent company guarantees.

The establishment of a form of security will be a significant issue for licensees and co-venturers, with respect to their obligations to one another. This issue will also be of interest to transferors in the event of a transfer or assignment of participating interests, when past licence holders hold residual liabilities; and governments will also wish to secure the compliance of licensees with regard to their decommissioning obligations.

4.4 Process planning etc

As discussed above, due to the complexity of decommissioning, planning is essential if success is to be assured and more easily attained, and difficulties reduced or eliminated. Matters relating to decommissioning should be addressed at the early stages of field development and not left until mid or late field life. The field development plan should address decommissioning, provision of financial security, indicative plans made for addressing liabilities, estimated costs, funding and execution of decommissioning activities.

The mapping of the regulatory framework is an important element of the plan, perhaps as important as the analysis and mapping of the stakeholders to be engaged in the process. A stakeholder engagement plan should be in place and address the required approvals and permits and wider society's concerns and expectations. The plan should also list the facilities to be decommissioned. This is not an easy task, considering the numerous materials and components, and the complexity of their integration.

The decommissioning process itself should begin with the setting up of a dedicated decommissioning team. The decommissioning team should as a minimum include (on a full- or part-time basis) personnel from both technical and support disciplines, such as finance, operations and maintenance, economics, logistics, well engineering, contracts, external affairs, tax, and legal.

The destination of hazardous materials (oil waste, asbestos, chromium and so on) must be properly addressed. Similarly, transportation and destination are sensitive matters to be considered, especially where it is planned to move waste across international borders. Equally important is the establishment of safe procedures for the workers or contractors who will deal with hazardous materials and those who will undertake the decommissioning activities in the field. Therefore, a health and safety programme should be put in place, following a risk assessment.

It is also important to engage with contractors at an early stage, to check their availability and the availability of vessels, materials, equipment and machinery necessary to undertake the decommissioning. Supply chain has an important role in the process and in activities such as subsea studies and site surveys, project management, facility decommissioning, well decommissioning and abandonment, disposal of structures, post survey and so on. The number of experienced and specialised contractors, who have the requisite technical capacity to undertake highly complex decommissioning operations, is small relative to the number of facilities to be decommissioned in the short to medium term.

The decommissioning plan will define the destination and possible usage of the items to be decommissioned. The possibilities include salvage, waste storage, recycling and reuse. Commercial possibilities will also be assessed, including carbon capture and storage, gas storage and pipeline reuse. A diagram of the major steps in such a plan is shown overleaf.

4.5 Other issues

Other factors to be considered when planning for decommissioning include health and environment, safety of navigation, age of installation, cost–benefit societal pressures, and public and stakeholder perceptions.

It is in the best interest of all stakeholders (oil companies, governments and governmental agencies, regulators, local communities and non-governmental organisations) that a clear and reasonable set of decommissioning obligations is

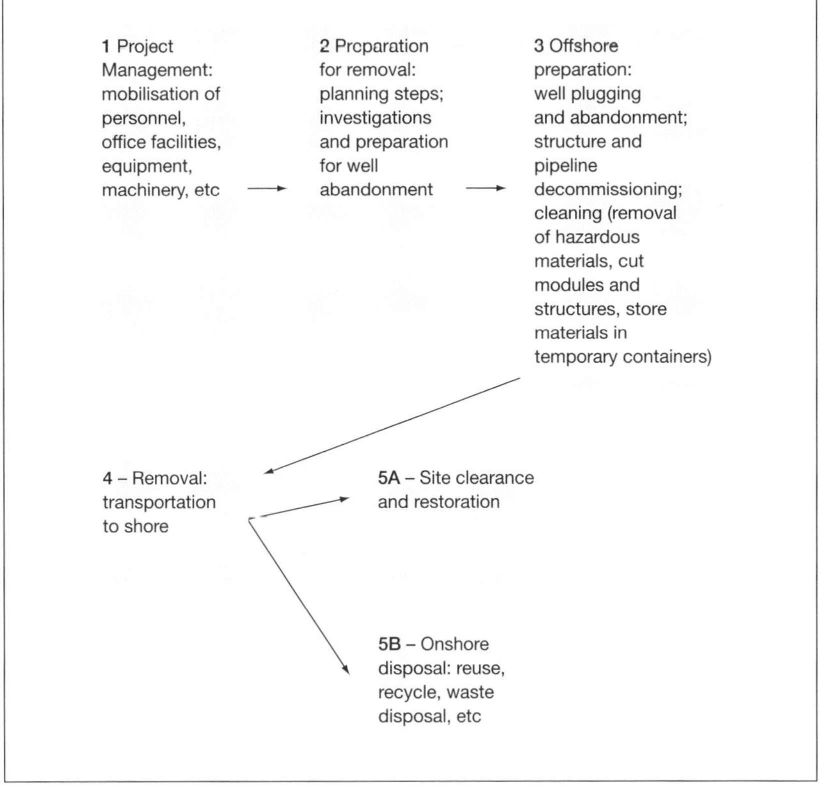

Decommissioning activities map[13]

established. At a minimum, they should include a definition of liabilities, details of either the funding mechanism or adequate provision (funds or provision to be cost recoverable, tax deductible and appropriate and sufficient), plans for sustainable development, impact on the environment and standards generally accepted in the international oil and gas industry to drive the decommissioning plans to be agreed and implemented.

5. Progress of international law on decommissioning

International law obligations and regulations relating to the disposal of disused offshore oil and gas installations progressed from the initial absolute-removal regime of Article 5(5) of the Geneva Convention on the Continental Shelf 1958, to the permissive provisions of Article 60(3) of the United Nations Law of the Sea Convention 1982 (UNCLOS). Article 5(5) was the first opportunity for international law to provide for the handling of disused offshore oil and gas structures. It provided simply that: "Due notice must be given of the construction of any such installations, and permanent means for giving warning of their presence must be maintained. Any installations which are abandoned or disused must be entirely removed."

13 *Source:* Shell UK Limited.

Although it would appear that the provisions of Article 5(5) were plain and unambiguous, a lively debate ensued as to the interpretation of the article. One school of thought contended that complete removal of disused offshore oil and gas installations was required, whilst another body of opinion argued that Article 5(5) permitted partial or less-than-complete removal (and in appropriate cases, even leaving in place disused installations). The vigorous debate formed the background to the negotiations on the subject of offshore decommissioning in the conferences and discussions that led to the finalisation and adoption of the United Nations Law of the Sea Convention (UNCLOS) in 1982. Article 60(3) of UNCLOS provides *inter alia* that:

> *"Any installations or structures which are abandoned or disused shall be removed to ensure safety of navigation, taking into account any generally accepted international standards established in this regard by the competent international organization. Such removal shall also have due regard to fishing, the protection of the marine environment and the rights and duties of other States. Appropriate publicity shall be given to the depth, position and dimensions of any installations or structures not entirely removed."*

UNCLOS had a number of significant implications for the evolution of international law on decommissioning of offshore oil and gas installations. First, its requirements are clearly less onerous than those of Article 5(5) of the 1958 Geneva Continental Shelf Convention. Secondly, it established, or admitted for the first time in unequivocal terms, the concept of partial or less-than-complete removal of disused installations. In view of the analysis of law and practice in a number of jurisdictions considered in this chapter, and the identification of customary international law on the subject, it can now be concluded for the purposes of international law that the less-than-complete-removal regime established by Article 60(3) of UNCLOS has now superseded the complete-removal regime set out in the 1958 Continental Shelf Convention. However, unlike the rather emphatic and conclusive provisions of Article 5(5) of the 1958 Convention, the provisions of Article 60(3) of UNCLOS are somewhat tentative to the extent that the setting of detailed rules or standards for offshore decommissioning was left to be established by an unspecified "competent international organization".

In 1989, and before UNCLOS came into force, the International Maritime Organization assumed the mantle of the unspecified "competent international organization" and consequently adopted the IMO Guidelines and Standards for the Removal of Offshore Installations and Structures on the Continental Shelf and in the Exclusive Economic Zone 1989.[14] The IMO Guidelines and Standards, though not legally binding, effectively give to coastal states considerable discretion to determine in what manner any particular disused facility may be dealt with on decommissioning. The guidelines set out a general principle that all abandoned or disused offshore installations or structures on the continental shelf should be removed except where non-removal or partial removal is consistent with the detailed standards.[15] The decision as to whether to allow a disused structure to remain on the seabed should be taken by the relevant coastal state after assessment to be

14 www.imo.org/home.asp.
15 IMO Guidelines, clause 1.1.

undertaken on a case-by-case basis.[16] One difficulty with the IMO Guidelines and Standards is that they are recommendatory in nature and not binding.[17] This may have been one of the many factors that contributed to the Brent Spar episode.

5.1 The Brent Spar episode

The Brent Spar was a cylindrical buoy (offshore the United Kingdom) owned and utilised by Shell and Esso, as an offshore storage and loading facility. The spar ceased operating in 1991 and was made ready for disposal. After numerous detailed studies, deep-sea disposal or dumping was thought the "best practicable option" and the UK government granted a permit for that purpose.[18] The spar was being towed to its final disposal site when Greenpeace activists boarded it. Greenpeace claimed that deep-sea disposal would damage the marine environment[19] and could set a bad precedent for other disused installations in the North Sea. An international furore followed. On the one hand, the UK government contended that it and Shell were acting properly and consistently under international law. At the same time, Greenpeace's protest attracted support from many western European countries (including some European governments). There followed a boycott of Shell products and petrol stations and, in a few instances, firebombing of stations. Eventually, Shell decided unilaterally to abandon deep-sea disposal and instead opted to scrap the spar onshore.

The implications of the Brent Spar episode for the development of international law and policy on offshore decommissioning were far-reaching and are beyond the scope of this chapter.[20] The episode turned out to be the defining moment for the development of international law and policy on decommissioning of disused offshore oil and gas installations. In the first place, it brought the issue of offshore decommissioning into the public arena. Secondly, the incident acted as a test of the prevailing international law on offshore decommissioning (as represented by the provisions of Article 60(3) of UNCLOS and the IMO Guidelines and Standards 1989). The Brent Spar episode suggested that the IMO Guidelines and Standards (and perhaps Article 60(3) to a lesser extent) were inadequate to meet the competing considerations relating to offshore decommissioning and therefore failed to be conclusive of rule-making on the subject.

Most of the policy and law developments relating to offshore decommissioning since Brent Spar have taken place in Europe. This is perhaps to be expected, in that the United Kingdom and other European countries in the North Sea area were those with the closest connection to the Brent Spar case. Furthermore, as seen earlier, the oil and gas sector in the North Sea has reached maturity, and planning has now begun in earnest for the decommissioning of many fields and installations.

5.2 OSPAR Decision 98/3

The Oslo and Paris Commission adopted the OSPAR Decision 98/3 on the Disposal of

---

16 IMO Guidelines, clause 3.4.

17 IMO Guidelines, preamble 2.

18 Shell UK, *North Sea abandonment Brent Spar disposal*, Shell Media Information, February 16 1995.

19 "Security Men Storm Oil Platform Held by Greenpeace", *The Times*, May 24 1995.

20 For a fuller examination, see Igiehon and Park, "Evolution of International Law on the Decommissioning of Oil and Gas Installations" (2001) *IELTR* 198.

Disused Offshore Installations, which came into force on February 9 1999. The decision set out detailed guidelines, standards and procedures to govern the decommissioning of disused offshore platforms in the North-East Atlantic area. The preamble to the decision provides the policy thrust underlying the guidelines and states:

"RECALLING the relevant provisions of the United Nations Convention on the Law of the Sea,

RECOGNIZING that an increasing number of offshore installations in the maritime area are approaching the end of their operational life-time ...

RECOGNIZING that reuse, recycling or final disposal on land will generally be the preferred option for the decommissioning of offshore installations in the maritime area,

ACKNOWLEDGING that the national legal and administrative systems of relevant Contracting Parties need to make adequate provision for establishing and satisfying legal liabilities in respect of disused offshore installations ..."

The OSPAR Decision 98/3 sets out very detailed guidelines emphasising the rule that complete removal of disused platforms is the norm.[21] Member states may grant permits allowing derogation or exception to the complete-removal regime, but, to ensure that derogation is not granted or exercised peremptorily, the allowable grounds are also clearly set out.[22] A procedure is also established for 32-week consultation periods preceding the decision by a member state to grant a permit of derogation, or exception to the complete-removal norm.[23] The consultation process[24] allows other states, apart from the state seeking to issue the permit, to contribute robustly and even object if they are of the opinion that there is no justification for the proposal to grant a partial-removal permit. Indeed, if a concerned state is unable to resolve the objections with the objecting state(s), then there are provisions for the executive secretary of the OSPAR Commission to convene a special consultative meeting, to consider the issues. Under the process for such a consultative meeting, the relevant state cannot simply ignore either the objections (of other objecting states) or the outcome of the consultative meeting. Where a final decision is taken to allow a disused platform to be left in place or partially removed, then the permit for such partial removal must cover a number of issues. Some of the issues which

---

21 Paragraph 2 thereof states: "The dumping, and leaving wholly or partly in place, of disused offshore installations within the maritime area is prohibited."

22 Paragraph 3:
"By way of derogation from paragraph 2, if the competent authority of the relevant Contracting Party is satisfied that an assessment in accordance with Annex 2 shows that there are significant reasons why an alternative disposal mentioned below is preferable to reuse or recycling or final disposal on land, it may issue a permit for all or part of the footings of a steel installation in a category listed in Annex 1, placed in the maritime area before 9 February 1999, to be left in place;
a concrete installation in a category listed in Annex 1 or constituting a concrete anchor base, to be dumped or left wholly or partly in place;
any other disused offshore installation to be dumped or left wholly or partly in place, when exceptional and unforeseen circumstances resulting from structural damage or deterioration, or from some other cause presenting equivalent difficulties, can be demonstrated."

23 Paragraph 4:
"Before a decision is taken to issue a permit under paragraph 3, the relevant Contracting Party shall first consult the other Contracting Parties in accordance with Annex 3."
Paragraph 5:
"Any permit for a disused offshore installation to be dumped or permanently left wholly or partly in place shall accord with the requirements of Annex 4."

24 Annex 3, OSPAR Decision 98/3.

every partial removal permit must cover[25] include:

- provision for independent verification that the conditions before disposal began are consistent with both the terms of the permit as well as with the information which was provided in order to secure the permit;
- arrangements and allocation of responsibility for monitoring the condition of the installation post disposal works; and
- identification of the owner(s) of those parts of the disused installation remaining in place for the purposes of meeting claims for future damages which might arise after abandonment.

At the same 1998 meeting, the Oslo and Paris Commission members also adopted new rules of procedure to govern the activities of the Commission.[26] One of the declared objectives of the new rules was "to facilitate the participation of NGOs in the work of the Commission, with the intention of enabling NGOs to participate at all levels of the Commission working structure".[27]

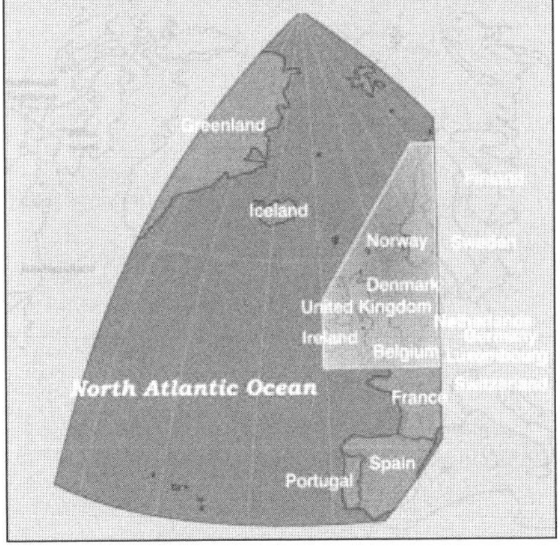

North East Atlantic States[28]

While only directly binding on North-East Atlantic States, there is evidence that OSPAR Decision 98/3 is well considered beyond the North-East Atlantic area. Though beyond the scope of this work, it is likely that OSPAR Decision 98/3 will become the basis of wider state practice beyond the North-East Atlantic region. If so, wide use of and adherence to OSPAR Decision 98/3 outside the Oslo and Paris Commission states could to some extent render the IMO Guidelines redundant. The proper determination of the role, status and use of OSPAR Decision 98/3 *vis-à-vis* the IMO Guidelines needs to be addressed and resolved.

25 See Annex 4 to OSPAR Decision 98/3.
26 Revised Rules of Procedure of the OSPAR Commission, 2001-6.
27 See: 1998 Ministerial Meeting of the OSPAR Commission Main Results, published on OSPAR Commission website.
28 Map used by the kind permission of OGP; © OGP International Association of Oil and Gas Producers: http://info.ogp.org.uk/Decommissioning/OSPAR/NorthSea.html.

5.3 Other international regulations

There are a number of other international law regulations relevant to offshore decommissioning, such as the Convention on the Prevention of Marine Dumping of Wastes and Other Matter 1972 (the London Dumping Convention), amended by its 1996 Protocol, and the OECD Decision on the Control of Transboundary Movements of Wastes Destined for Recovery Operations 2001, as amended in 2004. Among the limited number of decommissioning projects executed in the North Sea to date, there have been instances of disused installations removed from the continental shelf of the United Kingdom and taken away to Norway for recovery and scrapping. The OECD Decision closely regulates the movement of waste (including disused installations and their components) from the area of an exporting state to that of an importing state. Also relevant to decommissioning within the North East Atlantic Area is OSPAR Recommendation 2006/5 on a Management Regime for Offshore Cuttings Piles, which became effective on June 30 2006.[29] The Recommendation introduced a management regime for offshore drill cuttings piles, accumulations of which are typically to be encountered under or near offshore platforms and therefore forming part of materials to be handled or disposed of at decommissioning.

While the regulations discussed above are mainly applicable to North East Atlantic states, it is likely that they will have some influence in the establishment of decommissioning regulations in other regions of the world.

6. Decommissioning in national legislation and upstream agreements

National legislation on decommissioning in jurisdictions across the world is evolving. While some jurisdictions have well established and relevant laws or regulations in place, many others either have not yet established such laws or are still in the process of discussing what to adopt.[30] We are still a long way from having decommissioning properly provided for in national or regional regulation in all oil and gas producing countries.

For companies in the upstream offshore oil and gas industry, decommissioning obligations may arise out of national legislation (or regulation), a contractual framework or both. Aside from regulatory requirements, parties may commit to certain arrangements and obligations in anticipation of future decommissioning and related costs. Early oil and gas agreements (whether concession or other types) did not usually provide for decommissioning. Although references to well abandonment provisions are commonly found in early contracts, it is only in later agreements that decommissioning began to be specifically provided for.[31]

---

29 www.ospar.org.

30 In the North Sea area for example, the United Kingdom, Norway, the Netherlands, Germany, Ireland and Spain have specific legislation in place. Denmark has no specific national regulation but is signatory to most international conventions. In any event, under the relevant international regulations, all installations offshore from Denmark will have to be completely removed.

31 Bruce M Kramer and Gary B Conine, "Joint Development and Operations", p 646, in *International Petroleum Transactions*, Second Edition (Rocky Mt Min L Fdn, 2000): "Although some abandonment requirements, such as well plugging, have been in effect for many decades, widespread recognition of the environmental damage and health and safety hazards resulting from unreclaimed energy projects and the need to plan in advance for field abandonment did not occur until the 1970s and 1980s. For example, Norway did not enact special legislation dealing with abandonment of offshore facilities until 1985; Britain followed suit two years later."

Early joint operating agreements would simply provide for the operator's obligation to recover or dispose of all joint-venture property by the end of the economic life of the field, followed by the distribution of net proceeds to the joint account. Some later joint operating agreements would require an abandonment agreement to be executed by the parties (perhaps at a certain date, or on the occurrence of a certain event). Typical provisions in such abandonment agreements include how decommissioning works will be effected, by whom, who is liable to meet the costs of decommissioning and financial security arrangements towards meeting the costs of decommissioning.

Both the 1995 and the 2002 AIPN[32] Model International Operating Agreements address abandonment of wells and operations in their Article 10. Article 10 provides for an optional provision. According to this Article, depending on whether in the jurisdiction where the operations are undertaken the parties are liable for the costs of ceasing operations, when negotiating the field development plan they must agree on a security agreement.[33] Furthermore, according to both model forms, a withdrawing party remains liable for plugging and abandonment costs relating to wells in which it participated, and such withdrawing party may be requested to provide the remaining parties with security to satisfy them that such abandonment costs will be met to the extent legally required. In the event of transfer of interest or rights, the 1995 model form provides for the transferring party to remain liable before the other parties for obligations that have vested, matured or accrued prior to the transfer. In the 2002 model form, however, liability of the transferring party for costs of plugging and abandoning wells or portions of wells and decommissioning facilities in which the transferring party participated is subject to negotiation. Yet, the draft models suggest that if a well has been drilled as a joint operation and hydrocarbons have been produced as an exclusive operation, then the party that assumes it will bear the costs and liability of its plugging and abandonment, as required by applicable regulations.

AIPN also addressed decommissioning matters in its 2006 Model Form International Unitization and Unit Operating Agreement in its optional Article 12, Article 15.4 and in Exhibit D. Decommissioning costs and expenses are for the unit account. Parties are due to provide cash deposits in a decommissioning trust fund, or to provide an alternative security in lieu of such payment, all according to a decommissioning work programme and budget. The parties may unanimously agree alternative arrangements to the formation of a decommissioning trust fund. Such security and other related decommissioning matters are further specified in Exhibit D. In the case of termination of operations due to a group[34] default or a group

32 Association of International Petroleum Negotiators.

33 The AIPN 1995 Model International Operating Agreement defines security as a letter of credit issued by a bank or an on-demand bond issued by a surety corporation, or cash contributed to a trust fund. The 2002 Model slightly changed the definition of security to enlarge it, as follows:
"1.53 Security means (i) a guarantee or standby letter of credit issued by a bank; (ii) an on-demand bond issued by a surety corporation; (iii) a corporate guarantee; (iv) any financial security required by the Contract or this Agreement; and (v) any financial security agreed from time to time by the Parties; provided, however, that the bank, surety or corporation issuing the guarantee, standby letter of credit, bond or other security (as applicable) has a credit rating indicating it has a sufficient worth to pay its obligations in all reasonably foreseeable circumstances."

34 'Group' in this sense means the unit group, ie the parties that together form one of the parties to the unitisation and unit operating agreement.

withdrawal, the other group has the option to take over such operations, in which case they will inherit the related facilities and the liability for their decommissioning costs and will provide security for such obligation. The same principle applies to a single well to be abandoned by one unit group but taken over by another. Notwithstanding the provisions of Article 12.1 with respect to liabilities of the group taking over operations, in the event of a group's withdrawal or default, Article 15.4 establishes (among other obligations and liabilities) that a withdrawing party remains liable for its share of the costs of plugging and abandoning wells or portions of wells that formed part of a work programme and budget (or an authorisation of expenditure) prior to such party's notification of withdrawal. Such liability will be to the extent that decommissioning costs are legally required to be payable by the parties. The withdrawing party will be asked to provide security to the satisfaction of the other parties to fulfil obligations and liabilities for which it remains liable after the withdrawal. The decommissioning obligation will be one such continuing obligation.

7. Overview of national legislation

The following discussion of decommissioning legislation in a number of jurisdictions is not intended to be exhaustive, but it provides an overview of law and policy in the selected jurisdictions.

7.1 Brazil

The decommissioning obligations that the concessionaires[35] will be bound by are defined in the Brazilian Federal Petroleum Law,[36] in ANP,[37] by regulation[38] and in concession contracts. Furthermore, although IBAMA[39] is entitled to rule over this matter, they have not so far done so.

Concessionaires must present to ANP an installation deactivation programme, which will be discussed, agreed and approved by ANP. Such a programme should include a proposal for the plugging and abandonment of wells, and the deactivation and removal of plant, equipment and all other facilities. Title to all assets in respect of which acquisition costs are deductible for the calculation of the so-called 'special participation tax', which the ANP concludes is necessary for the continuity of production or are in the public interest, must revert to the Government of Brazil. Those assets that will not be subject to the said reversion are to be removed and disposed of.

The ANP may require a deactivation and abandonment guarantee, which must be in a form satisfactory to the ANP. Although actual costs or expenditure on decommissioning activities are tax deductible, their provision is not.

---

35 Brazil adopted the concession regime; hence oil companies that hold a participating interest in concession contracts are referred to as 'concessionaires'.

36 Federal Law 9,478 of 1997, article 28, §§ 1 and 2, article 43, VI.

37 'ANP' stands for *Agência Nacional do Petróleo, Gás Natural e Biocombustíveis* (National Agency for Oil, Gas and Biofules), the regulatory body.

38 Resolution 27/06 (Technical Rules for Decommissioning), Resolution 28/06 (Alienation and Reversion of Assets Procedures) and *Portaria* 25/02 (Technical Rules for Well Abandonment).

39 'IBAMA' stands for *Instituto Brasileiro do Meio Ambiente e dos Recursos Naturais Renováveis* (Brazilian Institute for the Environment and Natural Renewable Resources), a federal environmental body.

7.2 Kazakhstan

The Government of Kazakhstan has enacted rules that provide for the activities to be undertaken upon termination of the contract or of production.[40] Besides the obligations that arise out of laws and regulations, subsurface-use contracts also establish decommissioning obligations, such as the creation of an abandonment fund, the liquidation of environmental and other violations in the contract area, the restoration of the contract area for suitable further use, and the payment of compensation for environmental damage.

It is the responsibility of the licensee (or contractor, as the case may be)[41] to undertake the decommissioning activities and to bear the related costs and expenses. Licensees (or contractors) are jointly and severally liable for the decommissioning costs.

Contributions to the abandonment fund are recognised as expenditures and therefore are cost recoverable. If the abandonment fund is not sufficient to support all decommissioning activities, then the licensees (or contractors) must bear the additional costs. It is unclear whether payment of such additional costs is tax deductible, but it would be fair and reasonable to expect that the same principle and treatment applied for the contributions to the abandonment fund will be extended to such additional payments.

In the event of transfer of the totality of rights and interests, the seller does not retain residual liabilities (ie, the decommissioning obligations are transferred to the buyer). However, if the transfer is only partial, then the seller will remain liable for decommissioning costs to the extent that the licensees (or contractors) are jointly and severally liable.

7.3 Malaysia

Decommissioning obligations are in place in Malaysia, which typically utilises the production sharing contract upstream arrangements. The use of a decommissioning fund is required. If the end of the economic life of the field is reached during the term of the production sharing contract, then the contractor will be responsible for undertaking decommissioning activities; otherwise the national oil company will use the decommissioning fund to finance the decommissioning activities in the future. In 2000, Malaysia was one of the few countries in the region that adopted recoverable provisioning for decommissioning. Such costs are also tax deductible. Malaysia requires that all disused offshore installations should be removed, unless otherwise justifiable.

---

40 Article 66 of Subsurface Law of January 27 1996; article 16.3 of PSA Law, of July 8 2005; chapter 32 and article 268 of chapter 38 of the Ecological Code of January 9 2007; Unified Rules for the Development of Oil and Gas Deposits of the Republic of Kazakhstan and Unified Rules for Subsurface Protection in the Course of Development of Deposits of Minerals, Oil, Gas, and Subsurface Water in the Republic of Kazakhstan, approved, respectively by Government Resolutions no 745 of the Republic of Kazakhstan dated June 18 1996, and no 1019 of the Republic of Kazakhstan dated July 21 1999; Procedure for Termination or Suspension of Subsurface use Operations, approved by the Order of the Minister of Energy and Natural Resources of June 6 1997; and Rules on the Procedure for Liquidation of Oil, Gas, and Other Wells and Rules on the Procedure for the Plugging and Abandoning of Wells in Oil and Gas Deposit, Underground Gas Deposits and Thermal Water Deposits (both adapted from the Soviet era).

41 Production sharing agreement, tax royalty contract and service contract regimes coexist in Kazakhstan.

7.4 Nigeria

In Nigeria, there is a mix of joint ventures (with the national oil company as a necessary party) and production sharing contracts. Decommissioning laws are in place in Nigeria. An abandonment programme is required to be submitted to the Department of Petroleum Resources (DPR) for approval before its implementation. The Department of Petroleum Resources (DPR) will decide whether it wishes to acquire the installations. If the DPR does not exercise its option to take over the disused installations, then the licensee must proceed with decommissioning activities and restoration of the site. Complete removal is the rule in Nigeria.

A decommissioning fund can also be set up, though not mandatorily required by law. Contributions to the fund are recoverable.

7.5 Norway

The rule in Norway is also the complete removal of installations from offshore oil and gas fields, with partial removal only accepted in exceptional cases. Responsibility for decommissioning activities lies with the existing licensees jointly and severally. However, a change in the norm is expected to include the possibility of seeking such responsibilities from previous licensees, but limited to their respective participating interest at the time of transfer or assignment.

Licence holders are subject to residual liability for facilities or parts of facilities left in place. Financial securities are not usually required by the Norwegian authorities for decommissioning obligations. However, in the event of the transfer of a participating interest, the Ministry of Petroleum and Energy may require a guarantee from the transferee if its financial capabilities are not believed to be adequate to meet decommissioning obligations.

Future decommissioning costs must be accrued, but are not subject to tax deductibility until effectively incurred. Norway provides different treatment for abandonment (in this case removal of facilities) compared with the plugging and abandonment of wells.

A new fiscal law of June 2003, commonly called the 'grant method', provided for the state to cover part of the decommissioning costs in accordance with the average tax rate paid by the licensee over the life of the field. It also allows full tax deduction of decommissioning costs in the year activities are undertaken. In the case of a licensee exiting the country, cash payments will be made by the state for tax-loss carry forward caused by decommissioning costs.

7.6 Oman

In Oman, the operator is responsible for undertaking decommissioning activities, using funds contributed by the joint venturers. Contributions to an abandonment fund are required, and these are cost recoverable. Expenditure associated with decommissioning activities is also cost recoverable. Contributions to decommissioning funds and decommissioning expenditures are tax deductible.

In the case of continuity of production after the term of the licence and handover of the facilities and operations to the government, the abandonment fund will be transferred along with the decommissioning responsibility and liability.

7.7 United Kingdom

In the United Kingdom, the rule is the complete removal of installations from offshore oil and gas fields, with partial removal only accepted in exceptional cases that fall within the OSPAR derogations discussed above. It is primarily the responsibility of the licence holders to undertake decommissioning activities. This responsibility and liability is joint and several. In the event of default by current licence holders, previous licensees may be called upon to undertake the decommissioning.

There is residual liability for licence holders, and they will remain liable in perpetuity for the assets or parts of assets left in place. Currently, the regulator does not require from licence holders any form of financial security, except at the point of approval of a decommissioning programme. However, recent developments and legislative changes as contained in the Energy Act 2008[42] enabled the secretary of state to make all the relevant parties liable for the decommissioning of an installation or pipeline and, where a licence covers multiple sub-areas, clarifying which licensees will be liable.

The Energy Act 2008 also gave the secretary of state power to require decommissioning security at any time during the life of an oil or gas field if the risks to the taxpayer are assessed as unacceptable.

Furthermore, the Energy Act 2008 provides for protection of the funds put aside for decommissioning, in such a way that in the event of insolvency of the relevant party, the funds remain available to pay for decommissioning and the taxpayers' exposure is minimised.

This is an indication that in future, depending on the financial capacity of licensees, the government will be able at any time to require the licensees to submit security for meeting the eventual cost of decommissioning.

7.8 United States Outer Continental Shelf (OCS)

In the United States, lessees are required completely to remove all disused facilities from offshore oil and gas fields within one year of cessation of production.[43] However, exceptions have been granted for the formation of artificial reefs, partial removal or the re-use of facilities. 'Salvage' and 'abandonment' are terms commonly used in the United States. In the United States, where the lease regime is in place, the last lessee is primarily responsible for decommissioning costs. In the event of the default of the last lessees, then prior lessees are liable to meet the costs of decommissioning.

The Department of Interior Minerals Management Service requires lessees to provide bonds as a form of security towards meeting their decommissioning obligations. In the United States, the costs incurred for decommissioning are considered business costs and are tax deductible.

---

42 This Act passed into law on November 26 2008 and the decommissioning provisions therein came into force on January 26 2009.

43 30 CFR 250.5(a), 250.112(i).

7.9 Venezuela

Venezuela has recently changed its operating service contract scheme to a joint-venture system in which the national oil company is necessarily a party. The contracts then in place were terminated, and migration to the new system took place by way of the incorporation of new joint ventures with the national oil company, PdVSA.[44]

On termination of the granted exploration and production rights, the assets must revert from the joint venture to the government for continuity of activities, or else the production must be terminated and decommissioning undertaken in a manner that combines the most cost-effective way and meets environmental protection imperatives.[45] This is in line with Venezuelan oil industry concepts of rational use of hydrocarbons and maximising the ultimate recovery of the reservoirs.[46]

Decommissioning costs are treated as operational costs and, as such, are tax deductible.[47]

Decommissioning activities must be carried out by the joint venture and are subject to the supervision and approval of the Ministry of Energy and Petroleum. In terms of residual liabilities, environmental damage occurring after decommissioning is expressly considered an environmental crime and is subject to liabilities and sanctions.[48]

8. Challenges and opportunities for the future

Decommissioning presents a complex mix of technological, financial and legal challenges, particularly in light of the complexity of removal operations, high removal costs, the immature legislation of many jurisdictions, the level of liabilities involved (some of which will be uncertain, and most occurring in the future), and important health, safety and environmental considerations. However, development of innovative technology will no doubt, lead to less onerous decommissioning or removal processes (or extend the range of options for alternative uses for disused installations), whilst at the same time addressing other industry challenges and needs.

8.1 CO_2 sequestration as a re-use option

One such opportunity is the utilisation of depleted reservoirs as storage sites for greenhouse gases. Such carbon capture sequestration projects (CCS) are about capturing and underground storage or use of CO_2. The capture of and storing of CO_2 in underground reservoirs is now widely acknowledged as one of the viable ways of reducing CO_2 levels in the atmosphere and thus reducing greenhouse gas in the Earth's atmosphere. Further development of available carbon capture and storage technologies is progressing. Depleted oil and gas reservoirs (and associated disused installations) could act as effective underground storage sites for captured CO_2. Other storage-site options for storing CO_2 are deep saline reservoirs and un-mineable coal seams. Decommissioned oil and gas fields could be particularly attractive for the underground storage of CO_2, as oil and gas reservoirs are proven traps that have held

---

44 Petróleos de Venezuela, SA.
45 Organic Hydrocarbons Law, article 34.3(a).
46 New Hydrocarbons Law, article 19.
47 Income Tax Law, article 27.
48 Income Tax Law, article 27.

liquids and gases for thousands of years. The geology of such depleted reservoirs has become well known over the course of exploration and production lifecycles, as has the extent of the considerable storage capacity available. Some depleted reservoirs might therefore be modified for CO_2 storage.[49]

Even though there are already cases of carbon underground storage, there are still many technical, economical and legal challenges to be resolved. These challenges include finding adequate storage and transportation, developing an understanding of reservoir behaviour after injection, and issues as to economic viability, rights to proceed with the storage and clear definition of liabilities.

It is also worth noting that apart from underground storage of CO_2, captured CO_2 can also be utilised to enhance recovery of oil and gas from mature oil and gas reservoirs using an established CO_2-EOR (enhanced oil recovery) technique. The income from such CO_2-EOR schemes can prolong the life of a depleted oil and gas field.

Whilst offshore storage is the subject of international law, the storage of CO_2 in reservoirs under land is generally subject to national law and is beyond the scope of this chapter. Until recently, the offshore storage of CO_2 under the seabed was not permitted by international law, as CO_2 was not listed among the items that could be dumped under international conventions. By amendments adopted by the contracting parties on November 2 2006 to the 1996 Protocol to the Convention on the Prevention of Marine Pollution by Dumping of Wastes and Other Matter 1972 (the London Dumping Convention), which took effect from February 10 2007, storage of CO_2 under the deep seabed is now permitted by international law. The amendments (and further guidance) will regulate CO_2 storage in the seabed. The amendments prescribe that disposal of CO_2 can only be into sub-seabed geological formations; such CO_2 must consist overwhelmingly of carbon dioxide; and no waste or other matter may be added for the purpose of disposal. Disposal of CO_2 directly into the deep oceans is not permitted.

The combined effect of the amendments to the London Dumping Convention (and the detailed guidance adopted in November 2007 under the title *Risk Assessment Framework for CO_2 Sequestration in Sub-Sealed Geological Structures*) means that CO_2 storage or sequestration under the seabed will be subject to licences to be issued by governments under licensing regimes developed pursuant to the London Dumping Convention. Applicants for CO_2 storage licences will have to demonstrate that the CO_2 will remain permanently in place when placed or stored. Applicants will, therefore, have to prove the integrity of the proposed storage site and mitigation safeguards to be put in place.

The OSPAR Commission has recently adopted annexes to the OSPAR Convention.[50] By the amendments, storage of CO_2 in geological formations under the seabed in the OSPAR area is now permitted. However, the placement of CO_2 into the water-column of the sea and on the seabed remains prohibited.

49 See IEA Greenhouse Gas R&D Programme, *Putting Carbon Back into the Ground*, February 2001.
50 OSPAR Decision 2007/1 and OSPAR Decision 2007/2.

9. Current decommissioning projects, activities and technology

An overview of current decommissioning activities and projects reveals that whereas the majority of removals (in terms of numbers) are occurring in the Gulf of Mexico, at the rate of about 100 installations a year, the largest, most expensive, most complex and most challenging removal projects are in the North Sea. Currently, the three largest decommissioning projects in the North Sea are the Philips Petroleum-operated Ekofisk field, the Total-operated Frigg field and the BP-operated North West Hutton installation. Others recently commenced, or in which decommissioning planning is ongoing, include the Indefatigable field (operated by Shell),[51] the huge Brent field (operated by Shell)[52] and the Miller field (operated by BP).

9.1 Brent Redundant Facilities removal project

The decommissioning and removal of Brent Redundant Facilities (operated by Shell) has been completed. The project entailed the complete removal to shore of the Brent flare tower and six anchor blocks that previously held the Brent Spar in place. The Brent Redundant Facilities removal project was completed at a cost of around U$100 million. The redundant facilities were removed from their offshore location in the summer of 2005. The anchor blocks were re-used for land reclamation in Norway and the flare stack scrapped at the Aker Stord yard in Norway.[53]

9.2 Current decommissioning projects in the North Sea

The Ekofisk field located in the Norwegian sector of the North Sea comprises some 34 installations and is operated by Philips Petroleum. The Ekofisk decommissioning project is perhaps the largest removal project to date and is estimated to cost US$1.1 billion.[54] Removal will continue until about 2013. The operation is now in its first phase (flare and bridge removals). The contract for removal of the second phase covers 15 platforms and topsides. The Ekofisk tank was the first concrete structure granted derogation under OSPAR 98/3. Topsides have now been successfully removed by an engineering technique known as the 'piecesmall' technique (said to be a North Sea first).

The Frigg field straddles the United Kingdom and Norwegian sectors of the North Sea and comprised six installations. The governments of Norway and the United Kingdom jointly considered and approved Total's proposed decommissioning programme. Derogation under OSPAR 98/3 has been granted allowing four concrete structures (TCP-2, CDP-1, TP-1 and MCP-01) to be left in place. Aside from the derogations, the Frigg facilities are expected to be removed by the end of 2012 at an estimated cost of US$708 million (excluding pipelines). Removal of the topsides and jackets has been under way since 2006, with a major lift campaign under way in 2007

---

51 http://www.shell.co.uk/home/content/gbr/aboutshell/shell_businesses/e_and_p/facts_figures/decommissioning/indefatigable/dir_indedecom_25071530.html.

52 http://www.shell.co.uk/home/content/gbr/aboutshell/shell_businesses/e_and_p/facts_figures/decommissioning/brent_field_decomm_studies/dir_brentfield_decommissioning.html.

53 http://www.shell.co.uk/home/content/gbr/aboutshell/shell_businesses/e_and_p/facts_figures/decommissioning/brent_anchor_blocks/dir_brentdecom_14071040.html.

54 Petter Osmundsen, "Decommissioning of petroleum installations – major policy issues", *ScienceDirect* February 4 2003: www.sciencedirect.com.

involving large tandem lift of a module support frame (weighing more than 8,000 tonnes) backloaded onto a barge. Again, the latter is a new engineering challenge and achievement for the North Sea.

The NW Hutton field and installations in the United Kingdom continental shelf (operated by BP) are now in normally unattended mode, having ceased production in 2002. They are now awaiting final removal in the period 2008 to 2010. The decommissioning programme approved by the UK government under OSPAR requires the removal of all topsides and steel jackets down to the top of the jacket footings. Derogation was granted, permitting the jacket footings to be left in place. The first phase of the removal project was completed in 2008 and involved the removal of topside modules and other structures in preparation for removal of the jacket. The topsides were removed by heavy lift vessel and transported onshore to the United Kingdom for recycling and disposal. The decommissioning project is estimated to cost more than US$285 million.

10. The challenges of decommissioning in the United Kingdom

The legal and regulatory regime on decommissioning in the United Kingdom poses interesting challenges that have exercised the efforts of the oil and gas industry as well as the United Kingdom government over the past few years. These challenges have been described by *Oil and Gas UK* thus:

> *"The UK Petroleum Act 1998 ... puts a requirement on all these companies to eliminate the risk to government of any default on decommissioning obligations. It is in everyone's interest to ensure that joint ventures partners can cover their obligations and liabilities – but current government policy requirements drive particularly onerous security provisions for the UK oil and gas sector. The impact of this, by its nature, falls mainly on the smaller, less financially robust companies.*
>
> *This is further burdened by uncertainties concerning future tax relief, which requires companies to put up guarantees at a before-tax rate. There are also large uncertainties around the costs that need to be securitised. Together, these can create substantive barriers to negotiating asset transfers, which can hamper new investment for realising UK reserves.*
>
> *The major threat which decommissioning poses, however, is the shadow that the legacy liabilities cast over asset trading and investment today.*
>
> ...
>
> *Recent work ... has created a better understanding of the different effects that the UK offshore decommissioning liability is having on different stakeholders. This has resulted in a number of new initiatives that have the potential to significantly improve the situation."*[55]

Uncertainty in the estimation of costs for future decommissioning liability is another problem. This uncertainty arises largely as a result of decommissioning being relatively new and unexplored territory for the oil and gas industry, as well as for governments (at least in the North-East Atlantic area). Crucial to achieving more accurate estimates and reducing decommissioning costs will, first, be experience; secondly, development of new technology to help overcome engineering and

55 Paul Dymond, "Shadow Cast by Decommissioning Liability", 2006 *IELTR* 222 to 225.

technical challenges; and thirdly, finding ways to share learning across the industry whilst safeguarding the necessary liquid and competitive contractor market.

The oil and gas industry in the United Kingdom together with the relevant government departments have tried to address the challenges summarised above, and a number of initiatives are under way. These include the development of a standard decommissioning security agreement; common parameters for estimating decommissioning/removal costs; and consideration of new securitisation tools for decommissioning liability.

As this chapter was being written, the UK Parliament passed the Energy Act 2008. This will bring about significant changes to the legislative regime for decommissioning, by amending and supplementing the provisions of the Petroleum Act 1998 (which provided a statutory regime for decommissioning of disused offshore oil and gas installations). The Petroleum Act 1998 provides that the government, through the secretary of state, can require field owners to submit an abandonment programme setting out how they propose to deal with disused installations. The obligation of the field owners properly to remove and/or decommission disused installations in accordance with an approved programme is joint and several. Under the provisions of the Petroleum Act 1998, the secretary of state also has the power to require the parties to an approved decommissioning programme to establish financial security where the secretary of state is concerned about the ability of the parties to carry out the approved decommissioning programme. The Energy Act 2008 extends the powers of the secretary of state such that in future, he/she will be able to require financial security at any stage of field life, and even before the submission and approval of a decommissioning programme. The provisions of the new Energy Act 2008 will further enable the secretary of state to widen the net of relevant parties liable to undertake decommissioning of a disused installation. Furthermore, its provisions provide protection for funds set aside for decommissioning, so that even if any of the parties who have contributed or provided the security were to be become insolvent, the security will be protected against a liquidator.

Whether the oil and gas industry-led initiatives and the UK government's changes to the legislation on decommissioning as set out in the Energy Act 2008 and the Guidance Notes published by the Offshore Decommissioning Unit of the Department of Energy and Climate Change[56] Bill will resolve the existing difficulties in the United Kingdom's legal and regulatory regime on decommissioning remains an open question.

11. The unfinished business

The discussion in this chapter shows that the issues relating to offshore decommissioning and the adequacy of international law treaty and regulatory provisions as so sharply highlighted by the Brent Spar episode have now largely been resolved. There is now a settled body of international law (as well as some regional guidelines and regulations – for example in the North-East Atlantic area) regulating

56 https://www.og.berr.gov.uk/regulation/guidance/decommission.htm.

decommissioning. However, detailed guidelines do not yet exist and are not settled in many regions. Furthermore, many jurisdictions are yet to establish full complements of national statutes and regulations on decommissioning. Even in those jurisdictions with extant statutes, some of those statutes are now clearly inadequate and need to be revisited, with more thoroughgoing regulation put in place.

Although, as seen above, international law on offshore decommissioning is now well settled, the status of the IMO Guidelines and Standards 1989 is still somewhat unclear, as it could be argued that those guidelines have been rendered redundant by OSPAR Decision 98/3. There is a need for the International Maritime Organisation to reassess the status, utility and continued use of the IMO Guidelines and Standards. This is unfinished business.

In the United Kingdom at least, there are questions regarding the complex and onerous obligations placed by the national decommissioning legislation. This complexity has led to multiplication and duplication of security arrangements among upstream parties. There are ongoing efforts by both the government of the United Kingdom and the oil industry to bring about needed changes. The UK government has now passed the Energy Act 2008 with wide-ranging changes to aspects of existing legislation on decommissioning. But this remains unfinished business.

The least that can be concluded is that although decommissioning is now better understood and well provided for in many jurisdictions, compared with the state of knowledge and legislation in 1995 when the Brent Spar episode occurred, the number and magnitude of issues yet to be resolved and concluded (relating to legal, regulatory, technical and engineering, financial and tax challenges) across many regions and jurisdictions demonstrates that decommissioning will continue to be the subject of considerable legal, legislative and technical activity in the near future.

About the authors

Flávia Kaczelnik Altit
Senior Legal Counsel, Shell International BV
Flavia.Altit@shell.com

Flávia is senior legal counsel with Shell International BV in the Netherlands, supporting global E&P new business development and M&A activities. Previously, she was head of E&P Legal and a member of both the E&P and Legal coordination teams in Shell Brasil. Still with Shell Brasil, she managed legal corporate affairs with company secretary activities whilst also gaining experience in relevant downstream M&A transactions. Before joining Shell, she was legal chief with Banco BBM, a private investment bank. Flávia had six years of litigation experience with Ernst & Young and in private practice, with an emphasis on tax, civil and commercial law. She has been a guest lecturer at Shell and on external courses in Brazil and the Netherlands. Flávia has held a Bachelor's degree from the Law School of the University of Rio de Janeiro since 1993 and a post-graduate degree on business law from IAG-Master of Rio de Janeiro since 1996.

Danielle Beggs
Partner, Denton Wilde Sapte LLP
danielle.beggs@dentonwildesapte.com

Danielle Beggs is a senior partner in the energy, infrastructure and project finance department at Denton Wilde Sapte's London office. DWS is a leading international law firm, with a long-standing reputation as having a particular strength in the energy field. Danielle has extensive experience of working for a large number of international oil and gas and electricity industry clients, governments and regulators. Prior to starting work in private practice in 1995, Danielle worked for a number of years as legal adviser at British Gas plc. She has advised on major transactions in both upstream and downstream sectors. Danielle is recognised by Legal 500 and Chambers as a leading expert in the energy field.

Justyna Bremen
Professional Support Lawyer,
Denton Wilde Sapte LLP
justyna.bremen@dentonwildesapte.com

Justyna Bremen is a professional support lawyer in the energy, infrastructure and project finance department at Denton Wilde Sapte's London office. She has worked in the energy field for more than eight years. Prior to joining DWS in 2003, Justyna worked for five years at a multinational Australian law firm.

William E Browning
Partner, Infrastructure Development
Partnership LLP
wbrowning@infradev.co.uk

William E Browning has 25 years of experience in the oil and gas industry and is a partner with Infrastructure Development Partnership LLP in London; IDP provides an array of project development support activities including commercial, structuring, financing and environmental strategy.

Bill directed the legal work for the largest upstream development in the South Caspian Sea from inception to full production and for all export development from the South Caspian between 1995 and 2002. From 2002, Bill served as Baku–Tbilisi–Ceyhan pipeline's negotiations manager, concluding with its successful $2.6 billion project financing. More recently, he has provided project development advice for a number of developments, including a greenfield cross-border gas pipeline from Trinidad to other East Caribbean islands.

Bill is a member of the Texas Bar and holds a BA from Washington & Lee University and a JD from the University of Texas.

Thomas J Dimitroff
Oil and Gas Consultant
thomas.dimitroff@i2a.co.uk

Thomas J Dimitroff advises oil and gas companies and investors on upstream acquisitions, mid-stream developments and related strategy, financing and risk analyses and he works closely with Infrastructure Development Partnership LLP and i2a Consulting LLP (both based in the UK. From 1998 to 2005, Tom was a core member of the team that delivered the Baku–Tbilisi–Ceyhan (BTC) oil pipeline and the South Caucasus gas pipeline. In addition to being BTC's legal manager, Tom was legal advisor to the Azerbaijan government on Kazakhstan Cross Caspian oil transit negotiations and on the multilateral Energy Charter Transit Protocol negotiations. In addition, he served on the ECT Legal Advisory Task Force to draft model intergovernmental and host government agreements. In 2005, Tom became Regional Adviser to the BP Group for Russia, the Caspian, Turkey, the Middle East and Africa, advising on non-technical risks to a multiplicity of new ventures and existing operations across the region.

Tom is a member of the Illinois Bar, holds an MA in Law from St Edmund's College, Cambridge, a BCL from Jesus College, Oxford, and a JD from IIT Chicago-Kent College of Law.

Erin Dyer
Associate, Ashurst LLP
erin.dyer@ashurst.com

Erin Dyer is an associate in the energy, transport and infrastructure department at Ashurst, a leading international law firm with 12 offices in 11 countries and more than 1,500 employees. Erin is based in Ashurst's Singapore office and specialises in the energy and projects sector. She provides advice in respect of upstream, midstream and downstream oil and gas, LNG, mining, power projects and other infrastructure projects. She has worked for private companies, national oil companies and host governments in relation to upstream asset sales. Erin is a solicitor admitted in Western Australia.

Jubilee Easo
Senior Associate, Ashurst LLP
jubilee.easo@ashurst.com

Jubilee Easo is a senior associate in the energy, transport and infrastructure department of Ashurst. Jubilee specialises in corporate and project work in the oil and gas and wider energy sectors. She has particular expertise in the upstream and downstream oil and gas sectors and the LNG sector, having advised state oil and gas companies, international oil and gas companies, contractors, project companies and financial institutions on a wide range of upstream and downstream developments, LNG regasification projects and shipping projects.

Mhairi Main Garcia
Senior Associate, Ashurst LLP
mhairi.garcia@ashurst.com

Mhairi Main Garcia is a senior associate in Ashurst's energy, transport and infrastructure department and has been based in Dubai since 2001. Mhairi has a particular focus on energy and infrastructure projects and regional international law issues. She is key to the firm's public international law capability in the Middle East and has recently advised a number of international oil companies on proposed investments in the Middle East and Africa, including advice on constitutional questions, BITs, sanctions and territorial issues. Prior to moving to Dubai, Mhairi worked for more than three years in Belgium and France as a group adviser on the European Parliament's Legal Affairs and Internal Market Committee. Mhairi holds an LLM in International and Comparative Law (Vrije Universiteit Brussel), a Masters in International Politics specialising in territorial disputes (Université de Libre Bruxelles) and an LLB first-class honours (University of Aberdeen). Mhairi is admitted as an attorney and counselor at law in the State of New York and as a solicitor in England and Wales.

Charez Golvala
Partner, Chadbourne & Parke LLP
cgolvala@chadbourne.com

Charez Golvala is a corporate partner with Chadbourne & Parke in London. He focuses on transactions and projects in the energy industry. Mr Golvala has a broad corporate practice, advising clients from start-ups to multinationals on mergers, acquisitions and disposals, joint ventures, corporate finance and many other commercial transactions in a variety of industry sectors. He has acquired experience of doing deals in Russia, the CIS and the Middle East to add to his knowledge of regions as diverse as Trinidad & Tobago and the UK North Sea. Mr Golvala has more than 10 years' experience in the oil and gas and natural resources sectors, both in the United Kingdom and abroad. His energy and projects experience extends to many different upstream, midstream and downstream oil and gas agreements, project development contracts, abandonment arrangements, renewable energy projects and emissions trading developments.

Maine Stephan Goodfellow
Legal Intern, Baker Botts LLP
mainegoodfellow@mac.com

Maine Stephan Goodfellow attended Rice University in Houston, Texas, where he studied history, economics and photography. He is currently attending the University of Texas School of Law, from which he will graduate in May 2009.

George F Goolsby
Partner, Baker Botts LLP
george.goolsby@bakerbotts.com

George F Goolsby has more than 34 years of experience in the US and international oil and gas industries. In addition to handling traditional oil and gas work for operators, working interest owners and royalty interests, he has many years of experience in such post-production areas as processing, treating and marketing of natural gas. Mr Goolsby also specialises in cross-border hydrocarbon pipelines. He presently advises the Eastern Caribbean Gas Pipeline Project. Previously, he coordinated the legal team for the Baku–Tbilisi–Ceyhan (BTC) oil pipeline and advised the South Caucasus gas pipeline, which both traverse Azerbaijan, Georgia and Turkey.

Mr Goolsby is resident in the firm's Houston office. He is a member of numerous domestic and international legal and energy industry associations. He earned both his BA and JD degrees from the University of Texas at Austin.

Denys Hickey
Partner, Ince & Co
denys.hickey@incelaw.com

Denys Hickey is a leading member of the energy and offshore business group at Ince & Co. His main expertise is in oil and gas supply, transportation and trading, and he is also involved in offshore construction and general oil and gas work covering crude, products, LPG and LNG. Upstream oil and gas work has included

advising on offshore construction joint ventures, the financing of refinery projects, construction disputes, FPSO agreements, LNG vessels, oilfield redetermination problems, disputes arising out of the loss of offshore wells, pipeline disputes and oil and gas insurance matters.
Denys has advised on the supply and carriage of oil and gas and on shortage and contamination claims, and has been extensively involved in trading disputes and drafting long-term supply and offtake agreements. Denys also heads Ince's EU and competition team and has advised on the application of competition law in the oil and gas and shipping sectors.

Nina Howell
Associate, Hogan & Hartson
nhowell@hhlaw.com

Nina Howell is an associate in the London office of Hogan & Hartson. Nina practices in the corporate and commercial area, with a particular focus on international project development, project finance, and joint ventures in the energy sector. Nina's knowledge of the energy sector extends to oil and gas in both the upstream and downstream sectors, as well as electricity, renewables, power, and liquid natural gas projects. Nina advises governments, lenders, and public and private companies involved in the energy sector. Prior to joining Hogan & Hartson, Nina spent five years as an associate in the projects and project finance group in the London office of another major international law firm, which included a secondment to a leading global energy company. While working for a leading natural gas company in 2007, Nina was involved in a regasification project in Chile and a liquefied natural gas (LNG) project in Nigeria.

Mark Osa Igiehon
Senior Legal Counsel, Shell International BV
M.Igiehon@Shell.com

Mark Osa Igiehon is senior legal counsel with Shell International BV and since 2007 has been counsel to Shell companies in Kazakhstan. Mark holds a doctorate awarded jointly by Southampton Solent and Nottingham Trent Universities, as well as degrees from the Nigerian Law School and Bendel State University. Mark qualified in 1987 and was in private practice in Nigeria before joining Shell in 1996. Mark has worked with Shell companies in Warri, Port Harcourt, Aberdeen and Rijswijk. Mark's areas of practice principally cover upstream ventures, matters and contracts; construction; contracting and procurement; decommissioning; FPSOs and aviation. Mark was secretary to corporate Shell Nigeria Tenderboard and head of policies and procedures and led a team of lawyers dedicated to Shell Nigeria's major construction projects. Mark was counsel on many superlative projects including the Offshore Gas Gathering System, the EA Offshore project, the Odidi Associated Gas Gathering project and Shell Osubi Airport (execution phase). Mark's works have been published in many leading international legal journals.

Mark Morrison
Partner, Holman Fenwick Willan
mark.morrison@hfw.com

Mark Morrison is a partner in the trade and energy group at Holman Fenwick Willan, a global law firm advising on all aspects of international commerce. He has practised in the energy sector for more than 25 years, advising traders, major oil companies and financial institutions on the negotiation of contracts and the resolution of disputes under them. He handled a number of disputes arising out of the oil price crash in 1985 to 1986, and has more recently been involved in advising investment banks on contract terms for trading in the oil markets.

Daniel O'Neill
Partner, Ashurst LLP
daniel.o'neill@ashurst.com

Daniel O'Neill is a partner in the global energy team of international law firm Ashurst LLP, based in its Dubai office. Daniel specialises in advising clients in the energy and resources sector, with particular expertise in international oil and gas project development. Daniel has advised governments, companies, contractors and financial institutions on all aspects of the energy chain, including on exploration and production, pipelines, LNG, refining and petrochemical projects, as well as on acquisitions and disposals, joint ventures, supply, offtake and transportation arrangements and regulatory aspects of the oil and gas industry. He is a regular speaker at industry conferences and has published a number of legal articles on oil and gas matters. As well as being qualified in England and Wales, Daniel is also qualified in Western Australia, where he previously practised with a leading Australian law firm and worked for an international oil company based in Perth.

Garry Pegg
Partner, Hogan & Hartson
gjpegg@hhlaw.com

Garry Pegg is the managing partner of Hogan & Hartson's London office. His practice, which extends over 20 years, covers a comprehensive range of international corporate and commercial transactions. In particular, Garry focuses on corporate and project finance, mergers, share and asset acquisitions and disposals, and international joint ventures. He is recognised for the depth of his experience in a number of market sectors, most notably energy – oil, gas, and electricity. In the energy sector, Garry advises governments and public and private companies on a full range of international corporate and commercial matters including energy, commodity trading, and regulation. Garry has worked on major transactions in the energy sector in virtually every continent, frequently in developing countries. He also has significant experience in UK matters, particularly relating to North Sea oil and gas activities.

Geoffrey Picton-Turbervill
Partner, Ashurst LLP
geoffrey.picton-turbervill@ashurst.com

Geoffrey Picton-Turbervill is a partner in the energy, transport and infrastructure department in London and heads Ashurst's global energy team. Ashurst is an international commercial law firm with its head office in London and other offices in Europe, the Middle East, Asia and the United States. Ashurst has a dedicated energy practice and specialises in advising international energy companies, governments and government agencies, and financial institutions on international energy projects.

After qualifying as a lawyer, Geoffrey was seconded to an international oil and gas company where he gained wide experience of work in that sector, and in 1994 to 1995 he was based with his family in New Delhi, India, where he opened Ashurst's liaison office. He is a member of the Energy Institute, the International Bar Association, the UK Energy Lawyers Group and the Association of International Petroleum Negotiators, and is a regular speaker at international energy conferences.

Geoffrey has 22 years' experience of working in the international oil and gas industry, advising on mergers and acquisitions, greenfield projects and commercial agreements. Over the last couple of years Geoffrey has advised on transactions in many different jurisdictions, including the United Kingdom, Ireland, the Netherlands, Kuwait, Libya, Iran, Iraq, India, Brunei, Egypt and the former Soviet Union. He regularly acts for international energy companies and governments, and is recognised in independent guides as a leading energy lawyer.

Daniel Reinbott
Senior Associate, Ashurst LLP
daniel.reinbott@ashurst.com

Daniel Reinbott is a senior associate in the energy, transport and infrastructure group of the Singapore office of international law firm Ashurst. Daniel's practice focuses on advising project sponsors and lenders in relation to energy and infrastructure projects, with particular emphasis on the LNG, oil and gas and power sectors. His experience also includes seven months on secondment with a major international oil company in London, where he acted as an internal legal adviser to its gas and power business unit.

Nicholas Ross-McCall
Solicitor, Ashurst LLP
nicholas.ross-mccall@ashurst.com

Nicholas Ross-McCall is a solicitor in the energy group of Ashurst, based in the London office. He is a corporate and project finance lawyer specialising in upstream oil and gas financings, and projects in the power and petrochemical sectors. He has advised lenders and sponsors on numerous reserve-based lending transactions, including in the North Sea, South-East Asia, Russia and the Middle East.

Peter Taff
Independent Consultant
petertaff@gmail.com

Peter Taff is an independent consultant to the gas industry. He has spent most of his 30-year career working for the former British Gas and subsequently for Centrica. His experience ranges from the design and project management of underground gas storage in the United Kingdom (Hornsea salt cavities and conversion of the Rough field), through operational management and the negotiation of long-term gas purchase contracts, to setting up the new gas supply/trading operations department when British Gas split into separate transportation (Transco) and trading (Centrica) functions. In more recent years, as Head of European Operations at Centrica, he has had significant involvement in the development of many of the key processes and tools for trading gas in the European gas market. These include the UK–Belgian Interconnector and the Bacton Agent process, the trading hubs at Zeebrugge and TTF, membership of the EFET Hub Development Group and the founding and development of EASEE-gas.

Huw Thomas
Partner, Ashurst LLP
huw.thomas@ashurst.com

Huw Thomas is a partner at Ashurst specialising in the financing and development of upstream oil and gas assets and related infrastructure. Huw has worked on reserve-based lending transactions since the late 1980s and has been heavily involved in the development of that market, as it has moved from being initially North Sea focused to encompassing deals in many jurisdictions around the world including Russia, South-East Asia, India, Africa and the Middle East.

Huw was based in the firm's Singapore office from 1999 to 2002.

Richard Tyler
Partner, Lovells LLP
richard.tyler@lovells.com

Richard Tyler is an energy lawyer specialising in the areas of gas, LNG, power and renewables. Qualifying as a solicitor in 1991, Richard moved to work as in-house counsel for Amoco in 1995 and was responsible for drafting and negotiating the two allocation agreements (required respectively for the pipeline and gas-processing plant) of the Central Area Transmission System (CATS), one of the largest gas gathering systems in the UK North Sea. After joining Lovells LLP (and becoming a partner in 2001), he has worked on a downstream gas allocation agreement between two power plants (Baglan Bay), on the nomination and matching arrangements for the UK–Ireland gas interconnector, and drafted the standard master agreement for gas trading in Continental Europe for the European Federation of Energy Traders (EFET). He is a contributor to *UK Oil and Gas Law* by Daintith and Willoughby (specifically the downstream gas chapter).

Melanie Williams
Counsel, Ashurst LLP
melanie.williams@ashurst.com

Melanie Williams is a counsel in the energy, transport and infrastructure group of the Singapore office of international law firm Ashurst. Melanie specialises in energy projects and project financing (particularly upstream oil and gas). Prior to joining Ashurst, Melanie was a senior counsel at Doha-based Qatar Petroleum, where she worked across the upstream and downstream businesses. Melanie also worked for Woodside Energy Ltd, Australia's largest listed oil and gas exploration and production company, where she provided legal services to various divisions and worked in its Treasury department.

Sharon Wilson
Senior Associate, Freehills
sharon.wilson@freehills.com

Sharon Wilson is a senior associate in the corporate energy and resources group of Freehills, an Australian-based international law firm. Sharon is based in Perth, Western Australia. She is a commercial lawyer widely experienced in the energy and natural resources industries, with a particular emphasis on the oil and gas and LNG sectors. She has advised sponsors and host governments on upstream agreements, project development, offtake and marketing arrangements and M&A transactions throughout Asia, the Middle East, Australia and New Zealand. Sharon has also spent a significant period on secondment to an international oil and gas company advising on the management of its upstream oil and gas asset portfolio. Sharon is a solicitor admitted in England and Wales and also Western Australia.